COLONIAL LAND ENTRIES

in

NORTH CAROLINA

-1735-1752-

(Volume #1)

Compiled by:
Dr. A.B. Pruitt

Southern Historical Press, Inc.
Greenville, South Carolina

Please direct all correspondence and book orders to:
www.southernhistoricalpress.com
or
SOUTHERN HISTORICAL PRESS, Inc.
1071 Park West Blvd.
Greenville, SC   29611

Southernhistoricalpress@gmail.com

Originally Copyright: Albert Bruce Pruitt, 1994
Copyright Transferred 2026 to:
    Southern Historical Press, Inc.
ISBN #978-0-94499-252-4
Printed in the United Sattes of America

Introduction

This book is the first in a series of books containing abstracts of surviving land entries (or claims) in North Carolina during the colonial period. This first volume includes land entries between 1735 and 1752. These entries are found in the North Carolina Archives in the following books (or pieces of books): SS 1087 (entries 1-576), SS 591 folder 1 (entries 577-2763), and SS 591 folder 2 (2764-3341). Omitted from this book are abstracts of Bladen County entries previously published by Miles Philbeck. These abstracts are meant to complement the series of books published containing surviving land entries between 1778 and 1795.

Metes and bounds are given in entry 1768. Multiple tracts in one entry are found in entries 2960-2964, 3126, & 3129. Some unrecorded grants were found among the entries; these grants are between numbers 3139-3341.

It is intended to present in this book all information from the original records which would be of interest to a genealogist. The abstracted material (when mentioned in the original entry/warrant) in the book is in the following format:

(a) a sequential number assigned to each entry; this number is used in the index. When an entry/warrant

number appeared in the original, this "original" number is in parenthesis following the sequential number.

(b) a date. The date is the entry or warrant date indicated in the original book, or it is the date (month and

year) of the Council session at which the warrant was issued. Beginning about entry 1139, dates aren't

always mentioned in the original records so the date given is the last date mentioned.

(c) name of person claiming the land.

(d) number of acres. At one time, there was an attempt to confine claims to 640 acres each. But it can be seen

from this and succeeding books that this restriction wasn't always followed.

(e) county or precinct where the land was located.

(f) a water course (river, creek, swamp, etc).

(g) names of neighbors and indications if the claim includes any "improvements" (or signs of intent to make a

permanent settlement).

(h) additional dates, notes indicating a warrant for survey was issued, initials of officials who were paid

required fees, and (in very rare occasions) indications that counter claims (caveats) were made against the

entry (in which case no warrant was issued).

Persons interested in land entries in Bladen County (1735-1761), Mecklenburg County (1765-1768), Tryon County (1768-1774), or near the Broad River (1750-1760) should consult a series of land entry/warrant books published by Miles Philbeck. Persons interested in old Dobbs County should consult land entry/warrant books published by Bill Murphy.

Land grants began in North Carolina about 1663 when King Charles granted North Carolina, South Carolina, & Georgia to eight men who had helped Charles regain the throne for the House of Stuart. There are few surviving records of grants between 1663 and about 1735. Some copies are found recorded in county deed books, county loose records, or in Virginia records. A more formalized grant system began about 1715 with the passage of a new law creating a rent roll. In order to receive a land grant, a person notified a colonial land office of interest by paying a fee (or allowed someone to act as his agent to notify the land office), and the claim was noted. Copies of these claims (or entries) weren't always retained. Following the claim, a warrant was issued to the Surveyor General authorizing a survey. After the deputy surveyor was paid and other fees were paid, a "grant" could issue. It should be clear from this information that "grant" didn't imply a free gift of land. The grantee was required to cultivate 3 acres per 100 acres, build a house, and put 5 cattle on every 500 acres. People "owning" land prior to Jul. 25, 1729 were allowed to receive grants for 50 acres for each black or white person in the family or 100 acres for every 3 acres "cultivated or improved". Some of these requirements were formalized in 1736 when the Council decided to require that grants be registered with the Auditor General for tax purposes (see Colonial & State Records vol. 4 p. 180-189).

The earliest grants were issued by agents of the eight Lords Proprietor. After 1744, North Carolina was divided (for land grants) into two parts. Land in the northern part of the colony was granted by agents for the Earl of Granville. Grants in the southern part of the colony were issued by agents of the King. While copies of most of the grants survive, copies of land entries weren't always retained by colonial officials.

About 1735 Gov. Burrington was involved in a dispute about ownership of the Haw Fields (a tract of land in Orange County described in Miles Philbeck's book on Bladen County entries). One problem in determining ownership of the land was determining who had claimed (or entered) the land first. The person who made the first claim couldn't be determined from the records because copies of the entries weren't retained. The Governor decided to begin keeping a book listing the warrants as he signed them (see Colonial & State Records vol. 3 p. 336-337). The Surveyor General was to keep a similar book. These two copies could be compared with the Secretary's book to make sure errors weren't made. Descriptions of land were the same in land entries and land warrants. When the survey was complete a more "exact" description of the land was obtained; [the imprecise nature of colonial surveys still allowed for errors when compared to present day surveys]. In spite of official plans, there were still petitions to the Council indicating favoritism by the Governor (Colonial & State Records vol. 4 p. 115-119).

It appears no land entries prior to 1735 survive today. For some unknown reason there is a gap if the land entry/warrant books between 1738 and 1743, although grants were issued during this period. After 1743, more entries survive for the King's part of the colony than for Granville's part. As usual with old records it is unfortunate that only parts of some books survive and sometimes only parts of pages survive. In 1757 John Rice was authorized to record several grants (dated between 1735 and 1750) in the grant books because the grants weren't found in the grant books (see Colonial & State Records vol. 5 p. 814, 829, & 823 and CGP 5 folder 1758 in the Archives). In 1800 the Legislature authorized the Secretary of State of transcribe 13 old grant books (grants between 1663 and 1767). The Secretary was to place the old books in "a trunk" in the State Archives (see 1800 laws chapter 26). For this reason some early grants may be found in two grant books in the present Archives (or on microfilm).

For further research, one should try looking for a loose copy of the land warrant and/or land grant presently located in the North Carolina Archives. Part of these records can be searched by using the MARS computer system; in the future all grants and warrants will be included in this system.

A map is included to show the general location of counties in North Carolina. More detailed maps of the state are available (a) from the North Carolina Department of Transportation, (b) in a book of county maps (Puetz place, Landon Station, WI), (c) in a book of county maps (DeLorme Mapping Co, Freeport, ME), or (d) from the state Water Resources Department (maps divided into river basins).

In the index at the end of this book, the numbers are numbers assigned to each entry (not page numbers). Following the personal name index is an index of geographical locations--creeks, rivers, fords, swamps, etc.

The author thanks the North Carolina Archives for preserving the original records abstracted in this book. Thanks to the Archives staff for retrieving those records. Thanks also to Mrs. Grace Turner, Miles Philbeck, George Stevenson, & Mrs. Lee Albright for their assistance. Finally, thanks to the people who brought forth affordable computers, printers, & software without which the preparation of this book would have been much more arduous.

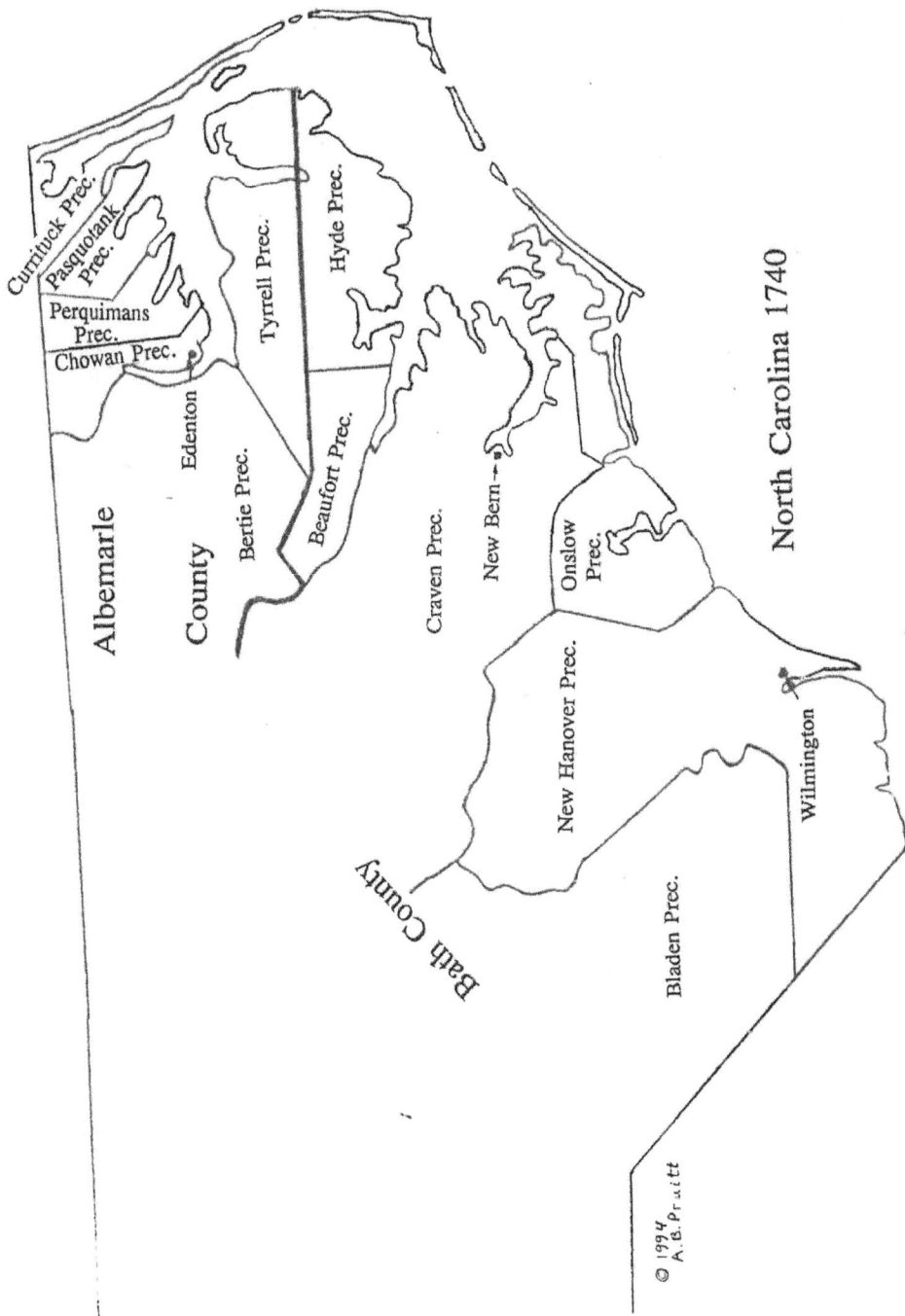

North Carolina 1740

Albemarle County

Currituck Prec.
Pasquotank Prec.
Perquimans Prec.
Chowan Prec.
Tyrrell Prec.
Hyde Prec.
Edenton
Bertie Prec.
Beaufort Prec.
Craven Prec.
New Bern →
Onslow Prec.

Bath County

New Hanover Prec.
Bladen Prec.
Wilmington

© 1994 A.B. Pruitt

North Carolina Land Entries 1735-1752

The following entries (1-576) are on 28 sheets (56 pages) which have been fastened together in box SS 1087 in the North Carolina Archives.

page 1

1. Nov. 6, 1735 Essex Bevil warrant for 640 ac in Edgecombe Prect, Albemarle Co on S side of Tar R and below mouth of Smiths Cr; certified Nov. 7, 1735; warrant to Jno Gray.

2. Oct. 16, 1735 Benjn Rowlins warrant for 150 ac in Edgecombe Prect, Albemarle Co on S side of Roanoke R; between Arthur Davis and William Benam; certified Nov. 4, 1735; warrant to Jno Gray.

3. Oct. 16, 1735 Benjn Joyner warrant for 580 ac in Edgecombe Prect, Albemarle Co on both sides of Beaverdam Br; certified Nov. 4, 1735; warrant to Jno Gray; warrant returned Oct. 1735.

4. Nov. 5, 1735 Willm Whitford warrant for 640 ac in Edgecombe Prect, Albemarle Co on Tar R; between Sam Tison and Cornels. Tison; certified Nov. 5, 1735; warrant to Robt Boyd; warrant returned Oct. 1735.

5. Oct. 16, 1735 Joseph Lane warrant for 300 ac in Edgecombe Prect, Albemarle Co; border: begins at a pine of the edge of Provider Marsh; certified Nov. 6, 1735; warrant to Jno Gray.

6. Oct. 16, 1735 Joseph Lane warrant for 200 ac in Edgecombe Prect, Albemarle Co; border: begins at a cyress on the side of Marsh Swamp; certified Nov. 6, 1735; warrant to Jno Gray.

7. Oct. 16, 1735 Joseph Lane warrant for 370 [written over 300] ac in Edgecombe Prect, Albemarle Co; border: begins at Mattw Rayford's corner and runs along said Lane's line; certified Nov. 6, 1735; warrant to Jno Gray; warrant returned Sept. 1737.

8. Nov. 4, 1735 George Carter warrant for 300 ac in Edgecombe Prect, Albemarle Co on E side of Beech Swamp; [being] the "plantation" where he lives; certified Nov. 6, 1735; warrant to Jno Gray.

9. Nov. 4, 1735 Gilbert Kinkead warrant for 550 ac in Edgecombe Prect, Albemarle Co on head of Connocounero Swamp; border: Joyn. McKinny; certified Nov. 6, 1735; warrant to Jno Gray; warrant returned Sept. 1737.

10. Nov. 4, 1735 Thos Goodwin warrant for 500 ac in Edgecombe Prect, Albemarle Co; border: Philip Raiford's upper line on Beech Swamp; certified Nov. 6, 1735; warrant to Jno Gray; warrant returned Sept. 1737.

11. Nov. 4, 1735 Andrew Johnson warrant for 200 ac in Edgecombe Prect,

Albemarle Co on S side of Deep Cr; border: begins at a poplar and runs "down"; certified Nov. 6, 1735; warrant to Jno Gray; warrant returned Feb. 1737.

12. Nov. 4, 1735 Elias Hodge warrant for 100 ac in Edgecombe Prect, Albemarle Co on S side of Morratoak R; border: a live oak on S side of Little Run Swamp of Deep Cr; certified Nov. 6, 1735; warrant to Jno Gray; warrant returned Oct. 1735.

13. Nov. 4, 1735 Joseph More warrant for 150 ac in Edgecombe Prect, Albemarle Co on S side of Moratok R; a pine on Reedy Br of Deep Cr; certified Nov. 6, 1735; warrant to Jno Gray; warrant returned Oct. 1735.

14. Nov. 4, 1735 Philip Raiford warrant for 200 ac in Edgecombe Prect, Albemarle Co on N side of Beech Swamp, S of Morratock R, & above Provendar Marsh; certified Nov. 6, 1735; warrant to Jno Gray; warrant returned Oct. 1735.

15. Nov. 4, 1735 Danl Crawley warrant for 280 ac in Edgecombe Prect, Albemarle Co on S side of Morratok R and in the fork made by said river and Quankey Cr; certified Nov. 6, 1735; warrant to Jno Gray.

page 2
16. Nov. 4, 1735 Thomas Howell warrant for 300 ac in Edgecombe Prect, Albemarle Co on S side of Tar R; certified Nov. 6, 1735; warrant to Jno Gray.

17. Nov. 4, 1735 Barny. McKinne warrant for 300 ac in Edgecombe Prect, Albemarle Co on W side of Fishing Creek Swamp; certified Nov. 6, 1735; warrant to Jno Gray.

18. Nov. 5, 1735 Robert Hill warrant for 300 ac in Edgecombe Prect, Albemarle Co on N side of Tar R and on both sides of the middle prong of Beech tree Swamp; certified Nov. 6, 1735; warrant to Jno Gray; warrant returned Feb. 28, 1738.

19. Nov. 6, 1735 John Pope warrant for 640 ac in Edgecombe Prect, Albemarle Co on Beaverdam Swamp and S side of Morratok R; border: Arthur Crawford; certified Nov. 6, 1735; warrant to Jno Gray; warrant returned Oct. 9, 1736.

20. Nov. 6, 1735 Willm Whitehead warrant for 400 ac in Edgecombe Prect, Albemarle Co on S side of Roanoke R and on a fork of Cahnkey Swamp; border: Richd Killingsworth; certified Nov. 6, 1735; warrant to Jno Gray.

21. Nov. 6, 1735 Willm Whitehead warrant for 640 ac in Edgecombe Prect, Albemarle Co on S side of Roanoke R and N side of Looking Glass Swamp; border: Jno Jacob and Henry Pope; certified Nov. 6, 1735; warrant to Jno Gray; warrant returned Oct. 9, 1736.

22. Nov. 6, 1735 Richd Lewis jr warrant for 300 ac in Edgecombe Prect, Albemarle Co on S side of Moratok R and Looking Glass Swamp; border: Capt.

North Carolina Land Entries 1735-1752

Whitehead, Richd. Lewis, & Mr. Jeffry; certified Nov. 6, 1735; warrant to Jno Gray; warrant returned Oct. 9, 1736.

23. Nov. 6, 1735 John Lean warrant for 190 ac in Edgecombe Prect, Albemarle Co on S side of Moratk R and on Beech Swamp; border: Philip "Rayford"; certified Nov. 6, 1735; warrant to Jno Gray; warrant returned Sept. 14, 1736.

24. Nov. 6, 1735 John Berret warrant for 400 ac in Edgecombe Prect, Albemarle Co; border: Jacob Brasswell's corner tree on N side of Tar R; certified Nov. 6, 1735; warrant to Jno Gray; warrant returned Sept. 14, 1736.

25. Nov. 6, 1735 Robert Warren warrant for 640 ac in Edgecombe Prect, Albemarle Co on S side of Morratok R and on Beach Swamp; certified Nov. 6, 1735; warrant to Jno Gray; warrant returned Oct. 9, 1736.

26. Nov. 6, 1735 Barny. McKinne warrant for 300 ac in Edgecombe Prect, Albemarle Co on W side of Fishing Creek Swamp; being a "plantation" improved by said McKinne; certified Nov. 6, 1735; warrant to Jno Gray; warrant returned Sept. 14, 1737.

27. Nov. 8, 1735 Charles Gaffing warrant for 450 ac in Edgecombe Prect, Albemarle Co on N side of Nuse R, on Falling Cr, & runs up Sandy Run; certified Nov. 8, 1735; warrant to Jno Gray "or" John Powell; warrant returned Jun. 27, 1738.

28. Nov. 5, 1735 George Carter warrant for 200 ac in Edgecombe Prect, Albemarle Co on S side of Murratok R; border: begins at mouth of Scotch Br and runs "up"; certified Nov. 8, 1735; warrant to Jno Gray; warrant returned Feb. 14, 1737/8.

29. Nov. 5, 1735 Deborah Williams warrant for 200 ac in Edgecombe Prect, Albemarle Co on N side of Swifts Cr; border: begins at the New Bridge and runs "down"; certified Nov. 8, 1735; warrant to Jno Gray.

30. Nov. 6, 1735 Ess Bevil warrant for 640 ac in Edgecombe Prect, Albemarle Co on S side of Tarr R and below mouth of Smiths Cr; certified Nov. 7, 1735; warrant to Jno Gray; warrant returned Sept. 14 [year omitted].

page 3
31. Nov. 5, 1735 Willm Bynum warrant for 300 ac in Edgecombe Prect, Albemarle Co on S side of Murratock R; border: begins on Panther Pocosson and runs down between Arthur Davis's lines to Looking Glass Swamp; certified Nov. 8, 1735; warrant to Jno Gray; warrant returned Oct 9, 1736.

32. Nov. 5, 1735 John Benbo warrant for 400 ac in Edgecombe Prect, Albemarle Co on N side of Kihaky Swamp and runs down the samp; certified Nov. 8, 1735;

warrant to Jno Gray; warrant returned Sept. 14, 1737.

33. Oct. 17, 1735 Francis Young warrant for 300 ac in Edgecombe Prect, Albemarle Co on N side of Fishing Cr; border: on lower side of Holland's line on Buffelows Br; certified Nov. 8, 1735; warrant to Jno Gray; warrant returned Oct. 9, 1736.

34. Oct. 17, 1735 Francis Young warrant for 150 ac in Edgecombe Prect, Albemarle Co; border: Holland's line on Buffalows Br and begins on the second fork & runs "up"; certified Nov. 8, 1735; warrant to Jno Gray.

35. Oct. 17, 1735 Francis Young warrant for 200 ac in Edgecombe Prect, Albemarle Co; border: begins 0.25 miles above the mouth of Buffelo Br on Fishing Cr; certified Nov. 8, 1735; warrant to Jno Gray; warrant returned Oct. 9, 1736.

36. Oct. 17, 1735 James Thompson warrant for 640 ac in Edgecombe Prect, Albemarle Co on Great Fishing Cr; border: on lower side of Ewd. Young; certified Nov. 8, 1735; warrant to Jno Gray.

37. Oct. 17, 1735 Mary Price warrant for 640 ac in Edgecombe Prect, Albemarle Co on Six pound Cr; border: near John Ghent's "plantation"; certified Nov. 8, 1735; warrant to Jno Gray; warrant returned Oct. 9, 1736.

38. Oct. 17, 1735 Samuel Williams warrant for 300 ac in Edgecombe Prect, Albemarle Co on S side of Stoney Cr; border: begins at mouth of a small branch and runs "up"; certified Nov. 8, 1735; warrant to Jno Gray.

39. Nov. 5, 1735 Edward Salter warrant for 640 ac in Edgecombe Prect, Albemarle Co in the fork of Checoe Cr and on S side of Pamplico R; certified Nov. 8, 1735; warrant to Jno Gray.

40. Oct. 16, 1735 Thomas Roberts warrant for 50 [or 500] ac in Edgecombe Prect, Albemarle Co on S side of Tar R and on N branch of Town Cr; border: at upper old field on N side of said branch; certified Nov. 8, 1735; warrant to Jno Gray.

41. Nov. 6, 1735 John Pope warrant for 400 ac in Edgecombe Prect, Albemarle Co on N side of Fishing Cr; border: Thos Pollock's corner tree; certified Nov. 8, 1735; warrant to Jno Gray.

42. Oct. 17, 1735 Francis Young warrant for 640 ac in Edgecombe Prect, Albemarle Co on Hub quarter Cr and at mouth of Redy Br; certified Nov. 8, 1735; warrant to Jno Gray; warrant returned Oct. 9, 1736.

43. Oct. 16, 1735 John Stafford warrant for 640 ac in Edgecombe Prect, Albemarle Co on head of Stephens Br; certified Nov. 8, 1735; warrant to Jno

North Carolina Land Entries 1735-1752

Gray.

44. Oct. 16, 1735 Capt. John Speir warrant for 320 ac in Edgecombe Prect, Albemarle Co on S side of Conoho Cr; certified Nov. 8, 1735; warrant to Jno Gray.

45. Oct. 17, 1735 Francis Young warrant for 200 ac in Edgecombe Prect, Albemarle Co on both sides of second fork of Buffelow Br; certified Nov. 8, 1735; warrant to Jno Gray.

46. Nov. 5, 1735 Thomas Howell warrant for 300 ac in Edgecombe Prect, Albemarle Co on S side of Tar R; [being] the "plantation" where he lives; certified Nov. 8, 1735; warrant to Jno Gray; warrant returned Sept. 14, 1737.

47. Nov. 6, 1735 Seth Pilkington warrant for 640 ac in Edgecombe Prect, Albemarle Co on N side of Pamplicoe R; between Tranchers [or Franchers] and Grindall Cr; border: joins land of said Pilkington; certified Nov. 10, 1735; warrant to Jno Gray; warrant returned Nov. 27, 1738.

48. Nov. 8, 1735 Lemuel Alexander warrant for 640 ac in Edgecombe Prect, Albemarle Co on E side of Scupperlong R and W side of Second Cr; certified Nov. 10, 1735; warrant to Jno Gray.

49. Nov. 28, 1735 Joseph Parker warrant for 200 ac in Edgecombe Prect, Albemarle Co on N side of Fishing Cr; border: E of John Speir and Short Swamp; certified Nov. 28, 1735; warrant to Jno Gray; warrant returned Oct. 9, 1736.

50. Dec. 1, 1735 John Nerme warrant for 640 ac in Edgecombe Prect, Albemarle Co on Maratock R; border: begins at an oak on the river and runs according to a former survey made by Jno Gray; certified Dec. 3, 1735; warrant to Jno Gray.

page 4
51. May 10, 1736 Coll. Byrd warrant for 1,000 ac in Edgecombe Prect, Albemarle Co; border: joins his land on Dan R; certified Jun. 15, 1736; warrant to John Gray.

52. Jun. 19, 1736 Joseph Cotton warrant for 640 ac in Edgecombe Prect, Albemarle Co on E side of Fishing Cr and at mouth of Beech Br; being the "plantation" where he lives; certified Jun. 21, 1736; warrant to Tho Carney [Jno Gray--lined out].

53. Jun. 19, 1736 Peter Johnston warrant for 200 ac in Edgecombe Prect, Albemarle Co on NE side of Beech Br; being the "plantation" where he lives; certified Jun. 21, 1736; warrant to Tho Carney [Jno Gray--lined out].

54. Jun. 19, 1736 Thos Gary [Gray--lined out] warrant for 260 ac in Edgecombe Prect, Albemarle Co on S side of Caucuonary Swamp; being the "plantation"

where he lives; certified Jun. 21, 1736; warrant to Tho Carney [Jno Gray--lined out].

55. Oct. 1, 1736 William Whitehead warrant for 200 ac in Edgecombe Prect, Albemarle Co on a fork of Deep Cr; border: begins at a white oak on N side of said creek and runs down the creek; certified Oct. 2, 1736; warrant to Tho Carney; warrant returned Nov. 16, 1738.

56. Oct. 2, 1736 Francis Parker jr warrant for 640 ac in Edgecombe Prect, Albemarle Co on W side of Sandy Run which falls into Swifts Cr on S side; border: begins at a marked white oak and runs up said creek; certified Oct. 2, 1736; warrant to Ben Rawlins; warrant returned Sept. 7, 1737.

57. Oct. 2, 1736 John Briges warrant for 200 ac in Edgecombe Prect, Albemarle Co on S side of Deep Cr; border: begins at a white oak and runs up said creek; certified Oct. 2, 1736; warrant to Ben Rawlins; warrant returned Sept. 7, 1737.

58. Oct. 8, 1736 Joseph Cotton warrant for 640 ac in Edgecombe Prect, Albemarle Co on S side of Fishing Cr; border: begins at a gum on said creek at mouth of Beech Swamp; certified Oct. 2, 1736; warrant to John Gray; warrant returned Oct. 12 [no year].

59. [no date] William Garey warrant for 200 ac in Edgecombe Prect, Albemarle Co on S side of Connicenaro Swamp and W side of Camp Br; border: a red oak; warrant to John Gray; warrant returned Oct. 12 [no year].

60. [no date] Thomas Hart warrant for 200 ac in Edgecombe Prect, Albemarle Co; border: a hickorey on Tarr R and runs NW up the river; warrant to John Gray; warrant returned Oct. 12 [no year].

61. [no date] John Tomkins warrant for 200 ac in Edgecombe Prect, Albemarle Co in the fork of Buffelow Br; border: a red oak on the North prong; warrant to John Gray; warrant returned Oct. 12 [no year].

62. Dec. 22, 1736 Thomas Mims warrant for 200 ac in Edgecombe Prect, Albemarle Co on S side of Beverdam Swamp, near Bear Marsh, on a "meddow", & runs down "the same"; certified Mar. 1, 1736; warrant to Ben Rawlins.

63. Feb. 14, 1737 John Lee warrant for 200 ac in Edgecombe Prect, Albemarle Co on upper side of Conetah Cr; border: begins at John Lee's upper corner on the creek and runs up the creek; certified Mar. 2, 1736; warrant to Ben Rawlins.

64. Mar. 5, 1737 Wm Cotton warrant for 200 ac in Edgecombe Prect, Albemarle Co on E side of Tostehot [sic] Swamp; border: above the land belonging [to] Lewes [sic] Conner on W side of Great Br "called" Buck Horn "Soup", "the branch from the mouth"; certified Mar. 2, 1736; warrant to Tho Carney or John

Williams; warrant returned Nov. 19, 1739.

65. Mar. 10, 1737 Wm Byrd esq warrant for 6,000 ac in Edgecombe Prect, Albemarle Co; being the land said Byrd had the late Gov. Burrington's warrant for 5,000 ac and the present governor's [warrant] for 1,000 ac; certified Mar. 2, 1737; warrant to Thomas Carney [William Mayo--lined out].

66. Sept. 8, 1737 Joseph John Alston warrant for 500 ac in Edgecombe Prect, Albemarle Co; border: begins at Geo Smith's corner tree on W side of Beverdam [Pond ?] and runs on each side of said pond; includes his improvement; certified Sept. 8, 1737; warrant to Thomas Carney; warrant returned Jun. 27, 1738.

67. Sept. 8, 1737 Joseph John Alston warrant for 13 ac in Edgecombe Prect, Albemarle Co in the fork of Butterwood [Swamp]; border: begins at Geo Smith's line and runs down the fork; certified Sept. 8, 1737; warrant to Thomas Carney.

68. Sept. 8, 1737 Joseph John Alston warrant for 300 ac in Edgecombe Prect, Albemarle Co on Baver Pond and in the fork of said pond of [sic] Fishing Cr; called Smiths Neck [Creek--lined out]; border: about a mile from said Alston's "plantation" and begins at a red oak; certified Sept. 8, 1737; warrant to Thomas Carney; warrant returned Jun. 27, 1738.

69. Sept. 8, 1737 Richard Cheek warrant for 640 ac in Edgecombe Prect, Albemarle Co; border: begins at head of a meadow about said Cheek's mer (?), runs a mile back from Tarr R, [page torn] mile "compleeting and senare for ye Co being ye run" [rest has page torn]; certified Sept. 8, 1737; warrant to Tho Carney or Robert Boyd; warrant returned Feb. 16 [no year].

page 5
70. Oct. 24, 1736 John Oxley warrant for 250 ac in Bertie Prect, Albemarle Co on W side of Beaverdam Swamp; border: joins late Thos Pollock's line and begins at a gum in the swamp; certified Oct. 24, 1735; warrant to Jno Pratt.
71. Nov. 7, 1735 John Dawson warrant for 250 ac in Bertie Prect, Albemarle Co on S side of Pollesasay Cr; border: joins widow Thomas' "plantation"; certified Nov. 7, 1735; warrant to Jno Pratt or Tho Kearny [sic]; warrant returned Jun. 7, 1739.

72. Nov. 7, 1735 Robt House warrant for 600 ac in Bertie Prect, Albemarle Co on Hunting Quarter Swamp; border: Ezekiel Fuller's "plantation", Wm Warr's "plantation", & "so along" to widow Lamb and Jno Basses; certified Nov. 7, 1735; warrant to Jno Pratt or Tho Kearny; warrant returned Jun. 7, 1739.

73. Nov. 6, 1735 Richard Merrick warrant for 300 ac in Bertie Prect, Albemarle Co on S side of Beaver pen Cr; certified Nov. 7, 1735; warrant to Jno Pratt.

74. Nov. 8, 1735 Willm Rogers warrant for 370 ac in Bertie Prect, Albemarle Co

on Chowan R; border: Wm Padget and Wm Maule; certified Nov. 8, 1735; warrant to Jno Pratt.

75. Nov. 19, 1735 Simon Herrin warrant for 100 ac in Bertie Prect, Albemarle Co on N side of Casky R and W side of Wills Quarter Swamp; border: James Curroy; certified Nov. 20, 1735; warrant to Jno Pratt.

76. Dec. 1, 1735 Patrick OQuin warrant for 640 ac in Bertie Prect, Albemarle Co on E side of waters of Toms Swamp; certified Dec. 1, 1735; warrant to John Pratt.

77. Dec. 12, 1735 Robt Hinds warrant for 150 ac in Bertie Prect, Albemarle Co on N side of Cushi [Swamp]; border: about 2 miles from Samuel Dickinson's "plantation"; certified Dec. 12, 1735; warrant to John Gray.

78. Mar. 1, 1735/6 Thomas Jackson warrant for 640 ac in Bertie Prect, Albemarle Co on W side of Chowan R; border: joins the land where he lives; certified Mar. 1, 1735/6; warrant to John Gray; warrant returned Sept. 10, 1737.

79. Jul. 3, 1736 Robert Forster warrant for 640 ac in Bertie Prect, Albemarle Co on W side of Chowan R, on upper side of mouth of Wickone Cr, & begins at mouth of said creek on Choewan [sic] R; certified Dec. 28, 1737; warrant to John Gray.

80. Jul. 3, 1736 Robert Forster warrant for 400 ac in Bertie Prect, Albemarle Co on N side of Oconeechey Swamp; being land formerly surveyed for said Forster by John Makinne [sic]; certified Dec. 28, 1737; warrant to John Gray.

81. Jul. 3, 1736 Robert Foster warrant for 640 ac in Edgecombe Prect, Albemarle Co; border: about 6 miles above Capt. Bryant on E side of Swifts Cr, a branch of Fishing Cr; certified Dec. 28, 1737.

82. Feb. 18, 1737/8 James Wright warrant for 100 ac in Bertie Prect, Albemarle Co on the Virginia line; border: begins at Nich. Boon's line; certified Feb. 18, 1737/8; warrant to John Gray.

83. Sept. 9, 1736 Henry Guston warrant for 300 ac in Edgecombe Prect, Albemarle Co on N side of Conway Cr and at a place called Dick Jackson's Mountan; certified Sept. 9, 1736; warrant to Tho Carney; warrant returned Jun. 27, 1738.

84. Jul. 3, 1736 John Winns warrant for 640 ac in Edgecombe Prect, Albemarle Co on Conways Cr, a branch of Fishing Cr; border: begins at upper and outer corner of Irwin's line; certified Dec. 28, 1737; warrant to John Gray.

85. [no date] William Pierson [or Piorson] warrant for 300 ac in Edgecombe Prect, Albemarle Co on S side of Stonehouse Cr; border: begins at Abraham

Maclemore's [sic] upper corner and runs up the creek; certified Feb. 23, 1737/8; warrant to John Gray.

page 6

86. Dec. 29, 1737 Bejamin Wall warrant for 150 ac in Edgecombe Prect, Albemarle Co on S side of Fishing Cr and the same side of White Oak Swamp; border: begins at a marked white oak at the mouth of a swamp and runs down said swamp; certified Feb. 17, 1737/8; warrant to Benjamin Rawlins; warrant returned Jun. 27, 1738.

87. Dec. 29, 1737 William Whitehead warrant for 100 ac in Edgecombe Prect, Albemarle Co on S side of Deep Cr; border: "on" Brigg's line and runs up the creek; certified Feb. 17, 1737/8; warrant to Benjamin Rawlins; warrant returned Jun. 27, 1738.

88. Dec. 29, 1737 William Whitehead warrant for 200 ac in Edgecombe Prect, Albemarle Co on NE side of Swift Cr and "near over against" mouth of Rocky Run; border: above Willm Busby's "plantation"; certified Feb. 17, 1737/8; warrant to Benjamin Rawlins; warrant returned Jun. 27, 1738.

89. Dec. 29, 1737 William Whitehead warrant for 200 ac in Edgecombe Prect, Albemarle Co on NE side of Swift Cr; between Thos Bryan & Wm Henry and begins at a white oak on said creek; certified Feb. 17, 1737/8; warrant to Benjamin Rawlins.

90. Dec. 29, 1737 William Whitehead warrant for 250 ac in Edgecombe Prect, Albemarle Co on S side of Swift Cr, on a branch called Rocky Run, near a place called Rocky Cabbin, & near the forks of said run; certified Feb. 17, 1737/8; warrant to Benjamin Rawlins; warrant returned Jun. 27, 1738.

91. Dec. 29, 1737 John Crowell warrant for 200 ac in Edgecombe Prect, Albemarle Co on N branch of Fishing Cr and at a place called Crowell's "house" alias Erwins Cr; certified Feb. 17, 1737/8; warrant to Benjamin Rawlins.

92. Dec. 29, 1737 Samuel Brown warrant for 150 ac in Edgecombe Prect, Albemarle Co on S side of Round oak [Cr ?], in the fork of Looking Glass Swamp, & on the marshes of said swamp; border: begins at a pine; certified Feb. 17, 1737/8; warrant to Benjamin Rawlins; warrant returned Jun. 27, 1738.

93. Dec. 29, 1737 William Reeves warrant for 400 ac in Edgecombe Prect, Albemarle Co on S side of Great Cr; cultivated by said William Reeves; certified Fcb. 17, 1737/8; warrant to Benjamin Rawlins; warrant returned Jun. 27, 1738.

94. Dec. 29, 1737 John Brown warrant for 250 ac in Edgecombe Prect, Albemarle Co on S side of Roanoke R; border: Pollock, Pope, Whitehead, & "near between" Looking Glass Swamp and Beaverdam Swamp; certified Feb. 17, 1737/8; warrant to Benjamin Rawlins.

95. Feb. 17, 1737/8 Capt. John Spier warrant for 160 ac in Edgecombe Prect, Albemarle Co on Great Contentiney Marsh; where Robert Radford lives; certified Feb. 18, 1737/8; warrant to Benjamin Rawlins; warrant returned feb. 22, 1738/9.

96. Feb. 16, 1737/8 Wm Speer warrant for 200 ac in Edgecombe Prect, Albemarle Co on N side of Swifts Cr; border: begins at the mouth of a branch and runs up the creek; certified Feb. 18, 1737/8; warrant to Benjamin Rawlins; warrant returned Jun. 27, 1738.

97. Feb. 16, 1737/8 John Speer warrant for 150 ac in Edgecombe Prect, Albemarle Co; border: begins at a marked red oak; being a "plantation" where William Midleton lives; certified Feb. 18, 1737/8; warrant to Benjamin Rawlins; warrant returned Jun. 27, 1738.

98. Feb. 16, 1737/8 Capt. John Speer warrant for 100 ac in Edgecombe Prect, Albemarle Co on N side of Deep Cr; being a "deserted plantation" where Robt Magee lived; certified Feb. 18, 1737/8.
99. Feb. 16, 1737/8 William Speer warrant for 150 ac in Edgecombe Prect, Albemarle Co; border: begins at a marked oak on Shorts Swamp and runs down the swamp; certified Feb. 18, 1737/8; warrant to Benjamin Rawlins.

100. Feb. 16, 1737/8 Joseph Lane warrant for 300 ac in Edgecombe Prect, Albemarle Co on S side of Burntcoat [Swamp]; border: begins at a maple marked "I L" at mouth of Reedy Br and runs "out and down"; certified Feb. 18, 1737/8; warrant to Benjamin Rawlins; warrant returned Jun. 27, 1738.

page 7
101. Oct. 15, 1736 memorandum: have sent the following warrants to Mr. Tho Carney enclosed in a letter by Mr. Ben Hill:
Wm Arington 100 ac in Bertie Prect; dated Mar. 29, 1733
John Pratt and Rowland Williams 200 ac Aug. 2, 1732
John Winn 640 ac Feb. 5, 1732
Joseph Mecham 300 ac Nov. 8, 1733
Col. Henry Gustin 600 [written over 640] ac Apr. 1, 1732
Richd. Killingsworth 200 ac Nov. 1, 1732
John Mulky 500 ac Dec. 13, 1732 Edgecombe Prect
Mr. Pickett 640 ac Jul. 29, 1732 Edgecombe Prect
"Geo Burrington" [written beside the above names]
and an order of the Council for a resurvey on Mr. Lovick's iseland [sic] dated Oct. 14, 1736 at the request of Mr. George Fenny esq.

page 8 [blank page]

page 9
102. Apr. 3, 1735 George Turner warrant for 320 ac in Currituck Prect, Albemarle

Co; at a place called Durrants Neck and at S end of Hatteras Banks; border: joins said Turner's land; certified Apr. 3, 1735; warrant to James Craven.

103. Oct. 12, 1736 Joseph Midget warrant for 300 ac in Currituck Prect, Albemarle Co near N end of Chikenocomock Island; formerly surveyed for Wm Wells; certified Oct. 13, 1736; warrant to Col. John Palin.

104. Sept. 30, 1737 Daniel Dowdy warrant for 340 ac in Currituck Prect, Albemarle Co; border: Capt. Norton & Saml Williams on Albemarle Sound and begins at a lightwood stump in a marsh; certified Feb. 25, 1737/8; warrant to James Craven.

page 10
[The heading is made out for Currituck Prect., but no warrants are listed.]

page 11
[The heading is made out for Pasquotank Prect., but no warrants are listed.]

page 12
105. Nov. 12, 1735 John Gilford warrant for 100 ac in Pasquotank Prect, Albemarle Co on N side of "the" river; border: Thos Merriday and Jno Simon; certified Dec. 9, 1735; warrant to James Craven; warrant returned 1737/8.

106. Nov. 12, 1735 Robert Cartwright warrant for 100 ac in Pasquotank Prect, Albemarle Co; border: Nathl Martyn [or Martyr], my own land, & runs down to Edmd Chanecy's [or Chamcy] land; certified Dec. 9, 1735; warrant to James Craven; warrant returned Feb. 14, 1737/8.

107. Nov. 12, 1735 John Jones warrant for 100 ac in Pasquotank Prect, Albemarle Co on N side of "the" river; called Harrisons or Butterworths Island; border: near the New Bridge on "said" river; certified Dec. 9, 1735; warrant to James Craven.

108. Nov. 12, 1735 John Jones warrant for 100 ac in Pasquotank Prect, Albemarle Co on N side of "the" river, on Red Oak Ridge, & at old pond in "the" Lake; certified Dec. 9, 1735; warrant to James Craven.

109. Sept. 23, 1736 Robert Hosea warrant for 75 ac in Pasquotank Prect, Albemarle Co; border: begins at Joseph Commander's corner gum in John Armer's [sic] line, runs SW to Elisha Tanton's gum, along Tanton's line to Armor's line, & along his line to the beginning; certified Dec. 24, 1736; warrant to James Craven.

page 13
110. Mar. 4, 1736/7 Nath Carruthers warrant for 200 ac in Perquimans Prect, Albemarle Co on Yawpim R; formerly known as Register's "plantation"; border: joins the land were he lives; certified Mar. 4, 1736/7; warrant to James Craven; warrant returned Feb. 14, 1737/8.

111. Mar. 7, 1736/7 Col. Rora Scarbrow warrant for 100 ac in Perquimans Prect, Albemarle Co; border: House's land and John Evans' "plantation"; certified Mar. 7, 1736/7; warrant to James Craven.

112. Jul. 1736/7 Jacob Docton warrant for 300 ac in Perquimans Prect, Albemarle Co; border: Thos Norfllet's [sic] line on head of Perquimans R and "the" E side; certified Jul. 1736/7; warrant to James Craven.

page 14
[The heading is made out for Perquimans Prect., but no warrants are listed.]

page 15
113. May 14, 1735 James Hazell esq warrant for 320 ac in New Hanover Prect, Bath Co; border: begins on Day's Landing on Rogers Cr and joins land where Nal. Moore "lately" lived; certified May 14, 1735; warrant to William Gray.

114. May 14, 1735 Richard Eagle esq warrant for 800 ac in New Hanover Prect, Bath Co; border: joins his own land at "the" forks formerly belonging to Mr. Nal. Moore; certified May 14, 1735; warrant to Willm Gray.

115. May 14, 1735 Richard Eagle esq warrant for 800 ac in New Hanover Prect, Bath Co between the forks of NW and NE Cape Fear Rivers; certified May 14, 1735; warrant to Willm Gray.

116. May 14, 1735 Archibald Nicholls warrant for 640 ac in New Hanover Prect, Bath Co on N side of Jevins [sic] Cr; border: begins at a pine tree on "the" marsh; certified May 15, 1735; warrant to Willm Gray.

117. May 15, 1735 Jehu Davis esq warrant for 300 ac in New Hanover Prect, Bath Co on an island opposite his house; certified May 15, 1735; warrant to Wm Gray.

118. May 15, 1735 Thomas Assop warrant for 640 ac in New Hanover Prect, Bath Co on lowermost northern branch of Old Town Cr; formerly surveyed for Charles Harrison; certified May 15, 1735; warrant to Wm Gray.

119. May 15, 1735 Ephraim Vernon esq warrant for 100 ac in New Hanover Prect, Bath Co on N side of NW River; formerly surveyed for Epm. Vernon and Nathl. Hill; between the "lands" of Point Vernon and Henry Neale; certified May 16, 1735; warrant to Jno Clayton.

120. May 15, 1735 Ephraim Vernon esq [rest is blank]; certified May 16, 1735.
121. May 16, 1735 Matthew Rowan esq warrant for 176 ac in New Hanover Prect, Bath Co on NW Cape Fear R; border: at an elm between the Governor's land and said Rowan's land; certified May 16, 1735; warrant to Jno Clayton.

North Carolina Land Entries 1735-1752

122. May 16, 1735 Matthew Rowan esq warrant for 144 ac in New Hanover Prect, Bath Co; between Randolph and said Rowan; border: begins at a water oak; certified May 16, 1735; warrant to Jno Clayton.

123. May 16, 1735 Capt. Hugh Blanning warrant for 170 ac in New Hanover Prect, Bath Co; border: begins at a gum joining Col. Halton's "to" a cypress, the lower corner tree is a bay, & "so" to the mouth of "the" creek; certified May 16, 1735; warrant to Jno Clayton.

124. May 16, 1735 Capt. Hugh Blanning warrant for 350 ac in New Hanover Prect, Bath Co between Long Cr and Turky Cr; border: opposite Capt. Ennis' "plantation" and runs up the creek above the first bluff; certified May 16, 1735; warrant to Jno Clayton.

125. May 15, 1735 [sic] James Espy warrant for 200 ac in New Hanover Prect, Bath Co on head of Governours Cr and 4 miles below Brunswick; certified May 16, 1735; warrant to Wm Gray.

126. May 15, 1735 James Espy warrant for 500 ac in New Hanover Prect, Bath Co on N side of a branch of Lockwoods Folley R and aout 3 miles above "the" inlet; certified May 16, 1735; warrant to Wm Gray.

page 16
127. May 15, 1735 Joshua Gabourell warrant for 1,920 ac in New Hanover Prect, Bath Co; called the mill land; border: joins the mill on a branch of Smiths Cr; certified May 16, 1735; warrant to Wm Gray; warrant returned 1736.

128. May 16, 1735 John Simmonds warrant for 250 ac in New Hanover Prect, Bath Co on the sound; between Shallot R and Little R; certified May 16, 1735; warrant to Wm Gray; warrant returned Jun. 8, 1736.

129. May 16, 1735 Jacob Simmonds warrant for 250 ac in New Hanover Prect, Bath Co on "the" fork of Shallot R; certified May 16, 1735; warrant to Wm Gray; warrant returned Jun. 9, 1736.

130. May 16, 1735 Joseph Meredith warrant for 160 ac in New Hanover Prect, Bath Co on NE River; border: Timothy Bloodworth and runs down the river; certified May 16, 1735; warrant to Da Evans.

131. May 16, 1735 Joseph Meredith warrant for 160 ac in New Hanover Prect, Bath Co on NE River; border: Rice Evans' corner tree and runs up the river; certified May 16, 1735; warrant to Da Evans.

132. May 14, 1735 James Baldwin warrant for 640 ac in New Hanover Prect, Bath Co on Waggomaw Swamp; border: Joseph Waters and begins on Waters' line; certified May 17, 1735; warrant to John Clayton.

133. May 15, 1735 Thomas Will warrant for 350 ac in New Hanover Prect, Bath Co on Rockfish Cr and on middle branch of NE River; certified May 17, 1735; warrant to Da Evans.

134. May 17, 1735 William Lewis warrant for 640 ac in New Hanover Prect, Bath Co; border: begins at Peter Watkins [line] and joins David Evans; certified May 17, 1735; warrant to Da Evans.

135. May 17, 1735 John Cook sr warrant for 640 ac in New Hanover Prect, Bath Co on S side of NE River; border: begins at a place called Dry Run; certified May 17, 1735; warrant to Da Evans.

136. May 16, 1735 James Espy warrant for 350 ac in New Hanover Prect, Bath Co on SW side of Cape Fear R and at head of Mr. Eleazr. Allen's Cr; certified May 17, 1735; warrant to Wm Gray; warrant returned Jun. 9, 1736.

137. May 17, 1735 George Gibbs warrant for 200 ac in New Hanover Prect, Bath Co on NW Cape Fear R; border: Capt. Rowan's land that is opposite the Thoroughfare; certified May 19, 1735; warrant to Jos Clark; warrant returned Sept. 5, 1736.

138. May 19, 1735 Stephen Mott warrant for 640 ac in New Hanover Prect, Bath Co on head of John Porters Cr; certified May 19, 1735; warrant to Willm Gray.

139. May 16, 1735 Cornelius Harnet warrant for 1,500 ac in New Hanover Prect, Bath Co; border: adjacent to his new saw mill; certified May 19, 1735; warrant to Will Gray.

140. May 16, 1735 David Roach warrant for 320 ac in New Hanover Prect, Bath Co; between Mullington and Cox; border: "against" Cabbage and Shole Inlets; certified May 20, 1735; warrant to Will Gray; warrant returned Jun. 9, 1736.

page 17
141. May 14, 1735 Joseph Waters warrant for 200 ac in New Hanover Prect, Bath Co; border: joins the land known as Thomas Hill's; certified May 20, 1735; warrant to Will Gray; warrant returned 1736.

142. May 17, 1735 Rice Evans warrant for 320 ac in New Hanover Prect, Bath Co on a branch of NE River and near Rattlesnake Br; certified May 22, 1735; warrant to Will Gray; warrant returned Jun. 9, 1736.

143. May 17, 1735 Richard Evans warrant for 300 ac in New Hanover Prect, Bath Co on Barnets Cr and on E side of NE Cape Fear R; certified May 22, 1735; warrant to Will Gray.

North Carolina Land Entries 1735-1752

144. May 17, 1735 Rev. Richd. Masden warrant for 1,000 ac in New Hanover Prect, Bath Co on head of Prince George Cr; certified May 22, 1735; warrant to Will Gray.

145. May 24, 1735 Michael Dyer warrant for 320 ac in New Hanover Prect, Bath Co; border: Mr. Watson's lower line on NE River and runs "down"; certified May 26, 1735; warrant to Will Gray.

146. May 27, 1735 James Marsh warrant for 640 ac in New Hanover Prect, Bath Co on the sound; between Little R and Shallot R; border: "to E on" Saml Master's land; certified May 31, 1735; warrant to Will Gray.

147. Jul. 17, 1735 James Baxter warrant for 640 ac in New Hanover Prect, Bath Co on E branch of Little R; border: begins on E side 12 chains W of a live oak and runs along said branch; certified Jul. 17, 1735; warrant to Will Gray.

148. Aug. 13, 1735 Richard Price warrant for 640 ac in New Hanover Prect, Bath Co on Rogers Cr; border: Mr. Hazel and runs up the creek; certified Aug. 15, 1735; warrant to Will Gray.

149. Jul. 13, 1735 Joseph Watters warrant for 100 ac in New Hanover Prect, Bath Co on S side of NW River; border: Wm Watters' East and South "line"; certified Aug. 16, 1735; warrant to Jos Clark.

150. May 14, 1735 Francis Thomas warrant for 350 ac in New Hanover Prect, Bath Co on NW River and SW branch of Hammonds Cr; certified Sept. 4, 1735; warrant to Jno Cleaton [sic].

151. May 14, 1735 Eleazar Allen warrant for 640 ac in New Hanover Prect, Bath Co; border: joins the land where he lives; certified Sept. 4, 1735; warrant to Will Gray.

152. Jun. 13, 1735 Jeremiah Bigfurd warrant for 150 ac in New Hanover Prect, Bath Co at Haw Hill on a fork of Town Cr [waters of] Cape Fear R; certified Sept. 4, 1735; warrant to Will Gray.

153. Aug. 13, 1735 Thomas Hill warrant for 200 ac in New Hanover Prect, Bath Co; border: P Palmer's land on Old Town Cr; certified Sept. 4, 1735; warrant to Will Gray.

154. Aug. 13, 1735 Thomas Hill warrant for 150 ac in New Hanover Prect, Bath Co; border: Wm Lewis' upper line on Old Town Cr; certified Sept. 4, 1735; warrant to Will Gray.

155. Jun. 13, 1735 John Lewis warrant for 300 ac in New Hanover Prect, Bath Co; border: Wm Lewis' upper line on Old Town Cr and runs "up"; certified Sept.

4, 1735; warrant to Will Gray.

156. Sept. 5, 1735 Solomon and John Ogden warrant for 640 ac in New Hanover Prect, Bath Co on Topsail Sound, oposite Broad Inlet, & on N side of Lees Cr; certified Sept. 8, 1735; warrant to Will Gray.

157. Sept. 5, 1735 William Lord warrant for 640 ac in New Hanover Prect, Bath Co on S side of Livingstons Cr; between Mr. Harnet and Capt. Blaning; certified Sept. 8, 1735; warrant to Will Gray; warrant returned Jun. 9, 1736.

158. Sept. 8, 1735 Lawrance Howley warrant for 575 ac in New Hanover Prect, Bath Co on New Topsail [Sound] opposite Rich Inlet; border: begins at Benj Mott's corner tree; certified Sept. 10, 1735; warrant to Will Gray.

159. Sept. 8, 1735 Laurance [sic] Howley warrant for 640 ac in New Hanover Prect, Bath Co; border: on back of a tract of said Howley on New Topsail Sound; certified Sept. 10, 1735; warrant to Will Gray.

page 18
160. Sept. 9, 1735 Capt. Willm Ford warrant for 320 ac in New Hanover Prect, Bath Co; border: on E side about 2 miles below Black R; certified Sept. 10, 1735; warrant to Will Gray.

161. Sept. 9, 1735 John Watson warrant for 640 ac in New Hanover Prect, Bath Co on the sound opposite Deep Inlet; were he lives; certified Sept. 10, 1735; warrant to Will Gray.

162. Aug. 12, 1735 James Espy warrant for 100 ac in New Hanover Prect, Bath Co about a mile N of Espys Cr and about 7 miles from mouth of Lockwoods Folly Inlet; certified Sept. 10, 1735; warrant to Will Gray.

163. Sept. 9, 1735 Thomas Clark warrant for 400 ac in New Hanover Prect, Bath Co on NW side of Smiths Cr; border: begins at Jos Stibbins' lower corner; certified Sept. 11, 1735; warrant to Will Gray; warrant returned Sept. 12, 1735.

164. Sept. 11, 1735 Rush Watts warrant for 100 ac in New Hanover Prect, Bath Co on the sound; between Goldsmith, Whitehouse, & George Bishop; certified Sept. 11, 1735; warrant to Will Gray.

165. Sept. 11, 1735 Agatha Blaning warrant for 320 ac in New Hanover Prect, Bath Co on E side of NW River; border: begins at an elm half a mile below Black R and "over against" Plumer's land; certified Sept. 11, 1735; warrant to Jos Clark.

166. Sept. 10, 1735 William Smith esq, Chief Justice warrant for 1,000 ac in New Hanover Prect, Bath Co on E side of NE River; between Mr. Dyer and Mr. Moor; certified Sept. 10, 1735; warrant to Jos Clark; warrant returned Sept. 11, 1735.

167. Sept. 8, 1735 John Marshall warrant for 640 ac in New Hanover Prect, Bath Co on S side of NE River; border: begins at "the" E line "whereon he lives"; certified Sept. 12, 1735; warrant to Will Gray.

168. Aug. 30, 1735 Mathew Rowan esq warrant for 230 ac in New Hanover Prect, Bath Co on SW side of NW River and opposite Long Island; between Benj Orman's two "half" tracts; certified Sept. 12, 1735; warrant to Jos Clark.

169. Sept. 11, 1735 David Burchard warrant for 500 a in New Hanover Prect, Bath Co on NE branch of Little R and near the head "thereof"; certified Sept. 12, 1735; warrant to Jos Clark.

170. Sept. 11, 1735 Jonathan Colkins warrant for 1,100 ac in New Hanover Prect, Bath Co on NE branch of Little R and N side "thereof"; border: begins at Col. Waters' NE corner and runs along the branch; certified Sept. 12, 1735; warrant to Jos Clark.

171. Sept. 8, 1735 Edward Wingate warrant for 640 ac in New Hanover Prect, Bath Co on NE branch of Lockwoods Folly R; border: joins a tract known as Edd. Lee's land; certified Sept. 13, 1735; warrant to Will Gray; "paid to Mr. W" [written in the margin].

172. Jun. 18, 1735 John Hodges warrant for 320 ac in New Hanover Prect, Bath Co on SW side of NW River; border: begins a "small" distance below Espys Cr and runs "down"; certified Sept. 13, 1735; warrant to Will Gray.

173. Sept. 12, 1735 Rees Evans warrant for 640 ac in New Hanover Prect, Bath Co on W side of NE River; border: begins at Da Evans' corner and runs "up South"; being the "plantation" where he lives; in New Hanover Prect, Bath Co warrant to Da Evans.

174. Sept. 17, 1735 Clement Machan warrant for 640 ac in New Hanover Prect, Bath Co; between Jos Watters and Jno Dallison; formerly Partridge's "plantation"; certified Sept. 17, 1735; warrant to Jos Clark.

175. Jun. 13, 1735 Thomas Mace warrant for 300 ac in New Hanover Prect, Bath Co on E side of the "entrance" of Dutchmans Cr; border: Jos Sherburn; certified Sept. 17, 1735; warrant to Wm Watters.

176. Sept. 17, 1735 Peter Byard warrant for 320 ac in New Hanover Prect, Bath Co on E side of NW River; border: about a mile above Job Howe; certified Sept. 17, 1735; warrant to Jos Clark.

177. Sept. 17, 1735 John Parry warrant for 600 ac in New Hanover Prect, Bath Co on "N" Topsail Sound; border: Parrys Cr and Rush Watt's land; certified Sept.

17, 1735; warrant to Wm Watters.

178. Sept. 3, 1735 Joshua Gabourel warrant for 1,280 ac in New Hanover Prect, Bath Co on NW River; border: begins at Welches Bluff and runs down the Thoroughfare certified Sept. 17, 1735; warrant to Jos Clark.

179. Sept. 17, 1735 [no name] warrant for 400 ac in New Hanover Prect, Bath Co on NE side of NE Creek of New Topsail [Sound]; border: Geo Bishop; certified Sept. 17, 1735; warrant to Michl. Clark.

page 19
180. Feb. 23, 1735/6 Thos Nixson warrant for 500 ac in New Hanover Prect, Bath Co; border: Wm Moris and on Nixsons Cr; certified Feb. 23, 1735/6; warrant to Wm Gray; warrant returned Sept. 10, 1737.

181. Feb. 23, 1735/6 Jean Husbands warrant for 320 ac in New Hanover Prect, Bath Co on the sound; between Capt. Cocke and Shole Inlet; being the land where she lives; certified Feb. 23, 1735/6; warrant to Wm Gray; warrant returned Jun. 9, 1736.

182. Feb. 21, 1735 Jonn. Pratt warrant for 400 ac in New Hanover Prect, Bath Co on W side of NE River; border: joins land where Thomas Hutchins lives; certified Feb. 21, 1735/6; warrant to Wm Gray.

183. Sept. 19, 1735 Jon. Taylor warrant for 400 ac in New Hanover Prect, Bath Co on head of Duchmans [sic] Cr and on the road to South Carolina from Brunswick; certified Feb. 23, 1735/6; warrant to Wm Gray [or] John Miller.

184. Jan. 14, 1735/6 Richd Hellier warrant for 350 [written over 300] ac in New Hanover Prect, Bath Co on SW side of Old Town Cr; according to a survey made by Paul Palmer; border: Robt Peter; certified Feb. 25, 1735/6; warrant to Wm Waters.

185. Feb. 18, 1735/6 Jon. Pickersgill and Bleak [sic] warrant for 300 ac in New Hanover Prect, Bath Co on N side of Goun Cr; where "he" lives; certified Feb. 25, 1735/6; warrant to Wm Waters.

186. Mar. 30, 1736 Edward Davis warrant for 300 ac in New Hanover Prect, Bath Co on the sound and about half a mile S of Cabbage Inlet Cr; border: on S of a tract formerly belonging to Henry Herby; certified Mar 30, 1736; warrant to Wm Gray; warrant returned Jun. 9, 1736.

187. Feb. 19, 1735/6 Evans Jones warrant for 1,280 ac in New Hanover Prect, Bath Co on W side of NE River; border: joins said Evans' land and "downwards"; certified Feb. 23, 1735/6; warrant to Wm Gray.

North Carolina Land Entries 1735-1752

188. May 17, 1735 Jno Edwards warrant for 320 ac in New Hanover Prect, Bath Co; border: begins at Reese Evans' land, joins a white oak, & runs down "the" branch; certified Feb. 24, 1735/6; warrant to Dad. Evans; warrant returned Jun. 9, 1736.

189. Feb. 24, 1735/6 Wm Gray sr warrant for 640 ac in New Hanover Prect, Bath Co on E side of NE Cape Fear R; border: begins at Edward Carter's upper corner on the river and runs up the river; certified Feb. 24, 1735/6; warrant to Jo Clark.

190. Feb. 24, 1735/6 Jno Gray warrant for 640 ac in New Hanover Prect, Bath Co; border: Wm Gray's entry "of this day" on E side of NE Cape Fear R and runs down the river; certified Feb. 24, 1735/6; warrant to Jos Clark.

191. May 21, 1735 [?] Lewis Bryan warrant for 640 ac in New Hanover Prect, Bath Co; border: begins at Edward Carter's lower corner on E side of NE Cape Fear R and runs down the river; certified Feb. 24, 1735/6; warrant to Jos Clark.

page 20
192. Feb. 18, 1735 Thos Bell warrant for 640 ac in New Hanover Prect, Bath Co on SW side of Lockwoods Folly R; border: begins 100 poles below Batchelors Cr and runs "up"; certified Apr. 9, 1736; warrant to Wm Gray; warrant returned Jun. 9, 1736.

193. May 10, 1736 James Murray warrant for 640 ac in New Hanover Prect, Bath Co on the sound; being the "plantation" where Fortune Holderby lately lives; certified May 14, 1736; warrant to Wm Gray; warrant returned Sept. 10, 1736.

194. Apr. 20, 1736 Nath. Rice esq warrant for 320 ac in New Hanover Prect, Bath Co on Old Town Cr; border: near Thos Hill and John Lewis; certified May 17, 1736; warrant to Joseph Clerk [Will Watters--lined out]; warrant returned Jun. 29, 1738.

195. Jun. 23, 1735 Hugh Campbell warrant for 640 ac in New Hanover Prect, Bath Co on E side of "the" river; border: joins the lower line "or" near Mr. Irby's land; certified May 26, 1736; warrant to Wil Gray; warrant returned Jun. 9, 1736.
197. Sept. 9, 1735 [?] John Hawes warrant for 100 ac in New Hanover Prect, Bath Co on a fork of Gevins' Cr and on the sound; border: opposite Baker's "plantation" on one side and A Nicholas' ["plantation"] on the other side; certified May 26, 1736; warrant to Will Gray.

198. Feb. 21, 1735/6 John Porter warrant for 200 ac in New Hanover Prect, Bath Co on E side of NE Cape Fear R, about 3 miles above Rocky point, & [on ?] Burkes [?] Br; between Edward Mosley and land said Porter bought of John Arthur; certified May 26, 1736; warrant to Will Gray; warrant returned Feb. 15, 1737/8.

199. Jun. 8, 1736 Jas Murray warrant for 400 ac in New Hanover Prect, Bath Co on E side of Cape Fear R; border: begins at Hugh Campbell's upper corner and runs up the river; certified Jun. 10, 1736; warrant to Wil Gray.

200. Jun. 8, 1736 Jas Murray warrant for 500 ac in New Hanover Prect, Bath Co on the sound; border: begins on John Hogeson's eastermost corner and runs to Edward Davis' line; certified Jun. 10, 1736; warrant to Wil Gray.

201. Jun. 17, 1736 Abraham Blackhall warrant for 640 ac in New Hanover Prect, Bath Co on W side of Waggamaw R; border: Lewis Johns lower line and runs down the river; certified Jun. 21, 1736; warrant to Wm Watters [or] John Miller; warrant returned Sept. 10, 1736.

202. Jun. 15, 1736 Rich Eagle warrant for 640 ac in New Hanover Prect, Bath Co; border: Henry Simonds, James Grange, & said Eagle's land; certified Jun. 21, 1736; warrant to Wm Gray; warrant returned Sept. 10, 1736.

203. Jun. 19 [24--lined out], 1736 Vincent Garen warrant for 640 ac in New Hanover Prect, Bath Co on Prince Georges Cr; where Armand DeRosset lives; border: joins upper part of Pontvint [sic] land; certified Jun. 24, 1736; warrant to Jon Miller; warrant returned Aug 20, 1736.

204. Jun. 19, 1736 Vincent Garen warrant for 640 ac in New Hanover Prect, Bath Co on Prince Georges Cr; being the "plantation" where Mr. Thomas Jones lives; certified Jun. 24, 1736; warrant to Jon Miller; warrant returned feb. 11, 1736 [sic].

205. Jun. 19, 1736 Mrs. Justinia Moor warrant for 640 ac in New Hanover Prect, Bath Co on both sides of "a" creek on E side of Cape Fear R, in a marsh opposite the end of Mr. Gray's Island, & runs "up"; certified Jun. 25, 1736; warrant to Will Watters.

206. Jul. 24, 1736 Mr. Rufus Marsden warrant for 400 ac in New Hanover Prect, Bath Co; border: begins on Capt. Joshua Gabourel's line and runs "towards" the sound; certified Jul. 30, 1736; warrant to Jothn. Miller; warrant returned Feb. 19, 1736/7.

207. Feb. 19, 1735/6 Sarah Rhoads warrant for 400 ac in New Hanover Prect, Bath Co on Topsail Sound and joins Beazleys Cr; certified Mar. 1, 1736/7; warrant to Michael Clerk; warrant returned Mar. 7, 1736/7.

page 21
208. May 20, 1736 John Lamb warrant for 350 ac in New Hanover Prect, Bath Co on E side of Black R; border: opposite Col. Halton's Island on NW; certified May 22, 1736; warrant to Willm Watters.

209. May 20, 1736 Thomas Rowan warrant for 350 ac in New Hanover Prect,

Bath Co on E side of Black R; border: opposite Col. Halton's Island on NW; certified May 22, 1736; warrant to Wilm Waters [sic].

210. Jun. 15, 1736 James Hesell warrant for 200 ac in New Hanover Prect, Bath Co; border: joins said Hesell's land on Rogers Cr; certified Jun. 16, 1736; warrant to Wm Watters.

211. Jun. 15, 1736 James Hesell warrant for 400 ac in New Hanover Prect, Bath Co; border: Rich Brice's corner; called "Buck head"; certified Jun. 16, 1736; warrant to Wm Watters; warrant returned Jun. 29, 1736 [?].

212. Jun. 15, 1736 James Hesell warrant for 200 ac in New Hanover Prect, Bath Co; border: joins "an entry of this date"; certified Jun. 16, 1736 warrant to Wm Watters; warrant returned Jun. 29, 1736 [?].

213. Jun. 15, 1736 Jehua Davis warrant for 640 ac in New Hanover Prect, Bath Co on Sturgeon Cr; border: Capt. Gabriel; certified Jun. 16, 1736; warrant to Wm Watters [or] John Miller; warrant returned Feb. 15, 1736/7.

214. Jun. 18, 1736 David Evans warrant for 640 ac in New Hanover Prect, Bath Co on W side of NE River; border: on N by Rev. Evans and on S by Wm Lee [or Lues]; certified Jun. 17, 1736 [sic]; warrant to Wm Watters.

215. Jun. 17, 1736 John Cooke warrant for 640 ac in New Hanover Prect, Bath Co on NE River; border: on head lines of David Evans and Rich Evans; certified Jun. 18, 1736; warrant to David Evans; warrant returned Mar. 1, 1736/7.

216. Jun. 18, 1736 Thomas Clark warrant for 300 ac in New Hanover Prect, Bath Co on E side of Cape Fear R; betwee Robert Halton esq and Christopher Bevis; certified Jun. 18, 1736; warrant to Wm Watters; warrant returned Feb. 21, 1736/7.

217. Jun. 17, 1736 Nal. Rice esq warrant for 320 ac in New Hanover Prect, Bath Co; border: said Rice's "plantation" on Old Town Cr where he lives; certified Jun 19, 1736; warrant to Jos Clark [Wm Watters--lined out]; warrant returned Feb. 11, 1736/7.

218. Jun. 17, 1736 Nal. Rice esq warrant for 320 ac in New Hanover Prect, Bath Co; border: Mr. Hesel's land on Mill Cr; certified Jun. 19, 1736; warrant to Jos Clark [Wm Watters--lined out].

219. Mar. 20, 1735/6 John Porter warrant for 400 ac in New Hanover Prect, Bath Co on a branch of Rockfish Cr and on NE Cape Fear R; certified Jun. 19, 1736; warrant to David Evans; warrant returned Sept. 10, 1737.

220. Mar. 30, 1736 John Anderson warrant for 640 ac in New Hanover Prect, Bath Co on NE branch of Long Cr; border: Thos Devne and on N side of NE Cape Fear

R; certified Jun. 19, 1736; warrant to David Evans; warrant returned Mar. 1, 1737.

221. [this one lined out] Jun. 17, 1736 Pheneas Stevens warrant for 400 ac in New Hanover Prect, Bath Co on Queens Cr; border: runs "back" [of] Slanton and Lea; certified Jun. 19, 1736.

222. Jun. 17, 1736 Richard Baker warrant for 640 ac in New Hanover Prect, Bath Co on Mine Cr; certified Jun. 19, 1736; warrant to Jos Clark.

223. Jun. 19, 1736 Wm Norton warrant for 200 ac in New Hanover Prect, Bath Co on Black R and below the meadow [Middle Br--lined out]; being the place where widdow Moore lived; certified Jun. 19, 1736; warrant to Wm Watters [or] John Miller; warrant returned Nov. 14, 1738 by W Gray.

224. Jun. 19, 1736 Wm Norton warrant for 100 ac in New Hanover Prect, Bath Co on N side of Black R; border: about 4 miles up the river from widow Moore's old "plantation"; certified Jun. 19, 1736; warrant to Wm Watters [or] John Miller.

225. Jun. 19, 1736 Jas Sherley warrant for 320 ac in New Hanover Prect, Bath Co on Jumping Run; border: begins a chain below "the" road and runs down the run; certified Jun. 19, 1736; warrant to Jos Clark; warrant returned Feb. 11, 1736/7.

226. Jun. 19, 1736 Jas Sherley warrant for 320 ac in New Hanover Prect, Bath Co on Jumping Run; border: joins "an entry of this date" and runs down "towards" Cheek Cr; certified Jun. 19, 1736; warrant to Jos Clark; warrant for Feb. 11, 1736/7.

227. Jun. 17, 1736 Samuel Plomer warrant for 640 ac in New Hanover Prect, Bath Co on E side of Wagamaw R, on South Carolina line, & runs up the river; certified Jun. 21, 1736; warrant to Wm Watters [or] John Miller; warrant returned Sept. 10, 1737.

228. Jun. 17, 1736 Samuel Plomer warrant for 640 ac in New Hanover Prect, Bath Co on W side of Waggamaw R [Swamp--lined out]; border: about 8 miles "by land" above Leus [sic] Johns beginning at a bay or creek and runs up the river; certified Jun. 21, 1736; warrant to Wm Watters [or] John Miller; warrant returned Sept. 10, 1737.

229. Jun. 17, 1736 Abraham Blackhall warrant for 640 ac in New Hanover Prect, Bath Co on W side of Waggamaw R; border: begins at a marked white oak at mouth of a creek about 2 miles below Leus Johns and runs up the river; certified Jun. 19, 1736; warrant to Wm Watters [or] John Miller; warrant returned Sept. 10, 1737.

page 22
230. Jul. 24, 1736 Mr. John Rice warrant for 320 ac in New Hanover Prect, Bath

Co on the main branch of Old Town Cr; border: begins about half a mile above Thomas Hill's "plantation" and runs up the creek; certified Oct. 1, 1736; warrant to Joseph Clark; warrant returned Feb. 11 [no year].

231. Jul. 24, 1736 Mr. John Rice warrant for 320 ac in New Hanover Prect, Bath Co; border: joins said Rice's entry of this date; certified Oct. 1, 1736; warrant to Joseph Clark; warrant returned Feb. 11 [no year].

232. May 19, 1736 Henry Bishop warrant for 400 ac in New Hanover Prect, Bath Co; where Nixon formerly lived; border: John Mott, William Morrice, & Richd Nixon; certified Oct. 28, 1736; warrant to William Gray; warrant returned Feb. 15, 1737/8.

233. Oct. 25, 1736 Joseph Jonson warrant for 300 ac in New Hanover Prect, Bath Co on White oak Swamp; border: Capt. Hyrnes [sic] and runs down said swamp to John Swann's line; certified Oct. 30, 1736; warrant to William Gray "or" Miller; warrant returned Mar. 1, 1737/8.

234. Nov. 27, 1736 Jerom Rowan warrant for 640 ac in New Hanover Prect, Bath Co on Hoods Cr; border: joins upper side of Math. Rowan's saw mill land; enters Dec. 13, 1736; warrant to John Clayton; warrant returned Mar. 1, 1737/8.

235. Nov. 27, 1736 Jerom Rowan warrant for 640 a in New Hanover Prect, Bath Co; border: begins at Matthew Rowan's corner tree on Hoods Cr and runs between said Rowan's land and Moore's land; certified Dec. 13, 1736; warrant to John Clayton; warrant returned Mar. 1, 1737/8.

236. Nov. 27 1736 James Miner warrant for 320 ac in New Hanover Prect, Bath Co between Little R and Waggamaw R; border: begins 3 miles from the Province line and runs N & E from a "cypras" tree; certified Dec. 13, 1736; warrant to Wm Gray "or" John Miller; warrant returned Sept. 10, 1737.

237. Sept. 5, 1736 John Taylor warrant for 320 ac in New Hanover Prect, Bath Co on Long Cr; border: John Anderson's eastermost line and runs N & S; certified Jan. 6, 1736/7; warrant to John Miller; warrant returned Jun. 29, 1738.

238. Jul. 26, 1736 William Maxwell warrant for 640 ac in New Hanover Prect, Bath Co on E side of NE Cape Fear R; border: begins at mouth of Limestone Cr and runs down the river; certified Feb. 21, 1736/7; warrant to Mr. William Gray; warrant returned Sept. 8, 1737.

239. Jul. 26, 1736 Christopher Becket warrant for 640 ac in New Hanover Prect, Bath Co on NW side of Waggamaw R; border: about 8 miles "by" land above Lewes John beginnings at Samuel Sabing Plummer's upper corner on the river and runs "up"; certified Feb. 21, 1736/7; warrant to Wm Gray; warrant returned Sept. 10, 1737.

240. Jul. 26, 1736 Christopher Becket warrant for 640 ac in New Hanover Prect, Bath Co on E side of Waggamaw R; border: begins on Sam Sabin Plummer's upper corner and runs "up"; certified Feb. 21, 1736/7; warrant to Wm Gray; warrant returned Sept. 10, 1737.

241. Jul. 26, 1736 Richd. Hellier warrant for 640 ac in New Hanover Prect, Bath Co on W side of Waccamaw [sic] R; border: begins on Cht. Becket's upper corner "warrant" of this date and runs "up"; certified Feb. 21, 1736/7; warrant to Wm Gray.

242. Jul. 1, 1736 William Symonds warrant for 640 ac in New Hanover Prect, Bath Co on the sound opposite Shalot Inlet; border: E of Lewes Johns; certified Feb. 21, 1736/7; warrant to Wm Gray.

243. Jul. 31, 1736 Jeremy Symonds warrant for 320 ac in New Hanover Prect, Bath Co on N [or NE] side of Saucepan Cr; border: Mr. Edward Hyrnes and Lewes Johns; warrant to Wm Gray; warrant returned Sept. 10, 1737.

244. Feb. 21, 1736 [?] Tho Evans warrant for 400 ac in New Hanover Prect, Bath Co on E side of Long Cr; border: John Swann's W line and runs to Armanda Rieusset's [sic] line; warrant to Mr. Wm Gray; warrant returned Sept. 10, 1737.

245. Dec. 15, 1736 Thomas Clark warrant for 640 ac in New Hanover Prect, Bath Co on Smiths Cr; border: begins at John Maultsby's upper line and runs up the creek; certified Feb. 21, 1736/7; warrant to Mr. Wm Gray.

246. Nov. 12, 1736 Nathann. Rice warrant for 320 ac in New Hanover Prect, Bath Co in "the" neck of Old Town Cr; border: Betsford [or Bekford] and said Rice; certified Feb. 5, 1736/7; warrant to Joseph Clark; warrant returned Feb. 11, 1736/7.

page 23-34 [These warrants are in Bladen Prect.; see Miles Philbeck's book for information about these warrants.]

page 35
247. Mar. 3, 1735 Rev. Jno Garzia warrant for 1,280 ac in Beaufort Prect, Bath Co on E side of S Dividing Cr "in" Pamlico; border: begins at Tarrapin Gut and runs up & down said gut; certified Mar. 31, 1735; warrant to Robt Boyd; warrant returned Oct. 4 [no year].

248. Sept. 6, 1735 Thomas Clendal warrant for 640 ac in Beaufort Prect, Bath Co; border: begins at a white oak on Loosing Swamp near the path to Neuse R; certified Sept. 6, 1735; warrant to Robt Boyd [or] John Powell; warrant returned Mar. 7, 1736/7.

North Carolina Land Entries 1735-1752

249. Sept. 6, 1735 Andrew Bass warrant for 500 ac in Beaufort Prect, Bath Co on N side of Neuse R; border: begins at a beech on the river and joins Cal. Metcalf; certified Sept. 6, 1735; warrant to Robt Boyd.

250. Oct. 2, 1735 Wyriot Ormond warrant for 640 ac in Beaufort Prect, Bath Co on side of "the" river; border: joins Philip Shute's "plantation"; known as Henderson's old field; certified Oct. 2, 1735; warrant to Robt Boyd.

251. Oct. 3, 1735 John Garzia warrant for 100 ac in Beaufort Prect, Bath Co; border: on Bath Town Commons [sic]; between Conert's and Cordent's "plantations"; certified Oct. 4, 1735; warrant to Robt Boyd.

252. Oct. 3, 1735 Josiah Jones warrant for 350 ac in Beaufort Prect, Bath Co on N side of Bay R and E side of Vandermore Cr; border: Francis Lingfield; certified Oct. 4, 1735; warrant to Robt Boyd; warrant returned Sept. 8, 1737.

253. Oct. 3, 1735 Josiah Jones warrant for 250 ac in Beaufort Prect, Bath Co on SW fork of Bay R; being a point in "the" fork and runs up southmost branch; certified Oct. 4, 1735; warrant to Robt Boyd; warrant returned Sept. 8, 1737.

254. Oct. 4, 1735 Willm Webster warrant for 565 ac in Beaufort Prect, Bath Co on S Dividing Cr; border: on back of Wm Lewis' land and joins Cypress Swamp; certified Oct. 4, 1735; warrant to Robt Boyd; warrant returned Feb. 14, 1737.

255. Oct. 4, 1735 Robt Dunbar warrant for 200 ac in Beaufort Prect, Bath Co on "the" fork of a creek; between Robt Compane and Robert Peyton; certified Oct. 4, 1735; warrant to Robt Boyd; warrant returned Jun. 27, 1738.

256. Oct. 4, 1735 Robt Dunbar warrant for 400 ac in Beaufort Prect, Bath Co on W side of Bear R; between Jas Hume and Wm Whitehouse; certified Oct. 4, 1735; warrant to Robt Boyd.

257. Oct. 4, 1735 Major Robt Turner warrant for 115 ac in Beaufort Prect, Bath Co on S side of Pamplico R and W side of S Dividing Cr; border: "other" of said Turner's land; certified Oct. 4, 1735; warrant to Robt Boyd.

258. Oct. 4, 1735 Henry Dyos warrant for 570 ac in Beaufort Prect, Bath Co on S side of Pamplico R, on W side of Blunts Cr, & in the fork of Dupois Cr; border: begins at a red oak; certified Oct. 4, 1735; warrant to Robt Boyd; warrant returned Feb. 21, 1738/9.

259. Oct. 4, 1735 Oliver Blackburn ad Henry Crafton warrant for 320 ac in Beaufort Prect, Bath Co; border: back of a "plantation" called Tyler's; certified Oct. 4, 1735; warrant to Robt Boyd; warrant returned Nov. 16, 1739.

page 36

North Carolina Land Entries 1735-1752

260. Oct. 4, 1735 Mary Perkins warrant for 640 ac in Beaufort Prect, Bath Co on N side of Pamplico R and W side of Duck Cr; border: Jno Brock's back line; certified Oct. 4, 1735; warrant to Robt Boyd; warrant returned Feb. 14, 1737/8.

261. Oct. 4, 1735 Simon Alderson warrant for 640 ac in Beaufort Prect, Bath Co on N side of Pamplico R; between head of Goose Cr and head of Machapungo Swamp; border: Mr. Worsley; certified Oct. 4, 1735; warrant to Robt Boyd; warrant returned Feb. 14, 1737/8.

262. Oct. 4, 1735 Nathl Draper warrant for 240 ac in Beaufort Prect, Bath Co on Aligator Gut; border: joins said Draper's former line; certified Oct. 4, 1735; warrant to Robt Boyd; warrant returned Sept. 8, 1737.

263. Oct. 4, 1735 Robert Boyd warrant for 30 ac in Beaufort Prect, Bath Co on W side of S Dividing Cr border: Abraham Prichard; certified Oct. 4, 1735; warrant to Doctor Maule; warrant returned Feb. 21, 1738/9.

264. Oct. 4, 1735 John Mills warrant for 600 ac in Beaufort Prect, Bath Co on S side of Pamplico R; border: Walter Dickson; certified Oct. 4, 1735; warrant to Robt Boyd.

265. Oct. 4, 1735 Peter Caila warrant for 640 ac in Beaufort Prect, Bath Co on E side of S Dividing Cr; border: Dr. Garzia's upper corner; certified Oct. 4, 1735; warrant to Robt Boyd.

266. Oct. 4, 1735 John Mayo warrant for 100 ac in Beaufort Prect, Bath Co; border: Robt Campane and Jno Prescot; certified Oct. 4, 1735; warrant to Robt Boyd; warrant returned Feb. 14, 1737/8.

267. Oct. 29, 1735 Wyriot Ormond warrant for 640 ac in Beaufort Prect, Bath Co on N side of Pamplico R; border: Solomon Adams' "plantation" and runs down the river; certified Oct. 29, 1735; warrant to Robt Boyd.

268. Nov. 6, 1735 James Perkins warrant for 200 ac in Beaufort Prect, Bath Co on N side of Bay R and on Vandimores [sic] Cr; border: Josiah Jones; certified Nov. 7, 1735; warrant to Robt Boyd.

269. Nov. 6, 1735 Saml Tyndall warrant for 370 ac in Beaufort Prect, Bath Co on S side of Bay R; between Tilmans Cr and Cabbin Cr; [being] the land where he lives; certified Nov. 7, 1735; warrant to Robt Boyd; warrant returned Feb. 21, 1738/9.

270. Nov. 6, 1735 Eliz. Proctor warrant for 250 ac in Beaufort Prect, Bath Co on S side of Bay R; border: Amos Chuthrill [sic]; certified Nov. 7, 1735; warrant to Robt Boyd; warrant returned Nov 16, 1739.

271. Nov. 6, 1735 John Riggs warrant for 640 ac in Beaufort Prect, Bath Co on S side of Bay R and on E side of Cabbin Cr; [being] the land where he lives; certified Nov. 7, 1735; warrant to Robt Boyd.

272. Nov. 6, 1735 Wm Carruthers warrant for 100 ac in Beaufort Prect, Bath Co on S side of Bay R and in the fork of Wanes Cr; certified Nov. 7, 1735; warrant to Robt Boyd; warrant returned Feb. 14, 1737/8.

page 37
273. Nov. 6, 1735 George Moy warrant for 200 ac in Beaufort Prect, Bath Co on N side of Pamplico R; border: begins on "the" creek and runs up Halling Run; certified Nov. 6, 1735; warrant to Robt Boyd; warrant returned Jun. 28, 1738.

274. Nov. 6, 1735 Josiah Jones warrant for 300 ac in Beaufort Prect, Bath Co on N side of Bear R and on head of Bear Cr; certified Nov. 7, 1735; warrant to Robt Boyd; warrant returned Feb. 14, 1737/8.

275. Nov. 6, 1735 George Moy warrant for 400 ac in Beaufort Prect, Bath Co on S side of Grindal Cr; border: begins at Reedy Br and runs "up"; certified Nov. 7, 1735; warrant to Robt Boyd; warrant returned Jun. 28, 1738.

276. Nov. 6, 1735 Jarvis Jones warrant for 100 ac in Beaufort Prect, Bath Co on S side of Bear R; border: David Whorton; certified Nov. 7, 1735; warrant to Robt Boyd; warrant returned Feb. 14, 1737/8.

277. Nov. 6, 1735 Josiah Jones warrant for 400 ac in Beaufort Prect, Bath Co; [being] the land where he lives; certified Nov. 7, 1735; warrant to Robt Boyd; warrant returned Feb. 14, 1737/8.

278. Nov. 6, 1735 Willm Carruthers warrant for 100 ac in Beaufort Prect, Bath Co on S side of Bay R; border: John Lintfield; certified Nov. 7, 1735; warrant to Robt Boyd; warrant returned Feb. 21, 1738/9.

279. Nov. 6, 1735 George Moy warrant for 500 ac in Beaufort Prect, Bath Co; [being] the land where he lives certified Nov. 7, 1735; warrant to Robt Boyd; warrant returned Jun. [Feb.--lined out] 28, 1738.

280. Nov. 6, 1735 Willm Carruthers warrant for 100 ac in Beaufort Prect, Bath Co on N side of Bay R and on head of Smiths Cr; certified Nov. 7, 1735; warrant to Robt Boyd; warrant returned Feb. 14, 1737/8.

281. Nov. 6, 1735 Willm Carruthers warrant for 110 ac in Beaufort Prect, Bath Co on N side of Bay R and in the fork of Bare Cr; certified Nov. 7, 1735; warrant to Robt Boyd.

282. Nov. 6, 1735 Willm Carruthers warrant for 400 ac in Beaufort Prect, Bath

Co on S side of Bay R and on head of Weans Cr; border: John Martin's land at Piney Point; certified Nov. 7, 1735; warrant to Robt Boyd; warrant returned Feb. 14, 1737/8.

283. Nov. 6, 1735 Willm Phips warrant for 150 ac in Beaufort Prect, Bath Co on N side of Bear R; [being] the land where he lives; certified Nov. 7, 1735; warrant to Robt Boyd; warrant returned Nov. 16, 1739.

284. Nov. 6, 1735 Amos Cuthrill warrant for 640 ac in Beaufort Prect, Bath Co on S side of Bay R and on head of Trent Cr; certified Nov. 7, 1735; warrant to Robt Boyd.

285. Nov. 6, 1735 Saml Tyndall warrant for 200 ac in Beaufort Prect, Bath Co on W side of Trent Cr and on S side of Bay R; certified Nov. 7, 1735; warrant to Robt Boyd.

286. Oct. 31, 1735 Israel Harding warrant for 300 ac in Beaufort Prect, Bath Co on N side of Tar R; border: opposite Thos Mills deceased; certified Nov. 7, 1735; warrant to Robt Boyd; warrant returned Feb. 21, 1738/9.

287. Oct. 30, 1735 John Chilley warrant for 30 ac in Beaufort Prect, Bath Co on N side of Pamplico R and W side of Broad Cr; border: Jno Jackson and Nichls. Smith; certified Nov. 7, 1735; warrant to Robt Boyd; warrant returned Dec. 22 [no year].

288. Nov. 5, 1735 Willm Dan warrant for 200 ac in Beaufort Prect, Bath Co on S side of Pamplico R; border: begins at Lee's head line, runs up "the" main branch, & back into the woods; certified Nov. 5, 1735; warrant to Robt Boyd; warrant returned Feb. 1, 1737/8.

289. Nov. 5, 1735 Harman Hill warrant for 300 ac in Beaufort Prect, Bath Co on S side of Pamplico R and on Hills Cr; border: joins a former survey; certified Nov. 5, 1735; warrant to Robt Boyd; warrant returned Sept. 8, 1737.

290. Nov. 6, 1735 Edmund Pearce warrant for 190 ac in Beaufort Prect, Bath Co on S side of Pamplico R and W side of Blounts C; border: Henry Dees [or Dies]; certified Nov. 6, 1735; warrant to Robt Boyd; warrant returned Nov. 22, 1738.

291. Nov. 6, 1735 Seth Pilkinton warrant for 640 ac in Beaufort Prect, Bath Co on S side of Pamplico R; border: Salter's land, begins at "his" back line, & run W; certified Nov. 6, 1735; warrant to Robt Boyd; warrant returned Feb. 22, 1738/9.

page 38
292. Nov. 11, 1735 Patrick Maule warrant for 180 ac in Beaufort Prect, Bath Co on N side of Pamplico R; being vacant land between Col. Carry and Lewis Conner's Bath Town Common; certified Nov. 12, 1735; warrant to Robt Boyd.

North Carolina Land Entries 1735-1752

293. Nov. 11, 1735 Patrick Maule warrant for 400 ac in Beaufort Prect, Bath Co on S side of Pamplico R and W side of "the" branch on head of S Dividing Cr; border: Robert Turner; certified Nov. 12, 1735; warrant to Robt Boyd.

294. Nov. 20, 1735 Thomas Worsley warrant for 200 ac in Beaufort Prect, Bath Co on S side of Deep Run; border: begins at a pine; certified Nov. 21, 1735; warrant to Robt Boyd; warrant returned Dec. 22, 1735.

295. Nov. 20, 1735 William Worsley warrant for 400 ac in Beaufort Prect, Bath Co on N side of "the" Beaver Dam; being pine land formerly surveyed for said Worsley; certified Nov. 21, 1735; warrant to Robt Boyd; warrant returned Dec. 22, 1735.

296. Nov. 20, 1735 William Worsley warrant for 500 ac in Beaufort Prect, Bath Co on N side of "the" Beaver Dam; border: begins at a pine by said dam; certified Nov. 21, 1735; warrant to Robt Boyd; warrant returned Dec. 22, 1735.

297. Nov. 20, 1735 William Worlsey warrant for 640 ac in Beaufort Prect, Bath Co on N side of eastermost branch of Broad Cr; certified Nov. 21, 1735; warrant to Robt Boyd; warrant returned Dec. 22, 1735.

298. Nov. 20, 1735 William Worsley warrant for 520 ac in Beaufort Prect, Bath Co on N side of "the" Beaver Dam and on head of Broad Cr; border: begins at a pin in the fork of the Beaver Dam; certified Nov. 21, 1735; warrant to Robt Boyd.

299. Nov. 20, 1735 William Worsley warrant for 400 ac in Beaufort Prect, Bath Co on W side of "the" Beaver Dam; border: begins at westermost "middle" fork of said dam; certified Nov. 21, 1735; warrant to Robt Boyd; warrant returned Dec. 22, 1735.

300. Nov. 20, 1735 James Worsley warrant for 640 ac in Beaufort Prect, Bath Co on E side of head of "the" Beaver Dam; border: begins at a pine; certified Nov. 21, 1735; warrant to Robt Boyd.

301. Nov. 20, 1735 John Worsley jr warrant for 240 ac in Beaufort Prect, Bath Co on E side of head of "Gooss" Cr; border: begins at a pine "of one of" Jacob Martin's line trees; certified Nov. 21, 1735; warrant to Robt Boyd.

302. Nov. 20, 1735 James Worlsey warrant for 640 ac in Beaufort Prect, Bath Co; border: begins at Mr. Odean's and Mr. Knight's lines; certified Nov. 21, 1735; warrant to Robt Boyd.

303. Nov. 20, 1735 Ebenezer Elliott warrant for 500 ac in Beaufort Prect, Bath Co; border: Henry Lucus and Thomas Batter; certified Nov. 21, 1735; warrant to Robt Boyd.

North Carolina Land Entries 1735-1752

304. Oct. 5, 1736 [sic] Cornelius Tison warrant for 300 ac in Beaufort Prect, Bath Co on E side of Swifts Cr; border: begins at a white oak and runs down "the" branch; certified Oct. 5, 1736; warrant to Robt Boyd; warrant returned Nov. 17, 1736.

305. Dec. 20, 1735 John Mandowell [sic] warrant for 300 ac in Beaufort Prect, Bath Co; border: Edward Peek and runs down Pantago Cr; certified "Oct. 19"; warrant to Robt Boyd.

306. Dec. 20, 1735 John Prescot warrant for 300 ac in Beaufort Prect, Bath Co; border: John Mark's land and begins at Conoho Path; warrant to Robt Boyd; warrant returned Nov. 16, 1739.

307. Dec. 20, 1735 John Smith warrant for 300 ac in Beaufort Prect, Bath Co on W side of "Pantico" R and W side of Gose Cr; border: begins at "the" side of Buting Sedge "Merch" and runs up Campbells Cr; warrant to Robt Boyd.

308. [no date] William Martin warrant for 300 ac in Beaufort Prect, Bath Co on N side of Pantico R and W side of Town Cr; border: Henry Woodward; warrant to Robt Boyd.

page 39
309. Nov. 20, 1735 Peter McDoule warrant for 200 ac in Hyde Prect, Bath Co on N side of Matchapungo R and E side of "Panlego" Cr; certified Nov. 21, 1735; warrant to Robt Boyd.

310. Mar. 3, 1736 Charles Buroughs warrant for 300 ac in Beaufort Prect, Bath Co on E side of Machapungo Swamp; certified Mar. 4, 1735; warrant to Robert Boyd.

311. Mar. 3, 1736 Joseph Barrow warrant for 640 ac in Beaufort Prect, Bath Co on N side of Pamplico R; border: Richard Barrow; certified Mar. 4, 1736; warrant to Robert Boyd; warrant returned Feb. 14, 1737/8.

312. Sept. 8, 1737 John Willson warrant for 300 ac in Beaufort Prect, Bath Co on N side of Pamplico R; being the land where he lives; certified Sept. 8, 1737; warrant to Robert Boyd; warrant returned Jun. 28, 1738.

313. Sept. 8, 1737 Tho Bonner warrant for 400 ac in Beaufort Prect, Bath Co; between Will Congolton and Set Pilkinton on Pamplico R; warrant to Robert Boyd warrant returned Jun. 28, 1738.

314. Sept. 8, 1737 Roger Jones warrant for 150 ac in Beaufort Prect, Bath Co on head of Duck Cr [waters of] Pamlico R; border: Thomas Worsley and joins "a savana back wards"; warrant to Robert Boyd; warrant returned Feb. 4, 1737/8.

315. Sept. 8, 1737 Tho Bonner warrant for 300 ac in Beaufort Prect, Bath Co; widdow Cooper, Wm Congleten, & runs across Herring Run; warrant to Robert Boyd; warrant returned Jun. 28, 1738.

316. Sept. 8, 1737 Adam Ivey warrant for 150 ac in Beaufort Prect, Bath Co; border: begins on N side of Timothey Harris' Mill Swamp and runs up the swamp; includes his improvements "within his lines"; certified Sept. 8, 1737; warrant to Robert Boyd; warrant returned Feb. 21, 1737/8.

317. Sept. 8, 1737 Henry Smith warrant for 300 ac in Beaufort Prect, Bath Co; border: begins at Wm Steven's line "up a medow side", runs up the medow to Wm Keeson's [or Reeson] line, to a marked tree, & includes said Smith's improvements to the beginning; warrant to Robert Boyd; warrant returned Nov. 16, 1739.

318. Sept. 8, 1737 Jacob Taylor warrant for 500 ac in Beaufort Prect, Bath Co; border: begins at the mouth of a branch on Cheekcod Cr and runs up said creek; warrant to Robert Boyd; warrant returned "Feb. 16".

319. Sept. 8, 1737 Mary Ward warrant for 300 ac in Beaufort Prect, Bath Co; border: begins in the fork of Conaghata Cr and runs up the creek; includes her "settlement"; warrant to Robert Boyd; warrant returned Feb. 8, 1737/8.

320. Nov. 4, 1737 Isack Buck warrant for 200 ac in Beaufort Prect, Bath Co up the N side of Great Bay and near Bear R; certified Nov. 4, 1737; warrant to Samuel Sinclare.

321. Nov. 4, 1737 Isack Buck warrant for 640 ac in Beaufort Prect, Bath Co on S side of Tarr R; border: begins at upper side of "a tract" belonging to Mr. Salter and runs S "up" to Jo Mills' lower line; certified Nov. 4, 1737; warrant to Robert Boyd; "J Make Croeare" warrant returned Nov. 17, 1738.

322. Sept 22, 1737 [sic] John Barrow warrant for 200 ac in Beaufort Prect, Bath Co on N side of Matchapungo Swamp; formerly Dr. Maule's "quarter"; certified Feb. 23, 1737/8; warrant to Robert Boyd; warrant returned Dec. 3, 1739.

323. Dec. 15, 1737 Thomas Worsley warrant for 300 ac in Beaufort Prect, Bath Co on S side of Pamplico R; border: begins at Horse pen Br and runs down "the" Beaverdam to Thos Worsley's old corner tree; certified Feb. 23, 1737/8; warrant to Robert Boyd.

page 40
324. Nov. 4, 1737 Isack Buck warrant for 160 ac in Hyde Prect, Bath Co on NE side of Matchapungo Cr; border: begins at Henry Eburn's upper line and runs up the main creek; certified Nov. 5, 1737; warrant to Samuel Sinclare.

325. Sept. 22, 1737 John Barrow warrant for 200 ac in Beaufort Prect, Bath Co on an oak ridge near Matchapungo Swamp; known as Long Acres; certified Feb. 23, 1737/8; warrant to Robert Boyd; warrant returned Oct. 3, 1739.

326. Feb. 18, 1737/8 John Lice warrant for 500 ac in Beaufort Prect, Bath Co; border: Josaha Little's "plantation" called Copess [or Capess] plantation on N side of Tarr R; certified Mar. 1, 1737; warrant to James Mackilwean; warrant returned Nov. 15, 1738

page 41

327. Apr. 9, 1735 George Roberts esq warrant for 640 ac in Craven Prect, Bath Co on both sides of Core Cr; border: Mr. Pollock's line "on lower side of the land upwards vacant"; certified Apr. 23, 1735; warrant to John Powell; warrant returned May 13, 1735.

328. Apr. 9, 1735 Goerge Roberts esq warrant for 3,000 ac in Craven Prect, Bath Co about 8 miles from head of Southwest Cr "bearing" about NW from head of said creek; "vacant"; certified Apr. 23, 1735; warrant to John Powell; warrant returned Sept. 26, 1735.

329. Apr. 9, 1735 Col. William Willson warrant for 400 ac in Craven Prect, Bath Co on N side of Trent R and on both sides of Willsons Cr; border: runs from the mouth of trhe creek "upwards" above High Germany; certified Apr. 23, 1735; warrant to John Powell or Richd Nixson; warrant returned Sept. 26, 1735.

330. May 14, 1735 Col. William Willson warrant for 500 ac in Craven Prect, Bath Co on both sides of Vine Swamp and runs up the swamp; certified May 14, 1735; warrant to Richd Nixson; warrant returned Sept. 26, 1735.

331. May 14, 1735 Col. Willm Willson warrant for 400 ac in Craven Prect, Bath Co on both sides of Beaver Cr at head thereof; certified May 14, 1735; warrant to Richd Nixson; warrant returned Sept. 26, 1735.

332. May 14, 1735 Col. Willm Willson warrant for 500 ac in Craven Prect, Bath Co at a place called Tuckahoe Marsh, above Cypress Cr, & on E side of Trent R; certified May 14, 1735; warrant to Richd Nixson; warrant returned Sept. 26, 1735.

333. May 15, 1735 Caleb Metcalf warrant for 400 ac in Craven Prect, Bath Co on N side of Nuce R; border: begins at a small gutt below Stone Town and runs "out" into the woods & down the river; certified May 20, 1735; warrant to John Powell.

334. Jul. 20, 1735 James Keith warrant for 400 ac in Craven Prect, Bath Co on N side of Neuse R, near "Stoneingtown", on the upper side of "the" Beaverdam, & runs up the river; certified Sept. 4, 1735; warrant to Jno Powell.

335. Jul. 20, 1735 James Keith warrant for 200 ac in Craven Prect, Bath Co on S

side of Neuse R, on lower side of Southwest Cr, & near Salsburry; certified Sept. 4, 1735; warrant to Jno Powell.

336. Jun. 13, 1735 Jacob Sheets warrant for 250 ac in Craven Prect, Bath Co; border: runs "up" from London Bridge along Bever Cr; certified Aug. 4, 1735; warrant to John Powell; warrant returned Nov. 21, 1735.

337. Sept. 5, 1735 Jon Hill warrant for 300 ac in Craven Prect, Bath Co on Swifts Cr; border: Wright; certified Sept. 26, 1735; warrant to Jno Powell.

338. Sept. 24, 1735 Willm Smith esq warrant for 640 ac in Craven Prect, Bath Co on N side of Nuse R at a place called Stony Town; border: begins at a white oak "a little" above Stony Town "old field" and runs "down"; certified Sept. 26, 1735; warrant to Jno Powell.

339. Sept. 24, 1735 Willm Smith esq warrant for 1,000 ac in Craven Prect, Bath Co on Round Neck and N side of Nuse R; border: begins at mouth of a small creek and runs up the river; certified Sept. 26, 1735; warrant to Jno Powell.

340. Sept. 24, 1735 Randolph Fisher warrant for 180 ac in Craven Prect, Bath Co on a branch of Smiths Cr; certified Sept. 26, 1735; warrant to Jno Powell.

page 42
341. Sept. 25, 1735 Thomas Fisher warrant for 200 ac in Craven Prect, Bath Co on Swifts Cr; border: Jas Jones; certified Sept. 26, 1735; warrant to Jno Powell.

342. Sept. 25, 1735 George Stringer warrant for 640 ac in Craven Prect, Bath Co on S side of Neuse R and upper part of Core Cr; border: Mr. Roberts; certified Sept. 26, 1735; warrant to Jno Powell; warrant returned Nov. 24, 1735.

343. Sept. 25, 1735 Abram. Taylor warrant for 300 ac in Craven Prect, Bath Co on W side of Core Cr; where he lives; certified Sept. 26, 1735; warrant to Jno Powell.

344. Sept. 25, 1735 Richd Elliot warrant for 200 ac in Craven Prect, Bath Co; border: Mr. Pollock's land about 1.5 miles from New Bern; certified Sept. 26, 1735; warrant to Jno Powell; warrant returned Sept. 9, 1737.

345. Sept. 26, 1735 Richd Johnson warrant for 200 ac in Craven Prect, Bath Co on Northwest Cr of Nuse R; certified Sept. 26, 1735; warrant to Jno Powell.

346. Jul. 20, 1735 Fredk. Islan warrant for 400 ac in Craven Prect, Bath Co on Trent R and on Nine Swamp; certified Sept. 26, 1735; warrant to Jno Powell; warrant returned Nov. 24, 1735.

347. Sept. 26, 1735 Howel Jones warrant for 100 ac in Craven Prect, Bath Co on

a branch of Loosing Swamp and on the high road between Catantney Cr and Nuse R; certified Sept. 26, 1735; warrant to Jno Powell.

348. Sept. 26, 1735 Thomas Branton warrant for 150 ac in Craven Prect, Bath Co between Neuse R and Catantney Cr on the high road; certified Sept. 26, 1735; warrant to Jno Powell.

349. Sept. 25, 1735 Philip Trapnell warrant for 250 ac in Craven Prect, Bath Co on S side of Nuse R and on Village Cr; border: Mr. Pollock; certified Sept. 27, 1735; warrant to Jno Powell.

350. Sept. 26, 1735 James Trotter warrant for 1,000 ac in Craven Prect, Bath Co; border: begins at a red oak on a large reedy branch, joins the upper side of Germany land, & runs down "the" river to the creek; certified Sept. 27, 1735; warrant to Jno Powell; warrant returned Nov. 24, 1735.

351. Sept. 26, 1735 William Gray warrant for 2,000 a in Craven Prect, Bath Co; border: begins at upper crner red oak of High Germany land and runs down "the" river to a large reedy branch; includes Great Tuckahoe Marsh; certified Sept. 27, 1735; warrant to Jno Powell; warrant returned Nov. 24, 1735.

352. Sept. 25, 1735 Martin Franks warrant for 3,000 ac in Craven Prect, Bath Co on S side of Trent R; called High Germany; certified Sept. 27, 1735; warrant to Richd Nixson.

353. Sept. 26, 1735 [sic] Martin Franks warrant for 1,000 ac in Craven Prect, Bath Co on N side of Trent R, at a place calld "Eel" Cr, & at head of Beaver Cr; certified Sept. 27, 1735; warrant to Richd Nixson; warrant returned Sept. 9, 1737.

354. Sept. 25, 1735 Martin Franks warrant for 1,000 ac in Craven Prect, Bath Co on N side of Trent R; at a place called Chinakapin; certified Sept. 27, 1735; warrant to Richd Nixson; warrant returned Nov. 24, 1735.

page 43
355. Sept. 26, 1735 John Vernam warrant for 350 ac in Craven Prect, Bath Co on S side of Nuse R and on Flat Swamp; border: Ferguson; certified Sept. 27, 1735; warrant to Richd Nixson.

356. Sept. 9, 1735 Nich Routledge warrant for 200 ac in Craven Prect, Bath Co on S side of Nuse R; border: joins back line of Peter Hand's land about 3 or miles from New Bern town; certified Sept. 27, 1735; warrant to Jno Powell.

357. Sept. 26, 1735 George Thomas [write over] warrant for 600 ac in Craven Prect, Bath Co on S side of Nuse R; border: begins at the Blue Banks; certified Sept. 27, 1735; warrant to Jno Powell; warrant returned Jun. 28, 1738.

358. Sept. 27, 1735 Francis Dawson warrant for 100 ac in Craven Prect, Bath Co on N side of Nuse R and at head of a branch coming out of Upper Broad Cr at E side of Great Savannah; certified Sept. 27, 1735; warrant to Jno Powell; warrant returned Oct. 26 [or 20], 1736.

359. Sept. 27, 1735 John Fonviele warrant for 200 ac in Craven Prect, Bath Co on Flat Swamp and near Fort Barnwell; border: Pollock; certified Sept. 27, 1735; warrant to Richd Nixson.

360. Sept. 26, 1735 Thomas Graves warrant for 350 ac in Craven Prect, Bath Co on Stony Br; border: near Capt. Hennis; certified Sept. 27, 1735; warrant to Richd Nixson; warrant returned Sept. 9, 1737.

361. Sept. 27, 1735 Richard Johnson warrant for 200 ac in Craven Prect, Bath Co on N side of Nuse R at "the" ferry; certified Sept. 27, 1735; warrant to Richd Nixson; warrant returned Sept. 9, 1737.

362. Sept. 25, 1735 [sic] Col. Willm. Willson warrant for 300 ac in Craven Prect, Bath Co on a branch of Brices Cr where said Willson has a saw "milne"; certified Sept. 27, 1735; warrant to Richd Nixson; warrant returned Nov. 24, 1735.

362. Sept. 26, 1735 Col. Willm. Willson warrant for 300 ac in Craven Prect, Bath Co on Raccoon Cr; border: back of Thos Pollock; certified Sept. 27, 1735; warrant to Richd Nixson.

363. Sept. 27, 1735 George Kenege warrant for 150 ac in Craven Prect, Bath Co at a place called Jacobs Wells on S side of Nuse R; certified Sept. 27, 1735; warrant to Jno Powell; warrant returned Nov. 24, 1735.

364. Sept. 24, 1735 [sic] George Roberts esq warrant for 320 ac in Craven Prect, Bath Co on N side of Southwest Cr and on a small branch about 5 miles from the mouth of the creek; certified Sept. 27, 1735; warrant to Jno Powell.

365. Sept. 24, 1735 George Roberts eq warrant for 200 ac in Craven Prect, Bath Co on E side of Southwest Cr and of Strawberry Br; border: begins near head of said branch and runs "down"; certified Sept. 27, 1735; warrant to Jno Powell.

366. Sept. 27, 1735 Thomas Smith warrant for 200 ac in Craven Prect, Bath Co; called Turky Quarter border: joins the land where he lives; certified Sept. 27, 1735; warrant to Jno Powell.

367. Sept. 27, 1735 John Taylor warrant for 200 ac in Craven Prect, Bath Co on E side of Southwest Cr; certified Sept. 29, 1735; warrant to Jno Powell; warrant returned Sept. 9, 1737.

368. Sept. 27, 1735 Robt Germain and Thos Smith warrant for 600 ac in Craven Prect, Bath Co on W side of Reed Br; border: joins a pocoson and meadow on S

side of Nuse R about 15 miles above Southwest Cr; certified Sept. 29, 1735; warrant to Jno Powell.

369. Sept. 29, 1735 Samuel Johnston warrant for 1,000 ac in Craven Prect, Bath Co; border: begins at Martin Franks' uper line on Chincopin Cr and runs up said creek "and branches"; certified Sept. 29, 1735; warrant to Jno Powell; warrant returned Nov. 4, 1735.

370. Sept. 29, 1735 Samuel Wodward warrant for 1,000 ac in Craven Prect, Bath Co; border: Martin Franks' land on "Eell" Cr & Bever Cr and runs up "said" creek; certified Sept. 29, 1735; warrant to Jno Powell; warrant returned Nov. 4, 1735.

371. Sept. 9, 1735 John Beasely warrant for 200 ac in Craven Prect, Bath Co on N side of Nuse R and begins at Whites Br; certified Sept. 29, 1735; warrant to Jno Powell; warrant returned Sept. 9, 1737.

372. Sept. 27, 1735 William Brice warrant for 200 ac in Craven Prect, Bath Co; border: joins the land where Col. Willson's mill stands; certified Sept. 29, 1735; warrant to Jno Powell.

page 44
373. Sept. 27, 1735 Solomon Smith warrant for 640 ac in Craven Prect, Bath Co on S side of Nuse R; border: John Lovick's upper line; certified Sept. 29, 1735; warrant to Richd Nixon.

374. Sept. 29, 1735 James Green warrant for 200 ac in Craven Prect, Bath Co; between his former line and Stony Br; border: begins at a red oak; certified Sept. 29, 1735; warrant to Richd Nixson.

375. Sept. 29, 1735 John Williams warrant for 300 ac in Craven Prect, Bath Co on Half Moon Swamp; border: Loftin; certified Sept. 29, 1735; warrant to Jno Powell; warrant returned Oct. 20 [written over 22], 1736.

376. Sept. 29, 1735 John Williams warrant for 100 ac in Craven Prect, Bath Co on S side of Southwest Cr of Nuse R; border: about a mile from Jno Taylor; certified Sept. 29, 1735; warrant to Jno Powell; warrant returned Oct. 20, 1736.

377. Sept. 27, 1735 Daniel Shine warrant for 200 ac in Craven Prect, Bath Co on N side of Nuse R and on the fork of Durhams Cr; certified Sept. 30, 1735; warrant to Jno Powell; warrant returned Oct. 20, 1736.

378. Sept. 27, 1735 Furnifold [or Turnifold] Green warrant for 200 ac in Craven Prect, Bath Co on N side of Nuse R; between Broad Cr and Goose Cr; border: joins a savannah; certified Sept. 30, 1735; warrant to Jno Powell.

379. Sept. 27, 1735 William Hancock warrant for 400 ac in Craven Prect, Bath

Co on S side of Nuse R; between Francis Nunn and Isaac Scadey; certified Sept. 30, 1735; warrant to Jno Powell.

380. Sept. 27, 1735 Lazarus Turner warrant for 640 ac in Craven Prect, Bath Co on S side of Nuse R; certified Sept. 30, 1735; warrant to Jno Powell.

381. Sept. 27, 1735 Jeremiah Murphy warrant for 200 ac in Craven Prect, Bath Co on N side of Trent R; border: on a branch between Jacob Sheets' and Thomas Humphry's "plantations"; certified Sept. 30, 1735; warrant to Jno Powell; warrant returned Nov. 17, 1738.

382. Sept. 27, 1735 William Pate warrant for 640 ac in Craven Prect, Bath Co at head of Cattantney Cr; certified Sept. 30, 1735; warrant to Richd Nixson.

383. Sept. 26, 1735 John Short warrant for 640 ac in Craven Prect, Bath Co on an island on N side of Nuse R; being a place called Core Landing; border: John Beesly; certified Sept. 30, 1735; warrant to Richd Nixson; warrant returned Oct. 20, 1737.

384. Sept. 26, 1735 Robert Bond warrant for 400 ac in Craven Prect, Bath Co on lower side of Upper Broad Cr and on Nuse R; certified Sept. 30, 1735; warrant to Richd Nixson; warrant returned Oct. 20, 1736.

385. Sept. 26, 1735 William Willson warrant for 100 ac in Craven Prect, Bath Co on Cattantney Cr at Rainbow Marsh; certified Sept. 30, 1735; warrant to Richd Nixson; warrant returned Oct. 20, 1736.

386. Sept. 26, 1735 Daniel Shines [sic] warrant for 200 ac in Craven Prect, Bath Co on "the" fork of Broad Cr and Nuse R; certified Sept. 30, 1735; warrant to Richd Nixson.

387. Sept. 25, 1735 [sic] George Linnington warrant for 200 ac in Craven Prect, Bath Co on S side of Nuse R and at mouth of Core Cr; certified Sept. 30, 1735; warrant to Richd Nixson; warrant returned Nov. 24, 1735.

388. Nov. 6 [written over 7], 1735 William Carruthers warrant for 100 ac in Craven Prect, Bath Co on N side of Nuse Cr, on Upper Broad Cr, & at head of Pine Tree Br; border: near Daniel Shine; certified Nov. 7, 1735; warrant to Jno Powell.

389. Nov. 6, 1735 Charles Howard warrant for 640 ac in Craven Prect, Bath Co in the fork of Lower Borad Cr; where he lives; certified Nov. 7, 1735; warrant to Jno Powell.

390. Nov. 6, 1735 Jno Withorington warrant for 200 ac in Craven Prect, Bath Co on S side of Nuse R and on E side of Clubfoots Cr; certified Nov. 7, 1735; warrant to Jno Powell.

391. Nov. [page torn], 1735 John Moore warrant for 300 ac in Craven Prect, Bath Co on head of Lower Broad Cr; border: Wm Hartford; certified Nov. 7, 1735; warrant to Jno Powell.

392. Nov. [page torn], 1735 Jacob Robinson warrant for 300 ac in Craven Prect, Bath Co on E side of Swift Cr; border: about 0.25 miles above "the" Great Bridge; certified Nov. 20, 1735; warrant to Geo Lennington [sic]; warrant returned Oct. 20, 1736.

393. Nov. [page torn], 1735 Ambrose Ariss warrant for 640 ac in Craven Prect, Bath Co on N side of Nuse R, on Falling Cr, & about 2.5 miles from the river; border: upper line of Jno Wiggins and runs "up"; certified Nov. 28, 1735; warrant to John Powel [sic].

394. Nov. [page torn], 1735 John Wiggins warrant for 300 [or 200--page torn] ac in Craven Prect, Bath Co on N side of Nuce R, on SW side of Falling Cr, & about 2.5 mles from the river, & [runs] up the creek; certified Nov. 28, 1735; warrant to Jno Powel [sic]; warrant returned Jun. 30 [no year].

page 45
395. Mar. 23 1735/6 Thos Murphy warrant for 300 ac in Craven Prect, Bath Co on Trent R; border: Tunicleft; being the "plantation" where he lives; certified Apr. 9, 1736; warrant to Jno Powell; warrant returned Sept. 27.

396. Jun. 15, 1736 Wm Herritage warrant for 500 ac in Craven Prect, Bath Co near head of Timmeys Cr; border: joins George Mills' back line; certified Jun. 19, 1736; warrant to Jno Powell; warrant returned Mar. 7, 1736/7.
397. Jun. 16, 1736 James Trotter warrant for 1,000 ac in Craven Prect, Bath Co on S side of Nuse R and opposite Roundabout Neck; certified Jun. 19, 1736; warrant to Jno Powell; warrant returned Mar. 7, 1736/7 [Sept. 30--lined out].

398. Jun. 19, 1736 James Trotter warrant for 1,000 ac in Craven Prect, Bath Co on S side of Trent R and on W side of Cypress Cr; certified Jun. 19, 1736; warrant to Jno Powell; warrant returned Sept. 23 [no year].

399. Jun. 19, 1736 John Parker warrant for 200 ac in Craven Prect, Bath Co on Trent R; border: John Roundtree and runs up the river; certified Jun. 19, 1736; warrant to Jno Powell; warrant returned Mar. 7, 1736/7.

400. Jun. 19, 1736 Thos Wardroper warrant for 900 ac in Craven Prect, Bath Co on E side of Mill Cr; certified Jun. 19, 1736; warrant to Jno Powell.

401. Jun. 19, 1736 Thos Wardroper warrant for 600 ac in Craven Prect, Bath Co on W side of Mill Cr; border: near Vandall Bliles; certified Jun. 19, 1736; warrant to Jno Powell.

North Carolina Land Entries 1735-1752

402. Jun. 19, 1736 Thos Wardroper warrant for 320 ac in Craven Prect, Bath Co; border: Pollock; where Wm Hunter lives on S side of Trent R; certified Jun. 19, 1736; warrant to Jno Powell.

403. Jun. 19, 1736 John Gillit warrant for 640 ac in Craven Prect, Bath Co on a branch running into Trent R; being the "plantation" where he lives; certified Jun. 21, 1736; warrant to Jno Powell; warrant returned Mar. 7, 1736/7 [sic].

404. Jun. 19, 1736 John Parker warrant for 200 ac in Craven Prect, Bath Co on Trent R; border: John Roundtree and runs up the river; certified Jun. 21, 1736; warrant to Jno Powell.

405. Jun. 16, 1736 Richard Lovett warrant for 320 ac in Craven Prect, Bath Co on N side of Tammys Cr; border: begins at mouth of the creek on N side of Trent R and runs "up"; certified Jul. 2, 1736; warrant to John Powell.

406. Feb. 2, 1735/6 (?) George Taylor warrant for 320 ac in Craven Prect, Bath Co on N side of Sluse R [sic] and on W side of Upper Broad Cr; border: begins on Jacob Kowes [or Kours] line; certified Jul. 2, 1736; warrant to John Powell; warrant returned Mar. 7, 1736/7.

407. Jun. 19, 1736 John Montgomery esq warrant for 500 ac in Craven Prect, Bath Co; border: Adam Moore's upper line on N side of Nuce R near Roundabout Neck and runs up said river; certified Oct. 13 [Jun. 19--lined out], 1736; warrant to John Powell; warrant returned Mar. 7, 1736/7.

408. Sept. 27, 1736 Andrew Bass warrant for 100 ac in Craven Prect, Bath Co; border: Mr. Medcalf and Tho Brenton on N side of Nuce R; certified Nov. 13 1736; warrant to John Powell; warrant returned Mar. 7, 1736/7.

409. Oct. 12, 1736 Wm Maxwell esq warrant for 640 ac in Craven Prect, Bath Co on N side of Trent R; border: begins at mouth of Chincopin Cr and runs up the creek; certified Oct. 13, 1736; warrant to John Powell; warrant returned Mar. 8, 1736/7.

410. Oct. 13, 1736 Eliazer Allen warrant for 320 ac in Craven Prect, Bath Co; border: Mr. "Culling" Pollock's back line; includes the vacant land between "the" pond and head of Lawsons Br; certified Oct. 13, 1736; warrant to John Powell; warrant returned Mar. 7, 1736/7.

411. Oct. 20, 1736 William Herritage warrant for 400 ac in Craven Prect, Bath Co; border: Richd Elliot on Lawsons Br; certified Oct. 25, 1736; warrant to John Powell; warrant returned Mar. [page torn].

412. Oct. 14, 1736 John Marshal warrant for 150 ac in Craven Prect, Bath Co on

E side of "the" fork of Broad Cr and "in" Nuce R and on upper side of [page torn]ld road; certified Oct. 26, 1736; warrant to Geo Lellington [sic].

page 46

413. Oct. 20, 1736 Edward Bryant warrant for 640 ac in Craven Prect, Bath Co on N side of Nuce R, on E side of Swifts Cr, & "aboute" Bave Br; certified Oct. 25, 1736; warrant to John Powell; warrant returned Sept. 9, 1737.

414. Oct. 20, 1736 George Bould warrant for 100 ac in Craven Prect, Bath Co; border: Pollock and Adam Moore on Trent R; being part of Great Marsh; certified Oct. 25, 1736; warrant to John Powell; warrant returned Sept. 9, 1737.

415. Oct. 20, 1736 John Slocomb warrant for 200 ac in Craven Prect, Bath Co on S side of Nuce R; border: begins at a red oak in Slocomb's and Moseley's line and near Handcocks Cr; includes the vacant land between "that" and Jack Skadre [or Skadies] and John Hoch [or Holk]; certified Oct. 25, 1736; warrant to John Powell; warrant returned Sept. 9, 1737.

416. Feb. 28, 1736/7 Robert Jones warrant for 200 ac in Craven Prect, Bath Co on N side of Trent R; called Jacobs Wells; certified "Do 1" [Mar. 1, 1736/7 ?]; warrant to John Powell; warrant returned Feb. 15, 1737/8.

417. Mar. 1, 1736/7 Richard Johnston warrant for 200 ac in Craven Prect, Bath Co on Shitten Bridge Swamp; border: on head of Lovick's line and runs down "the" Sand Hills; certified Oct. 2, 1736; warrant to John Powell; warrant returned Sept. 9, 1737.

418. Mar. 5, 1736/7 John Beckton warrant for 400 ac in Craven Prect, Bath Co; border: Owen ODonil's lnd on N side of Nuce R; certified "Mar."; warrant to John Powell; warrant returned Sept. 10, 1737.

419. Mar. 5, 1736/7 Benjamin Williams warrant for 200 ac in Craven Prect, Bath Co on S side of Nuse R and "amongst" the marshes above Mill Cr; certified "Mar."; warrant to John Powell; warrant returned Jun. 27, 1738.

420. Mar. 5, 1736/7 John Williams warrant for 640 ac in Craven Prect, Bath Co on S side of Nuse R and above mouth of Mill Cr; [being] a place called "the" fort ould fields; warrant to John Powell.

421. Mar. 5, 1736/7 John Beckton warrant for 640 ac in Craven Prect, Bath Co on S side of Nuce R and in the marshes above the "inhabitants"; warrant to John Powell.

422. Mar. 5, 1736/7 Thomas Williams warrant for 400 ac in Craven Prect, Bath Co on N side of Nuse R at Buffalo Cr; warrant to John Powell; warrant returned Sept. 9, 1737.

423. Mar. 5, 1736/7 Thomas McClendon [Francas Hopson-lined out] warrant for 640 ac in Craven Prect, Bath Co on N side of Nuse R and on Cypras Swamp; warrant to John Powell; warrant returned Sept. 9, 1737.

424. Mar. 5, 1736/7 Jon Beckton warrant for 420 ac in Craven Prect, Bath Co on Beverdam Swamp and N side of Little Catentney Cr; warrant to John Powell; warrant returned Sept. 9, 1737.

425. Mar. 7, 1736/7 John Willson warrant for 400 ac in Craven Prect, Bath Co on N side of Nuse R and on Loosing Swamp; certified Mar. 7, 1736/7; warrant to John Powell; warrant returned Sept. 9, 1737.

426. Mar. 7, 1736/7 Wm Brice warrant for 300 ac in Craven Prect, Bath Co; between Mill Cr and John Simonds; border: begins at a white oak beween White Oak [R] and Trent [R] Road; warrant to John Powell; warrant returned Sept. 9, 1737.

427. Mar. 7, 1736/7 Francis Stringer warrant for 220 ac in Craven Prect, Bath Co; border: Eleaxer Alen esq; warrant to John Powell; warrant returned Mar. 9, 1738 (?).

428. Mar. 7, 1736/7 Wm Petters warrant for 30 ac in Craven Prect, Bath Co in an island on N side of Nuse R and near Shorts Ferry; border: joins Short's line; warrant to John Powell; warrant for Sept. 9, 1737.

429. Mar. 7, 1736/7 Henry Owen warrant for 200 ac in Craven Prect, Bath Co on head of Garice [or Jorice] Br running into Stony town Cr on N side of Nuce R; warrant to John Powell; warrant returned Sept. 9, 1737.

430. Mar. 7, 1736/7 Abraham Basset warrant for 640 ac in Craven Prect, Bath Co on both sides of Crooked Run; where he lives; warrant to John Powell; warrant returned Sept. 9, 1737.

431. Mar. 7, 1736/7 Jeremiah Symons esq warrant for 1,000 ac in Craven Prect, Bath Co on S side of Trent R; border: John Gillet, Mathew Hase [or Chase], [page torn]Steel, & runs "towards" the river; being land where a German "letley" [or setler] lived; warrant to John Powell; warrant returned "Feb. 10".

page 47
432. Mar. 8, 1736/7 John Parker warrant for 100 ac in Craven Prect, Bath Co on S side of Trent R; border: John Simons on upper side; certified Mar. 8, 1736/7; warrant to John Powell; warrant returned Sept. 9, 1737.

433. Mar. 8, 1736/7 Lionel Lee warrant for 200 ac in Craven Prect, Bath Co on Durhams "Great" Br at "the" bridge on "the" road and on N side of Nuese R;

certified Mar. 9, 1736/7; warrant to James Mackelwean; warrant returned Sept. 9, 1737.

434. Mar. 9, 1736/7 Wm Brice warrant for 200 ac in Craven Prect, Bath Co on N side of Neuse R; [being] the first high ["bluff"--lined out] land above Capt. Hannesy; certified Mar. 9, 1736/7; warrant to James Mackelwean; warrant returned Sept. 10, 1737.

435. Mar. 9, 1736/7 Order of Council for resurvey of James Green's land in Craven Prect, Bath Co on Turkey Quarter at request of Thomas Smith; certified Mar. 9, 1736/7; warrant to James Mackelwean; warrant returned Sept. 10, 1737.

436. Mar. 9, 1736/7 Order of Council for resurvey of Keeth's [sic] and Andrew Bass's lands in Craven Prect, Bath Co; warrant to James Mackelwean; warrant returned Sept. 9, 1737.

437. Mar. 9, 1736/7 Moses Arnold warrant for 100 ac in Craven Prect, Bath Co; border: John Hill's "plantation" and near Peter Reel; certified Mar. 9, 1736/7; warrant to James Mackelwean; warrant returned Sept. 9, 1737.

438. Mar. 10, 1736/7 Mary Johnston warrant for 960 ac in Craven Prect, Bath Co; border: begins at a white oak, on "the" bank side, at the mouth of a branch which runs into "the" river; being near Martin Franks' [land] called High Germany; certified Mar. 10, 1736/7 [sic]; warrant to John Powell.

439. Mar. 10, 1736/7 Carolina Johnston warrant for 960 ac in Craven Prect, Bath Co; border: begins at a white oak, on "the" bank side, at the mouth of a branch which runs into "the" river and joins Mary Johnston's land; warrant to John Powell.

440. Mar. 10, 1736/7 Order of Council Tho Murphey's petition for a resurvey on land of Wm Tunicliff [or Funecleff] [is granted]; warrant to James Mackelwean; warrant returned Feb. 16, 1737/8.

441. Mar. 11, 1736/7 Matthew Rowan warrant for in Craven Prect, Bath Co; border: George Bould; being part of Great Marsh on Trent R; certified Mar. 11, 1736/7; warrant to James Mackelwean; warrant returned Sept. 9, 1737.

442. Mar. 11, 1736/7 William Powell and Osburn Powell warrant for 1,000 ac in Craven Prect, Bath Co on S side of Neuse R and on Broad Cr; certified Mar. 11, 1736/7; warrant to John Powel; warrant returned Sept. 10, 1737.

443. Jul. 27, 1737 Hugh Staniand warrant for 200 ac in Craven Prect, Bath Co on N side of Trent R; "between" a small branch below Mr. Maxwell's line; includes his "plantation" and run down the river; certified Mar. 11, 1736/7; warrant to James Mackelwean; warrant returned Sept. 10, 1737.

444. Sept. 7, 1737 George White warrant for 300 ac in Craven Prect, Bath Co on S side of Little Contentna Cr, above Tarr River Road, & on N side of Nuce R; certified Sept. 8, 1737; warrant to James Mackelwean; warrant returned Feb. 16, 1737/8.

445. Sept. 7, 1737 Henry Somerland warrant for 300 ac in Craven Prect, Bath Co on S side of Cotentna Cr and N side of Nuce R; certified Sept. 8, 1737; warrant to James Mackelwean; warrant returned Feb. 16, 1737/8.

446. Sept. 7, 1737 Francis Nune warrant for 200 ac in Craven Prect, Bath Co on N side of Nuce R and on Grindal Creek Br; certified Sept. 8, 1737; warrant to James Mackelwean; warrant returned Feb. 16, 1737/8.

447. Apr. 25, 1737 (?) James Cathcart warrant for 300 ac in Craven Prect, Bath Co on N side of Little Cotachne [sic] Cr and on Nuce R; border: on N side of the land where William Smith lives; certified Apr. 27, 1737; warrant to James Mackelwean; warrant returned Sept. 9, 1737.

448. Sept. 8, 1737 Joesph Worsley warrant for 250 ac in Craven Prect, Bath Co; border: begins at Joes Br on N side of Swifts Cr and [runs] on both sides of said branch; certified Sept. 9, 1737; warrant to James Mackelwean; warrant returned Feb. 22, 1738.

449. Sept. 8, 1737 Joseph Worlsey warrant for 250 ac in Craven Prect, Bath Co on both sides of Deep Br, on N side of Swifts Cr, & above Cantenengh [sic] [Cr ?] "both" on N side of Nuse R; certified Sept. 9, 1737; warrant to James Mackelwean; warrant returned Feb. 22, 1738.

450. Sept. 9, 1737 John Worsley warrant for 300 ac in Craven Prect, Bath Co on S side of Trent R and "by" the head of Mirey Br running into Trent R; "vacant land"; certified Sept. 19, 1737; warrant to John Powell; warrant returned Feb. 19, 1738.

451. Sept. 7, 1737 Geo Roberts warrant for 250 ac in Craven Prect, Bath Co on S side of Nuce R aout 4 miles above Southwest Cr; border: Turkey Medow; certified Sept. 9, 1737; warrant to Ja Mackelwean; warrant returned Feb. 16 [or 15], 1738.

452. Sept. 7, 1737 Wm Herritage warrant for 500 ac in Craven Prect, Bath Co on S side of Nuce R above Southwest Cr; certified Sept. 9, 1737; warrant to Ja Mackelwean; warrant returned "Feb."

453. Sept. 7, 1737 Geo Roberts warrant for 350 ac in Craven Prect, Bath Co in the fork of Southwest Cr and on S side of Nuce R; warrant to Ja Mackelwean.

454. Sept. 7, 1737 Wm Herritage warrant for 300 ac in Craven Prect, Bath Co

between Nuse R and Trent R; called Jacobs Wells; warrant to Ja Mackelwean; warrant returned "Feb."

455. Sept. 7, 1737 Josha Plat warrant for 150 ac in Craven Prect, Bath Co on head of Trent R and "in" Bowen fork; warrant to Ja Mackelwean.

456. Jun. 19, 1736 [sic] Resurvey [ordered] on Glover's land for Wm Herritage [on land] "entered" Sept. 14, 1737; [resurvey issued] to [page torn, maybe John Powell].

page 48

457. Sept. 10, 1737 Abraham Buffet warrant for 200 ac in Craven Prect, Bath Co; border: begins in a valley about 5 or 6 miles above Tuckahow Meddow and runs down Tuckahow R; certified Sept. 14, 1737; warrant to John Williams; warrant returned Feb. 17, 1737/8.

458. Sept. 8, 1737 John Precton warrant for 200 ac in Craven Prect, Bath Co on Stoney town Cr; border: above Robert Hodges on N side of Nuse R; certified Oct. 3, 1737; warrant to James Mackelwean; warrant returned Feb. 16, 1737/8.

459. Sept. 8, 1737 David Gurganous warrant for 300 ac in Craven Prect, Bath Co; border: begins on upper side of Jno Short's land on N side of Nuse R; certified Oct. 3, 1737; warrant to James Mackelwean; warrant returned Feb. 16, 1737/8.

460. Sept. 8, 1737 Christopher Harison warrant for 200 ac in Craven Prect, Bath Co on N side of Nuse R; between Bexleys [or Beseleys] Swamp and Bear Swamp; certified Oct. 3, 1737; warrant to James Mackelwean; warrant returned Feb. 16, 1737/8.

461. Sept. 8, 1737 Wm Smith warrant for 250 ac in Craven Prect, Bath Co on Cattle Swamp, on School Br, & on N side of Great Contentnaugh Cr; certified Oct. 3, 1737; warrant to James Mackelwean; warrant returned Jun. 29, 1738.

462. Sept. 8, 1737 Wm Smith warrant for 250 ac in Craven Prect, Bath Co on N side of Maple Swamp which makes out of S side of Little Contatitnaugh [sic] Cr; certified Oct. 3, 1737; warrant to James Mackelwean; warrant returned Jun. 29, 1738.

463. Sept. 8, 1737 James Roberts warrant for 200 ac in Craven Prect, Bath Co; where he lives at "the" roadway through Great Contenghtna [Swamp] and on N side of "the" river; certified Oct. 3, 1737; warrant to James Mackelwean; warrant returned Feb. 16, 1737/8.

464. Sept. 8, 1737 Edward Walmsley [sic] warrant for 20 ac in Craven Prect, Bath Co on NE side of Little Contentnaugh Cr and 2 miles above Tarr River Road; certified Oct. 3, 1737; warrant to James Mackelwean; warrant returned Feb. 16, 1737/8.

North Carolina Land Entries 1735-1752

465. Sept. 8, 1737 James Keith warrant for 50 ac in Craven Prect, Bath Co on N side of Nuse R and in Pocoson Island "against" State [or Slate] Landing; certified Oct. 3, 1737; warrant to James Mackelwean; warrant returned Feb. 22, 1738/9.

466. Sept. 8, 1737 Joseph Trewhitt warrant for 100 ac in Craven Prect, Bath Co on N side of Nuse R; border: begins at mout of Crooked Br "at" Richd. Carleton's; certified Oct. 3, 1737; warrant to James Mackelwean; warrant returned Feb. 16, 1737/8.

467. Sept. 9, 1737 John Hollingsworth warrant for 300 ac in Craven Prect, Bath Co on Swifts Cr; border: 2 miles below the fording place at Blunt's "plantation" on S side of said creek and N side of Nuse R; certified Oct. 3, 1737; warrant to James Mackelwean; warrant returned Feb. 16, 1737/8.

468. Sept. 9, 1737 James Mackelwean warrant for 640 ac in Craven Prect, Bath Co on both sides of Flat Swamp and on S side of Nuse R; border: Thomas Pollock's land and runs up "the" road; certified Oct. 3, 1737; warrant to John Powell; warrant returned Feb. 26, 1737/8.

469. Sept. 10, 1737 [sic] Rice Price warrant for 200 ac in Craven Prect, Bath Co; border: John Hills "plantation" on a branch of Swifts Cr, on N side of Nuse R, & upper side of Pamplico Road; certified Oct. 3, 1737; warrant to James Mackelwean; warrant returned Feb. 16, 1737/8.

470. Sept. 9, 1737 Tho Clark warrant for 200 ac in Craven Prect, Bath Co; called Conoe Neck; border: begins at Thomas Graves' line; certified Dec. 7, 1737; warrant to James Mackelwean.

471. Sept. 9, 1737 Francis Stringer warrant for 640 ac in Craven Prect, Bath Co on N side of Nuce R; border: begins at McRora Scarborough's upper line; being the "plantation" Wiggins "the Mullata" lived on; certified Dec. 7, 1737; warrant to James Mackelwean; warrant returned Feb. 16, 1737/8.

472. "Feb. 15" William Herritage warrant for 600 ac in Craven Prect, Bath Co on Contentney Cr and Mill Br; certified "Feb. 16"; warrant to James Mackelwean; warrant returned Mar. 2, 1738/9.

473. Mar. 3, 1736/7 [sic] Charles Hopton warrant for 400 ac in Craven Prect, Bath Co; border: joins the "plantation" where he lives; certified Sept. 8, 1737/8; warrant to James Mackelwean.

474. Mar. 4, 1736/7 Rice Price warrant for 200 ac in Craven Prect, Bath Co; border: John Hill, begins at Herring Run, & runs along Hill's line; includes Banks Island on Swifts Cr; certified Sept. 8, 1737; warrant to James Mackelwean.

475. Mar. 17, 1736/7 Daniel West warrant for 200 ac in Craven Prect, Bath Co on E side of Wild Cat Br; certified Sept. 8, 1737; warrant to James Mackelwean.

page 49
476. May 14, 1735 George Bishop warrant for 640 ac in Onslow Prect, Bath Co; border: [begins] on mouth of Middle Cr and [runs] up Topsail Sound to Mr. Ashe's land; certified May 16, 1735; warrant to Michael Clark; warrant returned Setp. 20, 1735.

477. May 15, 1735 George Bishop warrant for 520 ac in Onslow Prect, Bath Co on New Topsail Sound; border: begins "in" Elezer. Cr and runs up the sound; certified May 16, 1735; warrant to Michl Clark; warrant returned Set. 25, 1735.

478. Jul. 25, 1735 Edwd Morgan warrant for 640 ac in Onslow Prect, Bath Co; border: on lower side of Mr. Homes' land on S side of New R at Mithim Point and runs "down"; certified Jul. 28, 1735; warrant to Michl Clark.

479. Jul. 25, 1735 Ann Morgan warrant for 320 ac in Onslow Prect, Bath Co on NE New R; between Mr. Saml Jones and Mr. Richd. Russell and "so down"; certified Jul. 28, 1735; warrant to Michl Clark.

480. May 17, 1735 Richard Lovet warrant for 640 ac in Onslow Prect, Bath Co on Wallis Swamp; between White Oak R and New R on the main road; certified Sept. 4, 1735.

481. Sept. 11, 1735 John King warrant for 600 ac in Onslow Prect, Bath Co on W side of Goose Cr; border: Jno Wingate; certified Sept. 11, 1735; warrant to Michl Clark; warrant returned Sept. 20, 1735.

482. Sept. 11, 1735 Charles Harrison warrant for 200 ac in Onslow Prect, Bath Co on NE side of New R and on the fork of Kings Cr; certified Sept. 11, 1735; warrant to Michl Clark.

483. Sept. 9, 1735 Jacob Johnson warrant for 640 a in Onslow Prect, Bath Co on Turky Point Cr; border: Ezek. Johnston on "one" side and Michl King on the other side; certified Sept. 11, 1735; warrant to Michl Clark; warrant returned Oct. 6, 1735.

484. Sept. 13, 1735 Richd. Whitehurst warrant for 332 ac in Onslow Prect, Bath Co on N side of New R; "the ferry or fording place there"; certified Sept. 13, 1735; warrant to Michl Clark.

485. Sept. 15, 1735 John Williams warrant for 640 ac in Onslow Prect, Bath Co on NW New R; border: begins at a marked cypress at the mouth of Mill Run; certified Sept. 15, 1735; warrant to Michl Clark; warrant returned Feb. 15, 1738/9.

486. Sept. 25, 1735 Ishmael Taylor warrant for 583 ac in Onslow Prect, Bath Co on W side of White Oak R; border: Joseph Bell's land; certified Sept. 26, 1735; warrant to Michl Clark.

487. Sept. 25, 1735 Edmund Lowel warrant for 507 ac in Onslow Prect, Bath Co on S side of White Oak R; border: Fras. Thurley; certified Sept. 26, 1735; warrant to Michl Clark; warrant returned Mar. 7, 1736 "surveyed".

488. Sept. 26, 1735 Francis Brice warrant for 200 ac in Onslow Prect, Bath Co on SW side of White Oak R; border: Richd. Rushel's lower line; known as Morgans Neck; certified Sept. 27, 1735; warrant to [page torn, maybe John Powell].

[One entry erased at bottom of the page.]

page 50
489. Oct. 29, 1735 Jno Middleton warrant for 640 ac in Onslow Prect, Bath Co on SW side of White Oak R; border: begins at a marked pine near Ashes Cr and runs near Thick Br; certified Oc. 29, 1735; warrant to Michl Clark; warrant returned Mar. 22, 1736.

490. Nov. 7, 1735 Willm Shewbrige warrant for 640 ac in Onslow Prect, Bath Co on Hawlover [Cr]; between Holston and Gillets Creeks and near Little Inlet; certified Nov. 8, 1735; warrant to Michl Clark.

491. Nov. 7, 1735 Martin Holt warrant for 100 ac in Onslow Prect, Bath Co; called Rich Ridge; border: joins Great Savannah; certified Nov. 8, 1735; warrant to Michl Clark; warrant returned Jun. 29 [May 9--lined out], 1738.

492. Feb. 19, 1735/6 Richd Whithurst warrant for 640 ac in Onslow Prect, Bath Co on W side of New R; border: Alligood on upper side and runs up the river; certified Feb. 21, 1735; warrant to Michl Clark.

493. Feb. 21, 1735/6 Thos Tims warrant for 400 ac in Onslow Prect, Bath Co on N side of NW New R; border: begins at a red oak "right against the" cove; certified Feb. 21, 1735; warrant to Michl Clark; warrant returned Sept. 8, 1737.

494. Feb. 21, 1735/6 Char. Ratcliff warrant for 300 ac in Onslow Prect, Bath Co on "the" road "of" Smiths Cr and on S side of NW New R; certified Feb. 21, 1735; warrant to Michl Clark; warrant returned Jun. 29, 1738.

495. Feb. 20, 1735/6 Edwd Mashburn warrant for 250 ac in Onslow Prect, Bath Co on W side of New R; border: Col. Red's upper line certified Feb. 21, 1735; warrant to Michl Clark; warrant returned Sept. 7, 1737.

496. Feb. 19, 1735/6 Peter Parker warrant for 300 ac in Onslow Prect, Bath Co on SW side of New R and in the fork of Allegator Cr; certified Feb. 21, 1735; warrant

to Michl Clark; warrant returned Sept. 7, 1737.

497. Feb. 19, 1735/6 Peter Porry [sic] warrant for 300 ac in Onslow Prect, Bath Co on SW side of the "River of Bagde" and mouth of Pesimmon Br [and] Turkey Cr; where he lives; certified Feb. 21, 1735; warrant to Michl Clark; warrant returned Sept. 7, 1737.

498. Feb. 20, 1735/6 John Gess warrant for 640 ac in Onslow Prect, Bath Co on N side of New R and in the fork of Ryalls Cr; border: Ryall and William; certified Feb. 24, 1735; warrant to Michl Clark; warrant returned Sept. 8, 1737.

499. Feb. 20, 1735/6 Nath. Everet warrant for 640 ac in Onslow Prect, Bath Co; border: begins at mouth of Warrens Cr on S side of New R and joins Mors Prescoat's corner tree; certified Feb. 24, 1735; warrant to Michl Clark; warrant returned Mar. 22, 1736.

500. Feb. 19, 1735/6 Tristim Bullock warrant for 300 ac in Onslow Prect, Bath Co on S side of White Oak R; border: Burnop and Grant; certified Feb. 24, 1735; warrant to Michl Clark; warrant returned Mar. 1, 1736/7.

501. [page torn] Michl Clark warrant for 400 ac in Onslow Prect, Bath Co on W side of New R; border: Col. Red and joins the land where said Clark lives; certified [page torn].

502 [page torn] Arthur Mabson warrant for 640 ac in Onslow Prect, Bath Co n NE New R; certified [page torn]; warrant to Michl Clark.

page 51
503. Feb. 19, 1735/6 John Williams warrant for 640 ac in Onslow Prect, Bath Co on W side of New R and in "the" fork; being the land where he lives; certified Feb. 24, 1735; warrant to Michl Clark.

504. Feb. 19, 1735/6 John Wingate warrant for 450 ac in Onslow Prect, Bath Co on New Topsail Sound; border: John King; [being] the land where he lives; certified Feb. 24, 1735; warrant to Michl Clark.

505. Feb. 22, 1735/6 Geo Cockdale warrant for 320 ac in Onslow Prect, Bath Co on head of Bear Cr; border: joins said Cockdale's head line "in the woods"; certified Feb. 24, 1735; warrant to Michl Clark.

506. Feb. 19, 1735/6 Owen Hill warrant for 640 ac in Onslow Prect, Bath Co on Topsail Sound; border: John Wingate; certified Feb. 21, 1735 [sic]; warrant to Michl Clark; warrant returned Sept. 8, 1737.

507. Jun. 15, 1736 Zachaus Evans warrant for 600 ac in Onslow Prect, Bath Co on Blew Cr; border: above Charls. Ratclif [sic]; certified Jun. 16, 1736; warrant

to Michl Clark; warrant returned Sept. 8, 1737.

508 Jun 15, 1736 Michael Raizer warrant for 200 ac in Onslow Prect, Bath Co on N [sic] side of Nuse R; border: Lazaras Turner's land about 20 miles above Fort Barnwell; certified Jun. 16, 1736; warrant to John Powell.

509. Jun. 16, 1736 John Stokley warrant for 100 ac in Onslow Prect, Bath Co on "the" sound and on N side of Goose Cr; certified Jun. 16, 1736; warrant to Michl Clark; warrant returned Sept. 7, 1737.

510. Jun. 17, 1736 Pheneas Stevens warrant for 400 ac in Onslow Prect, Bath Co on Queens Cr; border: "runs back on" Stenton's [or Starton] and Lea [lines]; certified Jun. 19, 1736; warrant to Michl Clark; warrant returned Sept. 8, 1737.

511. Jun. 16, 1736 Mich King warrant for 640 ac in Onslow Prect, Bath Co on "Stunpy" Sound; border: begins on Jacob Johnston [line] and runs up "the" creek; certified Jun. 19, 1736; warrant to Michl Clark; warrant returned Sept. 8, 1737.

512. Jun. 19, 1736 Thos Petters warrant for 640 ac in Onslow Prect, Bath Co on the head of SW New R; border: begins at a red oak; certified Jun. 19, 1736; warrant to Michl Clark.

513. Jun. 19, 1736 Johathan Weridal [sic] warrant for 200 ac in Onslow Prect, Bath Co on E side of Beare [sic] Cr; border: Jno Huggins; being the land where he lives; certified Jun. 19, 1736; warrant to Michl Clark.

514. Jun. 19, 1736 Wm Morris warrant for 320 ac in Onslow Prect, Bath Co on upper side of Queens Creek Bridge; certified Jun. 21, 1736; warrant to Michl Clark.

515. Sept. 11, 1736 Francis Brice warrant for 200 ac in Onslow Prect, Bath Co on Rocky Run and NE side of New R; certified Oct. 26, 1736; warrant to [page torn].

516. Jul. 3, 1736 William Morice warrant for 300 ac in Onslow Prect, Bath Co on upper side of Queens Cr; certified Oct. 29, 1736; warrant to [page torn].

page 52
517. Feb. 17, 1736/7 William Fraser warrant for 200 ac in Onslow Prect, Bath Co at the mouth of New R; border: begins "and includes" a small island and runs E "on the banks"; "contains between" New River Inlet and Little Inlet; certified Feb. 21, 1736/7; warrant to Michael Clark.

518. Mar. 3, 1736/7 Samuel Jones warrant for 400 ac in Onslow Prect, Bath Co on NE fork of Queens Cr; certified Mar. 4, 1736/7; warrant to John Williams; warrant returned Feb. 17, 1737/8.

519. Mar. 2, 1736/7 [sic] Zarh. [or Farh] Evans warrant for 300 ac in Onslow

Prect, Bath Co above Bettys Vinyard; where he lives; certified Mar. 4, 1736/7; warrant to John Williams; warrant returned Jun. 29 [no year].

520. Mar. 2, 1736/7 Peter Lester [or Leister] warrant for 300 ac in Onslow Prect, Bath Co on SW New R; border: above "the habitents"; certified Mar. 4, 1736/7; warrant to John Williams; warrant returned Jun. 29 [no year].

521. Jul. 16, 1737 William Morgan warrant for 640 ac in Onslow Prect, Bath Co; border: begins a mouth of Ryals Cr and runs down NE New R; certified Jul. 19, 1736; warrant to John Williams "or" Mr. Lillington; warrant returned Sept. 8, 1737.

522. Jul. 16, 1737 John Guest warrant for 640 ac in Onslow Prect, Bath Co; border: begins at a poplar on the River Pocosen on N side of NE New R and runs up said river; certified Jul. 19, 1736; warrant to John Williams "or" Mr. Lillington; warrant returned Jun. 29 [no year].

523. Sept. 7, 1737 Peter Morton warrant for 640 ac in Onslow Prect, Bath Co; border: begins at mouth of Overs [sic] Cr and runs up NE New R; includes his improvements; certified Sept. 8, 1737; warrant to John Williams; warrant returned Jun. 29 [no year].

524. Sept. 8, 1737 Joseph Hart warrant for 640 ac in Onslow Prect, Bath Co on S side of NW New R; certified Sept, 8, 1737; warrant to John Williams.

525. Sept. 7, 1737 Wm Brice warrant for 300 ac in Onslow Prect, Bath Co on S side of White Oak R and in the fork of said river; border: begins at a cyprass swamp and runs up [down--lined out] the river; certified Sept. 9, 1737; warrant to John Powell; warrant returned Jun. 27 [no year].

526. Sept. 7, 1737 Christian Hidelbury warrant for 200 ac in Onslow Prect, Bath Co near Beasleys Bridge on "the" main road; certified Sept. 9, 1737; warrant to John Williams; warrant returned Feb. 17 [no year].
527. Sept. 9, 1737 Ezeekel Johnston warrant for 640 ac in Onslow Prect, Bath Co; border: begins at mouth of a maple swamp on "the" sound and runs up Turky Point Cr; certified Sept. 9, 1737; warrant to John Williams; warrant returned Feb. 17 [no year].

528. Sept. 7, 1737 William Mayner warrant for 640 ac in Onslow Prect, Bath Co on N [? faint] side of NW New R; border: begins on Trent Road and runs up the river; certified Sept. 10, 1737; warrant to John Williams; warrant returned Feb. 15, 1738/9.

529. [page torn] Ben Eason warrant for 320 [written over 300] ac in Onslow Prect, Bath Co; border: begins on Joseph Brooks' line on W side of Batchalers Delight Swamp and runs up both sides; certified Sept. 10, 1737; warrant to John Williams;

warrant returned Jun. 29 [no year].

530. [page torn] Edward Gerald warrant for 400 ac in Onslow Prect, Bath Co on "the" main road between White Oak R and New R at Horse Br and runs down both sides of the branch; certified Sept. 12, 1737; warrant to John Williams.

531. [page torn] Josias Waters warrant for 400 ac in Onslow Prect, Bath Co; border: begins at an oak in Col. Reed's [sic] land and runs up both sides of Stones Cr; certified [page torn]; warrant to John Williams; warrant returned Feb. 17 [no year].

532. [page torn] William Shewbridge warrant for 200 ac in Onslow Prect, Bath Co on W side of New R and on Wallases Swamp; border: begins on Ishmael Tayler's head lines and runs up said swamp; certified [page torn]; warrant to John Williams; warrant returned Jun. 29 [no year].

page 53
533. Sept. 24, 1735 John Webser warrant for 230 ac in Carteret Prect, Bath Co on White Oak R; border: begins aat John Garret's corner tree and runs "up"; certified Sept. 26, 1735; warrant to John Powell; warrant returned "Nov."

534. Sept. 26, 1735 Anthony Cox warrant for 300 ac in Carteret Prect, Bath Co on upper side of Black Swamp; certified Sept. 27, 1735; warrant to Jno Powell; warrant returned "Nov. 24".

535. Sept. 26, 1735 Francis Brice warrant for 400 ac in Carteret Prect, Bath Co on White Oak R; being the land where he lives; certified Sept. 27, 1735; warrant to Jno Powell; warrant returned "Nov. 24".

536. Sept. 26, 1735 Cary Godby warrant for 200 ac in Carteret Prect, Bath Co at mouth of Chester Cr; border: joins land formerly called Todd's; certified Sept. 29, 1735; warrant to Jas Winnright.

537. Sept. 29, 1735 William Burden warrant for 300 ac in Carteret Prect, Bath Co at mouth of Batchelors Cr on W side of Core Creek Run [sic]; border: runs across said creek to Reed's line; certified Sept. 29, 1735; warrant to Jas Winnright.

538. Sept. 29, 1735 Willm. Burden warrant for 490 ac in Carteret Prect, Bath Co; border: begins at a pine on Flaggy Cr "on" Harlows Cr and joins his own land; certified Sept. 29, 1735; warrant to Jas Winnright.

539. Sept. 29, 1735 Henry Stanton warrant for 480 ac in Carteret Prect, Bath Co; border: joins the head line of the land where he lives; certified Sept. 29, 1735; warrant to Jas Winnright.

540. Nov. 4, 1735 John Starkey warrant for 400 ac in Carteret Prect, Bath Co on

E side of White Oak R; border: begins at Bullock's corner and joins Hampton's land; certified Nov. 6, 1735; warrant to Jas Winnright.

541. Nov. 6, 1735 Willm. Burdon warrant for 640 ac in Carteret Prect, Bath Co on Core Cr; border: William Reed and said Burdon's land; certified Nov. 7, 1735; warrant to Jas Winnright.

542. Nov. 6, 1735 Arthur Mabson warrant for 340 ac in Carteret Prect, Bath Co on E side of Davisons or Harlows Cr; border: Shewbridge and Shepherd; certified Nov. 7, 1735; warrant to [page torn].

543. Feb. 19, 1735/6 Thos Harrison warrant for 140 ac in Carteret Prect, Bath Co on "Corse" Sound and Holsons Cr: border: [page torn]ense's land; certified Feb. 21, 1735/6; warrant to [page torn].

544. Feb. 22, 1735/6 Nich. Bryant warrant for 372 ac in Carteret Prect, Bath Co on E side of Newport R; border: [page torn]dal's and Stanton's lines; certified Feb. 24, 1735; warrant to [page torn].

545. Feb. 19, 1735/6 Geo Cummins warrant for 400 ac in Carteret Prect, Bath Co; border: Lee and Stark; where he lives; certified Feb. 24, 1735/6; warrant to [page torn].

546. Mar. 15, 1736/7 Hector Handcock warrant for 400 ac in Carteret Prect, Bath Co on North R and on Sappers (? faint) tree [page torn]; certified Mar. 25, 1737; warrant to [page torn].

page 54
547. [page torn] Charles Cogdell warrant for 422 ac in Carteret Prect, Bath Co on W side of Harlows Cr and joins Allegator Cr; certified Jun. 28, 1735; warrant to James Winright; warrant returned Oct. 13, 1735.

548. Jun. 16, 1735 David Shepherd warrant for 100 ac in Carteret Prect, Bath Co on S side of Newport R; border: Ephrim Chadwick; certified Jun. 28, 1735; warrant to James Winright; warrant returned Mar. 16, 1736/7.

549. Jun. 16, 1735 Josha Nash warrant for 233 ac in Carteret Prect, Bath Co on N side of Shepherds Cr; border: George Cogdale and Shepherd; certified Jun. 28, 1735; warrant to James Winright; warrant returned Sept. 8, 1737.

550. Jun. 16, 1735 Bryan McCullin warrant for 500 ac in Carteret Prect, Bath Co on N side of White Oak R and on head of Deep Cr; border: Morgan and Gillute [or Gilleete] and on both sides of said creek; certified Jun. 28, 1735; warrant to James Winright; warrant returned Mar. 10, 1736/7.

551. Jun. 16, 1735 Theophilus Norwood warrant for 640 ac in Carteret Prect, Bath

Co on W side of North R, on Gilbrto [or Gilberto] Cr, & runs up the creek & river; certified Jun. 28, 1735; warrant to James Winright; warrant returned Mar. 10, 1736/7.

552. Jun. 16, 1735 Henry Stanton warrant for 388 ac in Carteret Prect, Bath Co on Core Cr; border: Capt. Stanton's line and runs along Stanton's line to the "great station"; known as Gerry Point; certified Jun. 28, 1735; warrant to James Winright; warrant returned Feb. 2, 1736/7.

553. Jun. 16, 1735 John Jarrot [or Garrot] warrant for 320 ac in Carteret Prect, Bath Co in "the" straights and on head of Sunning Run; border: Mattox; certified Jun. 28, 1735; warrant to James Winright; warrant returned Feb. 2, 1736/7.

554. [page torn] William Davis warrant for 350 ac in Carteret Prect, Bath Co on W side of Core Sound, on S side of Oyster Cr, & runs along the sound to the "Table of Oakes"; certified Jun. 28, 1735; warrant to James Winright; warrant returned Mar. 10, 1736/7.

555. [page torn] Thomas Austin warrant for 640 ac in Carteret Prect, Bath Co; border: beings at Read's corner tree on E side of Core Cr and runs up said creek to Ja Took's line; certified [page torn]; warrant to James Winright; warrant returned Mar. 10, 1736/7.

556. [page torn] John Gillet warrant for 300 ac in Carteret Prect, Bath Co on N side of Petefors Cr and E side of White Oak R; certified [page torn]; warrant to James Winright; warrant returned Jun. 28, 1737.

557. [page torn] David Turner warrant for 200 ac in Carteret Prect, Bath Co on NE side of White Oak R; border: above Francis Brice; certified [page torn]; warrant to John Powell; warrant returned Sept. 9, 1737.

558. [page torn] Bell warrant for 200 ac in Carteret Prect, Bath Co on Bogue Sound; border: George Gibbs; certified [page torn]; warrant to James Winright; warrant returned Feb. 17, 1736/7.

559. [page torn] Kennedy warrant for 300 ac in Carteret Prect, Bath Co on W side of North R; border: Gilbert Shaw; certified [page torn]; warrant to James Winright; warrant returned Sept. 9, 1737.

560. [page torn] warrant for 640 ac on Core Sound and Oyster Cr; certified [page torn]; warrant to James Winright.

561. [page torn] warrant for [page torn]60 ac in Carteret Prect, Bath Co; border: begins at a cypress on White Oak R [faint] swamp and runs down the swamp; certified [page torn]; warrant to James Winright; warrant returned Jun. 28, 1737.

page 55

562. Nov. 25, 1735 Theophelus Pugh warrant for 280 ac in Chowan Prect, Albemarle Co; border: begin at a "ciprus" on E side of Sumertons Cr "in" the county line, runs a white oak of Deep Br, & down to said creek "as by a former survey"; certified Nov. 25, 1735; warrant to James [page torn].

563. Mar. 10, 1736/7 Francis Pugh warrant for 200 ac in Chowan Prect, Albemarle Co on Chowan R and near the mouth of Maherrinn R; certified Mar. 10, 1736/7; warrant to James [page torn].

564. Feb. 17, 1737/8 Kallam Ross warrant for 64 ac in Chowan Prect, Albemarle Co; border: begins at a pine "joining" John Everard's line and runs down Henry Baker's line; certified [blank]; warrant to James [page torn].

565. Sept. 30, 1738 (?) Thomas Blount warrant for 400 ac in Chowan Prect, Albemarle Co; border: begins at Emperor Pocosan "in" Chowan R, runs NE to George Capeheart's line, along his line to Cake Br, & along Cake Br to the river, & down the river; certified Feb. 25 [no year]; warrant to James [page torn].

566. Jul. 1, 1738 Col. Thomas Bonnar warrant for 400 ac in Chowan Prect, Albemarle Co on Bennets Cr; called Cow Island; includes all the "West" land within Patrick Lawley's patent; certified Jul. 1, 1738; warrant to Henry Bakar.

567. Sept. 7 [no year] Tho Nelson [William Shewbridge--lined out] warrant for 100 ac in Carteret Prect, Albemarle Co on "Coar" Banks; border: begins at a place called Whale bone "files"; certified "Sept. 14".

568. [no date] Tho Nelson warrant for 640 ac in Carteret Prect, Albemarle Co on S side of Ocrecock Inlet; border: begins at a place called three "hatts" and runs East; warrant to James Winwright.

page 56

569. [page torn] William Rhoads warrant for 50 ac in Edgecombe Prect, Albemarle Co on an island in Marratack R and near Wade Neck; certified [page torn]; warrant to John Gray.

570. [page torn] Francis Hopson warrant for 320 ac in Edgecombe Prect, Albemarle Co on N side of Flat Swamp; certified [page torn]: warrant to Robert Boyd.

571. [page torn] Edmond Smithwick warrant for 300 ac in Edgecombe Prect, Albemarle Co in the fork of Smithwicks Cr; border: near a swamp "of" Tho Spellar; certified "10th"; wrrant to Robert Boyd: warrant returned "Feb. 10".

572. [page torn] Edd. Smithwick warrant for 100 ac in Edgecombe Prect, Albemarle Co; [being] a swamp; border: joins his own "plantation" and John

Gardner; warrant to Robert Boyd; warrant returned "Feb. 10".

573. [page torn] Sam Smithwick warrant for 300 ac in Edgecombe Prect, Albemarle Co on both sides of Mill Swamp and near Smithwicks Cr; warrant to Robert Boyd; warrant for "Feb. 14".

574. [page torn] John Tennet warrant for 150 ac in Tyrrell Prect, Albemarle Co on Great Aligator R; known as the New land or Long Ridge; border: joins the river pocoson; certified Feb. 25, 1737/8; warrant to James Craven.

575. [page torn] James Craven warrant for 500 ac in Tyrrell Prect, Albemarle Co on E side of Scuppernung R and S side of Albemarle Sound; border: joins the sound and lines of Philips and Wimbey [or Wimbees] Point; includes Cowpen Bridges [sic]; certified Feb. 25, 1737/8; warrant to Robt Boyd.

576. [page torn] 30th Francis Hobson [sic] warrant for 400 ac in Edgecombe Prect, Bath Co on S side of Flat Swamp; formerly settled by Richard Barefield; border: begins at a red oak; certified Feb. 25, 1737/8; warrant to James Craven.

[The following entries (577-2763) are in the file SS 591 in the North Carolina Archives.]
page 1
577. [page torn] 23, 1743 Currituck [page torn] on Cypress Br near J [page torn] Sawyer's line and from there [page torn]line known by name of [page torn]; made out; paid.

578. Jul. 21, 1743 Theophs. Goodwin enters 250 ac in Edgecombe Co [page torn] side of Cabbin Br at a [page torn] down the branch to Sandy Cr and over [page torn] for complement; made out; paid.

579. Jul. 21, 1743 William "Sargeent" enters 200 ac in Edgecombe Co on [page torn] Hico Cr; border: a "Syrimo" [sycamore tree ?] [page torn] of a branch & so up the branch; [includes] his improvements; made out; paid "rites" returned.

580. Jul. 21, 1743 Osborne Jeffries enters 150 ac in Edgecombe Co [page torn] Ceder Cr; border: a white [page torn] of a branch and runs up the creek [page torn] cabbin for complement; made out; paid.

581. Jul. 21, 1743 Solo Fuller enters 300 ac in Northampton Co [page torn]; border: Wm Bon's land and runs [page torn] for complement; made out; paid.

582. Jul. 21, 1743 Jno Tyrrell enters 300 ac in Edgecombe Co [page torn] oak on S side of rear [page torn] of a branch; border: his own line [page torn] Wills for complement; made out; paid.

583. Jul. 21, 1743 Jno Tyrrell enters 200 ac in Edgecombe Co on both sides of Sandy Cr; border: a pine and runs "in" the falls near & above Pacos Tabb [page torn] "up" for a complement; made out; paid.

584. [page torn] Nathl. Martin enters 279 ac in [page torn] on W side of North R [page torn] Elias Alberdson's corner gum(? page torn) Moline [or "mo line"], runs [page torn] up the river to Jas Shaw's line, & from his [page torn]lbertson's; [page torn].

page 2
585. [page torn] enters 200 ac in Edgecombe Co on N [page torn] River; border: a red oak below Valentine [page torn] and runs up the river crossing Cypress [Cr ? page torn]; includes said Braswell's improvement; [page torn].

586. [page torn] enters 200 ac in Edgecombe Co at mouth of [page torn] creek [on] West side between "it" and Tar R [page torn]said Towend's claim; [page torn].

587. [page torn] Ricks(? page torn) enters 150 ac in Edgecombe Co on S side of [page torn] creek; border: a maple about 0.25 [page torn] below Cattail Marsh and runs down [page torn] for complement; [page torn].

588. [page torn]ms enters 300 ac in Edgecombe Co on lower side of [page torn] creek, on both sides of the road from [page torn] Conicanary to Marsh Island where [page torn] croses said creek, & runs for complement; [page torn].

589. [page torn]k enters 500 ac in Craven Co in the fork of [page torn] and Contentnea Cr; includes his own "plantation" for complement; [page torn].

590. [page torn] Smith sr enters 100 ac in Hyde Co on W side of Matchapungo R at upper end of [page torn]oap Pole Br, runs down River Swamp, & back; [page torn].

591. [page torn] Wyriot Ormand enters 150 ac in Beaufort Co on N side of Pamplico R near Dr. Maul's line on the bridge [page torn] creek and runs on both sides of the swamp; [page torn].

page 3
592. Jul. 21, 1743 Jno Smith jr enters 300 ac in Hyde Co [page torn] Ridge at head or fork of Matchapungo R; border: lower end of the ridge and runs up [page torn] for complement; made out; Forbes; "rites" returned.

593. Jul. 21, 1743 Lodwick Martin enters 150 ac in Hyde Co on S side of Lodwick Martin's Cr and runs between Jos Hall & Phillip Jolley; made out; Forbes; rites returned.

North Carolina Land Entries 1735-1752

594. Jul. 21, 1743 Jno Smith jr enters 100 ac in Hyde Co on N side of Matchapungo R; border: Shallops Cr, runs down the river, & back to the beginning; made out; Forbes; rites returned.

595. Jul. 21, 1743 Richd Alligood enters 150 ac in Beaufort Co on N side of Pamplico R, on Broad Cr, & Herring Run; border: runs between the run and Reedy Br; made out; Forbes; rites returned.

596. Jul. 21, 1743 Wm Webster enters 200 ac in Hyde Co on N side of Penlico [or Pinheo] Cr; border: Giddin, Hallaway, & Jones; made out; Forbes.

597. Jul. 21, 1743 Abraham Duncan enters 300 ac in Beaufort Co on S side of Tarr R; border: Jno Mills' corner tree, runs up Mills' "run", & back; made out.

598. Jul. 22, 1743 Jno Wynns enters 200 ac in Craven Co on S side of Ford [or Fort] Run of Great Cotnetnea Cr; border: John Beverly's line and runs "down"; made out.

599. [no date] Jas Kelley enters 200 ac in Edgecombe Co on M[page torn] Br; between Jn Leonard and [page torn]; made out; paid on "dect".

600. [page torn] Thos Hill enters 600 ac in New Hanover Co on the [page torn] between Shallot and Lockwoods folly [Rivers], on a [page torn] Shelley's land, & runs along the sound; [page torn].

page 4
601. [page torn] Jonathan White enters 300 ac in Edgecombe Co about a mile above "the" Western Path and on both sides of Tabs Cr; made out; [page torn].

602. "do" Jonathan White enters 150 ac in Edgecombe Co a mile below Western Path and on N side of Tabs Cr; made out; Kelley; rites returned.

603. "do" Jas Kelley enters 200 ac in Edgecombe Co; between Jonathan White's two tracts, on SW side of Tabs Cr, & near "the" trading path; made out; Conaeco.

604. "do" Jno Collins enters 200 ac in Edgecombe Co on S side "Nor" of Tar R about a mile above Green's Path and joins Crooked Cr; made out; paid; rites returned.

605. "do" Jno Collins enters 200 ac in Craven Co on S side of Cotentnea Cr; border: Thos Ivis [or Ive's] line and runs up the creek; made out; paid; rites returned.

606. "do" Wm Williamson enters 150 ac in Craven Co on S side of Cedar Cr; being a "plantation" where Edwd. Boker lives; made out; paid; rites returned.

607. "do" Chas Cavenot enters 200 ac in Edgecombe Co on N side of Tar R; border: Chas Coleman's line and runs "up"; "made"; rites returned.

608. "do" Wm Pugh enters 20 ac in Craven Co on S side of Slew bridge Swamp near Keatley's mill Marsh; made out; paid; rites returned.

609. [page torn] James Copland enters 550 ac in Chowan Co on E side of Chowan R; border: mouth of a branch above the "pitch" sand, runs S to Charles Jnkins [or Inkins] line, along his line to James [page torn] Henry Holland's line to the river, & up the river to the beginning; [page torn]; rites returned.

page 5
610. Jul. 23, 1743 Nathl. Everit enters 300 ac in Onslow Co on S side of New R; border: Edmd Ennet's corner red oak, runs to Edwd Mashburn's line, & back; made out; Swann; rites returned.

611. Jul. 23, 1743 Hen. Rhodes enters 150 ac in Onslow Co; border: Sam Moore's corner in Henry Rhodes' line, runs S along said line, & back; made out; Swan; rites returned.

612. Jul. 23, 1743 Danl Maodr(? write over) Orme [or Owne] enters 300 ac in Onslow Co; border: a black oak and runs E on Harris Cr; being the "plantation" where he lives; made out; Swann.

613. Jul. 25, 1743 Elisha Ballard enters 640 ac in Perquimans Co; border: mouth of "Arapeak" Swamp, said Ballard's line, & runs "towards or into" the desart and James Norfleet's line; made out; Swann.

614. Jul. 25, 1743 Alexr. Clark enters 200 ac in Bladen Co; border: Alexr McKay's upper corner about 2 miles above the "higher" Little R and "upwards"; made out; McCulloh; rites returned.

615. Jul. 25, 1743 Elisha Hunter enters 200 ac in Chowan Co; border: a pine in Isaac Hunter's and Robt Hunter's line, runs SE to a pine, S [SE--lined out] to a pine in Lassiters Br, down the branch to Isaac Hunter's line, & along said line to the beginning; made out; Crasen.
616. Jul. 25, 1743 William Bently enters 400 ac in Edgecombe Co on Tosneot [Swamp], at a pine runs "out", & up the swamp, made out; paid; rites returned.

617. Jul. 25, 1743 Thos Lane enters 400 ac in Craven Co on both sides of f[page torn] Run; border: a pine on N side of [page torn] and runs "acr" [or "on"] the run; made out; paid; rites returned.

page 6
618. Jul. 25, 1743 Benj Cullpepper enters 200 ac in Edgecombe Co on N side of a place called Peach Tree and near mouth of Pace's Br; made out; paid; rites

returned.

619. Jul. 25, 1743 Job Wilder enters 400 ac in Edgecombe Co on N side of a "place" called Peach Tree Cr; border: between Culpepper's line and runs across said creek; made out; paid; rites returned.

620. Jul. 25, 1743 Col. William Wilson enters 400 ac in Craven Co on upper side of Batchelors Cr, above "the" bridge, & runs "towards Tomyhauk" Br and the main creek; made out.

621. Jul. 25, 1743 Col. William Wilson enters 300 ac in Craven Co on lower side of Cries [or Bries] Cr; border: Thos Smith's upper corner tree and runs up the creek; being land formerly surveyed, but survey "by some means" was lost, prays a new one; made out.

622. Jul. 25, 1743 George Reed enters 300 ac in Carteret Co on Shepherd Cr; border: W on Joshua Nash's land, E "down the creek", & "so" back in the woods; made out; paid; rites returned.

623. Jul. 25, 1743 Joseph Pitman enters 100 ac in Craven Co on "the" side of Nuce R "in" Adams Cr; border: at the "outside" of a piece of land formerly Nathan Barrow's [or Barron] and joins Thos Nelson's line on both sides of Pinny Pine Br; made out; Lovick; rites returned.

624. Jul. 25, 1743 David Shepard enters 640 ac in Carteret Co on N side of Bogue Sound; border: Capt. Chas Cogdell's and Harman's line; made out; Lovick; rites returned.

625. [page torn] Thomas Martin enters 200 ac in Carteret Co on head of South R and S side of Southwest Cr; [page torn]; rites returned.

page 7
626. Jul. 25, 1743 Jno Hays enters 300 ac in Pasquotank Co on Sand Hill Swamp; border: Erasimus [or Erasunns] and Jno Ferrill; made out; Hodge; rites returned.

627. Jul. 26, 1743 Jos Jno Alston enters 150 ac in Edgecombe Co on N side of Contentnea Cr; border: mouth of a branch and runs "down" to include his improvements; made out; Kearny.

628. Jul. 26, 1743 Elias Fort enters 200 ac in Edgecombe Co on N side of Deep Cr; border: a gum above the path that leads to Col. Whitehead's and runs up the creek; made out; Kearny; rites returned.

629. Jul. 26, 1743 Ignatious Smallwood enters 300 ac in Craven Co on S side of Nuce R; border: a red oak near mouth of Lick Cr, below "the" trading path, & runs up the river; Jett.

630. Jul. 26, 1743 Wm Buim [or Berim] enters 500 ac in Northampton Co; border: Thos Maderies' corner on S side of Conroy [Swamp] and runs up the swamp; made out; Jett.

631. Jul. 26, 1743 Jno Swindel enters 900 ac in Currituck Co on Matamuskeet Lake and Mulberry Savannah; Herr.; rites returned.

632. [no date] John Smith sr enters 300 ac in Hyde Co; border: runs on John Smith's line that was formerly Ch. Smith's survey on head of Broad Neck on E side of Matchipungo R; rights "prd" before the "Councile".

633. [no date] Robt Edneg enters 150 ac in Pasquotank Co; known as Stag Park "by" the New found land; made out.

page 8
634. Jul. 26, 1743 Wm Walker enters 300 ac in Edgecombe Co; border: on upper side of Beaverdam Swamp, on S side of Fishing Cr at a red oak, & runs "out" and up the swamp; made out; paid; rites returned.

635. Jul. 26, 1743 Trueman Moor enters 250 ac in Perquimans Co on N side of "Pequamons" R; border: his own land, lower side of Thos Winslow, & upper side of Thos Jessop; made out; paid; rites returned.

636. Jul. 26, 1743 Richd. Hardgrove enters 200 ac in Edgecombe Co on N side of Little Nutbush Cr and between two branches; made out; paid.

637. Jul. 26, 1743 Geo Boid enters 100 ac in Bladen Co on NE side of NW River; border: Ben Singletary's lower line; made out; paid; rites returned.

638. Jul. 27, 1743 Richd. Wm Silvester enters 300 ac in Hyde Co; on Tinny [or Tumpy] Point Bay on "the" lake and sound; being land formerly surveyed by Mr. John Mann; made out; paid; rites returned.

639. Jul. 27, 1743 Jereal Lambert enters 150 ac in [no county mentioned] on head of Pasquotank R and NE side thereof "by" a Cypress Swamp; border: Cap. Burnham's land known as New found land; made out; Mr. Creavy [or Croevy] to pay.

640. Jul. 27, 1743 Peter West enters 100 ac in Bertie Co on Northern Br; border: his and Col. Frederick Jones' former lines; made out; Gould; rites returned.

641. Jul. 27, 1743 Edward Homes enters 300 ac in Bertie Co on W side of Canaan [Swamp]; border: William Wade; [page torn]; Gould; rites returned.

page 9

North Carolina Land Entries 1735-1752

642. Jul. 27, 1743 Elias Stallins enters 600 ac in Bertie Co; border: his own land, Thomas Baker, & on both sides of "the" Beaverdam; made out; Gould; rites returned.

643. Jul. 27, 1743 Elias Stallins enters 400 ac in Bertie Co; border: his NW corner, Benjamin Hollyman's corner, & runs up both sides of Great Branch of Canaan [Swamp]; made out; Gould; rites returned.

644. [no date] McRora Scarbo esq enters 250 ac in Perquimans Co; border: his own line and Thos Lone [or Long]; known as Oak Ridge; made out.

645. [no date] Jos Hemmg [or Heming] enters 300 ac in Chowan Co; border: land of "late" Mr. Boyd and John Woodward.

646. [no date] Thos Yeats sr enters 300 ac in Bertie Co; border: Jno Oxley's corner and runs along his line.

647. [no date] Isaac Odem enters 250 ac in New Hanover Co; border: Lewis' Br on S side; being land where Hen. Walker lives; made out; to get warrants next Court; McNaire.
648. [no date] Abra Odam enters 500 ac in New Hanover Co on E side of Little Pee Dee R; includes a large spring and Indian old fields; made out; McNaire.

649. [no date] Wm Boyd enters 100 ac in Craven Co; border: Jno Boyd and the sand hills on S side of Little R & N side of Nuse R; made out; McNaire.

page 10
650. [no date] Tho Raulings enters 100 ac in Craven Co on S side of Looseing Swamp; between his own land, Jas Herbert, & Thos McClendon; made out; McNaire.

651. [no date] Ricd. Brian enters 300 ac in Craven Co on S side of Nuse R; border: above Betty's land at Green's Path; being the land where he lives; made out; McNaire.

652. [no date] Jas N[ink blob] enters 300 ac in Craven Co on S side of Walnut Cr; border: Symons Br; being the land where he lives; made out; McNaire.

653. [no date] Niedham Bryan enters 50 ac in Craven Co on S side of Nuse R at the "coming out" of the marshes from Mr. Dee's land; made out; McNaire.

654. [no date] Wm Chambers enters 200 ac in Craven Co in Wiggons Neck on N side of Neuse R and on Long Br between Fallen and Styrrups Creeks; made out; McNaire.

655. [no date] Jos Sesnot enters 100 ac in Craven Co on S side of Nuce R; between

North Carolina Land Entries 1735-1752

Great Maroh and Kenry Ownes; made out; McNaire.

page 11
656. [no date] Thos Sasser enters 250 ac in Craven Co on N side of Little R;
between Jno Sacuer and Jno Ballard; being the land where he lives; made out;
McNaire.

657. [no date] Edwd Cumins enters 500 ac in Craven Co on N side of Trent R and
opposite Sollo [or Collos] Howard; being the land were he lives; made out;
McNaire.

658. [no date] Saml Martin enters 100 ac in Craven Co at mouth of Marchs [or
Marcks] Run, on upper side of the run, & N side of Swift Cr; made out; McNaire.

659. [no date] Thos Spinger [or Shinger] enters 400 ac in Craven Co on upper
Broad Cr; border: Jno Morgan's land "or thereabouts"; made out; McNaire.

660. [no date] Jno Carroway enters 200 ac in Craven Co about a mile above
Green's Path on "the" S Prong and on N side of S Prong; made out; McNaire.

661. [no date] Wm Mills enters 150 ac in Onslow Co on N side of NW New R;
border: a red oak and runs up the swamp; McNaire; "McNaire says this isn't his".

page 12
662. [no date] Joseph [or Gageph] Jordan enters 100 ac in Bertie Co on mouth [or
N] "Roadoke" R and upper side of Sohiky Cr; border: runs to head of the creek to
Cap. Gales line and the River Pecosen; being the "plantation" said Jordan "and
those under whom he claims" have "long" possessed; Next Court; this not to issue
until a hearing had on it.

663. [no date] Jno Lennon enters 640 ac in Bladen Co on SW side of White Oak
Br of Waggamaw Swamp; border: Capt. Rowan's upper line and runs "upwards";
"wart" made out; paid.

664. [no date] Mary McConkee enters 200 ac in Bladen Co on White Marsh;
border: upper corner of Jos Waters lower tract and runs up "the" branch; made
out; paid.

665. [no date] Thos Jones enters 100 ac in Bladen Co on E side of NW Cape Fear
R; between Jno Marhleer's Cr and Thos Locks Cr; made out; paid.

666. [no date] Thos Jones enters 200 ac in Bladen Co on E side of Pee Dee R
about 30 miles above the Great Cheraws "moeorass" [or marshes]; between great
falls & Mills Cr and runs "down"; made out; paid.

page 13

667. Nov. 8, 1743 James Smith enters 253 ac in Edgecombe and Tyrrell Cos; border: on both sides of the county line, on E side of Connetta Swamp, & begins at "the" side of the swamp between Danl McClam's and Wm Jackson's; made out; paid.

668. Nov. 8, 1743 Solo Mofort enters 250 ac in Craven Co on S side of Norhunty [Swamp] and on Low Br; being land were he lives; made out; paid.

669. Nov. 8, 1743 James Wiley enters 100 ac in Tyrrell Co on S side of Bark Poplar Swamp; made out; paid.

670. Nov. 8, 1743 Jno Powel enters 100 ac in Craven Co on S side of S side of Nuse R and on Bear Hill pecoson; between Isaac Williams and Jno Lee; made out; paid.

671. Nov. 8, 1743 Thos Mercor enters 200 ac in Craven Co in the fork of little Cotentnea Cr; border: the great branch which makes the fork; being where Jos Lambert lived; made out; paid.

672. Nov. 8, 1743 Jas Connor enters 200 ac in Craven Co on S side of middle prong of Keithly's mill Marsh; being where Maxwel [or Maxwit] lived; made out; paid.

673. Nov. 8, 1743 Jas Connor enters 150 ac in Craven Co on N side of Nuse R; between Ben Williams and Blackman; made out; paid.

page 14
674. Nov. 9, 1743 Robt Warren enters 350 ac in Northampton Co on S side of Meherrin R; border: a cypress in the cane ponds, runs up the cane ponds, & down Meherrin R; made out; paid.

675. Nov. 9, 1743 John Simmons enters 640 ac in Craven Co between Tar R and Nuse R on Richland Cr running into Nuse R; below "the" trading path that crosses Tar and Nuse Rivers; made out; paid; "N R" 40/.

676. Nov. 9, 1743 Wm Herbert enters 700 ac in Tyrrell Co on Croetar [or Cooetar] Point; border: Reuben's hamock, runs to the lake, along the lake to Peters Cr, along the creek to the sound, & to the beginning; made out.

677. Nov. 9, 1743 Math. Rowan enters 640 ac in Bladen Co on W side of NW Cape Fear R opposite Wm Rowan's land called Silver run; made out.

678. Nov. 9, 1743 George Cubbage enters 200 ac in Bladen Co on SE side of Little Pee Dee R about 6 miles from "the" line where he lives; made out; paid.

page 15

679. Nov. 9, 1743 George Cubbage enters 100 ac in Bladen Co on Gapway Samp about a mile from "the" line near Little Pee Dee R; includes the Cedar Swamp; made out; paid.

680. Nov. 9, 1743 Theophs Williams enters 100 ac in Onslow Co between Bogue Inlet and Weeks Island; made out.

681. Nov. 9, 1743 Owen Jones enters 50 ac in Onslow Co at mouth of White Oak R "fronting" his old patent land; made out.

682. Nov. 9, 1743 Andw Jno Feuben enters 150 ac in Onslow Co at mouth of Queens Cr; border: Snoad and Hall; made out.

683. Nov. 9, 1743 John Starkey enters 200 ac in Onslow Co; border: the "out" corner of the land where he lives and runs back of Sumpson; made out.

684. Nov. 9, 1743 Wm Cannon enters 400 ac in Beaufort Co on N side of Tar R and on Cannon Swamp; border: Mile Br, runs down the swamp, & back; made out; rites returned; paid.

685. Nov. 10, 1743 Jno Tuley enters 50 ac in Hyde Co on E side of Swan Quarter Bay; border: Thos Mason's upper line, runs up the bay, & back; made out; paid; on Wm Bocus rites.

page 16
686. Nov. 9, 1743 Wm Linniear enters 200 ac in Beaufort Co on E side of Horsepen Br; border: mouth of lower fork of the branch, runs up the branch, & back; made out; paid; rites returned.

687. Nov. 9, 1743 Henry Snoad enters 300 ac in Beaufort Co on N side of Pamplico R and E side of Whitehous' Cr; border: the upper open Beaverdam [Swamp], runs up the swamp, & back; made out; paid; rites returned.

688. Nov. 9, 1743 Simons Jones enters 200 ac in Beaufort Co on N side of Pamplico R and W side of Whitehous' Cr; border: Herring Run and "back"; made out; paid; rites returned formerly.

689. Nov. 10, 1743 Jno Bobbitt enters 400 ac in Edgecombe Co on N side of Reedy Cr, above the mouth of a great branch, & runs up said creek; made out; paid; rites returned.

690. Nov. 10, 1743 Garrat Wall enters 150 in Edgecombe Co; between his own land and Jno Parish on S side of Fishing Cr; made out; paid; rites returned.

691. Nov. 10, 1743 Wm Hixson enters 200 ac in Pasquotank Co on NE side of Pasquotank R; border: Latham Possel on SE side and runs NE from the river;

made out; rites returned.

page 17
692. Nov. 10, 1743 Wm Hixson enters 200 ac in Pasquotank Co on NE side of Pasquotank R; border: on NW side of Latham "Possell" and runs NE from the river; made out; rites returned.

693. Nov. 10, 1743 Margt. Haynes enters 200 ac in New Hanover Co on S side of main branch of Island Cr; made out; rites returned; crad. imd [or ined] book.

694. Nov. 10, 1743 Simon Holmes enters 200 ac in Craven Co on S side of Contentnea Cr; border: on the creek below mouth of Tosenut [Swamp], runs up Water Br, & crosses Saml Peacock's line; made out; paid; rites returned.

695. Nov. 11, 1743 Chas Gavin enters 600 ac in Craven Co on S side of Nuse R; border: a red oak and runs SE; made out.

696. Nov. 11, 1743 Thos Parker enters 300 ac in Edgecombe Co; border: a poplar on lower side of Paterson's Br on N side of Fishing Cr; made out; paid; rites returned.

697. Nov. 11, 1743 Wm Williams enters 640 ac in Onslow Co; border: Wm Wright's line and runs "towards" Jas Wright's line; made out.

698. Nov. 11, 1743 Col. Jno Simons enters 2,400 ac in Edgecombe Co on Rich Neck Cr; border: runs up the creek and joins Col. Moseley's line.

page 18
699. Nov. 11, 1743 Joseph Bradley enters 100 ac in Edgecombe Co on S side of "Roonoke" R; border: said Joseph Bradley's line "to" Patrick Lassley's line.

700. Nov. 11, 1743 Petr. Batson enters 100 ac in Carteret Co between Cedar Point Landing [and] Bartrim's on "Bougue" Sound; made out; paid; rites proved in Council.

701. Nov. 11, 1743 Jas Atkins enters 100 ac in Onslow Co; border: a pine near Lewis Trott's cabbin, on Shirlo's Br, & on S side of White Oak R, & runs up "the" swamp; made out; paid; rites paid in Council.

702. Nov. 11, 1743 Jas Hamilton enters 150 [written over 200] ac in Beaufort Co on S side of Gum Br, on Pamplico Road, & runs South; made out; paid; rites paid in Council.

703. Nov. 11, 1743 Christo. Dudley enters 200 ac in Onslow Co; border: on head of Jno Starkey's land, on Shirlo's Br, & on S side of White Oak R; made out; paid; rites proved in Council.

704. Nov. 11, 1743 Jas Dudley enters 200 ac in Beaufort Co on N side of Pamplico R and E side of Broad Cr; border: near Thos Worsley's old field, runs up Deep Run, & back; made out; paid; rites proved in Council.

705. Nov. 11, 1743 Wm Caron enters 100 ac in Beaufort Co on S side of Pamplico R; being the "plantation" where Jno Tyndhall formerly lived; made out; paid; rites proved in Council.

page 19
706. Nov. 11, 1743 Thos Jackson enters 400 ac in Chowan Co on E side of Chowan R; border: a cypress on the "brink" of said river marked with 3 notches on S side of said tree and a blaze fronting the river, runs down the river, & "out"; paid; rites returned.

707. Nov. 11, 1743 John Creekshanks enters 300 ac in Edgecombe Co; border: a white oak on N side of Little Shackoe Cr, runs "up", & "out"; rites proved in Council.

708. Nov. 11, 1743 Benja Kimboll enters 200 ac in Edgecombe Co; border: Cap. Young's line on Hub Quarter Cr and runs up both sides of the creek; paid; rites proved in Council.

709. Nov. 11, 1743 Richard Jones enters 400 ac in Edgecombe Co; border: a white oak at mouth of a branch "of" upper side of Six pound Cr and runs up both sides of the creek; paid; rites proved in Council.

710. Nov. 11, 1743 Joseph Kimboll enters 500 ac in Edgecombe Co; border: his own line, runs up his line, & joins Wm Saser on Six pound Cr; made out; paid; rites proved in Council.
711. Nov. 11, 1743 Thos Zackerry [or Lackerry] enters 300 ac in Edgecombe Co below his "plantation" on Little Shockoe Cr and runs "up" on both sides; made out; paid; rites proved in Council.

712. [no date] Benja Thomson enters 600 ac in Edgecombe Co; border: mouth of branch below Edward Jones and runs "down"; rites proved in Council.

713. Nov. 11, 1743 Wm Kimboll enters 500 ac in Edgecombe Co on N side of Great Fishing Cr; border: a great branch at a marked gum tree and runs up the creek; made out; paid; rites proved in Council.

page 20
714. Nov. 11, 1743 Wm Saser enters 300 ac in Edgecombe Co; border: a white oak on upper side of Six pound Cr and runs up the creek; made out; paid; rites proved in Council.

North Carolina Land Entries 1735-1752

715. Nov. 11, 1743 John Martin enters 100 ac in Edgecombe Co; border: a red oak on Abraham Bledsoe's line and runs "up & out"; made out; paid; rites proved in Council.

716. Nov. 11, 1743 Henry Best enters 200 ac in Craven Co on S of Norhunty Marsh; being the place where he lives; made out; paid; "x connor".

717. Nov. 11, 1743 Jas Cook enters 400 ac in Craven Co in fork of Great Cotentnea Cr and Norhunty [Swamp]; being the place where he lives; made out; paid.

718. Nov. 11, 1743 Ratlive [or Rattive] Boon enters 100 ac in Craven Co on S side of Spoil Conney Cr; border: "the" main road; made out; paid.

719. Nov. 11, 1743 Richd Wiggins enters 200 ac in Craven Co on N side of Nuse R; border: near Jno Blackman's land; made out; paid.

720. Nov. 11, 1743 Jno Whitly enters 100 ac in Craven Co on S side of Spoil Conney Cr; made out; paid.

721. Nov. 11, 1743 Jno Whitly enters 150 ac in Craven Co on both sides of Spoil Conney Cr; border: his "plantation".

722. Nov. 11, 1743 Jno Thomas enters 150 ac in Edgecombe Co; border: joins the land where he lives, Connen's land, & White Oak Swamp; made out; paid.

page 21
723. Nov. 11, 1743 Henry Davis enters 400 ac in Craven Co on S side of Norhunty [Swamp] above Wm Wiggins; being the place where he lives; made out; paid.

724. Nov. 11, 1743 Thos Long enters 200 ac in Craven Co on S side of Mill Marsh; being where Jas Bennet lived; made out; paid.

725. Nov. 11, 1743 Saml Harding enters 300 [written over 100] ac in Craven Co on S side of Contentnea Cr and on Turner's Swamp; made out; paid.

726. Nov. 11, 1743 Jas Bennet enters 400 ac in Craven Co on both sides of Stoney Cr; border: Jos Dawson and runs "down" from his line; made out; paid.

727. Nov. 11, 1743 Elias Bargeroon enters 200 ac in Craven Co on S side of Little Contentnea Cr; border: Corns. Tyson; made out; paid.

728. Nov. 11, 1743 Wm Taylor enters 150 ac in Edgecombe Co on N side of Conehoe Cr; border: said Taylor's own land; being where Henry Davis lived; made out; paid.

729. Nov. 11, 1743 Wm Wyndem [Rabn Beard--lined out] enters 200 [written over 150] ac in Craven Co on SW side of Little R; border: Col. Pollock's line and runs up the river; being where Rabi. Beard ["he"--lined out] lives; made out; paid.

page 22
730. Nov. 11, 1743 Jno Blackman enters 400 [written over 300] ac in Craven Co on a prong of Black R and near the head of "the" swamp; border: a beaver dam on N side of Black R; made out; paid; "here ends Connor's entries No. 15 nt paid for".

731. Nov. 11, 1743 Jno Williams enters 400 ac in New Hanover Co on the road from Rocky Point "to" between 13 and 14 miles "tree" on said road; made out; rites proved "formerly".

732. Nov. 11, 1743 David Evans enters 300 ac in New Hanover Co on a branch of Rockfish Cr; border: Timo Bloodworth's land; made out; rites proved "formerly".

733. Nov. 11, 1743 Henry "Momie" enters 200 ac in [blank] Co in fork of NW branch of Muddy Cr; border: about a mile above James Batchelor on E side of Cape Fear R; made out; rites returned.

734. Nov. 11, 1743 Andrew Wallice enters 200 ac in New Hanover Co on lower side of Limestone Cr, on both sides of Samners Br, & on NE side of NE Cape Fear R; border: about 3 miles above Richard Batchelor; made out; rites returned.

735. Nov. 11, 1743 Jno Keen enters 100 ac in New Hanover Co on a branch than makes out of Muddy Cr, on N side of a "creek" called Great Br, & on E side of NE Cape Fear R; made out; rites returned.

736. Nov. 11, 1743 David George enters 60 ac in Craven Co on N side of Trent R; being the place "one" Roberts sold to said George; made out; rites returned.

737. Nov. 11, 1743 David George enters 40 ac in Craven Co on N side of Trent R; being the place Richd Smith "went" to live(?) on; made out; rites returned.

738. Nov. 11, 1743 Wm Thomas enters 150 ac in New Hanover Co on lower side of Limestone Cr; border: below Wm Brice's lower corner tree on E side of NE Cape Fear R; made out; rites returned.

page 23
739. Nov. 12, 1743 Wm Kinchen sr enters 540 ac in Craven Co on N side of Norhunty [Swamp]; border: at "one" Sherrad's line and runs down the swamp; made out; rites returned.

740. Nov. 12, 1743 Wm Kinchen sr enters 100 ac in Edgecombe Co on W side of

Swift Cr; border: Spir's line and runs down the creek; made out; paid; rites returned.

741. Nov. 12, 1743 Wm Kinchen sr enters 200 ac in Craven Co; border: a white oak on SE side of Mill Marsh "a little" below a log house that James Bennet built and runs up the marsh; made out; paid; rites returned.

742. Nov. 12, 1743 Jos Thomas enters 300 ac in Edgecombe Co on both sides of Peachtree Cr; includes Geo Stevens' clearing; made out; paid.

743. Nov. 12, 1743 Wm Gourney enters 200 ac in Craven Co on N side of Nuse R above mouth of Little R; border: a pine by a branch and runs "up"; made out; paid.

744. Nov. 12, 1743 Nehemiah Joyner enters 200 ac in Edgecombe Co on S side of Tosneot [Swamp]; includes his improvements; made out; paid.

page 24
745. Nov. 12, 1743 Wm Herring enters 150 ac in Craven Co on N side of Tosneot [Swamp]; includes his improvement; made out; paid.

746. Nov. 12, 1743 Thos Farmer enters 300 ac in Craven Co on N side of Nuse R; border: a red oak above Arthr Blackman and runs up the river; made out; paid.

747. Nov. 12, 1743 Nichs. Boon enters 300 ac in Northampton Co on N side of Wildcat Swamp; border: a pine marked "N B", runs to the swamp, to Wm Bryant's line, & down the swamp; made out; paid; rites returned.

748. Nov. 12, 1743 Thos Walton enters 700 ac in Chowan Co on head of Indian Br; border: said Walton's upper line; made out; rites returned.

749. Nov. 12, 1743 Robt Ruffin enters 200 ac in Edgecombe Co on lower side of Hogpen Br and on S side of a "swamp in Tioncoe" [Tinoco Swamp ?]; border: a red oak and runs up the swamp; made out; paid.

750. Nov. 12, 1743 Wm Bently enters 200 ac in Edgecombe Co on N side of Tosneot [Swamp]; border: at Goffes Br and runs across the branch; includes his improvement; made out; paid; rites returned "before".

page 25
751. Nov. 12, 1743 Jacob Barnes enters 100 ac in Edgecombe Co in the fork of White oak Swamp; border: on N prong of White oak [Swamp]; includes his improvement; made out; paid; rites returned; on Nathan "Barns" rites.

752. Nov. 12, 1743 Nathan Barns enters 100 ac in Edgecombe Co on S side of main prong of White oak Swamp; includes his "complements"; made out; paid;

rites returned.

753. Nov. 12, 1743 Wm Chevers enters 200 ac in Edgecombe Co on S side of Tabs Cr, runs up the creek, & across "the same"; includes his improvement; made out; paid; rites returned "before".

754. Nov. 12, 1743 Richd Holland enters 200 ac in Edgecombe Co on both sides of Peachtree Cr; border: below Thos Horn in a savannah on W side of said creek; made out; paid.

755. Nov. 12, 1743 Richd Sumner enters 350 ac in Northampton Co on N side of Catawitsky Swamp; border: Davis' Pecoson and Jas Wood's land; made out; paid; rites returned.

756. Nov. 12, 1743 Alexr Campbel enters 400 ac in Northampton Co on S side of Yerahaw Swamp, runs "up" to Parker's line, & "out"; made out; paid; rites returned.

page 26
757. Nov. 12, 1743 Thoms. Bird enters 250 ac in Bertie Co on W side of Canaan Swamp; between his own land and Benja Holliman; made out; paid; rites returned.

758. Nov. 12, 1743 Thos McLendon enters 250 ac in Craven Co on N side of Nuse R and E side of "Brol" Swamp; border: Ambrose Agriss; made out; paid.

759. Nov. 12, 1743 Jno Wynns enters 200 ac in Craven Co on S side of Fort Run of Great Contentnea Cr; border: Jno beverly's line and runs down the run; made out; paid.

760. Nov. 13, 1743 Edwd. Jones enters 640 ac in Edgecombe Co; border: a white oak at the ford of Shacoe Cr on N side "thereof", above Jno Lysles, & runs down Shacoe Cr; made out.

761. Nov. 13, 1743 Jos Lane enters 400 ac in Edgecombe Co on N side of Conaconary Swamp; border: near head of Jos Watt's Br; includes his improvement; made out; paid; rites returned.

762. Nov. 13, 1743 Jos Lane enters 200 ac in Edgecombe Co "nigh" the head of middle prong of Tar R; includes his improvement; made out; paid.

page 27
763. Nov. 13, 1743 Geo Nicolson enters 640 ac in Edgecombe Co; border: a white oak on N side of Red bird Br, below "the" Beaver Pond, & runs up the branch; made out; paid; rites proved.

764. Nov. 13, 1743 Wm Williams enters 60 ac in Craven Co; border: a pine on

North Carolina Land Entries 1735-1752

Tycos Marsh in said Williams' own line and runs down both sides of the marsh; made out; paid; rites proved.

765. Nov. 13, 1743 Ralph [written over Chas] Mason enters 300 ac in Edgecombe Co; border: a blazed white oak near Tuckahee Br "of" the upper sides, runs to Swift Cr, down it, & up "both sides"; made out; paid; rites proved.

766. Nov. 13, 1743 Wallace Jones enters 350 ac in Edgecombe Co; border: Mr. Jno Edwards' line, runs up that line to said Wallace Jones' line, up to Jacob Rogers' line, along said line to a corner, & "off and down"; made out; paid; rites proved.

page 28
767. Nov. 14, 1743 Martin Gardiner jr enters 400 ac in Bertie Co on N side of Rackguis [or Rackquis] Swamp; border: Thos Wimberly, Abra Shepard, & said Gardiner; made out; paid; rites returned.

768. Nov. 14, 1743 Martin Gardiner jr enters 300 ac in Bertie Co on N side of "Raguis" [Swamp]; between James Roberts, Jas Williams, Samuel Herring, "Thos", & Wimberly; made out; paid; rites returned.

769. Nov. 14, 1743 Hugh Blaning enters 320 ac in New Hanover Co between NW River and Black R; border: about 2 or 3 miles from said Blaning's "plantation" on "the" NW; made out; chad.

770. Nov. 14, 1743 Rogr. Moore esq enters 300 ac in New Hanover Co; border: Mr. Thos Akin's land on Old Town Cr and upper tract of Mr. Jas Hasel on Mill Cr; made out; chad; rites proved "before".

771. Nov. 14, 1743 Jonathan Parker enters 600 ac in Chowan Co; border: E of the land belonging to Fras Spikes and on "the" side of the River Pecoson at a beach at lower end of Spikes Ridge; made out; paid; rites returned.

page 29
772. Nov. 14, 1743 Jno Davis enters 300 ac in Edgecombe Co on N side of Fishing Cr; border: mouth of Hogpen Br, runs "up", & "out" on [an] East course; made out; proved; rites returned.

773. Nov. 14, 1743 Jacob Lewis enters 640 ac in Onslow Co on W side of Glovers Cr and runs around a bay; border: Everitt's line and runs down "the same"; made out; chad.

774. Nov. 14, 1743 Ephraim Vernon enters 300 ac in Bladen Co on W side of Black R and on the river; being vacant land where said Vernon made "some" improvements; made out; rites proved "before".

775. Nov. 14, 1743 Robt Colley enters 200 ac in Bladen Co on Fishing Cr on W

side of Black R; made out; rites proved "before".

776. Nov. 14, 1743 Jno Davis enters 400 ac in Bladen Co on Fishing Cr; border: "nigh" Robt Colley and Ephraim Vernon; made out; rites proved "before".

777. [no date] Jas Green enters 250 ac in Onslow Co on NE side of SW New R; border: on Rattlesnake Br and runs up SW New R.

page 30
778. Nov. 15, 1743 Archd Mackilroy enters 250 ac in Craven Co on N side of Nuse R on Fishing Cr on "the" East side and runs up both sides of a branch of the creek; made out; paid; rites returned.

779. Nov. 15, 1743 Jno Herring jr enters 300 ac in Craven Co on N side of Nuse R; border: at No Sappony Cr and runs up Bogue Marsh to "the" beaverdam; made out; paid; rites returned.

780. Nov. 15, 1743 John Wilkins enters 200 ac in Chowan Co; border: Thos Ward's line and runs up "the" beaverdams or Thick Neck Swamp; made out; paid; rites returned.

781. Nov. 15, 1743 Jno Wilkins enters 200 ac in Perquimans Cr; border: on NE side of Tick Neck Swamp and runs up the swamp; made out; paid; rites returned.

782. Nov. 16, 1743 Andw Cary enters 100 ac in "C" County on S side of Campbels Cr; border: on E side of Jno Tyndhall's land; made out; Griff.

page 31
783. Nov. 16, 1743 Timo. Winslow enters 540 ac in Perquimans Cr; border: Jno Parish's corner tree at upper end of Burnt Glade, runs to Pine Glade, & joins Jno Nixon; made out; paid; rites proved.

784. Nov. 16, 1743 Needham Bryan enters 100 ac in Bertie Co on N side of Nuse R at Moor's camp; made out; Gould; rites returned.

785. Nov. 16, 1743 Jonathan Killeret enters 500 ac in Bertie Co on S side of Guize Hall at "a place" called Upper Horse Pond; made out; Gould; rites returned.

786. Nov. 16, 1743 Jos Edmondson enters 150 ac in Craven Co on NW side of Cashaw Cr; border: Cashaw bridge and runs up N side of Nuse R; made out; rites returned.

787. Nov. 16, 1743 Thos Devaughan enters 200 ac in New Hanover Co near "the" school house on the road to Long Cr; border: Capt. Innes and Saml Swann; made out.

North Carolina Land Entries 1735-1752

788. Nov. 16, 1743 Danl Marshburne enters 100 ac in Onslow Co on SW New R, about 0.5 miles above mouth of Harrys Cr, & runs down "the" SW [New R]; made out.

page 32
789. Nov. 16, 1743 Jos Portevint enters 300 ac in New Hanover Co on W side of Long Cr; border: below John Smith's land; made out.

790. Nov. 16, 1743 Jno Cockrene enters 200 ac in New Hanover Co on SW side of Black R and about 0.5 miles above Bridle's land; being where he dwells; made out; rites returned.

791. Nov. 16, 1743 Edmd Murphy enters 300 ac in Craven Co on W side of Hancocks Cr and on S side of Nuse R; border: a corner tree of land formerly Jno Slocumb's; made out; rites returned.

792. Nov. 16, 1743 Jas Wright enters 300 ac in Onslow Co; border: a white oak on E side of Millars Br and runs "down"; made out.

793. Nov. 17, 1743 Jno Roberts enters 300 ac in Craven Co; border: upper side of the "plantation" where he formerly lived; made out; rites returned.

794. Nov. 17, 1743 Jno Roberts enters 100 ac in Craven Co in the fork of Whitley Cr on S side of Nuse R; made out; rites returned.

page 33
795. Nov. 17, 1743 Jno Staniland enters 150 ac in Craven Co on little Chinkapin Cr on S side; border: Mart. Foutch; made out; rites returned.

796. Nov. 17, 1743 David Martan enters 300 ac in Craven Co; border: below Geo Shipper's land on N side of Nuse R; being where he lives; on Baucam's rites.

797. Nov. 17, 1743 Edwd Williams enters 300 ac in Craven Co in the Barron fork of Trent R and on both sides of Beaverdam Br; made out; rites returned.

798. Nov. 17, 1743 Levie Truehitt enters 800 ac in Craven Co between "the" Snow Hill and Moseley's Cr; made out; rites returned.

799. Nov. 17, 1743 Jas McLewaine enters 200 ac in Craven Co on both sides of Metts Br, S side of Southwest Cr, & S side of Nuse R; being where Jno "Wms" formerly lived; made out; rites proved.

page 34
800. Nov. 18, 1743 Hector McAlister enters 200 ac in Bladen Co on SW side of NW Cape fear R; border: Jno Owens' lower line and runs "down"; made out.

North Carolina Land Entries 1735-1752

801. Nov. 18, 1743 Henry Sims enters 400 ac in Edgecombe Co about 0.75 miles above Finches Cr on E side of Tar R and runs up Tar R; made out; paid; rites returned.

802. Nov. 18, 1743 Henry Sims enters 400 ac in Edgecombe Co on E side of Tar R; border: a place called West's cabbins; made out; paid; rites returned.

803. Nov. 18, 1743 Thos Jerman enters 100 ac in Craven Co on S side of Trent R; border: Chas Wilks; made out; paid; rites returned.

804. Nov. 18, 1743 Duncan McCoulsky enters 200 ac in Bladen Co on "a" creek; border: Hugh Campbell's upper line; made out; paid; rites returned.

page 35
805. Nov. 18, 1743 Neale Shaw enters 200 ac in Bladen Co on a small branch running into little Horseshoe Swamp; border: a black oak; made out; paid; rites returned.

806. Nov. 18, 1743 Thos Nince enters 200 ac in Edgecombe Co on E side of Peachtree Cr; border: about 0.5 miles below Jos Rigan's lower line; made out; paid; rites returned.

807. Nov. 18, 1743 Jno "Mcilroy" enters 100 ac in Craven Co on N side of Nuse R, on a branch of Falling Cr, & on "W side of N side of" the branch; being land on which he made "some" improvements; to be returned "agt" next Court rites not yet returned.

808. Nov. 18, 1743 Jno Herring jr enters 300 ac in Craven Co on N side of Nuse R and on W side of Bear creek Marsh; between Mart. Fryar and Christo. Hamson.

809. Nov. 19, 1743 Moses Tilman enters 100 ac in craven Co on "the road side" from Newbern up Nuse R; called Short's old field; made out.

page 36
810. Nov. 18, 1743 Thos Davis enters 100 ac in Bladen Co on NW side of NW Cape Fear R; "between" Edwd. Connon's land; made out.

811. [no date] Thos Roberson enters 50 ac in Bladen Co; border: Samson Wood's lower line and runs "down"; made out.

812. [no date] Thos Wallis enters 300 ac in Currituck Co; border: on NE of Silvester's land on Stumpy Point; made out.

813. [no date] Thos Devaughar enters 320 ac in New Hanover Co on W side of NE Cape Fear R, on a branch of Rockfish Cr, & about 2 miles back of John Squire's [or Sgenre] land on Black R; made out.

North Carolina Land Entries 1735-1752

814. [no date] Robt Halton esq enters 1,000 ac in Craven Co on Green's path, on Middle Cr on N side, & runs on both sides of Green's path; made out.

page 37
815. Nov. 21, 1743 John Horne enters 200 ac in Edgecombe Co on S side of Coneyhoe Cr; being the place where "he cleared on"; made out; Sec. paid.

816. Nov. 21, 1743 Jams. Smith enters 150 ac in Craven Co on a branch of little Conttentney Cr; being where Jesper Aldey lived; made out; paid.

817. Nov. 21, 1743 Jams. Smith enters 300 ac in Tyrrell Co; border: lower side of Griffin's land "it was" Johnston's in the fork of Great Coneyhoe and Little Creeks; made out; paid.

818. Nov. 21, 1743 Jams. Smith enters 200 ac in Edgecombe Co on Connetta Swamp; border: a pine marked "J S" and runs up the swamp; made out; paid.

819. [no date] Isaac Odam enters 250 ac in New Hanover Co at Lewis' Br on S side; being where "Henary" Walker lives; made out; paid.

page 38 [blank page]
page 39 Entry book of Warrants commencing Feb. 21, 1743/4

page 40
820. Feb. 21, 1743/4 James Henley enters 250 ac in Perquimans Cr; border: Saml Charles' line, runs up his line to Richard Sanders' line, to John Henley's line, & to the beginning; made out; rites returned.

821. Feb. 21, 1743/4 Fran. Spight enters 300 ac in Craven Co on N side of Cotentney Cr; border: Wm Smith's land; made out; rites returned.

822. Feb. 21, 1743/4 Tullee [or Jullee] Williams enters 600 ac in Tyrrell Co at a place called Mixon's Holly; border: a great pine on E side of Great Allegator R and on the River Pecoson about 2 miles up the river; made out; rites returned.

823. Feb. 21, 1743/4 "Talle" Williams enters 400 ac in Tyrrell Co on SE side of "the" lake about 2 miles "up" it; border: a poplar on the lake at a place known as Rich [or kich] lands; made out; rites returned.

824. Feb. 21, 1743/4 John Wilcocks enters 200 ac in Tyrrell Co on NE side of "the" lake; called Beasleys Camp; border: a black gum on the lake; made out; rites proved.

825. Feb. 21, 1743/4 Jams. Craven enters 500 ac in Tyrrell Co on SE side of Great Allegator R, about 3 miles up Mill Tail Cr, & on S side of said creek; made out;

rites proved.

page 41
826. Feb. 21, 1743/4 Wm Martin enters 250 ac in Hyde Co on Hyde Co on W side of Matchapungo R; known as Hog's entry and on S side of Lodwick Martin's Cr; made out; paid; rites returned.

827. Feb. 21, 1743/4 John Jordan enters 200 ac in Hyde Co on W side of Matchapungo R and S side of Jordans Cr; border: runs up his own line, Matchapungo R, & Jordans Cr; made out; rites proved in Court.

828. Feb. 21, 1743/4 Thos [written over Jno] Campean enters 200 ac in beufort Co on S side of Pamplico R at mouth of Oysters Cr; known as Piney Hamock; made out; proved; rites returned.

829. Feb. 21, 1743/4 Jno Wallace enters 150 ac in Beaufort Co on S side of Pamplico R; border: Robt Campean's line on Campbells Cr, runs down to Hunting Cr, & back; made out; proved; rites returned; Forbes.

830. Feb. 21, 1743/4 Jno Wallace enters 100 ac in Beaufort Co on S side of Pamplico R "on the river side" below Goose Cr; known as Piney Hamock [sic]; border: runs down the river and "back"; rites returned; Forbes [description and number of acres lined out].

page 42
831. Feb. 21, 1743/4 Henry Roberts enters 150 ac in Craven Co; border: above Jacob Taylor jr on S side of Nuse R; being the land Joseph Taylor has built on; made out; paid; rites returned; McNaire.

832. Feb. 21, 1743/4 Jno Wallace enters 100 ac in Beaufort Co on S side of Pamplico R at head of Eastermost Cr; border: near Jno Mayo's line and runs up "the" pecoson to in clude the ridge of oaks; made out; paid; rites returned; Forbes.

833. Feb. 21, 1743/4 Thos Smith enters 200 ac in Beaufort Co on S side of Pamplico R; border: Benja Rigney's corner tree, runs up Poley Bridge Br to a fork thereof, & "across"; made out; proved; rites proved in Court; Forbes.

834. Feb. 21, 1743/4 Darby McCarly enters 300 ac in Hyde Co on E side of Pantego Cr and runs to Thos Gearlor's and Fred Jones' lines; made out; paid; rites proved in Court; Forbes.

835. Feb. 21, 1743/4 Wm Bently enters 300 ac in Chowan Co on N side of Peters Cr; border: John Pipkins' line, runs "up" to Thos Jonekins' line, & to Robt Rogers' line; made out; paid; rites returned "before"; Forbes.

836. Feb. 21, 1743/4 Wm Carruthers enters 300 ac in Beaufort Co on N side of

Bay R and E side of Great Bear Cr; being the "plantation" where Wm Keaylon lives; includes Shaddock's Hamock; made out; paid; rites returned "before".

page 43
837. Feb. 21, 1743/4 Wm Carruthers enters 270 ac in Beaufort Co on N side of Bay R and W side of Great Bear "R"; being where Fras Caffery lives; made out; paid; rites returned "before".

838. Feb. 21, 1743/4 Wm Carruthers enters 200 ac in Beaufort Co on N side of Bay R and W side of Smiths Cr; border: Hen Lambert's corner tree; being where Elisha Cocks lives; made out; paid; rites returned "before".

839. Feb. 21, 1743/4 Wm Hunter enters 300 ac in Chowan Co; being an island on N side of Chowan R and in Cypress Swamp; made out; paid; rites proved in Court.

840. Feb. 21, 1743/4 Wm Gardiner enters 600 ac in Bladen Co [on] N side of Pee Dee R; border: a sycamore on lower part of an island and runs up & across a little creek; made out; paid; rites returned.

841. Feb. 21, 1743/4 Geo Turner enters 400 ac in Currituck Co on S side of "Maramuskeet" Lake; border: a gum at the lake side, runs "towards" SW end of the lake, & "back"; made out; paid; rites proved in Court; Forbes.

page 44
842. Feb. 21, 1743/4 Simon Holmes enters 400 ac in Craven Co on "Apletree" Br on N side, on Horse Marsh, & runs "up"; made out; paid; rites returned "before".

843. Feb. 21, 1743/4 Jno Ecles enters 200 ac in Beaufort Co between Pamplico R and Oyster Cr; border: at "the" thoroughfare and runs "upwards"; made out; Goulde.

844. Feb. 21, 1743/4 Miles Parker enters 640 ac in Bladen Co on NE side of NW Cape Fear R; border: on a creek "making out next above" Peter Parker's old "plantation", a plum tree "on" the mouth of a small branch, & runs up "both" creek and branch; made out; Goulde.

845. Feb. 21, 1743/4 Wm Kennedy sr enters 150 ac in Craven Co on S side of Nuse R and both sides of a spring branch; border: the line of Geo Roberts deceased; made out; paid; rites proved "before".

846. Feb. 21, 1743/4 Jno Fort enters 200 ac in Craven Co on S side of Burnt Swamp; border: mouth of a reedybranch at a white oak marked "I F" and runs "up"; made out; paid; rites returned; "J C".

page 45
847. Feb. 21, 1743/4 Edwd Stevens enters 100 ac in Craven Co on S side of Nuse

R and in the fork between Mill Cr & Nuse R; border: Robert Mill's line; made out; paid; rites returned; J C.

848. Feb. 21, 1743/4 Elias Stevens enters 250 ac in Craven Co on N side of upper prong of Falling Cr and runs "down"; made out; paid; rites returned "before"; J C.

849. Feb. 21, 1743/4 Jno Rhodes enters 200 ac in Bertie Co on E side of Sandy Run; border: Robt Mcleary's line and begins at a red oak; made out; paid; rites returned; J C.

850. Feb. 21, 1743/4 Mathew Reaford enters 640 ac in Craven Co on both sides of Beaverdam Swamp below Phillip Peirce's [or Puries]; border: near a crooked branch, runs "up", & on both sides; made out; paid; J C.

851. Feb. 21, 1743/4 Simon Peirce enters 100 ac in Craven Co on S side of Beaverdam Swamp and runs "down"; made out; paid; J C.

852. Feb. 21, 1743/4 Lewis Davis enters 300 ac in Tyrrell Co in Conekoe Island; border: Gainer's line and runs up the island; made out; paid; rites returned "before"; J C.

page 46
853. Feb. 21, 1743/4 Phillip Peirce enters 100 ac in Craven Co on Burden's Br of Nuse R; between Mockason Cr and Beaverdam Swamp; made out; paid; rites returned; J C.

854. Feb. 21, 1743/4 Jonathan Taylor enters 600 ac in Craven Co on N side of Goshen Swamp and on N side of a branch that comes out of Goshen Swamp; border: a long meadow; made out; paid; rites returned; J C.

855. Feb. 21, 1743/4 John Fort enters 550 ac in Craven Co on S side of "the" prong of Falling Cr and runs "up"; made out; paid; rites returned; J C.

856. Feb. 21, 1743/4 John Roufe [or Rouse] enters 300 ac in Craven Co on Maple Br above Cotentnauy path, on S side of Falling Cr, & on N side of Nuse R; made out; paid; rites proved in Council.

857. Feb. 21, 1743/4 Jno Clarke enters 850 ac in Bladen Co on lower end of Buffalo Island, runs up the island, then "out back", & down "the" river to the beginning; made out; rites returned; M Rowan.

858. Feb. 21, 1743/4 James Parker enters 400 ac in Chowan Co; border: John Williams and William Parker; made out; paid.

page 47
859. Feb. 23, 1743/4 Tarlow OQuin enters 600 [written over 640] ac in

Edgecombe Co; border: said OQuin's corner and runs up both sides of Cotentney Cr "on the N side"; made out; paid; rites returned.

860. Feb. 23, 1743/4 Wm Pool enters 300 ac in Craven Co on N side of Nuse R; border: "a little" below mouth of Jno Smith's mill Br; made out; paid; rites returned.

861. Feb. 23, 1743/4 Christopher Harrison enters 200 ac in Craven Co on Norhunty Swamp; border: "a little" below Ruffin's land on S side of said swamp; made out; paid; rites proved in Council.

862. Feb. 23, 1743/4 Seth Pilkington enters 200 ac in Beaufort Co on S side of Grindal Cr; border: Thos Pilkington's land and runs up the creek; made out; paid; rites returned "before".

863. Feb. 23, 1743/4 Thos Mealson [or Meolson] enters 300 ac in Perquimans Co; border: Jno and Phineas Nixon's land; made out; paid.

page 48
864. Feb. 23, 1743/4 Fras Brice enters 100 ac in New Hanover Co in the fork of Muddy Cr and on E side of NE Cape Fear R; known as Staffords Folley [or Shefford's Holley]; made out; paid; rites returned.
865. Feb. 23, 1743/4 Fras Brice enters 100 ac in Craven Co on E side of Mill Cr "without" [or outside of] Mr. Pollock's lines; made out; paid; rites returned.

866. Feb. 23, 1743/4 Fras Rountree enters 200 ac in Edgecombe Co on N side of Great Swamp and N side of Contentnea Cr; made out; paid; Conner.

867. Feb. 23, 1743/4 Fras Rountree enters 100 ac in Edgecombe Co on Cotentney Cr, on N side at mouth of Mill trak [or srak] Run, & about 5 miles above Great Swamp; made out; paid; Conner.

868. Feb. 23, 1743/4 Fras Rountree enters 100 ac in Edgecombe Co on S side of Cottentney Cr; being where he lives; made out; paid.

page 49
869. Feb. 23, 1743/4 Wm Hawkins enters 100 ac in Tyrrell Co on E side of "Srog" House Br; border: Wm Deacon; made out; paid; Conner.

870. Feb. 23, 1743/4 James "Connor" enters 200 ac in Tyrrell Co on both sides of Shepards Marsh; known as Jos Trovel's "place and" Saml Taylor's; made out; paid.

871. Feb. 23, 1743/4 Jno Harinton [or Harrenton] enters 400 ac in Beaufort Co on N side of Tar R; border: Wm Jones' line and runs between Wm Adams' and Wm Jones' lines; made out; paid; rites returned; Forbes.

872. Feb. 23, 1743/4 Wm Dunbar [or Dimbar] enters 300 ac in Beaufort Co; border: a white oak by the main road, runs across Round Pole Br, W to main branch of Blunts Cr, & down the same; made out; paid; rites returned.

page 50
873. Feb. 23, 1743/4 Wm Dunbar enters 100 ac in Beaufort Co; border: Jas Huind's [or Hinnd's] line and runs down "the" river to Rackoon Cr; made out; paid; rites returned.

874. Feb. 23, 1743/4 Jno Eckolls enters 500 ac in Beaufort Co on S side of Pamplico R and in a fork of Goose Cr; where Wm Jones formerly lived; proved; rites returned.

875. Feb. 23, 1743/4 Jas McWame [or McWaiane] enters 300 ac in Craven Co on S side of Little R; between Jas Chaney and Jno Boyd; proved; rites returned "before".

876. Feb. 23, 1743/4 John Monk [or Mouk] enters 300 ac in Craven Co on S side of Walnut Cr; border: James Simons' "plantation"; made out; paid; rites returned.

877. Feb. 23, 1743/4 John Monk enters 400 ac in Craven Co on S side of Walnut Cr; border: the "plantation" where he lives; made out; paid; rites returned.

878. Feb. 23, 1743/4 William Cain [John Rouse--lined out] enters 100 ac in Edgecombe Co on E side of Deep Cr; border: Richd Kemp's lower conrer and runs "down"; made out; paid; Conner.

page 51
879. Feb. 23, 1743/4 Samuel Jackson enters 200 ac in Edgecombe Co on S side of Little "Swam"; border: Joseph Cain; being the "plantation" where he lives; made out; paid; rites proved in Council; Conner.

880. Feb. 23, 1743/4 Benjamin Bridgen enters 200 ac in Edgecombe Co on S side of Swift Cr; border: a white oak and runs "down"; made out; paid; rites proved in Council; Conner.
881. Feb. 23, 1743/4 Jams. Dreak enters 200 ac in Edgecombe Co on S side of Swift Cr, both sides of Tumbling Cr, & runs "up"; made out; paid; rites proved in Council; Conner.

882. Feb. 23, 1743/4 Christo. Harrison enters 200 ac in Craven Co on S side of Nuse R; border: a pine on a high hill and runs up Nuse R; made out; paid; rites proved in Council.

883. Feb. 23, 1743/4 Wm Gardiner enters 100 ac in Craven Co on N side of Nuce R; border: mouth of Hellows mill Br, runs up the river, & "back"; made out; paid;

rites returned.

page 52
884. Feb. 23, 1743/4 Jacob Reasonover enters 200 ac in Craven Co on N side of Nuce R, South [or North--written over] side of Northwest Cr, & runs up the creek; made out; paid; rites proved in Council.

885. Feb. 23, 1743/4 Alexr McColvin enters 200 ac in New Hanover Co on Wild cat Br [Creek--lined out]; border: opposite Jno Warnor's land on E side of Black R; made out; rites proved; Skibbow.

886. Feb. 24, 1743/4 Jno Ballance enters 200 ac in Currituck Co; border: on E side of Evan Millar's line and W side of Jno Burton's line; made out; paid; rites returned.

887. Feb. 24, 1743/4 Jno Perkins enters 600 ac in Currituck Co; border: on W end of Mr. Donger's new survey, on Richd. Gregory's line, & runs W; made out; paid; rites returned.

888. Feb. 24, 1743/4 Saml Boutwel enters 200 ac in Beaufort Co in the fork of Pilkington's Br and on Geo Moy's "Herring run"; border: on the branch and runs back; made out; paid; rites returned "before"; Forbes.

page 53
889. Feb. 24, 1743/4 Benja Hodges enters 300 ac in Beaufort Co on N side of Pamplico R; border: Simon Jones' corner pine on the River Pecoson, runs to Grindal Cr, & "back"; made out; paid; Forbes.

890. Feb. 24, 1743/4 Jno Winfield enters 100 ac in Beaufort Co on N side of Little Cotentnea Cr; border: on lower side of Jno Tyson's line; made out; paid; a single man no rites.

891. Feb. 24, 1743/4 Isaac Giddens enters 100 ac in Beaufort Co on S side of Little Cotentnea Cr; border: on Abra. Giddens' lower line and runs down the creek; made out; paid.

892. Feb. 24, 1743/4 Wm Galloway enters 100 ac in Beaufort Co on N side of Little Cotentnea Cr; border: on "the" hickory ridge and runs "down and back"; made out; paid; no rites single man.

893. Feb. 24, 1743/4 Jno Reynolds enters 200 ac in Edgecombe Co on head of Hollands Br; border: Marmaduke Kimbro's corner tree and runs "downwards"; made out; rites returned; "R T".

page 54
894. Feb. 24, 1743/4 Robt Harris enters 350 ac in Edgecombe Co on upper side

of Poplar Cr; made out; rites returned; R T.

895. Feb. 24, 1743/4 Edward Carter enters 150 ac in Craven Co on S side of Nuce R; border: Wm Prescot's line at mouth of Panter Cr and runs on both sides of said creek; made out; rites proved in Council "before"; McCullo chd.

896. Feb. 24, 1743/4 Luke Whitefield enters 100 ac in Craven Co on S side of Nuce R; border: a line of the land he possesses, runs "off" from said line, & "back"; made out; ; McCullo chd.

897. Feb. 24, 1743/4 Chas Stevens enters 300 ac in Edgecombe Co on N side of Tar R; border: a red oak opposite Jno Collins' line; made out; paid; rites returned.

898. Feb. 24, 1743/4 Wm Taylor enters 200 ac in Edgecombe Co on N side of Tar R; border: a pine "up" Doomen's [or Doonren's] Br and runs up "the same"; made out; paid; rites returned "before".

899. Feb. 24, 1743/4 Robt "Wms" [Williams] enters 300 ac in New Hanover Co on Wildcat Swamp, at a pine near the head, & runs up both sides; made out; paid; rites returned.

page 55
900. Feb. 24, 1743/4 Thos Kirby enters 200 ac in Edgecombe Co on N side of Tar R; border: his own "plantation" land and Robt Hilliard; made out; rites returned "before".

901. Feb. 24, 1743/4 Jno Taylor enters 200 ac in Edgecombe Co on N side of Tar R; border: a red oak above [or "about"] Wm Strickland and runs "down"; made out; rites returned "before".

902. Feb. 24, 1743/4 Jno Williams enters 100 ac in New Hanover Co on N side of NE Cape Fear R; made out; rites proved in Council.

903. Feb. 24, 1743/4 Jno Williams enters 150 ac in Craven Co [sic] on S side of Nuse R; border: a cypress in "the" low grounds; made out; rites proved in Council.

904. Feb. 24, 1743/4 John Carroll enters 100 [written over 200] ac in Craven Co; border: Luke Whitfield's line and runs up the river; made out; rites returned.

905. Feb. 25, 1743/4 Wm [John--lined out] Bond enters 300 ac in Craven Co; border: on the back of Mr. McKlewean's "plantation" on or near head of Mill Br; made out; paid; rites returned.

906. Feb. 25, 1743/4 Geoge. Stevens enters 350 ac in Edgecombe Co on NE side of Maple Swamp; border: Robt Webb's line and runs to the swamp; made out; paid; rites returned.

907. Feb. 25, 1743/4 Jno Rackley enters 300 ac in Edgecombe Co on S prong of Cedar Cr; border: mouth of a large spring branch; includes his improvement; made out; paid; rites returned.

908. Feb. 25, 1743/4 Jno Rackley enters 300 ac in Edgecombe Co on N side of Tar R; border: a pine marked "I R"; made out; paid; rites returned.

page 56
909. Feb. 25, 1743/4 Richd. Cheeck jr enters 300 ac in Beaufort Co; border: a red oak on "the" river being his father's corner, runs between the meadow and river, to Hilliard's corner, to the river, & "up" to the beginning; made out; paid; rites proved; Jno McMek.

910. Feb. 25, 1743/4 Edwd Cumings enters 500 ac in Craven Co on N side of Trent R opposite Thos Harrell; being the land where said Cumings lives; made out; paid; rites returned; Jno McK.

911. Feb. 25, 1743/4 Thos Every enters 300 ac in Craven Co on upper side of Saml Smith's "plantation"; border: at or near Smith's upper line; made out; paid; rites returned.

912. Feb. 25, 1743/4 Saml Smith enters 100 ac in Craven Co on S side of Neuse R; border: opposite his "plantation"; made out; paid; rites returned.
913. Feb. 25, 1743/4 Saml Smith enters 200 ac in Craven Co on both sides of Swifts Cr, about 3 miles above Green's path, & on S side of Neuse R; made out; paid; rites returned.

914. Feb. 25, 1743/4 Wm Chamberlin [or Chamberlan] enters 200 ac in Craven Co in Wiggons Neck on N side of Neuse R, on Long R, & between Falling Cr [and] Sterup Creek Percoson; made out; paid; rites returned.

915. Feb. 25, 1743/4 Thos Lewis enters 100 ac in Craven Co on N side of Neuse R, on upper White Marsh, & lower side of Falling Cr; made out; paid; rites returned.

916. Feb. 25, 1743/4 Wm Hendrick enters 600 [written over 500] ac in Edgecombe Co on N side of Swift Cr; border: a white oak on E side of Great Br [in] Hardy Council's line and runs up the creek; made out.

page 57
917. Feb. 25, 1743/4 Wm Gregory enters 600 ac in Bertie Co on Roquiss Swamp; border: Richard Martin, widow Smith, & Robert Sticks [or Stieks] on or near Cashy R; made out.

918. Feb. 27, 1743/4 Thos Hall enters 100 ac in Onslow Co on S side of Queens Cr; border: a bridge and runs along the creek; made out; "for" Jno Starkey.

North Carolina Land Entries 1735-1752

919. Feb. 27, 1743/4 Alexr Steel enters 100 ac in Onslow Co on W side of Flat [or Fflat] Swamp and runs "upward"; made out; "for" Starkey.

920. Feb. 27, 1743/4 Saml Jones enters 100 ac in Onslow Co on S side of NW Queens Cr and begins below "the" Cypress Bridge; made out; "for" Starkey.

921. Feb. 27, 1743/4 Sarah Anderson enters 300 ac in Onslow Co on E side of NW New R; border: John Wallis' line and runs up the [NW] branch to "the" half moon [Creek]; made out; "for" Starkey.

922. Feb. 27, 1743/4 Saml Ramsay enters 300 ac in Onslow Co on "the" Sea Bank; between Little Inlet and New R; made out; Starkey.

923. Feb. 27, 1743/4 Wm Wickliffe enters 300 ac in Craven Co on Hancocks Cr; border: Marshall's line and runs up the creek; made out; Starkey.

924. Feb. 27, 1743/4 Thos Cumings enters 100 ac in New Hanover Co on Maxwells Cr about 2 miles below Jno Wms [Williams'] new road; made out; "chd pet"; rites proved in Council "before"; W F [or W T].

925. Feb. 27, 1743/4 Robt Colley enters 300 ac in Bladen Co on W side of Black R, N side of Fishing Cr, & about 2 miles up said creek; made out; rites returned "before"; W F [or W T].

page 58
926. Feb. 27, 1743/4 David Purseh enters 200 ac in New Hanover Co on E side of Black R; border: Jos Robinson's lower line and runs "down"; made out; rites returned ["before"--lined out]; W F [or W T].

927. Feb. 27, 1743/4 Jno Coles enters 5,000 ac in Chowan Co; border: the upper Sorraw [or Saraw] Town at the peach orchard, runs up & down both sides of Dan [sic] R, & joins upper part of Brunswick Co, VA; made out; Goulde.

928. Feb. 27, 1743/4 Wm McCannering [or McAnnering] enters 300 ac in Edgecombe Co on N side of Nuse R; border: a pine; made out; paid; rites returned.
929. Feb. 27, 1743/4 Jno Macon enters 300 ac in Edgecombe Co on Cabbin Br; border: near Wm Stroud's upper line and red oak on the branch; made out; paid; rites returned.

930. Feb. 27, 1743/4 Edmd Blount enters 250 ac in Tyrrell Co on Tottering bridge Br and runs along the main Desart; includes his own improvements and Wm Barret's; made out; rites returned.

page 59
931. Feb. 27, 1743/4 Jno Wiggons enters 200 ac in Edgecombe Co on S side of

White Oak Swamp and runs "out & down"; includes his improvements; made out; paid; rites returned.

932. Feb. 27, 1743/4 Hopkins Wilden enters 300 ac in Edgecombe Co on both sides of Swifts Cr, below mouth of a branch, & runs up and across both sides; includes his improvements; made out; paid; rites returned.

933. Feb. 27, 1743/4 Francis Mayberry enters 200 ac in Edgecombe Co on S side of Tar R; border: "nigh" or at mouth of Wolf Pit Br, below Wm Smith, & runs "out and down"; made out; paid; rites returned.

934. Feb. 27, 1743/4 Jno Phillips Shelley enters 100 ac in Edgecombe Co on S side of Swifts Cr and below Hopkin Wilder; includes his improvements; made out; paid; rites returned.

935. Feb. 27, 1743/4 Joseph Culpepper enters 300 ac in Edgecombe Co on N side of Swifts Cr, below mouth of Tuckahoe Br, & runs down and across the creek; includes both his improvements; made out; paid; rites returned.

936. Feb. 27, 1743/4 Thomas Hill enters 100 ac in Edgecombe Co on N side of Shaccoe [Swamp]; border: a red oak and runs "across" to Fishing Cr; includes his improvements in "the" neck; made out; paid; rites returned.

937. Feb. 27, 1743/4 Theops Goodwin enters 300 ac in Edgecombe Co on N side of Conway Cr; border: "the out" corner of his own line and runs "up"; made out; paid; rites returned.

938. Feb. 27, 1743/4 Joseph Bridges enters 200 ac in Edgecombe Co on N side of the falls of Cedar Cr and S side of Tar R "to include his complement"; made out; paid; rites returned.

939. Feb. 27, 1743/4 John Watson enters 200 ac in Edgecombe Co on both sides of Jacket Swamp [near--lined out] Francis Jones; includes his improvement; made out; paid; rites returned.

940. Feb. 27, 1743/4 Montfort Eelbeck [or Eclbeck] enters 300 ac in Edgecombe Co on both sides of Jacket Swamp [near--lined out] Francis Jones; includes his improvement; made out; paid; rites returned.

page 60
941. Feb. 27, 1743/4 Thos Jarnagan enters 300 ac in Edgecombe Co "on" the fork of White Oak Swamp; includes his improvement; made out; paid; rites returned.

942. Feb. 27, 1743/4 John Kennard [or Hennard] enters 150 ac in Craven Co on N side of Katenkney Cr above Wm Deloach; border: a pine on the creek and runs "out and up"; includes his improvements; made out; paid; rites returned.

943. Feb. 27, 1743/4 John Kennard [or Hennard] enters 200 ac in Craven Co on S side of Katankney Cr; border: Buckhorn Br and runs "up"; includes his improvement; made out; paid; rites returned.

944. Feb. 27, 1743/4 Thos Lane enters 200 ac in Craven Co on N side of Fort Run; border: his own corner and run "up"; made out; paid; rites returned.

945. Feb. 27, 1743/4 Benja Williams enters 150 ac in Craven Co on N side of Nuce R; border: a red oak at "the" side of a gut and runs "down"; made out; paid; rites returned "before".

946. Feb. 27, 1743/4 Jacob Wells enters 300 ac in New Hanover Co; border: an oak on upper branch of Iron mine Cr, Hedges' upper line, & runs up the creek; made out; rites not returned; McCullo chd pet.

page 61
947. Feb. 27, 1743/4 Steph. Williams enters 200 ac in Onslow Co; border: a red oak on a branch of Mill Run and runs up said branch [creek--lined out]; made out; rites returned; McCall's chas pet.

948. Feb. 27, 1743/4 Francis Parker jr enters 100 ac in Edgecombe Co on N side of Swift Cr; border: a "slept" red oak and runs up the creek; includes his improvements; made out; paid; rites proved in Council.

949. Feb. 27, 1743/4 Jno Lahoon enters 200 ac in Edgecombe Co on S side of Tar R; border: mouth of a branch at a hickory and runs "up"; made out; paid; rites proved in Council.

950. Feb. 27, 1743/4 Antho. Crocker enters 300 ac in Edgecombe Co on Pace's Path at a slept oak on Sandy Cr and runs down both sides of said creek; includes both his improvements; made out; paid; rites proved in Council.

951. Feb. 27, 1743/4 Edwd Powers enters 400 ac in Edgecombe Co on S side of Tar R, at mouth of Buffelo Cr, & runs up the river and "out"; made out; paid; rites proved in Council.

952. Feb. 27, 1743/4 James Farmer enters 100 ac in Craven Co; border: a blazed red oak on S side of Neuse R and runs down the river & "out"; includes his improvements; made out; paid; rites proved in Council.

953. Feb. 27, 1743/4 Sampson Williams enters 200 ac in Edgecombe Co; border: mouth of Cabbin Br, on S side of Crooked Cr at a white oak, & runs down the creek; made out; paid; rites proved in Council.

954. Feb. 27, 1743/4 Sampson Williams enters 640 ac in Edgecombe Co on N side of Tar R; border: a slept red oak near the river and runs down both sides of

the river; includes his improvements; made out; paid; rites proved in Council.

page 62
955. Feb. 27, 1743/4 James Mcilwean enters 200 ac in Craven Co on S side of Neuse R and above Michaels Cr; called Grassy Land; made out; paid; rites returned "before".

956. Feb. 27, 1743/4 Jno Faulk enters 200 ac in Edgecombe Co on both sides of Teonqueque [or Tconquque] Cr and below the upper beaverdam; made out; rites returned.

957. Feb. 27, 1743/4 Gideon Macon enters 400 ac in Edgecombe Co on S side of Shaccoe [Swamp] near the head; border: a blazed white oak and runs down both sides of Shaccoe [Swamp]; made out; paid; rites proved in Council.

958. [the following lined out] Saml Hilh [or Hill] enters 640 ac in Beaufort Co.

959. Feb. 28, 1743/4 John Williams enters 600 ac in Beaufort Co on N side of Tar R; border: a pine on N side of Pot Rack Swamp; made out; rites returned.

960. Feb. 28, 1743/4 John Moon enters 300 ac in Beaufort Co on N side of Tar R; border: Wm Mace's land on the great marsh; made out; paid; rites returned.

961. Feb. 28, 1743/4 James Adams enters 200 ac in Beaufort Co on W side of Blounts Cr, on S side of branch, & on Sheppards Run; made out; paid; rites returned.

962. Feb. 28, 1743/4 James Garey enters 200 ac in Edgecombe Co; border: on a branch above Peter Johnston's and runs "out & up"; made out; paid; rites proved in Council.

page 63
963. Feb. 28, 1743/4 Evan Jones jr enters 200 ac in Craven Co on Cahookey Cr and part of Wall's Neck, on Handcocks Cr, & on S side of Nuce R; paid; rites returned.

964. Feb. 28, 1743/4 Jacob Sheets enters 200 ac in Craven Co; border: Col. Pollock's line, said Sheets' line where Jacob Sheets lives, & runs down "the" swamp; paid; rites proved in Council "before".

965. Feb. 28, 1743/4 Edward Moor enters 200 ac in Edgecombe Co on N side of Sapponey Cr; border: mouth of a branch below the fork and runs "up"; made out; paid; rites proved in Council.

966. Feb. 28, 1743/4 Benja Flowers enters 200 ac in Edgecombe Co on N side of Tar R, near mouth of Saponey Cr, & runs to include "the" fork; made out; proved

in Council.

967. Feb. 28, 1743/4 Jacob Odam enters 300 ac in Chowan Co at a place called "the" in the main Cypress Swamp; surrounded "with" the swamp; made out; paid; rites proved in Council.

968. Feb. 28, 1743/4 Richard Bird enters 250 ac in Craven Co on E side of Falling Cr; border: Ambrose Agriss' line and runs up the creek; made out; paid.

page 64
969. Feb. 29, 1743/4 Marma. Norfleet enters 200 ac in Edgecombe Co; border: mouth of a great reedy branch on E side of Conotta Pecoson about a mile below [or "berd"] the Indian Paths; made out; paid; rites approved "before".

970. Feb. 29, 1743/4 Wm Hardy enters 500 ac in Craven Co; border: Stephen Calvert's line between Jumping Run and the beaverdams on Trent R; made out; on W Her. rites.

971. Feb. 29, 1743/4 Hen Deavour enters 200 ac in Craven Co on Cabbin Br, on S side of Tredlers [or Fudlers] Pond, & runs across the head of the branch; includes Seaen [or Scaen] Springs; made out; paid; rites proved in Council.

972. Feb. 29, 1743/4 Robt Dunbarr enters 300 ac in Edgecombe Co on S side of Tar R; border: Saml Sessum's line and runs up the river; made out; paid; rites returned.

973. Feb. 29, 1743/4 Joseph Howell enters 200 ac in Craven Co on S side of Catankney Cr and on Watery Br; border: below Saml Peacock and runs across the branch; made out; paid; rites returned.

974. Feb. 29, 1743/4 JohnHall enters 300 ac in Edgecombe Co on N side of Towne Cr, at the mouth of a branch, & runs "down"; made out; paid; rites returned.

page 65
975. Mar. 1, 1743/4 Marmaduke Norfleet enters 200 ac in Edgecombe Co on E side of Connetta Pecoson and on N side of uppermost reedy branch that runs into said pecoson; made out; paid; rites proved "before".

976. Mar. 1, 1743/4 James Ellison enters 200 ac in Beaufort Co on W side of Bath Town Cr; border: Jarvis and Wm Martin; made out; paid; rites returned.

977. Mar. 1, 1743/4 Abrahm. Boyd enters 200 [150--lined out] in Beaufort Co; border: Ambrose Ayress' upper survey on S side of Falling Cr; made out; paid; rites proved in Council.

978. Mar. 1, 1743/4 Abrahm. Boyd enters 100 ac in Beaufort Co on S side of

North Carolina Land Entries 1735-1752

Little Cr and on Great Catentney Cr; border: an oak; made out; paid.

979. Mar. 1, 1743/4 Abrahm. Boyd enters 100 ac in Beaufort Co inBucklesberry Percoson; made out; paid.

980. Mar. 1, 1743/4 Abrahm. Boyd enters 100 ac in Beaufort Co in the fork of Little Cr "in" Great Catentney [Swamp]; border: lower end of the fork; made out; paid.

981. Mar. 1, 1743/4 John Gyles enters 250 ac in Beaufort Co on N side of Neuse R and each side of Sterrup Br; border: at an oak; made out; paid.

982. Mar. 1, 1743/4 Jno Lott enters 200 ac in Edgecombe Co on N side of Tosneot Swamp; border: a red oak and runs up the swamp; made out; paid.

page 66
983. Mar. 1, 1743/4 Isaac Shavanesse enters 150 ac in Hyde Co on S side of Broad Cr, on E side of Deep Run, runs on Deep Run, & "back"; made out; paid; rites proved in Council.

984. Mar. 1, 1743/4 Wm Barnes enters 200 ac in Craven Co on N side of Catentney Cr; border: an oak; includes his improvement; made out; paid; rites returned.

985. Mar. 2, 1743/4 Sampson Pope enters 300 ac in Edgecombe Co on S side of Stoney Cr; being where he lives; made out; paid; rites proved in Council.

986. Mar. 2, 1743/4 Thomas Parker enters 300 ac in Edgecombe Co on N side of Little Fishing Cr; border: a red oak above his improvements and runs down to widow Patterson's improvements; made out last Court at Edeat.

987. Mar. 2, 1743/4 Garret Wall enters 150 ac inEdgecombe Co on S side of Fishing Cr; between his own line and Jno Parish's line; made out last Court at Edeat.

988. Mar. 2, 1743/4 George Portice enters 350 ac in Edgecombe Co on S side of Fishing Cr; border: a blazed red oak on the creek and runs "down"; made out.

989. Mar. 2, 1743/4 James Wyat enters 100 ac in Edgecombe Co on N side of Swift Cr and on head of Deep Run; includes the "plantation" where James Griffen lives; made out.

page 67
990. Mar. 2, 1743/4 Robert Baker enters 200 ac in Edgecombe Co on N side of Fishing Cr at Stephen Weaver's corner and runs "out"; made out.

North Carolina Land Entries 1735-1752

991. Mar. 2, 1743/4 Thos Smith enters 200 ac in Edgecombe Co on Rocky Swamp; border: on a branch of the swamp and runs up to Wm Jones' line on both of the swamp [line--lined out]; made out.

992. Mar. 2, 1743/4 Wm Fish enters 250 ac in Craven Co at the mouth of a branch above his improvements on Acocks Swamp and runs down the swamp; made out.
993. Mar. 2, 1743/4 Wm Fish enters 100 ac in Craven Co; border: a blazed pine on Marsh Br near Smith's Path and runs on both sides of the branch; made out.

994. Mar. 2, 1743/4 Jas Blount [or Bloint] enters 300 ac in Beaufort Co on S side of Pamplico R, in a fork of Blounts Cr, runs up Wolf pit Br, & "back"; made out; paid; rites proved in Council.

995. Mar. 2, 1743/4 Jno Lott enters 200 ac in Edgecombe Co on S side of Tosneot [Swamp], below mouth of a large branch, & runs "up"; made out; paid; rites returned.

996. Mar. 2, 1743/4 Wm Pick enters 700 ac in New Hanover Co; border: at Panthers Swamp "a little" above Indian Run and runs up said swamp; McCulloch chd. pet.

page 68
997. Mar. 6, 1743/4 Thos Kennon enters 200 ac in New Hanover Co on Maxwell Swamp at a dogwood; McCulloch.

998. [no date and lined out] Caleb Howell enters 200 ac in Beaufort Co; border: a pine on "the" Creek Swamp, runs 0.5 miles S to a pine, & "same distance" W to another pine.

999. Mar. 7, 1743/4 Jeremiah Swaine enters 400 ac in Tyrrell Co on E side of Scuppernong R; border: Geo Cooper's line and runs along "the same"; includes the rich level [or Aevel] called Beech ridge, runs with "the" Creek Pecoson, & includes the chesnut oak ground; made out; rites returned.

1000. Mar. 7, 1743/4 Cason Brinson enters 100 ac in Craven Co on Watering Pond, on NW side of Broad Cr, & about 2 miles below Jno Morgan's; made out; paid.

1001. Mar. 7, 1743/4 Nicholas Purefoy enters 200 ac in Craven Co on E side of main fork of Upper Broad Cr; border: John Marshall and George Graham; made out; paid.

page 69
1002. Mar. 7, 1743/4 Joseph Masters enters 150 ac in Craven Co at mouth of a branch, runs up "at" the head of Hancocks Cr, & on S side of Neuse R; made out.

North Carolina Land Entries 1735-1752

1003. Mar. 7, 1743/4 Garteam Howland enters 200 ac in Carteret Co on "the" banks near Point Lookout; border: Shacklesford's line; made out.

1004. Mar. 7, 1743/4 Jno Willison enters 100 ac in Carteret Co on Core banks; between Wm Davis and Drum Inlet; made out; rites returned.

1005. Mar. 7, 1743/4 Jacob Sheets enters 200 ac in Craven Co; border: Mr. Pollock's line and runs "down"; being where he lives; made out; chad.

1006. Mar. 7, 1743/4 Thos Banks enters 800 ac in Craven Co in the fork of Tysons Marsh [creek--lined out] and on S side of main prong of said marsh; made out.

1007. Mar. 7, 1743/4 Robt Monger enters 300 ac in Northampton Co on S side of Kerbys Cr; border: Thomas Williams' lower line and runs down the creek; made out; paid; rites returned.

1008. Mar. 7, 1743/4 Jno Smelley enters 100 ac in Northampton Co on N side of Corrory Swamp; border: mouth of Hunting Quarter Br and runs down the swamp; made out; paid; rites returned.

1009. Mar. 7, 1743/4 Jno Smelley enters 100 ac in Northampton Co on W side of Kirbeys Cr; border: Wm Crawford's lower line and runs down the creek; made out; paid; rites returned.

page 70
1010. Mar. 7, 1743/4 Wm Allen enters 250 ac in Northampton Co on N side of Potakasey Cr; border: a corner poplar and runs down the creek; made out; paid; rites returned "before".

1011. Mar. 7, 1743/4 Ozbn. Jeffreys enters 100 ac in Northampton Co on N side of Bridgen Cr; border: Col. Pollock's land; made out; paid; rites proved in Council "before".

1012. Mar. 7, 1743/4 John Pope enters 200 ac in Edgecombe Co; border: a white oak on N side of Tar R "a little" above mouth of Maple Swamp [creek--lined out] and runs up the swamp; made out; rites proved in Council "before".

1013. Mar. 7, 1743/4 James Hasel enters 640 ac in New Hanover Co in the forks of Assops Creek Branches; border: head of "said" Assop's land and runs between Musgrave's land and land that was "late" Robinson's; made out; chad. pet.

1014. Mar. 7, 1743/4 James Brickle enters 150 ac in Beaufort Co on E side of Jacksons Swamp; border: Mr. Ormand's line and the swamp; paid; rites proved in Council.

page 71

91

1015. [no date] John Ashe enters 140 ac in New Hanover Co on widow Moor's Cr and above & below the bridge on the road to Black R.

1016. [no date] Saml Swann enters 100 ac in New Hanover Co; border: below Jas Henery's and between land of "widdow" Marshal and said "Henry".

1017. [no date] Eliz Boushier enters 300 ac in New Hanover Co on Gum Br and on Island Cr; border: the River Swamp on NE Cape Fear R; made out; Walker chd. pet.

1018. [no date] Benja Befferet [or Beffnet] enters 200 ac in New Hanover Co on Maple Br running into Maxwells Cr; made out; Walker chd.

1019. [no date] Wm Gown enters 400 ac in New Hanover Co on or near Wm Lewis' Cr; border: near Jno Cook sr's land; made out; Walker.

1020. [no date] Jno Meazall enters 320 ac in Bertie Co on E side of Cypress Swamp; border: Jno Sowell's line; on Jno Wynn's rights; Goulde chad.

1021. [no date] Benja Holliman enters 300 ac in Bertie Co; includes a place called Pare Garden on an eastern branch of Connaritsa Swamp; on Richd Holly's rights; Goulde chad.

page 72
1022. [no date] Arinias Mackintosh enters 200 ac in Craven Co; border: Wilkinson's line and runs from Deep Br to Batchelors Cr; rites returned.

1023. [no date] Nathl Event enters 300 ac in Onslow Co; border: Ths Hallwood's [or Hellwood] corner white oak at head of Fullwoods Cr and joins Geo Pant [or Pan's] on E, Joshua Grainger on S, & Peter Parker on W.

1024. [no date] Jno Cowan enters 640 ac in New Hanover Co on NE Cape Fear R, near Golden Grove, & on a "branch of" Timo. Bloodworth's; rites returned.

1025. [no date] Roger Moor enters 300 ac in New Hanover Co on E side of Cape Fear R and opposite R Moor's "plantation"; border: Moor's land and Col. Moseley's land.

1026. [no date] Thos Cunningham enters 200 ac in New Hanover Co on Lockwoods folley R.

1027. [no date] Wm Boshier enters 200 ac in New Hanover Co on Lockwoods folley R.

page 73
1027A. [no date] James Hasel enters 100 ac in New Hanover Co.

North Carolina Land Entries 1735-1752

page 74 [blank page]

page 75

1028. Nov. 13, 1744 Luke gregory enters 200 ac in Chowan Co; border: Job Charleton's [page torn], joins his land, Nathl Ming, Thos Ming, [page torn] Yawpem Percoson; paid; rites returned.

1029. Nov. 13, 1744 Wm Wyatt enters 300 ac in Perquimans Co on Indian Cr; border: [page torn] Caruthers' line, said Wyatt, Jno Stepney [or Hopney], & land formerly belonging to John Banks and Jeremiah Pratt; rites returned; paid.

1030. Nov. 13, 1744 Wm Wyatt enters 200 ac in Perquimans Co on head of Pratt's Mill Swamp and near Peters Ponds; includes 1 or 2 ridges of land on each side of "the" swamp and includes Felt's land; rites returned; paid.

1031. Nov. 13, 1744 Susana. Anderson enters 200 ac in Edgecombe Co on N side of Dry [page torn] Br; border: Wm Green; rites returned; paid.

1032. Nov. 13, 1744 Jno Haywood enters 300 ac in Edgecombe Co; border: a blazed hickory on S side of main Island Cr, runs N up "the" branch to another branch, down the branch to the main creek, & up the creek to the beginning; rites returned; paid; "R F".

1033. Nov. 13, 1744 Wm Acock enters 500 ac in Northampton Co; border: Arthur Cavenah's [page torn] on Roanoke R, runs up S[faided] Cr, & join Gaddis' line; includes Kendall's Neck; rites returned; paid; R F.

1034. Nov. 13, 1744 Saml Brock enters 600 ac in Edgecombe Co on N side of Fishing Cr; border: James Wyatt; includes the vacant land above [faided] Wm Kerby's land; rites returned; paid; R F.

1035. Nov. 13, 1744 Wm Baleaa [or Balead] enters 200 ac in Edgecombe Co; border: a marked red oak [page torn] a branch of H[page torn]; rites returned; paid; R F.

page 76

1036. Nov. 13, 1744 Robt [or Rost] Harris enters 400 ac in Edgecombe Co on N side of Tar R and in the great Low Grounds; border: a blazed red oak and runs up the river; rites returned "before"; paid; R F.

1037. Nov. 13, 1744 Wm Mears enters 500 ac in Edgecombe Co on S side of Fishing Cr; border: Thomas Drake and James Cane; rites returned; paid; R F.

1038. Nov. 13, 1744 James Hendrick enters 200 ac in Edgecombe Co; border: a blazed poplar on S side of Carolls Cr and runs down the creek; includes his improvement.

1039. Nov. 13, 1744 John [or Felix] Richards enters 200 ac in Edgecombe Co; border: a poplar on S side of Shaccoe Cr and runs up both sides; rites proved "now"; paid; R F.

1040. Nov. 13, 1744 James Reves enters 300 ac in Edgecombe Co on S side of "Qunkee" Swamp; border: lower side of the fork of Watery Br, runs up the branch, & down the swamp; rites returned; paid; R F.

1041. Nov. 13, 1744 Saml Williams enters 100 ac in Edgecombe Co; border: a pine on "the" side of his mill dam, joins Mr. Karney, & on W side of "the" Mill Swamp; paid; R F.

1042. Nov. 13, 1744 Montfort Eclbeck enters 640 ac in Edgecombe Co on Quankee Cr; border: near Peter Richardson's line and begins at a red oak on S side of said creek; rites assigned to him and returned; paid; R F.

1043. Nov. 14, 1744 Jno Becton enters 50 ac in Craven Co; border: on NW side of Isaac Adams' land and joins Kitt Snowden; rites returned; paid.

1044. Nov. 14, 1744 Jno Becton enters 200 ac in Craven Co on Indian Wells [Swamp--lined out] at White Oak Pecoson and runs on both sides; paid.

page 77
1045. Nov. 14, 1744 Jas Terry enters 400 ac in Edgecombe Co on both sides of Swift Cr; border: a great stone and runs down the creek; paid.

1046. Nov. 14, 1744 Wm Kennedy enters 400 ac in Craven Co on both sides of Little Cotentnea Cr; border: the end of a meadow about a mile above Jno Ward's survey; paid.

1047. Nov. 14, 1744 Jas Smith enters 100 ac in Tyrrell Co on Conetta Swamp on N side and runs E on the swamp; paid.

1048. Nov. 14, 1744 Wm Hall enters 200 ac in Craven Co on Apple Tree Swamp; border: Holmes' ford and runs up the swamp on S side of great Cotentnea Cr; paid.

1049. Nov. 14, 1744 Elias Fort enters 400 ac in Craven Co on Cohera Swamp; being where Elkanah Peacock formerly lived; "X".

1050. Nov. 14, 1744 Geo Moore enters 320 ac in Bladen Co on NW side of Black R and on lower side of Lake Cr; border: a blazed pine and runs up the creek; X.

1051. Nov. 14, 1744 Geo Moore enters 320 ac in Bladen Co on NW side of Black R and upper side of Lake Cr; border: mouth of said creek and runs "up"; X.

North Carolina Land Entries 1735-1752

1052. Nov. 14, 1744 Geo Moore enters 320 ac in Bladen Co on NW side of Black R and on a lake about 2 miles from the river; border: a blazed pine and runs "down" [on upper side of said lake at a blazed pine and runs back--lined out]; X.

1053. Nov. 14, 1744 Geo Moore enters 320 ac in Bladen Co on NW side of Black R and on a lake about 2 miles from said river; border: on [page torn] of said Moor's of todays date; X.

page 78
1054. [no date] Leonard Loftin enters 200 ac in Craven Co; border: upper corner tree of his old "plantation" at a pine on W side of Handcocks Cr; includes the vacant land between said old "plantation" and Bounding Cr; rites returned; paid.

1055. [no date] Benja Sanderson enters 600 ac in Hyde Co on E side of Matchepungo R; border: on SE side of said Sanderson's patent land; known as Sanderson's Piney neck; S Swann.

1056. [no date] Benja Sanderson enters 150 ac in Craven Co on S side of Brices Cr; border: joins land where he lives; X.

1057. [no date] Josh Jno Alston enters 600 ac in Edgecombe Co on S side of Reedy Cr at the mouth of Fanny's Delight and runs up "the" branch & creek; paid.

1058. [no date] Josh Jno Alston enters 500 ac in Edgecombe Co at mouth of Beaverdam Br on S side of Fishing Cr, in the fork of Buffelo Br, & runs up each branch; border: Frank Young; paid.

1059. [no date] Josh Jno Alston enters 100 ac in Edgecombe Co on S side of Fishing Cr; border: a little branch [at] Bobbit's line; paid.

1060. [no date] Phillip Alston enters 600 ac in Edgecombe Co on N side of Fishing Cr; border: Capt. Alston's line and runs up the creek & swamp; paid.

page 79
1061. [no date] Wm Ferris enters 50 ac in New Hanover Co; being a neck of land on "the" Sound near Joshua Graneg [or Graney] and Jno Motts; "made out thus far".

1062. [no date] Wm Gillam enters 200 ac in Northampton Co; border: Wm Clanton's line on Little Pidgeon Roost Cr and runs up both sides of said creek; rites returned "before"; paid.

1063. [no date] John Lysle enters 300 ac in Edgecombe Co on N side of Fishing Cr, at mouth of Danl Fluquimore's Spring Br, & runs down the branch; rites returned "before"; paid.

North Carolina Land Entries 1735-1752

1064. [no date] Thos Dudley enters 300 ac in Onslow Co on Queens Cr; border: Hawkins' back line and a blazed pine; rites returned; paid; Starky.

1065. [no date] Wm Barber enters 300 ac in Onslow Co on NE New R and on Poplar Br; border: Joseph Barnes' upper line and runs "up"; rites returned; paid; Starky.

1066. [no date] And Jno Febin enters 150 ac in Onslow Co on mouth of Queens Cr; border: Snoad's line and runs "up"; rites returned "before"; paid; Starky.

1067. [no date] Jno Starkee enters 300 ac in Onslow Co; between Saml Jones and Jno Simpson; "rites before"; paid; Starky.

1068. [no date] Jno Starkee enters 300 ac in Onslow Co on N side of Horse Swamp; border: a pine and runs "up"; paid; Starky.

page 80
1069. [no date] Wm Bush enters 300 ac in Craven Co on S side of Nuse R, mouth of Brush Br above Rocky point, & runs down the river; on Becton's rites; paid.

1070. [no date] Edwd Stevens enters 200 ac in New Hanover [Bladen--lined out] Co on a branch of Black R; at a place called Cohera Swamp and a branch running into Black R; rites returned "before"; paid.

1071. [no date] Wm Moore enters 200 ac in Craven Co; border: about 0.5 miles above nest Bevill's cabins on head of Little R and joins the Bever ponds; rites returned "before"; paid.

1072. [no date] Wm Stroude enters 200 ac in Edgecombe Co at mouth of Cabbin Br and runs up both sides of said branch; rites returned; paid.

1073. [no date] Wm Paskall enters 150 ac in Edgecombe Co; border: a white oak on Stroude's North line, runs N down Powells Cr, & "back over" said creek; rites returned; paid.

1074. [no date] Henry Heaton enters 150 ac in Craven Co on head of Sycomore Br; known as "the" islands; rites returned; paid.

1075. [no date] Henry Gibbons enters 200 ac in Craven Co on S side of Eagle Br; border: about a mile above Richd Lovet's land; rites returned; paid.

page 81
1076 (1). [no date] Abraham Sheperd enters 400 ac in Craven Co on S side of Cottentney Cr; border: Rountree's line, the creek, & runs down the creek; rites "sent"; paid.

1077 (2). [no date] Henery Everat enters 300 ac in Craven Co on S side of Nuce R; border: Mackelwain's line and runs down; rites sent; paid.

1078 (3). [no date] Henery Everat enters 150 ac in Craven co on S side of Nuce R and on N side of Swifts Cr; known as Morrough's "complement"; rites sent; paid.

1079 (4). [no date] Jams. Tyner enters 200 ac in Craven Co on N side of Nuce R; border: a beaver branch below Joseph Boon; paid.

1080 (5). [no date] William Hooks enters 200 ac in Craven Co on both sides of Buck Swamp; border: his own land; rites in Mr. Foster's hands proved; paid.

1081 (6). [no date] Joseph Boon enters 200 ac in Craven Co on N side of Nuce R and on upper side of Spoil Cunt Cr; rites in Mr. Foster's hands proved; paid.

1082 (7). [no date and lined out] John Becton enters 300 ac in Craven Co on S side of Nuce R and about 0.25 miles above Rockey hill; paid.

1083 (8). [no date and lined out] John Becton enters 150 ac in Craven Co on S side of great Cottentney Cr; border: "Littell" Cr; rites in "the" office both these entrys; paid.

page 82
1084 (9). [no date] John Johnson enters 200 ac in Beaufort Co on N side of Grindel Cr; rites sent; paid.

1085 (10). [no date] Joseph Seiler enters 100 ac in Craven Co on S side of Appletree Cr; border: a beaver dam; being [where] John Cleark lived; paid.

1086 (11). [no date] Richd Pierce enters 100 ac in Craven Co on N side of "Littel" R and on Sazer Eyes Swamp; paid.
1087 (12). [no date] Simon Flowers enters 100 ac in Craven Co on S side of Norhunty [Swamp]; between Garreld and best; paid.

1088 (13). [no date] Solomon Johnson enters 200 ac in Craven Co on N side of Bear Cr and on lower side of Peters Br; rites in "the" office; paid.

1089 (14). [no date] Richd Barfiel enters 500 ac in Craven Co on NE side of Franks Swamp and at "the" mouth; being where "one" Pendry lives; rites in Mr. Forester's hands; paid.

1090 (15). [no date] William Gurley enters 200 ac in Craven Co on N side of Mackison Cr; border: his first survey; rites in "the" office; paid.

1091 (16). [no date] Elias Fort enters 150 ac in Craven Co on S side of Falling Cr; between Arthur Fort and William Cush [or Cuth]; rites in "the" office; paid.

1092 (17). [no date] Joshua Lam enters 100 ac in Craven Co on N side of Black Cr; being where he lives; paid.

pag 83
1093 (18). [no date] Thoms. Lam enters 100 ac in Craven Co in the fork of Black Cr and Great Swamp; paid.

1094 (19). [no date] Jacob Lam enters 100 ac in Craven Co on N side of Black Cr and at mouth of a small branch; paid.

1095 (20). [no date] Edwd. Bass enters 200 ac in Craven Co on N side of Black Cr; being where he lives; rites in Mr. Forester's hands; paid.

1096 (21). [no date] William Dreak enters 100 ac in Edgecombe Co on head of Spiers' Br and N side of Coneyhoe Cr; paid.

1097 (22). [no date] Jams. Conner enters 300 ac in Craven Co on both sides of Marsh Br and N side of Falling Cr; "ye" know my rites in "the" office; paid.

1098 (23). [no date] Patrick menture enters 100 ac in Craven Co; border: Mr. Pollock, Kindom, great marsh, & begins at a poplar; paid.

page 84 [blank page]
page 85
1099. [no date] John Barrow enters 400 ac in Beaufort Co on N side of Forked Swamp; bthe ridge "to" Pungo Swamp and runs down "the same"; rites returned; paid.

1100. [no date] Wm Tipps [or Fipps] enters 100 ac in Beaufort Co on head of Brown's Cr; border: Wm Carruthers on both sides of the swamp; Carruthers; paid.

1101. [no date] Wm Cooper enters 300 ac in Beaufort Co on head of Masons Cr and on S side of Bay River; Carruthers; paid.

1102. [no date] Robt Howel enters 100 ac in Bertie Co on S side of Buck Swamp; border: James Parker and his own line; rites returned; paid.

1103. [no date] John Williams enters 100 ac in New Hanover Co in a fork of a branch of Cohera Swamp where "one" Peacock was killed by a tree; rites returned "before"; paid.

1104. [no date] John Williams enters 400 ac in New Hanover Co on a branch of Cohera Swamp and runs up both sides of said branch.

1105. [no date] Thos Moor enters 100 ac in Craven Co on S side of Swift Cr, on

North Carolina Land Entries 1735-1752

Wolf Pit Ridge, & on N side of Nuce R; paid.

1106. [no date] Dennis McClendon enters 300 ac in Craven Co on N side of Cotentnea Cr; between Jno Rasberry and Wm Sims [or Jones] on a marsh; rites not proved.

page 86
1107. [no date] Robt Mitchel [write over] enters 150 ac in Edgecombe Co; border: Robt Mitchel's line on Island Cr and runs up Great Island Cr; on Henderson rites; paid.

1108. [no date] Jno Grenade enters 300 ac in Craven Co on Mill Cr; border: Pollock's line and runs up the creek into "the Paradise"; rites returned; paid.

1109. [no date] Neal McNeil enters 100 ac in Bladen Co on SW side of NW River; border: about 140 yards below "one" McNeal's lower line and runs "down"; rites before; McCullo.

1110. [no date] Martin Trentham enters 400 ac in Bladen Co on SW side of NW River; border: back of John Holton's land [on] Lids [or Sids] Cr, begins at an oak, & runs "up"; rites returned; McCullo.

1111. [no date] Evan Jones enters 200 ac in New Hanover Co on the main branch of Rockfish Cr about 4 miles from Mr. James' [or Jannes'] land; border: an oak and runs "up"; rites returned; McCullo.

1112. [no date] Evan Jones enters 200 ac in New Hanover Co on main branch of Maxwels Cr about 7 miles from Jno Cook's; border: an oak and runs "up"; rites returned; McCulloh.

page 87
1113. [no date] Jno "Carrold" enters 200 ac in Craven Co on Panther Cr; border: Baron's upper line and runs "up"; rites proved in Court "before"; McCulloh.

1114. [no date] John Brook enters 200 ac in Bladen Co; border: joins upper part of his "plantation" and runs up "the" river; rites returned.

1115. [no date] Michl Ram enters 200 ac in Craven Co on both sides of Beaver Cr; border: Mr. Sheets and runs down the creek; paid; rites "before".

1116. [no date] John Worsley jr enters 200 ac in Beaufort Co; border: his own survey on E side of "the" Beaver dam, runs "on" Cutler's survey, & the head of the Beaver dam; rites returned; fees paid.

1117. [no date] Phillip Mew enters 200 ac in Craven Co; border: begins 50 yards below Mew's bridge; includes his improvement and runs up Southwest Cr; rites returned; paid.

1118. [no date] Jno Fonvielle enters 150 ac in Craven Co on Southwest Cr where Phillip Mew ["he"--lined out] formerly improved at a branch below said improvements; rites "before"; paid.

1119. [no date] Jno Fonvielle enters 300 ac in Craven Co; being said Fonvielle's surplus land on S side of Neuse R; between Major Hannis' land and his own land; rites "before"; paid.

page 88
1120. [no date] Jno Nelson enters 50 ac in Craven Co on E side of the road from Neuse R to Pamplico R and near North end of Juniper Swamp; Lovet.

1121. [no date] Thos Nelson enters 640 ac in Carteret Co on Coxe Banks near Ocacock Inlet; Lovet.

1122. [no date] Thos Nelson enters 300 ac in Carteret Co on E side of South R and N side of Eastermost Cr; Lovet.

1123. [no date] Levi Alderson enters 100 ac in Beaufort Co; border: a branch between an old settlement of Chas Pedon's on Forked Swamp and runs up the same; includes the old settlement; Goulde.

1124. [no date] Robt Walker enters 320 ac in New Hanover Co; border: joins land belonging to Thos Hutchins on Long Cr and between said land & land now in possession of said Walker; rites "before"; Rowan.

page 89
1125. Nov. 15, 1744 Osborne Jeffries enters 500 ac in Craven Co in "the" fork and lower side of NE prong of Flat R; border: the river; on Solo. Fuller's rites; paid.

1126. Nov. 15, 1744 Osborne Jeffries enters 150 ac in Northampton Co on a branch or swamp that runs into Potecasy Cr; border: a red oak and runs "up"; on Solo. Fuller's rites; paid.

1127. Nov. 15, 1744 Osborne Jeffries enters 400 ac in Edgecombe Co on N prong of Tar R, above "the" trading path, & on Plumtree Br; border: a red oak and runs "up"; on Solo. Fuller's rites; paid.

1128. Nov. 15, 1744 Jno Ferrill enters 200 ac in Craven Co on Horse Cr; includes his mill; paid.

1129. Nov. 15, 1744 Ignats. Smallwood enters 200 [written over 800] ac in Craven Co on Beaver Pond Cr; includes his improvement; paid.

1130. Nov. 15, 1744 Littleson Spivey enters 400 ac in Edgecombe Co on Reedy Br that makes out a branch of Tabs Cr; paid.

1131. Nov. 15, 1744 Wm Pearson enters 350 ac in Edgecombe Co; border: his "plantation" on Stonehouse Cr; paid.

1132. Nov. 15, 1744 Jno Sherun enters 500 ac in Edgecombe Co; border: a white oak on Lyons Cr "on both sides"; on Ben Kymbal's rites; paid.

page 90
1133. Nov. 15, 1744 Jacob Jarnagan enters 100 ac in Craven Co on S side of Neuse R; border: a pine on said Jarnagan's line and runs along his line; rites returned; fees paid.

1134. Nov. 15, 1744 John Echolls enters 500 ac in Beaufort Co on S side of Pamplico R and on a fork of Goose Cr where Wm Jones formerly lived; rites returned; paid; "paid for this" last Feb. Bath.

1135. Nov. 15, 1744 John Forbes enters 500 ac in Beaufort Co on S side of Tar R; border: Wm Ham's [or Hamp] back line and runs "up & back"; rites in "the" office.

1136. Nov. 15, 1744 David Dun enters 100 ac in Craven Co; between Peter Reel and Jno Robinson on lower prong of Swifts Cr; "Single man"; paid.

1137. Nov. 15, 1744 Richd Hart enters 100 ac in Craven Co on W side of Pometa [Swamp] at the first "Great" Br above a place called Bull going over; rites returned; paid.

1138. Nov. 15, 1744 Jas McWaine esq enters 400 ac in Craven Co on Great Cotentnea Cr at "the" fording place on S side "thereof"; rites assigned from Wm Dehe; paid.

page 91
1139. Nov. 15, 1744 Sampson Underwood enters 200 ac in Northampton Co; border: a corner pine on S side of Patty's delight and runs up the swamp; rites returned; paid.

1140. Nov. 15, 1744 Chas Jordan enters 200 ac in Northampton Co; border: a blazed pine on Kates hole Swamp, on upper side of "the" pine meadow, & each side of the swamp; rites returned; paid.

1141. Nov. 15, 1744 Chas Jordan enters 200 ac in Northampton Co; border: at the county line where it crosses the middle prong of Spring Swamp and runs down the county line; rites returned; paid.

North Carolina Land Entries 1735-1752

1142. Nov. 15, 1744 Carrolos Anderson enters 60 ac in Northampton Co; border: Chas Kerby's lower line and runs down Kerby's Cr; rites returned; paid.

1143. Nov. 15, 1744 Mathew Strickling enters 300 ac in Northampton Co; border: Robt Monger's upper corner tree and runs "out"; rites returned; paid.

1144. Nov. 15, 1744 Stephens Lee enters 100 ac in Tyrrell Co in the fork of a mill pond; border: Capt. Downing's land "deced." commonly called new land; rites returned; paid.

1145. Nov. 15, 1744 Jno Watson enters 100 ac in Edgecombe Co; border: a percimon tree on S side of Red bird Br, runs across, & up both sides of "a" branch; rites returned "before"; paid.

page 92
1146. Nov. 15, 1744 Saml Williams enters 300 ac in Edgecombe Co on S side of Peachtree Cr and on a branch; border: runs across the creek and down the creek; includes his improvements; rites not proved; paid.

1147. Nov. 15, 1744 Hopkin Wilder enters 300 [written over 200] ac in Edgecombe Co on N side of Tar R, on Collin's Cr, & runs down the river; rites to be proved; paid.

1148. Nov. 15, 1744 Jos King enters 300 ac in Edgecombe Co on S side of Tar R; border: above said King's "plantation" on S side and runs across the river; rites to be proved; paid.

1149. Nov. 15, 1744 Wm Wilder enters 100 ac in Edgecombe Co on Peachtree Swamp and runs on N side; includes his improvements; rites to be proved; paid.

1150. Nov. 15, 1744 Moses Dean enters 100 ac in Tyrrell Co on Flat Swamp on S side; border: on lower side of Jno Johnston's line; rites not proved; paid.

1151. Nov. 15, 1744 Wm Williamson enters 200 ac in Edgecombe Co on N side of Town Cr and on a large reedy branch; being the "plantation" where George Gardiner lives; rites proved "before"; paid.

page 93
1152. Nov. 15, 1744 Thos Brown enters 200 ac in Edgecombe Co on S side of Tar R; border: a white oak and runs "up"; rites returned; paid.

1153. Nov. 15, 1744 Joshua Lee enters 500 ac in Edgecombe Co on N side of Cotentnea Cr; border: a white oak on the creek and runs up to include the "plantation" where he lives; rites returned; paid.

1154. Nov. 15, 1744 Wm Johnston enters 100 ac in Craven Co on the fork of Brices Cr in an island; border: a great branch and runs down; rites to be proved; paid; "made out this far".

1155. Nov. 15, 1744 Jas Cane enters 100 ac in Edgecombe Co on S side of Fishing Cr and near the mouth of Beaverdam Swamp; "p".

1156. Nov. 15, 1744 Wm Gardiner enters 300 ac in New Hanover Co on S side of Cohera Cr; between the creek and Black R; border: a pine; rites returned "before"; paid.

1157. Nov. 15, 1744 Wm Gardiner enters 200 ac in New Hanover Co on N [written over "S"] side of Cohera Cr; border: runs up the creek from a pine; paid.

page 94
1158. Nov. 15, 1744 Jno Rouse enters 200 ac in New Hanover Co in the fork of Black R and on N side of said river; border: runs up the river from a red oak.

1159. Nov. 15, 1744 Wm Johnston enters 400 [written over 600] ac in New Hanover Co on S side of Cypress Swamp and runs on both sides; rites returned; paid.

1160. Nov. 15, 1744 Rice Price enters 200 ac in Craven Co on N side of Nuse R; border: joins the land where he lives.

1161. Nov. 15, 1744 Anthy. Cocks enters 400 ac in New Hanover Co on Beaverdam Swamp running into Black R; rites returned; paid.

1162. Nov. 15, 1744 Mathew [write over] Whitfield enters 100 ac in New Hanover Co on E side of Middle Cr and runs down the same; rites returned; paid.

1163. Nov. 15, 1744 Luke Whitfield enters 200 ac in Craven Co on S side of Nuce R, on Falling Cr, & runs "up"; paid.

1164. Nov. 15, 1744 Wm Prescot enters 200 ac in New Hanover Co on E side of NE Swamp and near Buck Marsh; rites returned; paid.

page 95
1165. Nov. 15, 1744 Jno Clark enters 150 ac in Craven Co on N side of Nuce R and on Falling Cr; border: runs down from an oak; paid.

1166. Nov. 15, 1744 Robt Surl enters 100 ac in Craven Co on N side of Nuce R and Falling Cr; border: near John Ronce's land; paid.

1167. Nov. 15, 1744 Wm McIlroy enters 100 ac in Craven Co on N side of Nuce R and on Ground Nut Marsh; paid.

1168. Nov. 15, 1744 John Stringer enters 100 ac in Craven Co; border: Abra Odam's [or Adam] land; paid.

1169. Nov. 15, 1744 Jas Collins enters 200 ac in Craven Co on N side of Nuce R and on N side of Fyce's [or Tyce's] Marsh; rites returned; paid.

1170. Nov. 15, 1744 Robt Savage enters 600 ac in Bladen Co on E side of Cape fear R; border: a gum, runs to Pokeberry Cr, & down the river; paid.

1171. Nov. 15, 1744 Wm Pool enters 200 ac in Craven Co on N side of Swift Cr "a little" above Green's Path at Murray's Camp; paid.

1172. Nov. 15, 1744 Edwd. Matchitt enters 200 ac in New Hanover Co on S side of Goshen Swamp at Bullen's Camp; rites returned; paid.

1173. Nov. 15, 1744 Jas Cheyne enters 200 ac in Craven Co on N side of Vine Swamp at Turky Point; paid.

page 96
1174. Nov. 15, 1744 Wm Hall enters 200 ac in Craven Co on Filds [or Files] Marsh; border: Howel's land; paid.

1175. Nov. 15, 1744 George McCarty enters 10 ac in Craven Co; being the surplus land between Tunaclif's [or Funaclif] land and the river.

1176. Nov. 15, 1744 Saml Gillyard enters 500 ac in Craven Co at mouth of and N side of Beaver Cr; rites returned; paid.

1177. Nov. 15, 1744 John Wade enters 640 ac in Edgecombe Co on S side of Great Shaccoe Cr; border: mouth of first branch above Frank Young's ford, runs to John Gant's line, & down the creek; rites assigned from Jno Hodghill [or Stodghill]; fees paid.

1178. Nov. 15, 1744 John Wade enters 500 ac in Edgecombe Co; border: mouth of first branch above Paces' ford on S side of Shacco Cr and runs "down"; rites to be paid; fees paid.

1179. Nov. 15, 1744 John Clark enters 200 ac in Edgecombe co on S side of Shaccoe Cr; border: mouth of lower Beaver Pond Br and runs up the branch & creek; rites to be proved; fees paid.

1180. Nov. 15, 1744 Wm Taylor enters 300 ac in Edgecombe Co near the head of Island Cr; rites returned; fees paid.

page 97
1181. Nov. 15, 1744 Wm Taylor enters 200 ac in Edgecombe Co on S side of

Roanoke R; rites returned; fees paid.

1182. Nov. 17, 1744 Jno Collins enters 150 ac in Craven Co on S side of Swifts Cr; border: mouth of a large reedy branch and runs up the creek; rites proved "before"; paid.

1183. Nov. 17, 1744 Thos Dowle enters 500 ac in Craven Co.

1184. Nov. 17, 1744 Thos Turner enters 300 ac in Edgecombe Co at mouth of Jumping Run and runs up Deep Cr; rites to be proved.

1185. Nov. 17, 1744 Antonie Duboise enters 400 ac in New Hanover Co on the upper part of Indian Bluff and on Long Cr; border: begins at a pine; rites returned; fees paid.

1186. Nov. 17, 1744 John Powel enters 400 ac in Craven Co on Wherrys Br; border: Pollock, Peter Haw, & "back"; rites returned; paid.

page 98
1187. Nov. 17, 1744 Robt Jones e200 ac in Craven Co on S side of Nuce R, on N side of White Oak Pecoson, & at a place called Indian Wells; rites returned; paid.

1188. Nov. 17, 1744 Anthy Williams enters 200 ac in New Hanover Co on Mathew's Br and runs down NE "Swamp of" Cape Fear R; rites returned; paid.

1189. Nov. 17, 1744 Pat Stanuland [or Stantland] enters 100 ac in Craven Co at a place called Mount Pleasant; border: upper end of the land he lives on; rites returned "before"; paid.

1190. Nov. 17, 1744 Robt Coutney enters 150 ac in Onslow Co on Half Moon Br, on N side of New R, & runs up both sides of the branch; rites returned; paid.

1191. Nov. 17, 1744 Jno Blalock enters 640 ac in Onslow Co on S side of New R and runs up both sides of the "stream"; rites returned; paid.

1192. Nov. 17, 1744 Jno Hinton enters 150 ac in Onslow Co on S side of New R; border: joins the land where he lives; rites "before"; paid.

page 99
1193. Nov. 17, 1744 Michl. French enters 100 ac in Craven Co; border: George Skipper's land and runs on both sides of "the" river; rites not proved; paid.

1194. Nov. 17, 1744 Mark Morgan enters 400 ac in Bladen Co on "the" S branch of New hope Cr called Morgans Cr running into Cape Fear R; rites returned "before" [rites not proved--lined out]; paid.

North Carolina Land Entries 1735-1752

1195. Nov. 17, 1744 Stephe. Clayton enters 500 ac in Craven Co on a run on E side of Richland Cr and runs up the same; rites not proved; paid; "made out to this".

1196. Nov. 19, 1744 Nichs. Culbert enters 250 ac in Craven Co on Moseleys Cr; border: mouth of Folley Br; rites [to be--lined out] returned; paid.

1197. Nov. 19, 1744 Chas. Adams enters 200 ac in Craven Co; border: Wilkinson's line and runs from Deep Br to Batchelors Cr; rites not proved.

1198. Nov. 19, 1744 Benja Payton enters 200 in Beaufort Co on S side of Pamplico R; border: West's line on Blunts Cr; rites proved [in] Council.

page 100
1199. Nov. 19, 1744 Jno Plowman White enters 250 ac in Craven Co on S side of Rainbow Swamp and runs up the swamp; rites to be returned.

1200. Nov. 19, 1744 Benja Rush enters 200 ac in Edgecombe Co on both sides of Flat Rock Cr and on Lyon Cr; border: an oak; includes his improvements; rites returned; paid.

1201. Nov. 19, 1744 Jas Derham enters 100 ac in Craven Co on head of Mill Br and on Batchelor's Cr; border: near Col. Wilson's land; rites [ink blob] proved in Council; paid.
1202. Nov. 19, 1744 Martin Frank enters 300 ac in Craven Co on E side of Beaver Cr and on N side of trent R; being where Churchill lived; rites returned "before"; paid.

1203. Nov. 19, 1744 Wm Bullen enters 100 ac in Craven Co on Beavers Br; border: back of Beaver's and John Rowse's land on N side of Neuse R; single man [to be proved--lined out]; paid.

1204. Nov. 19, 1744 Benja Cooper sr enters 250 ac in Craven Co on both sides of Harry's Br and S side of Neuse R; rites returned; proved.

1205. Nov. 19, 1744 Thos Davis enters 250 ac in Craven Co on N side of Catenknee Cr; between Wm Curlee and Wm Mear's "plantation"; paid.

1206. Nov. 19, 1744 George Michl. Wolf enters 150 ac in Craven Co on N side of Neuse R, on Tyce's Marsh, & on S side of Catanknee Cr; rites returned; paid.

page 101
1207. Nov. 19, 1744 Henry Owen enters 100 ac in Craven Co on S side of Neuse R; between Josha Sessantt and Rawlins; single man; paid.

1208. Nov. 19, 1744 Richd Johnston enters 200 ac in Craven Co; border: Michl

Raisher's land on S side of Nuce R; rites "before"; paid.

1209. Nov. 19, 1744 Theops. Williams enters 150 ac in New Hanover Co; border: below John McDaniel now in possession of Saml Everage on Moors Cr; rites returned; paid.

1210. Nov. 19, 1744 Thos Pierce enters 150 ac in Bertie Co on S side of Conerika Cr; border: Jas Woods' line and runs down the pecoson; rites proved [in] Council; paid.

1211. Nov. 19, 1744 Fredk. Holms enters 200 ac in Edgecombe Co on Little Nutbush Cr and runs up N side of the same; rites returned [in] Council; paid.

1212. Nov. 19, 1744 Thos Barfield enters 300 ac in Edgecombe Co about 2 miles below the beaver ponds on Great Island Cr; rites proved [in] Council; paid.

1213. Nov. 19, 1744 Wm Burton enters 200 ac in Craven Co; border: Jacob Reasonover's corner pine and runs S with his line across "the" branch; includes a beaverdam near Trent R; rites proved [in] Council; paid.

page 102
1214. Nov. 19, 1744 Jas Mulkey enters 100 ac in Bladen Co; border: a pine on S side of New hope Cr in the edge of "the" low ground about a "small" mile above Mark Morgan's cabin; rites proved [in] Council; paid.

1215. Nov. 19, 1744 Robt Clary enters 200 ac in Edgecombe Co; border: a pine below Evans' ferry on N side of Tar R and runs up the river; rites proved [in] Council; paid.

1216. Nov. 19, 1744 Wm Burton enters 50 ac in Craven Co on N side of Trent R about 50 yards below Cordies Landing and runs down the river; includes the improvement of Frederick's; Mackelwean to pay.

1217. Nov. 19, 1744 John Murphy enters 100 ac in Craven Co; border: at the two forks of Deep Gullys back of his own lines and runs up Myrry Glade; paid.

1218. Nov. 19, 1744 Jno Johnston enters 100 ac in Onslow Co on Reedy Br on the upper side, near mouth "thereof", & runs "back"; paid.

1219. Nov. 19, 1744 Robt Hooks enters 100 ac in Onslow Co on S side of Cypress Br at a place called "the" Lake; paid.

page 103
1220. Nov. 19, 1744 Jno Mathews enters 200 ac in Craven Co on Black Cr on S side; border: a poplar and runs down the creek; rites returned; paid.

1221. Nov. 19, 1744 Henry Smith enters 200 ac in Craven Co on S side of Swift Cr and runs up "the" swamp; being the "plantation" where John Rogers lives; rites proved; paid.

1222. Nov. 19, 1744 John Hardy enters 400 ac in Beaufort Co on S side of Tarr R; border: his own line, runs down the river, & "back"; rites proved; paid.

1223. Nov. 19, 1744 Saml Tindall enters 400 ac in Beaufort Co on S side of Bay R; border: Yawpan Hamock; includes Davis' Island; rites proved; paid.

1224. Nov. 19, 1744 John Murfey enters 150 ac in Craven Co on N side of Neuse R; border: the thoroughfare and runs on John Gatlin's line; rites proved; paid.

1225. Nov. 19, 1744 Wm Foreman enters 100 ac in Beaufort Co on S side of Pamplico R and on the open Beaver Dam; border: Wm Martin; rites proved; paid.

1226. Nov. 19, 1744 Luke Forteskue enters 100 ac in Hyde Co on W side of Matchapungo R and runs in the fork of Rites Cr; rites proved; paid.

1227. Nov. 19, 1744 Willowby Adams enters 200 ac in Hyde Co on N side of Matchapungo R; border: John Smith; includes Wm Dick's improvement; rites proved; paid.

1228. Nov. 19, 1744 Wm Giddins enters 100 ac in Hyde Co in New Curratuck [Twsp] on head of Chappel Cr; border: Henry Slade and runs up "the" swamp; rites proved; paid.

page 104
1229. Nov. 19, 1744 Eliza Snoad enters 300 ac in Beaufort Co on S side of Tarr R; border: lower side of Forbes' Br, runs down the branch, & back; rites proved; paid.

1230. Nov. 19, 1744 Christn. Guin enters 200 ac in Edgecombe Co on E side of Deep Cr, on Tar R, runs down the creek, & back; rites proved; paid.

1231. Nov. 19, 1744 Christn. Guin enters 200 ac in Beaufort Co on S side of Tarr R; border: above Tar Landing, runs down the river, & "back"; rites proved; paid.

1232. Nov. 19, 1744 Isaac Buck enters 200 ac in Beaufort Co on S side of Tar R; border: runs on Salter's line and "the" branch of Grays Cr.

1233. Nov. 19, 1744 Richd. Bassett enters 150 ac in Beaufort Co on W side of Mouse Harbour Bay and near head thereof; rites proved; paid.

1234. Nov. 19, 1744 Roger Hodges enters 300 ac in Beaufort Co in the fork of Pamplico R; bruns on Saml Botewell's upper line, the River Swamp, &

Chockawinnety Bay; rites proved; paid.

1235. Nov. 19, 1744 Wm Taylor enters 200 ac in Beaufort Co on S side of Tarr R; border: Seth Pilkinston and runs "back"; rites proved; paid.

1236. Nov. 19, 1744 Josha. Saterthwite enters 100 ac in Hyde Co on E side of Matchapungo R and in a fork of Ruckman's Cr; being the "plantation" where he lives; rites proved; paid.

1237. Nov. 19, 1744 John Wayne enters 200 ac in Craven Co in John James' Neck on Swift Cr; border: George Fisher and John James; being the "plantation" where he lives; rites proved; paid.

page 105
1238. Nov. 19, 1744 Roger Mason enters 100 ac in Hyde Co in the "ced" of "the" savanna; border: John tooley and runs on Papa Ridge; rites proved; paid.

1239. Nov. 19, 1744 Darby McCarty enters 600 ac in Hyde Co on E side of Matchapungo R; border: his own line and Saml Slade; being part of Benja Sanders' claim; rites proved; paid; "pet" granted.

1240. Nov. 19, 1744 Anthy. Wherry enters 200 ac in Beaufort Co on N side of Swift Cr; border: Clayroot Swamp, runs up the swamp, & "back"; rites "proved proved"; paid.

1241. Nov. 21, 1744 Roger Moore esq enters 320 ac in New Hanover Co on Mill Cr a branch of Old Town Cr; border: Nathl. Rice, James Hazell's upper tract, & said creek.

1242. Nov. 21, 1744 Roger Moore esq enters 200 ac in New Hanover Co near head of Lockwoods folley Sound and near a place called Horse pen.

1243. Nov. 21, 1744 Henry Simons enters 600 ac in Bladen Co on a branch of Hamonds Cr and near the road from Miller's on NW River to Brown Marsh; rites [proved in] Council.

1244. Nov. 21, 1744 Abraham [Jno--lined out] Busset enters 200 ac in Craven Co on S side of Trent R; border: on Indian Graves Br and runs down; rites returned; paid.

1245. Nov. 21, 1744 Jno Hilliard enters 250 ac in Craven Co on S side of Trent R at a place called long branch and runs about 0.5 miles up Trent R; rites returned; paid.

page 106
1246. Nov. 21, 1744 Phillip Miller enters 200 ac in Craven Co on N side of Trent

R and in the fork of Johns Folley; rites returned; paid.

1247. Nov. 21, 1744 James Denson enters 500 ac in Bladen Co on N side of Great Pedee R at a place called Red bluff; border: a red oak and runs "down"; rites returned; Mr. McCulloh Dr.

1248. Nov. 21, 1744 Richd. McClure enters 300 ac in Currituck Co; border: John Ballance's new survey, Mr. Parker, Josias Nicholson, & "the" great swamp; rites returned.

1249. Nov. 21, 1744 Mary Edwards enters 300 ac in Craven Co on S side of Neuse R; border: a red oak on S side of Buck Swamp about 2 or 3 miles from Williams' Camp and runs down said swamp; Mr. McCulloh; "made out to this".
1250. Nov. 22, 1744 Moses Houston enters 300 ac in Carteret Co; between Nichs. Hunter's head line and Bryan McCullen's line; proved in Council "before"; made out; Starkey.

1251. Nov. 22, 1744 Hope Willets enters 200 ac in New Hanover Co on Doe cr; border: Schinkg. Moore's corner tree, runs along his line, & then South; rites [proved] inCouncil; made out; R Moor.

1252. Nov. 22, 1744 Jno Wallis enters 100 ac in Onslow Co on NE side of NW New R; border: joins the land where he lives; rites to be proved; made out; paid.

page 107
1253. Nov. 22, 1744 Jos Strickland enters 200 ac in Edgecombe Co on N side of Deep Cr; border: Nichs. Smith's lower line; rites R F to return; paid; made out.

1254. Nov. 22, 1744 Jos Strickland enters 300 ac in Edgecombe Co on S side of Deep Cr; border: Thos Bryant's line and runs down the creek; rites R F to return; paid; made out.

1255. Nov. 22, 1744 Jno Watson enters 100 ac in Tyrrell Co on Connetta Road and on Wolf pen [or "peb"] Ridge; single man; paid; made out.

1256. Nov. 22, 1744 Richd. Allen enters 200 ac in Edgecombe Co in the low ground "again" his own land; border: Foreman; rites R F to return; paid; made out.

1257. Nov. 22, 1744 Geo Downing enters 150 ac in Edgecombe Co on S side of Deep Cr; between two pieces of land belonging to Jno Oneal and joins Ben Bridges; rites R F to return; paid; made out.

1258. Nov. 22, 1744 Wm Faulk enters 100 ac in Tyrrell Co inthe low ground below Popler point; border: Mead's back line; known as Poplar Ridge; single man; paid; made out.

1259. Nov. 22, 1744 Wm Smith enters 100 ac in Edgecombe Co on N side of Little Conneta Cr; being where he lives; single man; paid; made out.

1260. Nov. 22, 1744 Jas Smith enters 100 ac in Tyrrell Co on SW side of Connetta Swamp; being the place he has "lately" improved; single man; paid; made out.

1261. Nov. 22, 1744 Jno Everitt enters 200 ac in Edgecombe Co on Maple Swamp and on SW side of Connehoe Cr; paid.

page 108
1262. Nov. 22, 1744 Jas McDowel enters 200 ac in Bertie Co; border: thos Ashburne; [being] the "plantation" that formerly belonged to Abra Herring and now [belongs] to himself; rites returned; made out.

1263. Nov. 22, 1744 John Peters [or Ceters] enters 10 ac in Craven Co on mouth of Cattail Br, on N side of Neuse R, & above John Hollingsworth; rites returned; paid; made out.

1264. Nov. 22, 1744 Richd. Sessnitt enters 100 ac in Craven Co between Aligator Pond and upper Bogue Marsh on N side of Nuse R; rites returned; paid; made out.

1265. Nov. 22, 1744 Robt Parks enters 100 ac in Craven Co on Black Walnut Cr; border: Wm Stanley and runs up & "over" the creek proved [in] Council "1 rite"; paid; made out.

1266. Nov. 22, 1744 Abra Herring enters 150 [written over 100] ac in Craven Co; border: Jno Rouce "of" Bear Cr and runs down the savannah to Wolf trap Br; rites returned; paid; made out.

1267. Nov. 22, 1744 Wm Herritage enters 300 ac in Craven Co; border: upper corner tree "of" the back line of his own land whereon Gilbert Deaver lives and runs to Wm Belk's line; rites proved "before" [paid--lined out]; made out.

page 109
1268. Nov. 22, 1744 Thos Parker enters 200 ac in Edgecombe Co on S side of Beaverdam Cr; border: near the head of Burny Coole [or Coote] and begins at a red oak; rites returned; paid; Forster; made out.

1269. Nov. 22, 1744 Thos Parker enters 300 ac in Edgecombe Co on N side of Fishing Cr; border: a red oak and runs "down"; includes his improvements; rites returned "before"; paid; made out.

1270. Nov. 22, 1744 John Demant enters 250 ac in Edgecombe Co on N side of Fishing Cr; border: Henry West's line and runs to Christo. Green's line; rites returned; paid; made out.

1271. Nov. 22, 1744 David Ward enters 250 ac in Edgecombe Co on N side of Fishing Cr; between Robt West, Thos Hart, & Robt Hudnal; includes his improvements; rites returned; paid; made out.

1272. Nov. 22, 1744 Thos Keanry [or Kearny] enters 300 ac in Edgecombe Co on N side of Elke Marsh; border: Jno Low's corner white oak, runs along his line to his head corner, & down to Henry Sims' line; rites returned "before"; paid; made out.

1273. Nov. 22, 1744 Israel Robinson enters 600 ac in Edgecombe Co; border: at the little creek above Stroud's Path that leads to Thos Howel's and runs up both sides; rites returned; paid; made out.

page 110
1274. Nov. 22, 1744 Robt Hill jr enters 200 ac in Edgecombe Co; border: a white oak on S side of Peachtree Swamp and runs up both sides thereof; on Mr. Dawson's rites; paid; made out.

1275. Nov. 22, 1744 Abner Hill enters 200 ac in Edgecombe Co on N side of Turky Cr; border: a blazed red oak and runs up the creek; on Mr. Dawson's rites; paid; made out.

1276. Nov. 22, 1744 Jno Lynch enters 300 ac in Northampton Co; border: Virginia line and runs up the county [sic] line; known as "little Lizard"; rites returned; Griff; made out.

1277. Nov. 22, 1744 Jno Lynch enters 300 ac in Edgecombe Co on Tar R at "the" shoals and runs up both sides; rites returned; Griff; made out.

1278. Nov. 22, 1744 Jos Clark enters 200 ac in Bladen Co on Beaverdam Cr above Capt. Blaning's mill and runs up both sides of the creek; rites returned; paid; made out.

1279. Nov. 22, 1744 Adam Moor enters 200 ac in Craven Co; border: the back line of his own line and runs up to Wm Herritage's line on Jemys [or McGungs] Cr; rites proved in Council; paid; made out.

page 111
1280. Nov. 22, 1744 Adam Moor enters 200 ac in Craven Co on S side of Trent R, Barren fork, & on Trent R between Trent R and Tuckahoe Cr; rites proved in Council; paid the above; paid; made out.

1281. Nov. 22, 1744 Jno Demant enters 250 ac in Edgecombe Co on N side of Fishing Cr; between Jas Wyat and Francis Spivey; includes his improvements; rites returned; paid; made out.

North Carolina Land Entries 1735-1752

1282. Nov. 22, 1744 Phil Bradford enters 250 ac in Edgecombe Co on Reedy Br and on N side of Fishing Cr; border: a red oak on the branch and runs on both sides; rites returned "before"; paid; made out.

1283. Nov. 22, 1744 Jno Oats enters 500 ac in New Hanover Co on a branch of NE Cape Fear R and runs on both sides of the branch; rites proved in Council; paid; made out.

1284. Nov. 22, 1744 Wm Marshmont [write over] enters 200 ac in Onslow Co; border: Anderson's line and runs on both sides of Half Moon Br; includes the "plantation" where he lives and Jos Sumners; paid; made out.

1285. Nov. 22, 1744 Jno Hart enters 200 ac in Northampton Co on N side of Poteusy Cr; between Panter's Swamp and Wm Vince's line; rites returned; paid; made out.

page 112
1286. Nov. 22, 1744 Jno Bryan enters 100 ac in Craven Co on S side of Coor Cr and above Green Ponds; rites returned "before"; McWaine; made out.

1287. Nov. 22, 1744 Richd. Banfield enters 200 ac in Craven Co on S side of Black Cr; being where he lives; rites returned; paid; made out.

1288. Nov. 22, 1744 Hen. Roberts enters 250 ac in Craven Co on S side of Nuce R, on N side of Southwest Cr, & below Trotter's land; McWaine; made out.

1289. Nov. 22, 1744 Geo Turnage enters 200 ac in Craven Co on S side of N branch of Little Cotentnea Cr; beting where Saml Lamberson lives; McWaine; made out.

1290. Nov. 22, 1744 Phillips Kerkins enters 250 ac in Craven Co on both sides of Falling Cr; border: below Jno Rouce's land; paid; made out.

1291. Nov. 22, 1744 Jas Everit enters 100 ac in Edgecombe Co on Little Swamp and above the mouth of "aruning" branch; single man; paid; made out.

1292. Nov. 22, 1744 Wm Brice enters 100 ac in Craven Co; border: a corner tree on head of Cyprus Cr, S side of Trent R, & joins James Trotter's head line; rites returned; paid; made out.

page 113
1293. Nov. 22, 1744 Hen. Bull enters 100 ac in Craven Co on N side of Spoillonney Cr and N side of Neuce R; rites to be proved.

1294. Nov. 22, 1744 Nichs. Gregenis enters 100 ac in Onslow Co on N side of SW New R.

113

1295. Nov. 22, 1744 David Miles enters 300 ac in Bladen Co on S side of Little R about 8 or 10 miles from the mouth at an old field and runs "down"; rites returned; paid; made out.

1296. Nov. 22, 1744 David Miles enters 300 ac in Bladen Co; border: his other tract and runs down Little R; paid; made out.

1297. Nov. 22, 1744 David Miles enters 200 ac in Bladen Co on SW side of Great P D River; border: Solo. Hughes' corner tree and runs "down"; paid; made out.

1298. Nov. 22, 1744 Jno Hamone enters 100 ac in Bladen Co on SW side of Great P D River; being the land where he lives; single man; paid; made out.

1299. Nov. 22, 1744 Fras. McClendon enters 600 ac in Craven Co; border: Jno Crew's line on Sandy Run and runs down "the" swamp; rites returned; paid; made out.

page 114
1300. Nov. 22, 1744 John Small sr enters 100 ac in Carteret Co on the branches of Black Cr; border: Col. Thos Lovick's land; rites returned; warrant made out; Col. Lovick to pay.

1301. Nov. 22, 1744 John Smison enters 200 ac in Onslow Co on head of White Oak R "a little" above Fields' head line; being the upper most survey; rites proved in Council; made out.

1302. Nov. 22, 1744 Jno Clark enters 640 ac in Bladen Co; border: upper end of Bear Island on N side of Great P D River, runs "out", & down the river; on Geo Moor's rites; Geo Moor [sic]; made out.

1303. Nov. 22, 1744 Jno Clark enters 300 ac in Bladen Co; border: back of Swan Pond, runs "out", & up "the" river; on Wm Walston's rites; Geo Moor; made out.

1304. Nov. 22, 1744 Jno Clark enters 200 ac in Bladen Co above mouth of Turky Cr, runs "out", & "down"; on Wm Walston's rites; Geo Moor; made out.

1305. Nov. 22, 1744 Peter Adams enters 500 ac in Chowan Co; border: Truelove's line, "his" line, Thos Ming, on "the" Great desart, & "along" to halfway tree on Yawpin Road; rites returned; Ja Crave; paid; made out.

page 115
1306. Nov. 22, 1744 Jas Blount enters 300 [written over 400] ac in Tyrrell Co on Morratuck R; border: Wm Rhodes' line, runs along his line to Garret's line, down to Welches Cr, to Morratuck R, & along the river to the beginning; rites returned; paid; Ja Craven; made out.

1307. Nov. 22, 1744 Isaac Hunter enters 150 ac in Bertie Co; border: Wm Pugh, Caleb Stevens, & on "the" River Pecoson; rites returned; paid; Ja Craven; made out.

1308. Nov. 22, 1744 John Halsey enters 400 ac in Chowan Co; border: Jno Vail, Thos Blount, & "one" Houghton; called Gaulberry Pecoson; rites returned; paid; Ja Craven; made out.

1309. Nov. 22, 1744 Thos Taylor enters 300 ac in Pasquotank Co on head of Pasquotank R and called Horsepen Necks; rites returned; paid; Ja Craven; made out.

1310. Nov. 22, 1744 Theophs. Pugh enters 2,000 ac in Chowan Co at a place called Sand Banks; border: mouth of Sumeston's Cr, runs "out" to the nearest survey, joins Ballard, King, Hook, "Spight", Ross, Taylor, & "other outward" surveys, runs down said Sand Banks to a pine, across said banks to Chowan R, & up the river; includes Barefield's Marsh and "all" the vacant land; rites returned; paid; Ja Craven.

page 116
1311. Nov. 22, 1744 Walter Lane enters 200 ac in Craven Co on Vine Swamp; border: lower bounds of Robt White's land and runs down on both sides; rites returned; Mr. Griff to pay; made out.

1312. Nov. 22, 1744 Wm Carruthers enters 200 ac in Beaufort Co in the fork of Bay R and on "the" main road; border: on both sides of the long Cypress Bridge; made out.

1313. Nov. 22, 1744 Thos Graves enters 200 ac in New Hanover Co on S side of NE Cape Fear R, on head of a branch, & runs up both sides of the branch; paid; made out.

1314. Nov. 22, 1744 Eleazr. Allen esq enters 1,000 ac in Onslow Co on a branch of SW New R; includes the place called the Springs; made out.

1315. Nov. 22, 1744 Wm Peyton enters 300 ac in Beaufort Co at Green Swamp and runs up "the" branch of the swamp; Peyton; paid; before Council; made out.

1316. Nov. 22, 1744 Coleman Row enters 400 ac in Beaufort Co; border: Jas Blount's line and runs along his line; rites returned; paid; Peyton; made out.

page 117
1317. Nov. 22, 1744 George Mauarthy enters 300 ac in Craven Co; border: a red oak joining his "plantation" on N side of Vine Swamp and runs up th swamp; rites returned; made out.

1318. Nov. 22, 1744 Wm Blake enters 300 ac in Edgecombe Co on N side of Fishing Cr; border: mouth of a branch below his own land and runs down the creek; on Mr. Jno Alston's rites; fees paid; made out.

1319. Nov. 22, 1744 Jno Demant enters 250 ac in Edgecombe Co on N side of Fishing Cr; border: Hen. West's line and runs to Christo Green's line; rites returned "before"; entd. before in a preceeding page [may refer to No. 1281 above] [paid made out--lined out].

1320. Nov. 22, 1744 Jos Anderson enters 400 ac in Edgecombe Co at mouth of a branch on S side of Reedy Cr; border: a red oak and runs up the branch and creek; made out.

1321. Nov. 22, 1744 Jos Anderson enters 300 ac in Edgecombe Co on N side of Fishing Cr; border: mouth of a branch near Phill. Alston's line; made out.

1322. Nov. 22, 1744 Wm Bennett enters 450 ac in Edgecombe Co on NE prong of Tar R; border: a hickory and runs down both sides; made out.

page 118
1323. Nov. 22, 1744 David Marlow enters 270 ac in Craven Co on N side of Nuce R; border: a black walnut on the river side on George Skipper's line; made out.

1324. Nov. 22, 1744 Wm Baron enters 200 ac in Craven Co on Batchelors Cr; border: Benja Fordam's corner and runs down the creek to Col. Wilson's line; rites returned; paid; made out.

1325. [following lined out] Jno Boyd enters 100 ac in Bladen Co; border: joins lower side of Ben [sic].

1326. Nov. 22, 1744 Wm Fulsher enters 100 ac in Craven Co on N side of Nuce R and E side of Pean's Cr; border: "near" the creek; paid; made out.

1327. Nov. 22, 1744 Wm Coleman enters 200 ac in Craven Co on N side of Catanknee Cr; being where he lives; rites proved "before"; paid; made out.

1328. Nov. 22, 1744 Othniel Staughan enters 200 ac in New Hanover Co on Elder Cr 3 miles above "the" road; made out.

1329. Nov. 22, 1744 Robt Walker enters 200 ac in New Hanover Co; being marsh land; border: his land on Long Cr and between his & David Morgan's lands; made out.

1330. [following lined out] Garret Wall enters 150 ac in Edgecombe Co on S side of Fishing Cr; between his own line and John Parish.

North Carolina Land Entries 1735-1752

page 119
1331. Nov. 22, 1744 Jas Burns enters 300 ac in Onlsow Co on E side of Queen Cr; between Jno Simpson and Saml Jones; paid; made out.

1332. Nov. 22, 1744 Joseph Winns enters 100 ac in Chowan Co on N side of Chowan R; bmouth of Muddy Cr and runs up the river & creek; being a marsh; rites returned; paid; made out.

1333. Nov. 22, 1744 Thos Walker enters 400 ac in Bertie Co; border: John Elk's corner at center of 3 pines and joins said Elk's land; rites returned; paid; made out.

1334. Nov. 22, 1744 Thos Oddam enters 200 ac in Bertie Co; border: Richd Williford's corner on Harts Delight "Pacoson"; rites returned; paid; made out.

1335. Nov. 22, 1744 Richd Williams enters 150 ac in Craven Co on N side of head of Great Catankney Cr or Mockerson Swamp; border: a sweet gum in "the" low grounds; rites returned; paid.

1336. Nov. 22, 1744 Wm Outlaw enters 200 ac in Bertie Co on S side of Quioccasan Swamp; border: John Howell jr at a place called Peggys neck; rites returned; paid; made out.

1337. Nov. 22, 1744 Saml Saban. Plumer enters 200 ac in Currituck Co on the North Banks; known as Robt Jones' Point; border: Hendrick on S side and Cederhouse on N side; Anderson; made out.

pages 120 and 121 [blank pages]
page 122
1338 (5) Dec. [blank], 1788 Rd Greenwood enters 200 ac in New Hanover Co about 1.5 miles from land granted to Richd Hellier on Waggamaw R.

1339 (7). Feb. 28, 1744/5 Nath. Rice and Ephrm. Vernon enter 400 ac in New Hanover Co on N side of Hoods Cr; border: on or near the mill land of Mat. Rowan esq and "to or towards" Ro Moor esq "his" line at Rattlesnake Br.

1340. Feb. 28, 1744/5 Nathl. Rice and Ephrm. Vernon enter 400 ac in New Hanover Co; border: joins their entry of this date and the mill land of Mat. Rowan.

1341 (8). Feb. 28, 1774/5 Nathl. Rice and Ephrm. Vernon enter 500 ac in New Hanover Co; border: "Mrs." Rowan's mill land on the "first beginning of her head line of her mill land" on S side of Levingston's Cr and runs with her head line.

page 123
1342 (1). Nov. 15, 1744 Richd James enters 300 ac in New Hanover Co on a branch of black R about 600 miles from the mouth thereof, near the branches of

North Carolina Land Entries 1735-1752

Rockfish Cr, & "distant" from any "plantation"; made out.

1343 (2). Nov. 15, 1744 Richd James [and Benjamin Fuzzel--lined out] enters 200 ac [in New Hanover Co]; border: Benja Fuzzel and [land that was formerly Peter Watkins--lined out] his own "plantation" on NE Cape Fear R; made out.

1344 (3). Nov. 15, 1744 Richd James enters 300 ac [in New Hanover Co]; being the land that was formerly called Peter Watkins' "joins" [blank]; made out.

1345 (4). Nov. 15, 1744 John Williams enters 200 ac in New Hanover Co; between Mr. Thos Clark and Rd James' "plantation"; made out.

1346 (6). Jan. 23, 1744/5 Edwd Moseley esq enters 1,500 ac in New Hanover Co on or near head branches of Elizabeth R and "thereabouts"; "to be laid out in small tracts or parcels"; made out.

1347. Jan. 27, 1744/5 Mat. Rowan enters 500 ac ["in New Hanover Co on Alligator Cr; border: joins his mill land and on NW River"--lined out]; entered in a "following" page [may refer to No. 1361 below]; made out.

1348. Jan. 27, 1744/5 Geo Moore enters ["500 ac in New Hanover Co on Alligator Cr; border: joins his mill land on NW River"--lined out]; entered on a "following" page [may refer to No. 1362 below]; made out.

1349 (10). Mar. 6, 1744/5 Thos Hall enters 100 ac in Onslow Co where the road parts going from Stephen Williams to "the" Healing Springs and on the left hand [side] of the path to the Springs as "they" go out of the great Country Road; made out.

1350 (11). Mar. 14, 1744/5 Henry Heaton enters 250 ac in Craven Co; border: George Lane on Neuse R and at or near Fort Barnwell; made out.

page 124
1351 (21). Mar. 20, 1744/5 Robt Cowlehane enters 200 ac in Craven Co; border: Lazarus Peirce's upper line on Eastmost Br of Swift Cr, runs back of Coulehan's "plantation", & down the creek; made out.

1352 (9). Mar. 4, 1744/5 John Lewis enters 200 ac in Bladen Co on White Marsh and on Welches Cr; border: upper side of Welch's land; made out.

1353 (12). Mar. 22, 1744/5 Job Howe enters 500 ac in New Hanover Co on the boundary "next to" South Carolina, about 2 miles from "the" Boundary House, & joins said line; made out.

1354 (13). Mar. 22, 1744/5 Job Howe enters 500 ac in New Hanover Co; border: Calkin's "back" tract of 400 ac; includes a place called Cypress Swamp; made out.

North Carolina Land Entries 1735-1752

1355 (14). Mar. 22, 1744/5 Job Howe enters 500 ac in New Hanover Co; border: about 0.5 miles from Mr. Moo[page torn]y's corner of his "front" tract on E branch of Little R; made out.

1356 (15). Mar. 22, 1744/5 James Batchelor enters 100 ac in [blank] Co on N side of N fork of Muddy Cr; border: the swamp and runs "up"; made out.

1357 (16). Mar. 22, 1744/5 John Hawkins enters 300 ac in New Hanover Co on Rockfish Cr; border: joins land of Fuzzel and James; made out.

page 125
1358. Apr. 1, 1745 Saml Mackubin enters 400 ac in Craven Co on Batchelors Cr, opposite Johnston the miller, on the other side of the creek, & about 3 miles from said McKubbins [written over McCubbins]; border: Bryan's upper corner on mouth of Deep Br; made out.

1359 (17). Apr. 2, 1744 Frances Rowan enters 1,200 ac in New Hanover Co on Livingstons Cr within her own patent land; being surplus; made out.

1360 (18). Apr. 2, 1744 Jas Baldwin enters 200 ac in Bladen Co on White Marsh; border: Welch's land formerly surveyed for said Baldwin; made out.

1361 (19). Apr. 2, 1744 Mat. Rowan enters 500 ac in New Hanover Co on Alligator Cr; border: his mill land on NW River; made out.

1362 (20). Apr. 2, 1744 Georg Moor enters 500 ac in New Hanover Co on "Aligator" Cr; border: his mill land on NW River; made out.

1363. Apr. 2, 1744 John Sanderson enters 350 ac in Hyde [written over Beaufort] Co on E side of Matchapungo R; border: on E side of his father's old patent land and joins "his plantation"; made out.

1364. Apr. 2, 1744 Robt Ryley enters 200 ac in [blank] Co on N side of Nuce R; between Ryley's land and the river; border: David Jonecan and runs down the river; paid; made out.

page 126
1365. Apr. 2, 1744 Thos McClendon enters 550 [written over 500] ac in Craven Co on S side of Nuce R; border: above Thos Branton's line at a pine and runs up "the" road; rites returned; made out.

1366. Feb. 20, 1744/5 Henry Heaton enters 150 ac in Craven Co on S side of Neuce R and N side of Southwest Cr; made out.

1367. Mar. 20, 1744/5 Wm Martin enters 400 ac in Beaufort Co on N side of

Pamplico R and on W side of Bath Town Cr; between a former survey of Joel Martin, "between said line" and Aldersons Br, & runs down the branch and a line of Town Cr; being the "plantation" where he lives; made out.

1368. [entire entry lined out] Feb. 20, 1744/5 Wm Brice enters 100 ac in Craven Co; border: on W side of Slocum and joins Wm Hancock's upper line; known as Dogwood Neck.

1369. Feb. 22, 1744/5 Job Rogers enters 450 ac in Edgecombe Co on S side of Tar R, runs across the river, & "up"; rites returned; made out.

1370. Feb. 22, 1744/5 Jno Lawhane enters 400 ac in Edgecombe Co on S side of Tar R, near mouth of Crooked Cr, runs across the river, & "up"; made out.

page 127
1371. Feb. 10, 1744/5 Joseph Balch enters 200 ac in Craven Co on N side of Nuce R and on Robins Camp Br; border: a little meadow on E side of "thereof" and runs "up"; made out.

1372. Mar. 10, 1744/5 Wm Downing enters [blank] ac in Tyrrell Co; between Stephen Lee and said Downing; known as Springs Neck; made out.

1373. Mar. 6, 1744/5 Edward Phelps enters 300 ac in Tyrrell Co on E side of Scuppernong R, on W side of Beaver Cr, & runs up the river and creek; rites returned; made out.
1374. Mar. 15, 1744/5 Benja Peyton enters 640 ac in Beaufort Co; border: his last survey, runs along Row's line, & "up"; made out.

1375. Mar. 18, 1744/5 Nathl. Rice enters 350 ac in Craven Co; border: Nichs. Routledge's "side" line on W, Doctr. Jno Bryan on E, runs into a swamp, & back between said lines; made out.

1376. Mar. 20, 1744/5 Benja Griffin enters 300 ac in Craven Co on E side of Pametta Swamp, at the old road that use to land to Pamplico R, & at a "place" called Gum Br; made out.

page 128
1377. Mar. 18, 1744/5 Robt Ryley enters 250 ac in Craven Co on N side of Nuce R "on the river"; between said Ryley's land and the river; made out.

1378. Mar. 18, 1744/5 Andw. Morgan enters 100 ac in Craven Co on NW Run of Upper Broad Cr and runs up the run; rites returned; made out.

1379. Mar. 18, 1744/5 John Fonvielle enters 250 ac in Craven Co between Green pond Br and Hardys Cr on E side of Core Cr; paid; made out.

North Carolina Land Entries 1735-1752

1380. Mar. 19, 1744/5 John Fonvielle enters 150 ac in Craven Co on Jumping Run; border: Thos Truihitt's line and runs up Jumping Run; paid; made out.

1381. Mar. 18, 1744/5 Benja Sanderson enters 150 ac in Craven Co on S side of Nuce R; border: Benja Sanderson's line and runs up Brices Cr; made out.

1382. Mar. 21, 1744/5 Jno Crews jr enters 100 ac in Craven Co on mouth of Cowford Br, on S prong of Little Cotentnea Cr, on "each side", & runs up the branch.

page 129
1383. Mar. 21, 1744/5 Robt Parks enters 400 ac in Craven Co; border: Solomon Mofort's land on [ink blob] branch on S side of said branch and runs "up and over"; "chd"; made out.

1384. Mar. 21, 1744/5 Robt Parks enters 400 ac in Craven Co; border: Wm Kinchen's line on Button Br, runs into Nohunty [Swamp], & runs up both sides; "chd"; made out.

1385. Mar. 23, 1744/5 Robt Parks enters 640 ac in New Hanover Co on Cohera Swamp, on W side of Beaverdam Br, & below mouth of Long Marsh; chd; made out.

1386. Mar. 26, 1744/5 Nichs. Purifoy enters 200 ac in Craven Co on N side of Nuce R, on head of Upper Broad Cr, & at a place called Markpeach Neck; made out.

1387. Mar. 26, 1744/5 David Smith enters 200 ac in Bladen Co; called Bare Island on upper side of Lower Little R and on SW side of NW Cape Fear R; rites returned; made out.

page 130
1388. Mar. 24, 1744/5 John Rice enters 400 ac in Craven Co; border: Glover's land; between him and Otter Cr about 0.5 miles back from the river; made out.

1389. Apr. 4, 1745 Wm Mannering enters 300 ac in Craven Co on S side of Neuse R; border: a blazed oak on the river side and runs up the river; made out; R F.
1390. Apr. 4, 1745 Edwd Bryan enters 400 ac in Craven Co on N side of Nuce R, on E branch of Swifts Cr, & on W side of "the" main swamp; being a place called Hill's Neck; border: near Hill's line, above Hopton's tar kiln, & runs up the ridge between the savanna and main swamp; made out.

1391. Apr. 4, 1745 Edwd Bryan enters 250 ac in Craven Co on E side of Swifts Cr; being a place called James Neck; border: John James & John Waines "bounds" and runs up the neck; includes the vacant land of the neck, runs "over" the Beverdam to Christian Ipach's line, along his line to a branch, & "up"; made out.

page 131

1392. Apr. 5, 1745 Benja Martin enters 200 ac in Hyde Co; between Thos Baily, John Jordan, & Joseph Foreman; paid; J Forbes; made out.

1393. Apr. 5, 1745 Simon Burney enters 400 ac in Beaufort Co on S side of Tarr R; border: his own line; paid; J Forbes; made out.

1394. Apr. 5, 1745 Jno Robt Lanier enters 300 ac in Tyrrell Co on S side of Smithwicks Cr and runs on both sides of Nairns Beaverdam Swamp; paid; J F; made out.

1395. Apr. 5, 1745 John Worsley enters 320 ac in Beaufort Co on head of "the NW" of Old Town Cr; being the part of the surplus land in his part of an old patent; paid; J F; made out.

1396. Apr. 5, 1745 Wm Watkins enters 400 ac in Beaufort Co on S side of Checod Cr; border: runs on Gray's line and "back"; paid; J F; made out.

1397. Apr. 5, 1745 Abra Easter enters 200 ac in Hyde co on S side of Swan Quarter Bay; between Roger Mason and John Joly; known as Negroe Ridge; paid; J F; made out.

1398. Apr. 5, 1745 John Slaughter enters 200 ac in Beaufort Co on lower side of Guindall Cr; border: Jno Smith, runs up the creek, & back; paid; J F; made out.

1399. Apr. 5, 1745 Saml Vines enters 100 ac in Beaufort Co on E branch of Swift Cr; border: up "the" swamp above Nisby Mills, runs on the swamp, & "back"; paid; J F; made out.

1400. Apr. 5, 1745 James Gumley enters 320 ac in Craven Co on N side of Neuse R and E side of Broad Cr; called Whistlers Ridge and Panthers Ridge; border: runs "towards" the savanna; paid; J F; made out.

1401. Apr. 5, 1745 Jno Worsley jr enters 350 ac in Beaufort Co on N side of Pamplico R; border: his line on "the" Beaverdam, joins Andrew Simons, &runs to the fork of Deep Run; paid; J F; made out.

page 132

1402. Apr. 5, 1745 John Trudall [or Tindall] enters 200 ac in Beaufort Co on S side of Pamplico R; between Goose Cr and Oyster Cr; border: the great marsh and Thos Campain; paid; J F; made out.

1403. Apr. 5, 1745 Jno Russell enters 200 ac in Craven Co on S side of Neuse R; border: John Smith on a branch of Long Cr; rites to prove; paid; made out.

1404. Apr. 5, 1745 Jno Mills enters 150 ac in Craven Co at head of Powells Cr on N side of Neuse R; betweenJno Nellson and Wm Morgan; rites proved; made out.

1405. Apr. 1, 1745 Edward Bryan enters 400 ac in Craven Co on E side of Swift Cr; border: on head of Watry Br, runs over the ridge by a bond and savannah, to head of Gum Br, & "over and down" to Parmetta Swamp; paid; made out.

1406. Apr. 1, 1745 Hardy Bryan enters 400 ac in Craven Co in the fork of Water Br that makes out of E side of Pameta Swamp; border: a blazed pine on S prong and runs up the fork; paid; made out.

1407. Apr. 1, 1745 Hardy Bryan enters 400 ac in Craven Co at the horsepen on N side of Water Br, runs 0.5 miles up the branch, & across to Gum Br; paid; made out.

1408. Apr. 1, 1745 Hardy Bryan enters 200 ac in Craven Co on E side of Swift Cr and on both sides of Pametta Swamp; border: "up" Jas Rigney's head line and runs up both sides of Pametta Swamp; paid; made out.

page 133
1409. Apr. 2, 1745 Wm Eaton enters 200 ac in Edgecombe Co on the upper meadows of Grassy Cr; border: a red oak marked "W E"; paid; made out.

1410. Apr. 2, 1745 Jno Rose enters 200 ac in Craven Co on N side of Little Cotentnea Cr; known as Pine Long Swamp; paid.

1411. Apr. 3, 1745 Fras Dawson enters 250 ac in Craven Co on N side of Nuce R and on E side of head of Orchard Cr; border: Bond and Fulcher on head of Pearces Cr; rites returned "before"; paid; made out.

1412. Apr. 3, 1745 Jno Becton enters 200 ac in Bladen Co above mouth of Taylor's hole on Cape Fear R and runs up to Armstrong's line; paid; on J Giles rites returned before; made out.

1413. Apr. 3, 1745 Jno Becton enters 200 ac in Bladen Co below Taylor's hole and runs down "the" river; paid; on J Giles rites returned "before"; made out.

1414. Apr. 3, 1745 John Rose enters 350 [400--lined out] ac in Edgecombe Co on S side of Tar R, at mouth of a branch, & runs "down"; made out.

page 134
1415. Apr. 3, 1745 John Giles enters 200 ac in Craven Co on Cow Br of Cotentnea Cr and runs on both sides; paid; made out.

1416. Apr. 3, 1745 John Giles enters 200 ac in Craven Co on N side of Nuce R; border: joins the land where he lives; paid; made out.

1417. Apr. 3, 1745 John Giles enters 200 ac in New Hanover Co on Bare Marsh [written over "creek"]; border: Jonathan Taylor's land on N side of Goshen Swamp; paid; made out.

1418. Apr. 3, 1745 Mark Philips enters 350 ac in Craven Co on S side of Nuce R; border: a spanish oak near mouth of Miln Cr and runs up the river; includes his improvement; paid.

page 135
1419. Apr. 3, 1745 John Lancaster Lovick enters 200 ac in Carteret Co on N side of Newport R; border: the "going over" place on Deep Cr; paid; made out.

1420. Apr. 3, 1745 Jno Simpson enters 500 ac in Onslow [written over Carteret] Co in the fork of Queens Cr; "partly" bounded by Jno Starky and Jalz. Spooner; paid; made out.
1421. Apr. 3, 1745 Josh. Pilman enters 100 ac in Craven Co; border: Jos Mar's line, runs SE, joins a piece of land called Jeremy's, Gould's line, from Gould's to Thos Martin's, & runs the "back" line; includes a place called Peter Chrasty's old field; paid; made out.

1422. Apr. 3, 1745 Jno Egerton enters 300 ac in Edgecombe Co on Nutbush Cr; includes Johnson's folley land; rites returned; paid; made out.

1423. Apr. 3, 1745 Wm Person enters 400 ac in Edgecombe Co near the fork of "the" Country Road, on the branches of Butterwood Cr, & runs down on both sides of said road; paid; made out.

page 136
1424. Apr. 3, 1745 Thos Benson enters 200 ac in Edgecombe Co on Bens Cr; includes his "plantation"; paid; made out.

1425. Apr. 3, 1745 Richd Chrason [or Chaason] enters 300 ac in Onslow Co on NE branch of Turky Cr and runs up both sides of Dirt Bridge Swamp; rites returned; J Starky; made out.

1426. Apr. 3, 1745 Jno McCasslin enters 200 ac in [blank, New Hanover or Bladen] Co; border: Miss Sarah Groves, Edmd. Rourk, & said McCasslin "on the front", runs "back" East from main branch of Wacomaw R; rites returned; made out.

1427. Apr. 3, 1745 Abra Odam, of Tar R, enters 100 ac in Edgecombe Co on S side of Sapony Cr and "on" a "plantation" of Wm Kersy; border: a red oak; rites returned "before"; paid; made out.

page 137

North Carolina Land Entries 1735-1752

1428. Apr. 4, 1745 Fras Spivey enters 100 ac in Edgecombe Co on N side of Fishing Cr; border: the back of Christo. Guin's patent land; single man; paid; made out.

1429. Apr. 4, 1745 Roger Moore enters 320 ac in New Hanover Co; border: "the" sound, Deep Inlet, & Cox's land; R M; made out.

1430. Apr. 4, 1745 Jas Grange enters 500 ac in Bladen Co on Carvers Cr; border: above Charles Benbow's "plantation"; R M; made out.

1431. Apr. 4, 1745 John Sanders enters 300 ac in Carteret Co on Eastermost Br of Deep Cr and begins at a small branch above the upper "going over"; rites returned; R L; made out.

1432. Apr. 4, 1745 Chas Harrison enters 320 ac in New Hanover Co on the branches back of a cypress pond on "the" Sound Road; border: a bay tree on the fork branches; made out.

1433. Apr. 4, 1745 Chas Harrison enters 200 ac in New Hanover Co on SW side of "a" large Springy Savannah; border: a pine by a bay branch "in the woods" back of "the" Sound Road; made out.

page 138
1434. Apr. 4, 1745 Chas Harrison enters 100 ac in New Hanover Co on E side of my swamp where I lived; border: a pine on Meadow Br and runs towards "the" Sound; made out.

1435. Apr. 4, 1745 Robt Young enters 300 ac in Edgecombe Co on Peek Basket Cr; border: a pine and runs "out and back"; rites returned; paid; G G; made out.

1436. Apr. 4, 1745 Jno Davis enters 1,000 ac in New Hanover Co near "the" Boundary [state] line and joins a branch of Waggamaw R; made out.

1437. Apr. 4, 1745 Jacob Reasonover enters 100 ac in Craven Co on S side of Nuce R; border: Jacob Slanbuck's back line and Brices Cr; rites returned "before"; paid; made out.

1438. Apr. 4, 1745 Thos Martin enters 400 ac in Craven Co; border: John Gould's head corner gum, runs along his line to Wm Hodgson's head line, & into the woods; paid; made out.

1439. Apr. 4, 1745 Jacob Taylor enters 100 ac in Craven Co; border: Wm Brice's upper corner sweet gum on head of Slocumbs Cr, across "the" swamp to mouth of Black Swamp, & to Wm Hancock's line below Dogwood Neck; made out.

page 139

1440. Apr. 5, 1745 John Fowler enters 400 ac in Edgecombe Co; border: Virginia line at Haw tree Cr and runs up both sides; paid; made out.

1441. Apr. 5, 1745 Nichs. Golifler enters 400 ac in Edgecombe Co; border: Jno Fowler's line and runs up "the" creek & both sides of his line; paid; made out.

1442. Apr. 5, 1745 Rave Ratsbeth enters 640 ac in Edgecombe Co on the branches of Great Cr; paid; made out.

1443. Apr. 5, 1745 David Douglas enters 400 ac in Northampton Co on Pidgeon roost Cr; border: the Virginia line and runs "down both sides"; paid; made out.

1444. Apr. 5, 1745 Wm Sison enters 300 ac in Edgecombe Co; border: Phil Hawkins' lower corner on "the" river bank, runs down to a great branch, to John Hawkins' line, & down to Johnston's line; paid; made out.

page 140
1445. Apr. 5, 1745 Wm Duke enters 300 ac in Edgecombe Co on Possom Quarter Cr and below Edwd. Jones' Path at head of a branch; paid; made out.

1446. Apr. 5, 1745 Wm Duke enters 300 ac in Edgecombe Co on Reedy Cr at Brantly's Path andruns down the creek; paid; made out.

1447. Apr. 5, 1745 Peter Kersy enters 100 ac in Edgecombe Co on lower fork of Stone House Cr and runs up both sides; paid; made out.

1448. Apr. 5, 1745 Jas Paine enters 640 ac in Edgecombe Co at a great [branch--lined out] Spring on Deep Cr a branch of Neuse R, near head of Tar R, & runs "upwards"; paid; made out.

1449. Apr. 5, 1745 Levi Alderson enters 150 ac in Beaufort Co; border: a branch in a savanah near Mr. Martin's Beaverdam line, runs up both sides of the branch to the head, to Mr. Simons' line, & to the fork of Deep Run; paid; made out.

page 141
1450. Apr. 5, 1745 Saml Swann enters 800 ac in Tyrrell Co being an island or ridge of land on W side of "Alligeter" R about 6 or 7 miles from said river and about a mile back from said river through a swamp or "pacoson"; between Second Cr and Goose Cr; made out; Mr. Speakr. Dr.

1451. Apr. 5, 1745 John Grenade enters 60 ac in Craven Co on E side of Mill Cr; border: a red oak in a neck above a beverdam and runs up the creek; surveyed in 1737 for John Symons; paid; made out.

1452. Apr. 5, 1745 John russel enters 150 ac in Craven Co on S side of Neuse R and on "the" branches of Long Cr; border: Reid and Smith; made out.

1453. Apr. 5, 1745 James Green enters 100 ac in New Hanover Co on Angola Cr at head of James Murry's land, runs up the creek, & "back"; made out.

1454. Apr. 5, 1745 John Butler enters 100 ac in Onslow Co near Muddy Cr; border: widow Hill, between two tracts of Hiddleberry's, & runs "back"; made out.

1455. Apr. 5, 1745 Stephn. Hollingsworth enters 600 ac in New Hanover Co on Muddy Cr and runs up both sides; includes his improvement; made out.

page 142
1456. Apr. 5, 1745 Simon Herring enters 600 ac in New Hanover Co on W side of Cohera Cr at a place called round marsh; paid; made out.

1457. Apr. 5, 1745 Wm Rogers enters 200 ac in Craven Co on S side of Nuse R and in the fork of Whitly Cr; being the land where he lives; paid; made out.

1458. Apr. 5, 1745 Andrew Killet enters 200 ac in Onslow Co on N side of NW New R, on Ash Br at the mouth, & runs "up"; made out.

1459. Apr. 5, 1745 Jonathan Melton, in behalf of orphans of Edwd Smellage, enters 300 ac in Onslow Co on N side of NE New R; border: How's land and runs up said NE New R from How's corner.

page 143
1460. Apr. 5, 1745 Edwd. Brown enters 450 ac in Edgecombe Co on N side of Cypress Swamp of Coneho Cr; known as Beaverdam [Coneho--lined out]; paid; made out.

1461. Apr. 5, 1745 Jno Wiggons enters 200 ac in Edgecombe Co on mouth of Harrels Br and on N side of Coneho Cr; border: Richd. Wiggon and Wm Taylor; paid; made out.

1462. Apr. 5, 1745 Robt. Hatcher enters 250 ac in Craven Co on S side of Falling Cr; being the place where he lives; paid; made out.

1463. Apr. 5, 1745 Wm Everet enters 200 ac in Craven co on S side of Neuse R; between Henry Everet and John Smith.

1464. Apr. 5, 1745 Robt. Rayford enters 150 ac in Craven Co on N side of Little R and above Ballard's; paid; made out.

1465. Apr. 5, 1745 Wm Watson enters 200 ac in Craven Co on N side of Little R; between Little Buffelow and great Buffelow Creeks; being where he lives; paid; made out.

1466. Apr. 5, 1745 Henry Jarnagin enters 200 ac in Edgecombe Co on a branch of White Oak Cr; where George Elms lives; paid; made out.

1467. Apr. 5, 1745 Abra. Sheppard enters 200 ac in Craven Co on S side of Cotenkney Cr; between Frances Roundtree's land and his own land; paid; made out.

1468. Apr. 5, 1745 Moses Horn enters 350 ac in Edgecombe Co on N side of Coneho Cr and on Cypress Swamp; paid; made out.

1469. Apr. 5, 1745 Thos Long enters 300 ac in Craven Co on S side of Norhantey [Swamp]; between his own land, Pugh, & Conner; paid; made out.

1470. Apr. 5, 1745 Geo Demy [or Dency] enters 200 ac in Craven Co on Watrey Br of great Cotenkney Cr; being where he lives; paid; made out.

1471. Apr. 5, 1745 Wm Horn enters 150 ac in Edgecombe Co on N side of Coneho Cr; border: opposite Jno Wiggon's land; paid; made out.

1472. Apr. 5, 1745 Saml Rusten enters 100 ac in Edgecombe Co on Sapponee Cr; border: mouth of Poplar Cr "down the creek"; paid; made out.

page 144
1473. Apr. 5, 1745 Saml Rustin enters 300 ac in Edgecombe Co on Deep Cr; border: Wm Bryan's line at a large white oak [and runs] down the creek; paid; made out.

1474. Apr. 5, 1745 Wm Taylor enters 300 ac in Edgecombe Co on S side of Roanoke R; border: Hopson's lower line and Ballard's upper line; paid; made out.

1475. Apr. 5, 1745 Jos Cotton enters 300 ac in Edgecombe Co; border: his own land, Cowhall, & Conner; paid; made out.

1476. Apr. 5, 1745 Wm McGee enters 250 ac in Edgecombe Co on both sides of Coneho Cr; border: Joseph Moor and above Wm Drake; paid; made out.

1477. Apr. 5, 1745 Wm Andrews enters 450 ac in Edgecombe Co on S side of Roanoke R; border: Lor's line and runs up the river to his own line; paid; made out.

1478. Apr. 5, 1745 George Cannon enters 150 ac in Beaufort Co on S side of Grendall Cr; border: "a little" above the great meadow above James Barrow's; paid; made out.

1479. Apr. 5, 1745 Wm Andrews enters 550 ac in Edgecombe Co on Kehukee

North Carolina Land Entries 1735-1752

[Swamp]; border: Abraham Due and Gray; made out.

page 145
1480. Apr. 5, 1745 Jno Forbes enters 320 ac in Beaufort Co on S side of Tarr R; border: "the" line formerly Saml Tyson's & now Corns. Tyson's and runs back of his own line; rites proved; paid; made out.

1481. Mar. 6, 1744/5 Edmd. Smithwick enters 300 ac in Tyrrell Co on W side of Smithwicks Cr; border: runs up the creek to Jno Willard's & John Swain's lines and "back"; rites before; paid; made out.

1482. Mar. 6, 1744/5 Thos Kearny enters 200 ac in Edgecombe Co on S side of Beverdam Swamp; border: Edwd. Poor's corner and runs up the swamp; paid; made out.

1483. Mar. 6, 1744/5 Thos Kearny enters 200 ac in Edgecombe Co on N side of Beaverdam Swamp; border: Jos Jno Alston's [write over] corner and runs up the swamp; made out.

1484. Mar. 6, 1744/5 Richd. Wilifore enters 250 ac in Bertie Co in Hearts delight Pecoson and Ridge; border: a pidgeon oak on NE side of Fort Br; rites returned; made out.

1485. Apr. 6, 1745 Anthy. Herring, son of Saml Herring, enters 640 ac in Craven Co; border: upper Bogue Swamp and runs down; rites returned; paid; made out.

page 146
1486. Apr. 6, 1745 Wm Reddick enters 300 ac in Craven Co; border: on head of John White's line on Horns Swamp and runs on Wm Smith's line; rites proved in Council; paid; made out.

1487. Apr. 6, 1745 Jas Johnson enters 200 ac in Carteret Co on Core Banks; border: Jno Willis; rites proved; paid; made out.

Giles entries:
1488. Apr. 6, 1745 Saml Smith enters 200 ac in Craven Co on S side of Nuce R and N side of Swifts Cr; border: his survey; made out.

1489. Apr. 6, 1745 Hardy Hinton enters 300 ac in Craven Co on N side of Nuce R; includes "plantation" where he lives; made out.

1490. Apr. 6, 1745 Alexr. Every enters 600 ac in Craven Co; border: a white oak on S side of Swifts Cr; made out.

1491. Apr. 6, 1745 Absalom Tyler enters 300 ac in Craven Co on N side of Swifts Cr; border: Wm Every's corner white oak; made out.

1492. Apr. 6, 1745 Mark Philips enters 275 ac in Craven Co on Mill Cr; border: joins the land where he lives; made out.

1493. Apr. 6, 1745 Wm Cockrum enters 100 ac in Craven Co on S side of Nuce R; border: joins the land where he lives; made out.

1494. Apr. 6, 1745 Benja Balling enters 200 ac in Bladen Co on Balling Cr; includes the "plantation" where he lives; made out.

1495. Apr. 6, 1745 Jno Paterson enters 300 ac in Bladen Co; border: joins land where he lives; made out.

1496. Apr. 6, 1745 Jas Forest enters 400 ac in Craven Co on Little R above Trading [Paths--lined out] "Sides" Path South fork; "called" Beaverdam Cr; made out.

1497. Apr. 6, 1745 Henry Johnston enters 100 ac in Craven Co on Little R above "the" Trading Path; made out.

1498. Apr. 6, 1745 Jas Dinkin enters 200 ac in Craven Co on Lick Cr running into Flat R; made out.

1499. Apr. 6, 1745 Joseph Cates enters 200 ac in Craven Co on W side of Lick Cr running into Flat R; made out.

1500. Apr. 6, 1745 Geo Lane enters 200 ac in Edgecombe Co on N side of Capt. Alston's mill Swamp running into Fishing Cr; made out.

1501. Apr. 6, 1745 Isom Sims enters 200 ac in Craven Co; border: Wm Mew's line on Little R and runs on both sides; made out.

1502. Apr. 6, 1745 Wm Middleton enters 300 ac in Craven Co on N side of Neuse R, on "great" Creek, & runs on both sides of the creek; includes the "plantation" where he lives and where Morgan & Matthews formerly lived; made out.

1503. Apr. 6, 1745 James Barton enters 100 ac in Craven Co on N side of Neuse R; being where John Bletsoe formerly lived; made out.

1504. Apr. 6, 1745 James Boon enters 100 ac in Craven Co on N side of Neuse R and on a beaver dam; made out.

1505. Apr. 6, 1745 Joseph Boon enters 100 ac in Craven Co on N side of Neuse R and on Spoil Coney Cr; border: joins land where he dwells; made out.

1506. Apr. 6, 1745 Richd Kemp enters 400 ac in Craven Co on N side of Neuse R and on Richland Cr; border: Clayton's line; includes "his plantation"; made out.

1507. Apr. 6, 1745 John Brown enters 200 ac in Craven Co on N side of Neuse R; border: mouth of Horse Cr and runs down the river; made out.

page 149
1508. Apr. 8, 1745 George Jordan enters 150 ac in Edgecombe Co being an islan in "the" river; border: above Rawlins ford; made out.

1509. Apr. 8, 1745 River Jordan enters 200 ac in Edgecombe Co; border: Thos Good's upper line and runs up both sides of Indian Cr; made out.

1510. Apr. 8, 1745 Robt Hilliard enters 600 ac in Edgecombe Co on N side of Tar R; border: his own line and runs down the river; made out.

1511. Apr. 8, 1745 Edwd. Roberson enters 400 ac in Edgecombe Co; border: joins his own line; includes both sides of S prong of Marsh Swamp; made out.

1512. Apr. 8, 1745 Robt Hilliard enters 200 ac in Edgecombe Co on S side of Roanoke R; border: below Benja Foreman's line and runs down the river; made out.

1513. Apr. 8, 1745 Lodiwick Tanner enters 200 ac in Edgecombe Co on S side of Shacoe [Swamp]; border: a beech tree above "the nark" branch, runs "out", & down the branch; made out.

page 150
1514. Apr. 8, 1745 James Cane enters 200 ac in Edgecombe Co on N side of Swift Cr and on a small branch; being on Wm Whitehead's land; made out.

1515. Apr. 8, 1745 John Jones enters 300 ac in Edgecombe Co on Roanoak R; border: Gabriel Peckering's upper corner and runs up the river; includes his improvements; made out.

1516. Apr. 8, 1745 Garret Wall enters 100 ac in Edgecombe Co on S side of Fishing Cr; between his own land and John Parish's; made out.

1517. Apr. 8, 1745 Jno Smith enters 150 ac in Craven Co on Coats Cr "the" East branch; border: his own land and runs up the creek; rites returned "before"; paid; made out.

1518. Apr. 8, 1745 Foster Jarvis enters 100 ac in Hyde Co on E side of Oyster Cr and on Swan Quarter Bay; paid; made out.

1519. Apr. 8, 1745 John Barrow enters 150 ac in Beaufort Co on N side of Pamplico R and W side of Deep Run; border: near the "up" River Road, runs up Deep Run to the fork, & "back"; rites proved; made out.

1520. Apr. 8, 1745 James Jenkins enters 300 ac in Edgecombe Co on SW prong of Deep Cr and E side of "the" swamp; border: above John Phillips and at a pine blazed with a cross; rites proved; made out.

page 151
1521. Apr. 8, 1745 Frans. Bellis enters 200 ac in Edgecombe Co on a branch on S side of Tar R and at Sassafras ford; rites proved; made out.

1522. Apr. 8, 1745 Thos Tyson enters 200 ac in Craven Co on N side of Little Cotentnea Cr; border: a swamp "side" and runs up the creek; made out.

1523. Apr. 8, 1745 Abra Wanen [or Wawen] enters 100 ac in Craven Co on N side of Nuce R; border: mouth of White Oak Br and runs on "the" fork of High bridge Br; rites returned "before"; paid; made out.

1524. Apr. 8, 1745 Mich. Blocker jr enters 200 ac in Bladen Co between the two Little Rivers, about 0.25 miles back of "the" middle Beverdam, & on NW River; Jo Clark to "take out"; made out.

1525. Apr. 8, 1745 Chas Williamson enters 200 ac in Onslow Co on SW New R; border: mouth of Rattlesnake Br, runs up the river, & "back"; on Gren's rites; J Rice; made out.

1526. Apr. 8, 1745 Jno Moy enters 300 ac in Edgecombe Co on N side of Tar R, on lower side of Indian Cr, runs down the river, & "back"; rites to be proved in Council; paid; made out.

page 152
1527. Apr. 9, 1745 Jno Conoway enters 200 ac in Craven Co; being the surplus land of the tract where he lives; paid; made out.

1528. Apr. 9, 1745 Saml Harwell [or Hanwell] enters 200 ac in Edgecombe Co on E side of Tar R, at mouth of a great branch, & runs up the river; paid; made out.

1529. Apr. 9, 1745 Ambrose Jackson enters 200 ac in Edgecombe Co on W side of Tar R; border: a hickory above Henry Horn's land and runs up the river; paid; made out.

1530. Apr. 9, 1745 Wm Hester enters 200 ac in Bladen Co on Welches Cr; border: back of Jas Welch's land on NE side of White Marsh; rites to be returned; paid; made out.

North Carolina Land Entries 1735-1752

1531. Apr. 1, 1745 [sic] John Rice enters 400 ac in Craven Co on the main branch of Batchelors Cr; border: runs along Wilkins' line to said creek; includes the land between Col. Wilson deceased's land and Wilkinson's land; paid; made out. page 153

1532. Apr. 9, 1745 David Journagin enters 100 ac in [Craven Co ?] on N side of Neuse R; border: Henry Owens' & Richard Johnson's land and between said land & the river; made out.

1533. Apr. 9, 1745 Richd Johnston enters 600 ac in Bladen Co on Cape Fear R; between mouth of New [or Mew] hope Cr and Deep R, runs "on both sides", & "down"; made out.

1534. Apr. 9, 1745 James Noleyboy enters 200 ac in Edgecombe Co on N side of Swift Cr; border: runs "down" from a white oak; rites proved; made out.

1535. Apr. 9, 1745 Capt. James Speirs enters 350 ac in Edgecombe Co on S side of Fishing Cr; border: his own land and runs "up"; rites proved; made out.

1536. Apr. 9, 1745 Wm Pugh enters 200 ac in Edgecombe Co on S side of Tarr R; border: his own land and runs "up"; rites proved; made out.

1537. Apr. 9, 1745 Wm Williamson enters 200 ac in Craven Co on "the" fork of Bear Cr, at mouth of a branch, & runs "up"; rites proved; made out.

1538. Apr. 9, 1745 Isaac Devenport enters 300 ac in Edgecombe Co on S fork of Tarr R and on the path that runs from Shelton's to Grice's; border: runs "up" from a red oak; made out.

1539. Apr. 9, 1745 Marmaduke "Norflite" enters 200 ac in Edgecombe Co on E side of Curnecats Pocoson and on both sides of Indian Path; border: a "markt" pine in the edge of the pocoson and runs "up"; made out.

page 154

1540. Apr. 9, 1745 Wm Hilliard enters 400 ac in Northampton Co on SW side of Pottecasy Cr near mouth of a large branch "Barnaby Thomas' line", runs up the branch, & down "the" swamp; includes Danl Oquin's "plantation"; made out.

1541. Apr. 9, 1745 Thos Morat enters 650 ac in Northampton Co on N side of Kerbys Cr; border: his own line and runs "up"; made out.

1542. Apr. 9, 1745 Nicholas Tyler enters 200 ac in Northampton Co in the fork of Patterson's delight and joins the same; made out.

1543. Apr. 9, 1745 Osborn Jeffries enters 150 ac in Tyrrell Co on lower side of Conneten Swamp; border: Eldridge's lower line on S side of said swamp and runs "down"; made out.

1544. Apr. 9, 1745 Richd. Braswel enters 100 ac in Edgecombe Co on Conneta Swamp; made out.

1545. Apr. 9, 1745 Arthr. Jordan enters 400 ac in Northampton Co on N side of Roanoke R; border: a red oak on upper side of Dogwood Run; paid; made out.

1546. Apr. 9, 1745 Wm Lindsay enters 50 ac in Beaufort Co on S side of Pamplico R "a branch in" South Dividing Cr "on East side"; between Richd. Hany and John Bond.

1547. Apr. 9, 1745 Thos Matchell enters 100 ac in Craven Co on N side of Nuse R, in the fork of Pine tree Br, & runs over N side of the branch; border: Edwd. Mathers; paid; made out.

page 155
1548. Apr. 9, 1745 Charles Covenate enters 200 ac in Edgecombe Co on N side of Saponey Cr, at a small branch, & runs "up"; rites proved; made out.

1549. Apr. 9, 1745 John Terrel enters 300 ac in Bladen Co on Pritted Cr and runs on both sides of "the" river & creek; made out.

1550. Apr. 9, 1745 John Terrel enters 400 ac in Bladen Co on N side of Prity Crocked Cr, S side of Haw R, & about 6 miles from Haw [written over Hard] R; made out.

1551. Apr. 9, 1745 John Terrel enters 400 ac in Bladen Co on New Warrey Cr and runs "down"; "in" P D River; made out.

1552. Apr. 9, 1745 John Terrel enters 400 ac in Bladen Co on S side of Deep R [Creek--lined out], above mouth of Little R, & runs into Cape Fear R [on] S side; made out.

1553. Apr. 9, 1745 Timoty. "Terrell" enters 600 ac in Bladen Co in main fork of New Hope Cr and runs "up"; made out.

1554. Apr. 9, 1745 Timoty. Terrell enters 600 ac in Bladen Co on a branch of Indian Cabbin Cr and on S side of Haw R; made out.

1555. Apr. 9, 1745 Timoty Terrell enters 600 ac in Bladen Co on a branch of Little R making out of N side of Deep R; made out.

1556. Apr. 9, 1745 Timoty Terrell enters 150 ac in Bladen Co on an island "of" Haw R and runs over to the South side; made out.

North Carolina Land Entries 1735-1752

1557. Apr. 9, 1745 Jno Thornton enters 400 ac in Edgecombe Co on S branch of Shackoe Cr and runs up both sides of the branch; made out.

page 156

1558. Apr. 9, 1745 Jno Clark enters [blank] ac [in Bladen Co a tract surveyed by Thos Jones for Jno Grady on S side of Peedee R; "if not returned it's Mr. Clerk's desire to enter said land"--lined out].

1559. Apr. 9, 1745 [Josh. Jno Alston in trust for--lined out] Phil Mulkey, son of Phil Mulkey deceased, enters 300 ac in Edgecombe Co; border: a chesnut white oak on Beaver pond Swamp; includes all improvements made by Phil Mulkey deceased and Jno Patterson; made out.

1560. Apr. 9, 1745 Jos Hare enters 200 ac in Craven Co on N side of Swifts Cr above Worsley's survey; paid; on Jos Bryan's rites; made out.

1561. Apr. 9, 1745 Thos Sutton enters 200 ac in Craven Co on N side of Swift Cr, E side of Clayroot Swamp, on "the" Spring Br, & runs "down"; paid; on Jos Bryan's rites; made out.

1562. "Jno Anderson" [rest of entry blank]

page 157

1563. Apr. 10, 1745 Robt Halton esq enters 300 ac in New Hanover Co; border: on head of his own line on "the" main road to Wilmington; made out.
1564. Apr. 10, 1745 Daniel McGuffee "s s" enters 100 ac in New Hanover Co on W side of the main branch of Long Cr at a place called Hickory hill; made out.

1565. Apr. 10, 1745 Christn. Dudley [Andrew Gillet--lined out] enters 100 ac in Onslow Co on E side of Middle Br of Beazleys Cr; border: Beazley's and Sadberry's line; made out.

1566. Apr. 10, 1745 Francs. Alexander "s s" enters 280 ac in New Hanover Co "fronting" the "plantation" where he dwells; made out.

1567. Apr. 10, 1745 James Duncan "s s" enters 300 ac in New Hanover Co on Mulberry Br above Capt. Janes' [or Jurens'] land; made out.

1568. Apr. 10, 1745 Robt Hill sr enters 200 ac in Edgecombe Co; border: Emanl. Rogers' line at a blazed red oak and runs "up & down" Rogers' line; Dawson; made out.

1569. Apr. 10, 1745 Nicks. Baggot enters 500 ac in Northampton Co on NE side of Catawetskee Cr; border: "Izrael" Campbell; Campbell; made out.

1570. Apr. 10, 1745 Jno Muzell enters 300 ac in Bertie Co on E side of Cypress

Cr; border: John Sowell [or Lowell]; Campbell; made out.

1571. Apr. 10, 1745 Edwd. Roberts enters 400 ac in Bertie Co on N side of Ahotsky [Swamp] and joins the mouth & lower side of Turkey [Ahotsky--lined out] Swamp; Campbell; made out.

1572. Apr. 10, 1745 Benja Holliman enters 300 ac in Bertie Co on Bear Garden [Swamp] "the" Eastern branch of Conoreterat [Swamp]; Campbell; made out.

page 158
1573. Apr. 10, 1745 Anthony Herrin enters 300 ac in Craven Co on N side of Nuce R, on upper side of "Boag" Swamp, & runs up Boag Swamp; made out.

1574. Apr. 10, 1745 Robt Howard enters 200 ac in Craven Co; border: at the Haw Ponds and runs into the low grounds of the river & creek on S side of Trent R; made out.

1575. Apr. 10, 1745 Thos Fisher enters 200 ac in Craven Co on "the" branches of Swifts Cr; border: John Gatlin's survey; paid; made out; ["ditto 250 ac" on next line before No. 1576].

1576. Apr. 10, 1745 Saml Williams enters 300 ac in Currituck Co "on" mouth of North R on E side; border: Gibin's line; called "brd" [or Crd (broad ?)] Neck; rites returned; paid; made out.

1577. Apr. 10, 1745 Geo Eason enters 200 ac in Perquimans Co; border: Lamuel Powel's land "in" a small island in "Pequimans" R; paid; made out.

1578. Apr. 10, 1745 Benja Perry enters 50 ac in Perquimans Co; border: Jno Holloway, his own land, & Dismal [Swamp]; paid; made out.

page 159
1579. Apr. 10, 1745 Moses Tyson enters 500 ac in Beaufort Co on S side of Tar R; border: Jno Hardy, runs up the river, & "back"; being the "plantation" where he lives; rites to be proved; paid; made out.

1580. Apr. 10, 1745 Fras. Hodges enters 200 ac in Craven Co; border: Simon Bright's survey on N side of Briery Br and runs down the branch below the survey; rites to be proved in Council; Dr Chd; made out.

1581. Apr. 10, 1745 John Wright enters 640 ac in New Hanover Co on Goshen Swamp and NE Cape Fear R; border: near Mr. Archd. Hamilton; rites proved; Dr; made out.

1582. Apr. 10, 1745 John Wright enters 640 ac in New Hanover Co on Goshen Swamp and on NE Cape Fear R; border: near Mr. Hamilton and his own land;

rites proved; Dr; made out.

1583. Apr. 10, 1745 Archd. Hamilton enters 640 ac in New Hanover Co on Goshen Swamp at mouth of a large branch; border: runs "down" from an oak; Dr; made out.

1584. Apr. 10, 1745 Archd. Hamilton enters 1,500 ac in New Hanover Co on Goshen Swamp; border: an oak at mouth of a large branch and runs "up"; Dr; made out.

page 160
1585. Apr. 11, 1745 Jno Swann enters 500 ac in New Hanover Co on lower side of Widow Moors Cr; border: John Ashe's line and runs up the creek; Dr; made out; Rd. McClure.

1586. Apr. 11, 1745 Benjn. Cowell jr enters 150 ac in Currituck Co at Powells Point; border: Thos Gibson and "back"; paid; made out.

1587. Apr. 11, 1745 Evan Miller enters 150 ac in Currituck Co; border: John Ballance, his own [land], Thos Lowther, & Thos Taylor; R McClure; paid; made out.

1588. Apr. 11, 1745 Jacob Paul enters 300 ac in Bladen Co on N side of Pedee R, above mouth of Hedgecock Cr, & on both sides of said creek; paid; made out.

1589. Apr. 11, 1745 Bryant Ward enters 300 ac in Bladen Co on N side of "P D" River; border: on lower side of John Mark's "plantation"; paid; made out.

1590. Apr. 11, 1745 Jacob Paul enters 50 ac in Bladen Co being an island in P D River "a little" above mouth of Hedgecock Cr; paid; made out.

1591. Apr. 11, 1745 Owen Reec's [sic] enters 250 ac in Pasquotank Co; border: Cartright's line on Middle Swamp, runs to Little fork Swamp, & up th swamp; paid; made out.

page 161
1592. Apr. 11, 1745 Jos Jno Alston enters 640 [written over 700] ac in Edgecombe Co on S side of Reedy Cr; border: near his own line, runs "off, & down"; rites "before"; paid; made out.

1593. Apr. 11, 1745 Chas. C Harrison enters 200 ac in New Hanover Co on the road from "the" sound back of Clist's [or Clifs]; border: on S side of a pond at a pine; Dr; made out.

1594. Apr. 11, 1745 John Fonvielle enters 400 ac in Craven Co being marsh land "fronting" said John Fonvielle's land; paid; rites "before"; made out.

1595. Apr. 11, 1745 Wm Curlee enters 200 ac in Craven Co on both sides of Mill Cr; where said Curlee has "his frame up" on S side of Cotanknee Cr; made out. [Gibbon Jennings--lined out]
1596. Apr. 11, 1745 Joell Lashley enters 200 ac in Craven Co on N side of Little Cr; between James Jones' old survey and his new survey; border: Owen ODaniel's land; made out.

1597. Apr. 11, 1745 Wm Shergold enters 150 ac in Pasquotank Co; border: a poplar at Jones' old line; includes Griffin's old field "so called"; paid; made out.

1598. Apr. 11, 1745 Wm Daniel enters 200 ac in Chowan Co; border: on W & NW sides of Baker's land and joins Baker's "line"; made out.

pag 162
1599. Apr. 11, 1745 Jos Bryan enters 200 ac in Craven Co on N side of Nuce R, N side of Swifts Cr, & E side of Maul Run; border: John Gray's corner tree and runs up the swamp; rites "before"; paid; made out.

1600. Apr. 11, 1745 Edwd. Bryan enters 400 ac in Bladen Co on SW side of great Peedee R; border: Goodman's line and runs "out & down"; paid; made out.

1601. Apr. 11, 1745 Hugh Lorrimore enters 400 ac in Bladen Co on NE side of great PeeDee R; border: an "Allebie" line on the great river, runs "out, & up"; paid; made out.

1602. Apr. 11, 1745 Wm Routledge [Alexr McCulloh--lined out] enters 400 ac in New Hanover Co; border: a line of the land where he lives, runs to a Maple Swamp, over the same, & runs "up and back"; rites proved; made out.

1603. Apr. 11, 1745 Rogr. Moor enters 400 ac in New Hanover Co on Waggamaw Lake; border: joins his own land; made out.

page 163
1604. Apr. 11, 1745 John Carruthers enters 100 ac in Craven Co on N side of Nuce R; border: Simon Bright's upper line and on N side of Briery Br; made out.

1605. Apr. 11, 1745 John Rice enters 100 ac in Craven Co on N side of Nuce R; border: John Carruthers on N side of Briery Br; made out.

1606. Apr. 11, 1745 Charles Taylor sr enters 100 ac in Pasquotank Co; border: on head of John Bayley's line and "back"; Richd. McClure; made out.

1607. Apr. 11, 1745 Robt. Coulehare enters 400 ac in Bladen Co on S side of great Pee Dee R below mouth of [great--lined out] Crown Cr; rites "before"; paid; made out.

1608. Apr. 11, 1745 Isabella Phillips enters 400 ac in Craven Co on N side of Nuce R; border: Henry Sumerland and runs up Bear Pecoson; made out.

1609. Apr. 11, 1745 Robt Parks enters 400 ac in Bladen Co on S side of great Pee Dee R, at Walker's Island, & runs "out and up"; paid; made out.

page 164
1610. Apr. 11, 1745 Robt Parks enters 300 ac in Craven Co on S side of Bear Creek Marsh and on S side of Haris Br; border: runs down the marsh to John Herring's line and "back"; chd; made out.

1611. Apr. 11, 1745 Jas Monk enters 640 ac in New Hanover Co on Goshen Swamp and on NE Cape Fear R; border: near John Wright; made out.
1612. Apr. 11, 1745 Chas Monk enters 640 ac in New Hanover Co on Goshen Swamp and on NE Cape Fear R; border: near Jas Monk and John Wright; made out.

1613. Apr. 11, 1745 Wm Maynor enters 640 ac in Onslow Co on S side of NW New R; border: Wm Sloan and Jethro Marshburne; rites returned; McWaine; made out.

1614. Apr. 11, 1745 Alexr. McCullo enters 300 ac in New Hanover Co on Panther Swamp; border: an oak "a little" above the Indian Path and runs "up"; made out.

page 165 [blank page]
page 166 [random adding, only, on this sheet]

page 167 "Entries of Warrants Commencing" May 6, 1745 [sic, entries on p. 169 are of later date]

page 168 "An account of the returns made by the Surveyor General Sept. [20--lined out], 1745"
25th   returned 56
26th   returned 22

page 169
1615. "Aug. 17" George Hamegee enters 400 ac in Craven Co on N side of Nuce R and on S side of Richland Swamp; border: Thos McClendon's lines on "each" side.

1616. "Aug. 17" Rice Price enters 150 ac in New Hanover Co on Angola Br of Holley Shelter Cr on W side of the creek.

1617. "Aug. 17" John Phillips enters 300 ac in Craven Co on N side of Nuce R; between the lines of John Derham.

1618. "Aug. 17" Geo Nettles enters 200 ac in Craven Co on Richland [Hico--lined out] Cr; border: Richd. Kemp's line and runs "up".

1619. "Aug. 17" Geo Nettles enters 200 ac in Craven Co above mouth of Marsh Cr and runs "down".

1620. "Aug. 17" Abra. Bledsoe enters 300 ac in Craven Co; border: a red oak below Richland Cr and runs up both sides.

1621. "Sept. 13" John Hawkins enters 200 ac in Craven Co on N [W--lined out] side of Trent R; known as Joshua's "Resolution" or Stanly's old place.

page 170
1622. May 10, 1745 Wm Hill enters 200 ac in Chowan Co on SW side of Bennets Cr opposite Chowan Indian town; Mr. Anderson; rites returned.

1623. [entry lined out] May 10, 1745 Wm Smith enters 300 ac in Craven Co on S side of Nuce R and E side of Slocumbs Cr; border: Mr. Slocumb; between Slocumb's and Handcocks Cr.

1624. May 10, 1745 Wm Davis enters 200 ac in Craven Co in the forks of great Chinkapin [Swamp] and W side of White Oak Pecoson; at a place where Wm Ledman formerly lived.

1625. May 10, 1745 John Vernam enters 150 ac in Craven Co on S side of Nuce R; border: on the back of Luke Russel's and joins Jas Derham; rites proved.
1626. May 10, 1745 John Vernam enters 100 ac in Craven Co on S side of Nuce R and on the islands of Harrys Br.

1627. May 10, 1745 John Powel enters 200 ac in Craven Co on N side of Nuce R, on S side of Loosing Swamp, & runs up the swamp.

1628. May 10, 1745 Lemuel Harvey enters 100 ac in Craven Co on E side of Low Cr; border: Geo Stringer and Wm Herritage.

page 171
1629. May 10, 1745 John Row enters 200 ac in Craven Co in the fork of Falling Cr and Ground nut Marsh on N side of Nuce R.

1630. May 10, 1745 Richd. Sarsnut enters 100 ac in Craven Co on E side of Bog Marsh; border: John Heming's line and runs "up"; to R Parks.

1631. May 10, 1745 John Marshal enters 200 ac in Craven Co; border: Whitford's corner treek, runs NW, & down "the" swamp; paid 40/.

North Carolina Land Entries 1735-1752

1632. May 10, 1745 Wm Rice enters 100 ac in Craven Co; border: Jas Robertson's line on N side of Nuce R and runs E.

1633. May 10, 1745 Wm Morgan enters 100 ac in Craven Co on head of Smiths Cr on N side and on N side of Nuce R; rites not proved; single man.

1634. May 10, 1745 John Brown enters 200 ac in Craven Co on N side of Pamplico R and S side of Gum Swamp that runs into Tranters Cr; paid.

page 172 [blank page]

page 173 "Entry Book of Warrants" for Sept. Court 1745
page 174 [blank page]

page 175
1635. Sept. 25, 1745 John Rice enters 400 ac in Craven Co on N side of Trent R; border: near Hugh Stanaland's "plantation"; being where Christo. Tew lived.

1636. Sept. 25, 1745 Lodowick Alford enters 600 ac in Edgecombe Co on S side of Crooked Cr; border: a red oak marked "L A"; rites returned "now"; R F to pay.

1637. Sept. 25, 1745 Thos Williams enters 640 ac in New Hanover Co on S side of Kerbys Cr; border: his own corner white oak; rites returned "now"; R F to pay.

1638. Sept. 25, 1745 Cason Brinson enters 150 ac in Craven Co on N side of Nuce R and W side of Upper Broad Cr; border: Mr. Shine.

1639. Sept. 25, 1745 Joseph Fulcher enters 250 ac in Craven Co on W side of Upper Broad Cr; border: Cason Brinson's line, runs down "the" swamp, & joins Danl Shine.

1640. Sept. 25, 1745 Joseph Carruthers enters 100 ac in Craven Co on N side of Nuce R, E side of Loosing Swamp, & W side of Sow Ponds; border: runs towards Becton's and Rawlins' lines.
1641. Sept. 25, 1745 John Rice enters 400 ac in Craven Co on N side of Nuce R and on Briery Br; border: above Simon Bright's land.

1642. Sept. 25, 1745 John Rice enters 200 ac in Craven Co on S side of Nuce R, on Falling Cr, & near the fork of said creek.

page 176
1643. Sept. 25, 1745 Patrick Stanly enters 200 ac in Craven Co on N side of Trent R, on a "place" called John Jones Br, &runs up both sides of said branch; border: Jacob Sheets.

1644. Sept. 25, 1745 George bell sr enters 200 ac in Carteret Co on Core Banks

141

and about 0.75 miles E of a place called Whalebone Hamock; between Thos Nelson and John Nelson; Col. Lovick Dr.

1645. Sept. 25, 1745 Jacob Brawler enters 300 ac in Craven Co on N side of Nuce R; border: on Beards Creek Swamp, runs across said creek at the head, & runs up the middle branch.

1646. Sept. 25, 1745 Chas Howard sr enters 100 ac in Craven Co being marsh land at a place called Piney Point on N side of Nuce R.

1647. Sept. 25, 1745 Jno Gatlin sr enters 100 ac in Craven Co on N side of Nuce R and between two small runs; between said Gatlin and Fras. Linkfield; known as Fulches Neck.

1648. Sept. 25, 1745 Thos Smith enters 200 ac in Craven Co at a place known as Indian Camps at head of Great Swamp.

1649. Sept. 25, 1745 Philip Trapnah enters 100 ac in Craven Co on S side of Nuce R and on a branch; border: on "the" main road about 0.5 miles from John Tutan's.

1650. Sept. 25, 1745 Philip Trapnah enters 200 ac in Craven Co on S side of Nuce R; at a place known as "the" Islands and Snakehole Br or Harrys Br.

page 177 [entries 1651-1669 same as entries 1615-1634 above]
1651. Sept. 25, 1745 George Harnege [or Hamege] enters 400 ac in Craven Co on N side of Nuse R and E side of Richland Swamp; border: Thos McClendon's lines on each side.

1652. Sept. 25, 1745 Rice Price enters 150 ac in New Hanover Co on "Angole" Br of Holley Shelter Cr and W side of said creek.

1653. Sept. 25, 1745 John Philips enters 300 ac in Craven Co on N side of Nuce R; "between" the lines of John Derham.

1654. Sept. 25, 1745 George Nettles enters 200 ac in Craven Co on Richland Cr; border: Rd Kemp's line and runs "up".

1655. Sept. 25, 1745 George Nettles enters 200 ac in Craven Co above mouth of Marsh Cr and runs "down".

1656. Sept. 25, 1745 Abra. Bledsoe enters 300 ac in Craven Co; border: a red oak below Richland Cr and runs up both sides.

1657. Sept. 25, 1745 John Hawkins enters 200 ac in Craven Co on N side of Trent R; known as Joshua's "Resolution" or Stanly's old place.

1658. Sept. 25, 1745 Wm Hill enters 200 ac in Chowan Co on SW side of Bennets Cr opposite Chowan Indian town; Mr. Anderson; rites returned "now"; Mr. Anderson Dr.

1659. Sept. 25, 1745 Wm Davis enters 200 ac in Craven Co in the forks of great Chinkapin [Swamp] and W side of White Oak Pecoson; at a place where Wm "Leedman" formerly lived.

page 178
1660. Sept. 25, 1745 John Vernam enters 150 ac in Craven Co on S side of Nuce R; border: on the back of Luke Russell's [sic] and joins Jas Derham; rites returned "before".

1661. Sept. 25, 1745 John Vernam enters 100 ac in Craven Co on S side of Nuce R and on the islands of Harrys Br; rites returned "before".

1662. Sept. 25, 1745 John "Powell" enters 200 ac in Craven Co on N side of Nuce R, on S side of Loosing Swamp, & runs up the swamp; paid "per note".

1663. Sept. 25, 1745 Lemuel Harvey enters 100 ac in Craven Co on E side of Low Cr; border: Geo Stringer and Wm Herritage; paid "per note".

1664. Sept. 25, 1745 John Row enters 200 ac in Craven Co in the fork of Falling Cr and Ground nut Marsh on N side of Nuce R; paid "per note".

1665. Sept. 25, 1745 Richd. Sarsnut enters 100 ac in Craven Co on E side of "Bogg" Marsh; border: John Heming's line and runs "up"; R Parks.

1666. Sept. 25, 1745 John "Marshall" enters 200 ac in Craven Co; border: Whitford's corner tree, runs NW, & down "the" swamp; paid "per note".

1667. Sept. 25, 1745 Wm Rice enters 100 ac in Craven Co; border: James Robertson's line on N side of Nuce R and runs E; paid "per note".

page 179
1668. Sept. 25, 1745 Wm Morgan enters 100 ac in Craven Co on head of Smiths Cr on N side and on N side of Nuce R; paid "per note".

1669. Sept. 25, 1745 John Brown enters 200 ac in Beaufort [sic] Co on N side of Pamplico R and S side of Gum Swamp that runs into Tranters Cr; rites returned "now"; paid.

1670. Sept. 25, 1745 Thos Cox enters 200 ac in Craven Co on S side of Nuse R and lower side of Falling Cr; border: Wm Bush and runs up the creek; paid "per note".

1671. Sept. 25, 1745 Thos Cox enters 300 ac In Craven Co on S side of Nuse R and lower side of Falling Cr; border: Wm Bush's corner tree, runs "off", & down the river; paid "per note".

1672. Sept. 25, 1745 Saml Collins enters 200 ac in Craven Co on S side of Nuce R; border: John Collins; paid.

1673. Sept. 25, 1745 Jas Ellison enters 100 ac in Beaufort Co on N side of Pamplico R; border: James Dudley's survey, on W side of Deep Run, & joins John Barrow; rites "before"; paid; "down".

1674. Sept. 25, 1745 Jas Ellison enters 200 ac in Beaufort Co on N side of Pamplico R; border: John Worsly jr, Robt Cutler, & Juniper Swamp.

page 180.

1675. Sept. 25, 1745 Jas Elar [or Elarz] Clitheral enters 100 ac in Carteret Co in and near mouth of North R; border: near James Shackleford's houses on "his" Banks, E of the main channel leading from Beaufort Inlet to Tilas' Point, "through" the main creek, "towards" NW part of said Clitheral's land, & joins Joseph Wilkins; J [or "Og] Clitheral's rites; J C Dr.

1676. Sept. 25, 1745 Wm Wilkison enters 200 ac in Beaufort Co; border: Thos Campain's line, runs down "the" creek, runs across a point of marsh to Deep Bay, runs up Hog Bay "a Canpain line", & up the creek; rites returned "now"; paid.

1677. Sept. 25, 1745 Thos Nelson enters 50 ac in Carteret Co on Ocricock Banks; within 6 or 7 miles of the inlet called Bunch of Busles "or" Bunch of Evergreen; border: near said Nelson's survey called the whalebone; rites returned "before"; Rd Lovet Dr.

1678. Sept. 25, 1745 Thos Nelson enters 50 ac in Carteret Co on W side of Nelsons Cr at "the" Hunting Quarters; rites returned "before"; Rd Lovet Dr.

1679. Sept. 25, 1745 Jacob Farrow enters 640 ac in Currituck Co on Hatteras Banks; border: a live oak on Follys Cr, runs along the creek to the sound, & along Pamplico Sound and Wm Bryan's line to the seashore on Hrdka [or Rrdba] Farrow's line; rites proved "before"; Rd Lovet Dr.

page 181

1680. Sept. 25, 1745 Mathew Casewell enters 100 ac in Tyrrell Co; border: his own line; [being] an island called Rd Adison and Sam's Island, part of Juniper Swamp, & a line formerly called John Hasell's; single person; paid.

1681. Sept. 25, 1745 Elias Hodges enters 640 ac in Beaufort Co between head of Hunting Run and Briery Swamp; border: at an Indian Springs, runs down the run, & "back"; Lords pt; paid.

1682. Sept. 25, 1745 Wm Cason enters 200 ac in Beaufort Co on N side of Grindal Cr, on the Creek Swamp, & runs "up and back"; Lords pt; paid.

1683. Sept. 25, 1745 Archd. Campbel enters 300 ac in Beaufort Co on S side of Pamplico R and at head of Juniper Run; border: Peter Morr's corner, runs back in the fork, & across the Western Run; Lords pt; paid.

1684. Sept. 25, 1745 Isaac Buck enters 100 ac in Beaufort Co on S side of Tar R, at Crog [or Cros] Swamp, runs up the main branch of Churd Cr, & "back"; Lords pt; paid.

1685. Sept. 25, 1745 Isaac Buck enters 200 ac in Beaufort Co on N side of Pamplico R; border: a small gut below Israel Harding's house in the low grounds of the river, runs down the river, & "back"; Lords pt; paid.

page 182
1686. Sept. 25, 1745 Mathias Tyson enters 300 ac in Beaufort Co on N side of Little Cotentnea Cr; border: below John Winfield's, runs down the swamp, & "back"; rites returned "before"; Lords pt; paid.

1687. Sept. 25, 1745 John Slade enters 150 ac in Craven Co on E side of Little Cotentnea Cr, on "the" Beaverdam, & runs "down and back"; rites returned "before"; "down"; paid; 10/ due.

1688. Sept. 25, 1745 Moses Tyson enters 100 ac in Beaufort Co on "the" fork of Pine log Swamp and on Little Cotentnea Cr; border: begins at the fork and runs on Pine log Swamp; Lords pt; paid; Forbes Dr 10/.

1689. Sept. 25, 1745 Wm Adams enters 300 ac in Beaufort Co on N side of Pamplico R and runs on upper fork of Horsepen Br; rites returned "before"; Lords pt; paid; Forbes Dr 10/.

1690. Sept. 25, 1745 Thos Richards enters 300 ac in Beaufort Co on S side of Pamplico R and upper side of Chukawindy Cr; border: a great branch on said creek, runs down the swamp of the creek, & "back"; Lords pt; paid.

1691. Sept. 25, 1745 George Graham enters 200 ac in Craven Co on E side of Upper Broad Cr; border: his own line and Archs. Purefoy; called Graham's "addition"; rites returned "before"; paid; "down".

page 183
1692. Sept. 25, 1745 Fras. Caffrey enters 50 ac in Beaufort Co three miles up Great Bay; called Perkins' old field; Jno Carruthers Dr; made out.

1693. Sept. 25, 1745 Andrew Ross enters 150 ac in Edgecombe Co on N side of Sapponey Cr and on Haw tree Br; border: runs "up" from a red oak; rites returned "now"; Lords pt; paid; made out.

1694. Sept. 25, 1745 Andrew Ross enters 150 ac in Edgecombe Co on S side of Stoney Cr; being a clearing of Charls. Plenty; Lords pt; paid; made out.

1695. Sept. 25, 1745 Josh. Barradell enters 200 ac in Bertie Co on E side of Wildcat Br; border: Josh. Watsford's corner pine; rites returned "before"; R F; Lords pt; made out.

1696. Sept. 25, 1745 Thos Mann enters 200 ac in New Hanover Co on N side of Gowshain Swamp; border: a red oak marked "T" and runs down the swamp; rites returned "before"; paid 10/ due to J C; "down"; made out.

1697. Sept. 25, 1745 Robt Dickinson enters 150 ac in Edgecombe Co; border: a red oak on N side of Conoway Cr and runs up both sides; rites assd. from And Ross; Lords pt; paid J R; made out.

1698. Sept. 25, 1745 Gregory Stallins enters 200 ac in Edgecombe Co at mouth of a branch on Bear head Pocoson and runs along the pocoson; rites assd. from And Ross; Lords pt; paid to J R; made out.

page 184
1699. Sept. 25, 1745 Richd. Green enters 200 ac in Edgecombe Co on S side of Tar R; border: Record's line and runs up the river; Lords pt; paid to J R; rites to be proved now; made out.

1700. Sept. 25, 1745 Thomas Hollyman enters 150 ac in Edgecombe Co on S side of Tyankowky Cr; border: his own land; Lords pt; paid to J R; rites to be proved now; made out.

1701. Sept. 25, 1745 Hopkin Wilder enters 100 ac in Edgecombe Co; border: a popler on S side of said Wilder's Mill Br, runs across the mill branch, & up both sides; includes Walter Gibson's improvements; rites returned "before"; paid; Lords pt; made out.

1702. Sept. 25, 1745 Timothy Harris enters 300 ac in Beaufort Co on S side of Tar R, on S side of Lamberts Cr, runs back from the creek, & across the same and "back"; rites returned; paid; Lords pt; 10/ due to J R; J Forbes; made out.

1703. Sept. 25, 1745 George Norris enters 300 ac in Craven Co on Cow Br; being where Chas McDonohow lived; rites returned "before"; paid; made out; "down".
1704. Sept. 25, 1745 Wm Davis enters 500 ac in Craven Co on N side of Norhunty [Swamp] and on a place called Dead old Fields; between George Fort and John Fort; rites returned "before"; paid; pet. made out.

1705. Sept. 25, 1745 Benjn. Lambert enters 200 ac in Craven Co in the fork of

North Carolina Land Entries 1735-1752

Little Cotentny Cr; being where George Hartly lived; rites returned "before"; paid; pet. made out; "down".

page 185
1706. Sept. 25, 1745 Wm Bennet enters 200 ac in Craven Co; border: a small branch [oak--lined out] on S side of Slew Swamp above Wm Pugh's land and runs "up"; rites returned "before"; paid; made out.

1707. Sept. 25, 1745 Robt. Parks enters 200 ac in Bladen Co on S side of great Pedee R above "the" falls; border: Solomn. Hews; Mr. Parks Dr; chd; made out.

1708. Sept. 25, 1745 Robt. Parks enters 500 [written over 200] ac in Bladen Co on S side of great Pedee R, below Walker's Island, & begins on Young's Island; Mr. Parks Dr "to" four entrys; chd; made out.

1709. Sept. 25, 1745 Robt. Parks enters 200 ac in Craven Co in the forks of Black Walnut Cr; Mr. Parks Dr; chd; made out.

1710. Sept. 25, 1745 Robt. Parks enters 300 ac in New Hanover Co in one of head forks of NW Cape Fear R; Mr. Parks Dr; chd; made out.

1711. Sept. 27, 1745 Robt. Parks enters 300 ac in Bladen [Craven--lined out] Co on S side of Little R and near John Elleby's land; border: a white oak and runs "up"; Mr. Parks Dr; chd; made out.

1712. Sept. 27, 1745 John Cheek enters 400 ac in Bladen Co at John Cheek's Island, runs across a creek, "up, across, & down"; rites "before"; paid; "P" made out.
[the following three lined out at bottom of page]
Thathirow Harris enters 408 ac in Craven Co
Abra Duncan enters 3 [blank]
John Carruthers enters [blank] in Craven Co

page 186
1713. Sept. 27, 1745 Caleb Howel enters 400 ac in Bladen Co at a place called Mount Pleasant on S side of P D River, runs "out, & back"; rites "before"; paid; "P" made out.

1714. Sept. 27, 1745 Jas Brickle enters 150 ac in Bladen Co on S side of P D River; border: Gilaspy's line and runs up the river; rites "before"; paid; "P" made out.

1715. Sept. 27, 1745 Cathrine Hamais [or Harrais] enters 463 ac in Craven Co on S side of Nuce R; border: her own land where she lives; rites "before"; "P" made out.

147

1716. Sept. 27, 1745 Wm Stone enters 400 ac in Bladen Co on S side of great P D River, on S side of Little R, runs "out and down", & to "the" river; on Smith's rites; paid; 10/ due; "P" made out.

1717. Sept. 27, 1745 Wm Cheek enters 400 ac in Bladen Co near mouth of Town Cr, runs up to an Indian old field, "across, & down"; on Smith's rites; paid; 10/ due; "P" made out.
[first line of No. 1719 lined out at bottom of page]

page 187
1718. Sept. 27, 1745 Wm Webster enters 150 ac in Hyde Co on W side of Matchapungo R and at mouth of Cedar Cr; border: runs between Cattar [or Callar], Flyn, & his own line; rites "before"; paid; "P" made out.

1719. Sept. 27, 1745 Wm Foskew enters 100 ac in Hyde Co on E side of Matchapungo R and S side of Slades Cr; 82 ac of which is surplus land found in a survey "lately" made for said Foskew; the rest is vacant land; rites proved; paid; "P" made out.

1720. Sept. 27, 1745 Robt. Parks enters 300 ac in Bladen Co on S side of great P D River; border: Young's line and "up"; Parks Dr; chd; "P" made out.

1721. Sept. 27, 1745 Jas Green enters 200 ac in Bladen Co on S side of great P D River; border: above Cartlidge's line and runs "up"; rites before; J Green Dr; "P" made out.

1722. Sept. 27, 1745 John Smith enters 200 ac in Bladen Co on S side of great P D River, on the river, & runs down the same; rr "now"; paid; "P" made out.

page 188
1723. Sept. 27, 1745 Willis Ship enters 100 ac in Craven Co on E side of Beselys [or Bexlys] Swamp; border: Nun's line; rites returned "before"; paid; "P" made out.

1724. Sept. 27, 1745 Jas Nelson enters 200 ac in Craven Co on E branch of Swifts Cr and above Peter Reel's line; rites before; paid; "P" made out.

1725. Sept. 27, 1745 Hugh Larrimore enters 300 ac in Bladen Co on S side of great P D River, above Mount Pleasant, & runs up the river; rites "before"; paid; "P" made out.

1726. Sept. 27, 1745 Jas Connor enters 300 ac in Bladen Co on S side of great P D River; border: above Jasper King's line, runs "out, & up"; rites "before"; paid; "P" made out.

1727. Sept. 27, 1745 Fras. McWaine enters 300 ac in Bladen Co on S side of great

North Carolina Land Entries 1735-1752

P D River; border: Col. Parks' line, runs "up, & out"; on his father's rites; paid 10/ due; "P" made out.

1728. Sept. 27, 1745 Wm Smith enters 300 ac in Bladen Co on S side of great P D River, below mouth of Brown Cr, & runs "down"; rites returned; paid; "P" made out.

1729. Sept. 27, 1745 John Nelson enters 80 ac in Craven Co on N side of Nuce R; border: a gum, runs to a juniper, & the "several courses" to the beginning; rites "before"; Lovet Dr; "P" made out.

page 189
1730. Sept. 27, 1745 John Nelson enters 319 ac in Craven Co on N side of Nuce R; border: a gum on Cashoe Cr, runs up said creek, & "back"; rites "before"; Rd Lovet Dr; "P" made out.

1731. Sept. 27, 1745 John Fitzgerrald enters 200 ac in Craven Co; border: on or near Jas McWaine's land "above" Little R; Mr. Griffith Dr; "P" made out.

1732. Sept. 27, 1745 Thos Cunningham enters 200 ac in New Hanover Co; border: on back of his own line "the half tract" he bought of Chas. Harrison; being where he lives; R Moor Dr; rites "before"; "P" made out.

1733. Sept. 27, 1745 Donald McKikin enters 320 ac in Bladen Co; border: his own land; R Moor Dr; "P" made out.

1734. Sept. 27, 1745 Solomon Ogden enters 100 ac in New Hanover Co about 4 miles back of Waggamaw R on a small lake and on W side of the river; R Moor Dr; rites "before"; "P" made out.

1735. Sept. 27, 1745 Jno Struckberry [or Stouchberry] enters 200 ac in Bladen Co at Solomons Cr on N side of P D River; paid; "P" made out.

1736. Sept. 27, 1745 Christo. Putnell enters 100 ac in Beaufort Co on S side of Pamplico R and S side of Goose Cr; at Putnell's Ridge; rites to be proved by Ben Peyton who is Dr; "P" made out.

page 190 [only one entry on this page]
1737. Nov. 24, 1745 Fras. Stringer enters 200 ac in Craven Co between Flat Swamp and Cose [or Core] Cr; border: Robt Taylor and Edwd. Herring.

page 191
1738. Nov. 24, 1745 Wm Wilkison enters 100 ac in Craven Co; border: Jas Cheyn's line on Vine Swamp and runs to Anto. Calvert's line; "P" made out.

1739. Nov. 24, 1745 Benoni Loftin enters 50 ac in Craven Co on S side of Nuse

R and on both sides of Salisburry Swamp; between Geo Roberts and Henry Eaton; "P" made out.

1740. Nov. 24, 1745 Martin Bender enters 100 ac in Craven Co on both sides of Simon's Run; "P" made out.

1741. Nov. 24, 1745 Saml Pacey enters 300 ac in Craven Co on Goose Cr on W side; border: Robt. Pits on N side of Nuse R; "P" made out.

1742. Nov. 24, 1745 Mary Peyton enters 640 ac in Beaufort Co; border: Jas Blunt's line, runs on Coleman Row's, & Ben Peyton's [lines]; "P" made out.

1743. Nov. 24, 1745 Danl Sullivan enters 200 ac in New Hanover Co on upper end of Buck Marsh on E side; known as Holleys Spring; "P" made out.

1744. Nov. 24, 1745 Geo Kernegee [or Kemegoo] enters 50 ac in New Hanover Co on lower end of Buck Marsh on E side and runs "up"; "P" made out.

1745. Nov. 24, 1745 Jas Keith enters 320 ac in Bladen Co between New Hope Cr & Haw R and "down" in the main fork; border: at mouth of New Hope Cr and runs up the river & fork; "P" made out.

page 192
1746. Nov. 24, 1745 William Cookson enters 100 ac in Craven Co; border: Jacob Sheets' corner tree, runs up GravelyRun, down the W side, & up Bever Cr; "P" made out.

1747. Nov. 24, 1745 Joshua Sarsnutt enters 100 ac in Craven Co on S side of Nuce R; border: on the first high land above Capt. Powel's and a "little" below Sleepy Cr; "P" made out.

1748. Nov. 24, 1745 Anto. Herring enters 600 ac in Craven Co on both sides of Bogue Marsh Creek; between Bogue Marsh and Nuse R on S side; "P" made out.

1749. Nov. 24, 1745 Henry Oberry enters 350 ac in Bladen Co on S side of Cohera R; border: a pine in the fork of Smith's Swamp and runs up both sides of Reedy Marsh; "P" made out.

1750. Nov. 24, 1745 Saml Smith enters 100 ac in Craven Co on S side of Trent R; known as Steel's Run; border: Math. Reasonover; "P" made out.

1751. Nov. 24, 1745 Jacob Ipock enters 150 ac in Craven Co on W side of Trent R; border: a white oak "joining" Rocky Ridge, runs to "the" River Pecoson, & up the river; "P" made out.

1752. Nov. 24, 1745 Jos Harper enters 320 ac in Craven Co on S side of Trent R;

border: Martin Frank's line on "the" Permany land; "P" made out; "W" made out.

1753. Nov. 24, 1745 Armwel Howard enters 200 ac in Craven Co on W side of Trent R and W side of Wilsons Cr; border: Wm Suggs; "P" made out.

1754. Nov. 24, 1745 Danl Quillen enters 100 ac in Craven Co on W side of Trent R and E side of Wilsons Cr; "P" made out.

1755. Nov. 24, 1745 Jonatha. Sanderson enters 100 ac in Craven Co on N side of Trent R; border: Mrs. Wilson's land and runs "down"; "P" made out.

page 193
1756. Nov. 24, 1745 Francis Stringer enters 300 ac in Craven Co on [SE side--lined out] Falling Cr and SE side of Great Marsh; border: Petit; "P" made out.

1757. Nov. 24, 1745 Francis Stringer enters 200 ac in Craven Co on N side of Nuse R; being Beaslys Island below Trapnel [Swamp ?]; "P" made out.

1758. Nov. 24, 1745 Fracis Stringer enters 150 ac in Craven Co on Vine Swamp; between Moseleys Cr and said swamp; "P" made out.

1759. Nov. 24, 1745 Robt. Ryley enters 250 ac in Craven Co on Dover Gum Swamp; between "Moslelys" Cr and Vine Swamp; "P" made out.

1760. Nov. 24, 1745 Robt. Ryley enters 200 ac in Craven Co on Falling Cr, on N side of a little marsh, an Indian old field, & runs down to Crooked Run; "P" made out.

1761. Nov. 24, 1745 Jno Edwards enters 200 ac in Bladen Co on S side of Cape Fear R, on N side of Fryars Swamp, & at Nathl. Moor's old "markt" Path; "P" made out; paid.

1762. Nov. 24, 1745 Jno Spier enters 150 ac in Craven Co on S side of Nuse R; border: a marked cypress beside a place known as Pitch kettle and runs down the river; "P" made out.

1763. Nov. 24, 1745 Thos West enters 130 ac in Craven Co on N side of Nuse R, on E side of Swift Cr, & on S side of Bear Br; border: Jno Gatlin; "P" made out.

1764. Nov. 24, 1745 Jno Harris enters 100 ac in Craven Co on N side of Trent R, on Jacobs Br, on Bever Cr, & runs up "the" creek; "P" made out.

1765. Nov. 24, 1745 Wm Whitford enters 400 ac in Craven Co on N side of Nuse R, SW side of "Crd" [Crooked] Cr, on Jumping Br, & runs up "the" swamp; "P" made out.

page 194

1766. Nov. 24, 1745 George Kernegee enters 100 ac in New Hanover Co on NE Cape Fear R, about 0.25 miles above "the" great marsh, on NE side of "the" swamp, & "against" Barefield's; "P" made out.

1767. Nov. 24, 1745 Jno Counce enters 250 ac in Craven Co; border: Counce's line at mouth of Chinkapin Cr and runs down "the" river; "P" made out.

1768. Nov. 24, 1745 Jno Fonvielle enters 300 ac in Craven Co on S side of Nuse R; border: his own corner "ring" oak, runs N60W 240 poles to a red oak, S43W 330 poles to a hickory, & down his own line; "P" made out.

1769. Nov. 24, 1745 Henry Barlow enters 200 ac in Craven Co on S side of Neuse R and on Falling Cr at "the" upper beverdam; "P" made out; paid.

1770. Nov. 24, 1745 Jno Brooks enters 200 ac in Craven Co on S side of Nuse R and on Falling Cr; border: Andw Bass; "P" made out; paid.

1771. Nov. 24, 1745 Jas Burns enters 400 ac in Bladen Co on SE side of Little R at a place called "the" Lake and on N side of Great P D River; border: about 0.5 miles above "the" mouth and runs down to Great P D River; "P" made out.

1772. Nov. 24, 1745 Solo Grant enters 400 ac in Bladen Co near Rocky ford and runs up both sides of Little R; "P" made out; paid.

1773. Nov. 24, 1745 Malcolm McNeil enters 200 ac in Bladen Co on Baptized Neck, on N side of Horseshoe Swamp where there's a hutt with four "crotches" and four crosssticks; "P" made out.

page 195

1774. Nov. 24, 1745 Jno Roberson enters 200 ac in Craven Co on E branch of Bare Cr and runs "over" Seneca Cr; rites proved "before"; paid; "P" made out.

1775. Nov. 24, 1745 Jno Bryan enters 350 ac in Craven Co on W side of Goose Cr; known as Cahoon's rich land; rites proved "before"; paid; "P" made out.

1776. Nov. 24, 1745 Abra. Easter enters 100 ac in Hyde Co on E side of Swan Quarter Bay; between Jno Tuly and Roger Mason; rites proved "before"; paid; "P" made out.

1777. Nov. 24, 1745 Willeby Richards enters 100 ac in Hyde Co; border: Jno Leath's land and runs of Swinging Ridge; paid; "P" made out.

1778. Nov. 24, 1745 Bailey McCarty enters 100 ac in Hyde Co on E side of Matchapungo R; border: runs between Darby McCarty, Thos Jewel, & his own line; rites proved "before"; paid; "P" made out.

1779. Nov. 24, 1745 Thos Richards enters 300 ac in Beaufort Co on S side of Pamplico R, on upper side of Chickowinity Cr, runs down the swamp of the creek, & "back"; rites returned; paid; "P" made out.

1780. Nov. 24, 1745 Jas Conner enters 400 ac in Bladen Co on N side of P D River, on lower side of "the" rich low grounds, & runs up the river; rites proved "before"; paid; "P" made out.

page 196
1781. Nov. 24, 1745 Jno Blackston enters 300 ac in Craven Co on S side of Little Cotentney Cr and at the three prongs of the Marked land Pecoson; being the place where he lives; rites proved; paid; "P" made out.
1782. Nov. 24, 1745 Saml Johnston esq enters 640 ac in Onslow Co on NW side of New R and on SW branch [of New R]; border: a marked pine on said branch; "P" made out.

1783. Nov. 24, 1745 Richd. Lovet enters 200 ac in Craven Co on NW side of Trent R; border: Wm Franks, "Carneege", & Thos Allen; "P" made out.

page 197 [blank page]
page 198 "rights proved and warrants granted and 1745" [sic]

page 199 "Entry Book begun at Bath Mar. 11, 1745"
page 200 [blank page]

page 201 "Lands entered at Bath Mar. 11, 1745
1784. Mar. 11, 1745/6 Robt Parks enters 450 ac in Craven Co on N side of Neuse R, "a little" above mouth of Beaverdam Br at a red oak, & runs up the river; rites returned "before"; R S; chd.

1785. Mar. 11, 1745/6 Robt "Parke" enters 200 ac in Craven Co on S side of Neuse R and on Sleepy Cr; border: back of Powell's "plantation", begins "a little" below "the" road, & runs on both sides of the creek; rites returned "before"; chd.

1786. Mar. 11, 1745/6 Robt Parke enters 400 ac in Bladen Co on S side of Great P D River, at lower end of Young's Island, & runs down the river; rites returned "before"; chd.

1787. Mar. 11, 1745/6 Robt Parke enters 640 ac in Bladen Co on S side of Great P D River; border: a branch on SE side of Browns Cr and runs up the branch; chd.

1788. Mar. 11, 1745/6 Robt Parke enters 300 ac in Bladen Co on N side of Great P D River; border: a branch below Walston's cabins and runs up the river; chd.

1789. Mar. 11, 1745/6 Robt Parke enters 400 ac in Bladen Co on S side of Deep R; border: a white oak below "the" roundabout and runs up; includes the roundabout; chd.

1790. Mar. 11, 1745/6 Robt Parke enters 300 ac in Bladen Co on N side of Deep R; border: a white oak below Brigman's cabins and runs up the river; chd.

page 202
1791. Mar. 11, 1745/6 Hugh Brown enters 100 ac in Bladen Co on S side of NW Cape Fear R; border: Rowan's corner tree and runs "down"; paid.

1792. Mar. 11, 1745/6 Wm Kemp enters 640 ac in Bladen Co on S side of Great P D River; border: a white oak at Canoe Landing and runs up the river; rites not yet proved.

1793. Mar. 11, 1745/6 John Hornbeck enters 400 ac in Bladen Co on S side of Great P D River; border: mouth of Walker's Gut [or Gat] and runs up the river; rites to prove.

1794. Mar. 11, 1745/6 Jno McCoy enters 300 ac in Bladen Co on N side of Great P D River and on N side of Little R; border: a red oak and runs "up"; includes his improvement; rites to prove.

1795. Mar. 11, 1745/6 Thos Red enters 350 ac in Bladen Co on S side of Great P D River at a place called Mount Pleasant; rites to prove.
1796. Mar. 11, 1745/6 Thos Red enters 200 ac in Bladen Co on N side of Great P D River; border: Thomas Jones' line and runs down the river; rites to prove.

1797. Mar. 11, 1745/6 Jno Gyles enters 300 ac in Bladen Co on S side of Great P D River; border: an oak on the river bank at mouth of Dry Cr and runs up the river.

1798. Mar. 11, 1745/6 Joseph Bryan enters 250 ac in Craven Co on S side of Neuse R, below mouth of Core Cr, & runs "down"; R P.

page 203
1799. Mar. 11, 1745/6 Mathew Allen enters 300 ac in Craven Co on S side of Great Catenknee Cr; border: "against" the [or "Her"] little Fort and runs down; R P.

1800. Mar. 11, 1745/6 Jno Ratcliffe enters 50 ac in Craven Co on N side of Falling Cr; border: John Herring's line and runs "up"; R P.

1801. Mar. 11, 1745/6 Rt Fellows enters 50 ac in Craven Co on S side of Neuse R; border: Robert's corner pine and runs "down"; R P.

1802. Mar. 11, 1745/6 Danl Herring enters 100 ac in New Hanover Co on a branch of NE Cape Fear R, on S side of Juniper Marsh, & runs "down"; R P.

1803. Mar. 11, 1745/6 Bryan Conner enters 200 ac in Bladen Co on W side of Horseshoe Br; known as Long Br and near Brown Marsh; called Bryan Conner's land; M Rowan Dr.

1804. Mar. 11, 1745/6 Gartian [or Garkan] Benbo enters 150 ac in Bladen Co on Fryars Swamp and near the Lake Path; M Rowan Dr.

1805. Mar. 11, 1745/6 Gartian Benbo enters 200 ac in Bladen Co on head of Parkers or Carvers Cr and near the Beaver Pond; M Rowan Dr.

1806. Mar. 11, 1745/6 Edmd Rorke enters 300 ac in Bladen Co on Brown Marsh Swamp; border: Bryan's land; M Rowan Dr.

1807. Mar. 11, 1745/6 [Thos McClendon--lined out] Jas Burns enters 200 ac in Bladen Co on N side of Great P D River, on Mountain Cr, & at a place called Poplar "Nck"; paid.

page 204 [blank page]
page 205
1808. Mar. 12, 1745/6 Thos Armstrong enters 300 ac in Bladen Co on N side of Deep R; border: "a little" above Mr. Campbell's land and runs "up"; Mr. McCull. Dr; "P" made out.

1809. Mar. 12, 1745/6 Felix Kannon enters 240 ac in New Hanover Co; border: on a branch of Black R at a red oak near Mr. McCulloh's line, on W side of Turkey Br, & runs up the branch; Mr. McCull. Dr; "P" made out.

1810. Mar. 12, 1745/6 Wm Faris enters 200 ac in New Hanover Co; border: Caleb Grainger's land on the great road from Wilmington about 4 miles from his "milns", joins "his" SW line, & runs "towards" said milns; Dr; "P" made out.

1811. Mar. 12, 1745/6 Benja Fuzzel enters 300 ac in Bladen Co on S side of Little R of Great Pedee R, at a branch "just" below "the" falls, & runs "down"; "P" made out; N R.

1812. Mar. 12, 1745/6 Jas Cook enters 300 ac in New Hanover Co on the main branch of Rockfish Cr; border: opposite Rd James; "P" made out; N R.

1813. Mar. 12, 1745/6 Jas Hasel enters 100 ac in New Hanover Co on N side of Cabbage Inlet; border: the inlet; "P" made out; N R.

1814. Mar. 12, 1745/6 Timo. Allen enters 250 ac in Hyde Co; border: at a branch of Jones Cr on W side of Matchapungo R, runs to head of Crooked Cr, then to

North Carolina Land Entries 1735-1752

Duck Cr, & with "the water courses" to the beginning; "P" made out; paid.

1815. Mar. 12, 1745/6 Pheba and Mary Lyten enter 300 ac in Craven Co; border: Jno Leister [Wm Herritage--lined out] and Adam Moore; paid; "P" made out.

page 206 [blank page]
page 207
1816. Mar. 12, 1745/6 Jno Benson enters 300 ac in Craven Co on S side of a little creek that runs out of Trent R "just by" New bern town and opposite a piece of land Mr. Herritage sold to Mr. Lister.

1817. Mar. 12, 1745/6 Wm Macoy enters 300 ac in Bladen Co on S side of P D River; border: a red oak and runs down the river; being the land where he lives; Giles Dr; "P" made out.

1818. Mar. 12, 1745/6 Jno Macoy enters 300 ac in Bladen Co on N side of Little R; border: a red oak, runs "up", & "into" Cheeks Island; Giles Dr; "P" made out.

1819. Mar. 12, 1745/6 Anto. Cox enters 180 ac in Craven Co on N side of Nuse R; border: a cyprus and joins the "plantation" where he formerly lived; Mr. McWaine Dr; "P" made out.

1820. Mar. 12, 1745/6 David and Isaac Fonvielle, orphans of John Fonvielle deceased, enter 250 ac in Craven Co; being marsh land fronting Jno Fonviell's [sic] land; border: mouth of a little creek between said Fonviell's and Peter Hendy's; Griffis [or Grittis] Dr; "P" made out.

1821. Mar. 12, 1745/6 Thos Hilliard enters 200 ac in "Brau" [Beaufort ?] Co; border: Jacob Evans and Saml Swearingham; being the land where he lives on S side of Pamplico R; Mr. McWaine Dr; "P" made out.

1822. Mar. 12, 1745/6 Fras. Nunn enters 150 ac in Craven Co on lower side of Half Moon Swamp; border: mouth of said swamp and joins the land formerly Fras. Nun's [sic]; paid; "P" made out.

page 208
1823. Mar. 12, 1745/6 Wm Houston enters 150 ac in New Hanover Co on E side of S branch of Black R; border: Alex. McCulloh's head line and runs "up"; McCulloh Dr; "P" made out.

1824. Mar. 12, 1745/6 Alexr. McCulloh enters 640 ac in New Hanover Co on E side of S branch of Black R; border: a gum on said branch and runs "up"; Dr; "P" made out.

1825. Mar. 12, 1745/6 John Warner enters 600 [written over 400] ac in Beaufort Co on S side of Campbells Neck; border: Carin's survey and runs up the creek to

North Carolina Land Entries 1735-1752

Echoll's survey; rites returned; paid; made out.

1826. Mar. 12, 1745/6 Edmond Pierce enters 300 ac in Beaufort Co on E side of Swifts Cr, above mouth of Pometto Swamp, runs up the creek, & "back"; rites returned; paid; made out.

1827. Mar. 12, 1745/6 Wm Devil enters 150 ac in Hyde Co; between Goten [or Galen] Smith and Henry Eborn; rites returned; paid; made out.

1828. Mar. 12, 1745/6 Henry Eborn enters 100 ac in Hyde Co on S side of Pungo Cr and W side of Lawrel Swamp; border: runs on Jas Barrow's line and "back"; paid; made out.

1829. Mar. 12, 1745/6 James Brickle enters 300 [or 400, a blob] ac in Beaufort Co on head of Jacksons Swamp; border: Mr. Ormand's head line; paid.

page 209
1830. Mar. 14, 1745/6 John Hardy enters 640 ac in Bladen Co on N side of S fork of Cape fear R called Deep R; border: a red oak marked "I L" at Beaverdam Swamp a branch of Rockey Cr; rites proved "before"; R F; W made out.

1831. Mar. 14, 1745/6 Wm Williams enters 200 ac in Onslow Co on NW New R at a place called War Tom; border: a red oak and runs "down"; Mr. McCulloh Dr; W made out.

1832. Mar. 14, 1745/6 Wm Williams enters 200 ac in Onslow Co on E side of NW New R at a place called the Vinyard; border: a red oak on Bever Swamp and runs "down"; Mr. McCulloh Dr; Wt made out; P made out.

1833. Mar. 14, 1745/6 Joseph Blake enters 200 ac in New Hanover Co on a branch of Rockfish Cr; border: Thos Corbett's lower line; paid; P made out.

1834. Mar. 14, 1745/6 Joseph Bishop enters 50 ac in New Hanover Co called Waters' Point; between Woodman Sudberry and Wm Waters; paid; P made out.

1835. [the following lined out] Miles Gole jr enters 400 ac "being an island" [no county indicated].

1836. Mar. 14, 1745/6 Anto. Lewis enters 640 ac in Onslow Co on NW New R; border: the river and said Lewis' land; P made out; S Swann Dr.

1837. Mar. 14, 1745/6 Corns. Harnett enters 200 ac in New Hanover Co; border: his own land at Pinch Gut Cr a branch of Lockwoods folly R; P made out.

page 210 [blank page]
page 211 [only one entry on this page]

157

1838. Mar. 14, 1745/6 Wm Williams enters 300 ac in Onslow Co on NW New R on W side and on N side of Miln Br; border: his own land; paid; P made out.

page 212 [blank page]

page 213 "Book of Entries for June Court 1746" [and some random arithmetic]
page 214 [blank page]

page 215
1839. Jun. 10, 1746 Danl Simons enters 200 ac in Craven Co on S side of Trent R; border: his own land & Cullen Pollock at Long Br and runs down the marsh; paid.

1840. Jun. 10, 1746 Joseph Morgan sr enters 200 ac in Onslow Co on N side of S fork of Bear Cr; rites returned.

1841. Jun. 10, 1746 Valentine Wallace sr enters 150 ac in Carteret Co; between Bartrim's line and Bogue Sound; rites returned.

1842. Jun. 10, 1746 Edwd. Ward sr enters 200 ac in Onslow Co on W side of Kings Road & Cowhead Br and runs to Cogdales Br.

1843. Jun. 10, 1746 Alexr. Fraizer [or Traizer] enters 100 ac in Carteret Co; between John Roberts and his own line; being where he lives.

1844. Jun. 12, 1746 Henry Smith sr enters 300 ac in Carteret Co; border: David Bailey's land and near Thos Nelson's land; rites returned; Col. Lovick Dr.

1845. Jun. 12, 1746 Martin Bender enters 640 ac in Craven Co on NE side of White Oak R in "the" fork and on "the" great branch.

1846. Jun. 12, 1746 Thos Norwood enters 200 ac in Craven Co on both sides of Lawsons Cr, runs "up", & across "the" road; rites returned; McWaine Dr.

page 216
1847. Jun. 12, 1746 John Kinsey enters 100 ac in Onslow Co on NE [side] of White Oak R near the head; border: about a mile above John Taylor's line and between two swamps.

1848. Jun. 12, 1746 John Benson enters 40 ac in Craven Co; border: a tree formerly Edwd. Bryan's near John Kig's [sic] "plantation", runs with Johnston's line to Deep Br, & up Batchelors Cr.

1849. Jun. 12, 1746 Jno Moor enters 100 ac in Craven Co; between Vine Swamp and Jacobs Wells; border: joins Storey's.

North Carolina Land Entries 1735-1752

1850. Jun. 12, 1746 Gershom Wiggins enters 300 ac in Craven Co on N side of Nuse R; at a place known as Sloop Landing on upper side of Falling Cr; border: "begins at a white oak and ends at a maple" on the upper end of "the" land.

1851. Jun. 12, 1746 Jno Spicer enters 100 ac in Craven Co on N side of Nuse R; between Beards [or Beasds] Cr and Duck Cr.

1852. Jun. 12, 1746 John Fitzgerald enters 150 ac in Craven Co on N side of Nuse R and S side of Little R; border: Jno Page's back line and Rd Boss' [or Bass].

1853. Jun. 12, 1746 Morrice Walker enters 200 ac in Craven Co on mouth of Broad Cr; between said creek and Goose Cr on N side of Nuse R.

1854. Jun. 12, 1746 Morrice Walker enters 200 ac in Craven Co on N side of Nuse R at Broad Creek Bridge.

page 217
1855. Jun. 12, 1746 Saml Smith enters 100 ac in Craven Co on S side of Nuse R, on head of Slocum's Cr, & on Core Swamp; "rights" proved and made out.

1856. Jun. 12, 1746 Jno Becton enters 100 ac in Craven Co near Jacobs Wessl on S side of Nuse R; border: runs along Robt Jones' line and "out"; includes Jacobs Wells and part of "the" savanna; made out.

1857. Jun. 12, 1746 Edwd. Outlaw enters 200 ac in New Hanover Co; border: Jonathan Taylor jr "his" line on Cow hole Swamp and run "up"; Mr. McCulloh Dr; made out.

1858. Jun. 12, 1746 John Rouce enters 200 ac in Craven Co on SW side of Falling Cr, on N prong of Falling Cr, & on both sides of Stanlys Marsh; Mr. McWaine Dr; made out.

1859. Jun. 12, 1746 Thos Jonacan enters 150 ac in Craven Co on S side of Neuse R and on Slocombs great Marsh; Mr. McWaine Dr.

1860. Jun. 12, 1746 David Smith enters 400 ac in Craven Co on Nuse R; between Henry Owens & Edwd. Rawlins and runs "back"; Mr. McWaine Dr; made out.

1861. Jun. 13, 1746 Francis Holton enters 200 ac in Bladen Co on NE side of NW Cape Fear R, at Falling Run, & "a little" below a "plantation" of Thos Lock's.

page 218
1862. Jun. 13, 1746 Alexr. McCallester enters 200 ac in Bladen Co on SW side of NW Cape Fear R; between James Carver and Saml Swann; border: a white oak and runs "downward"; made out.

159

North Carolina Land Entries 1735-1752

1863. Jun. 13, 1746 Henry Bradley enters 100 ac in New Hanover Co on NE side of Black R, on a mirey branch on Green's Path, & about 2 miles from the "foard" of Black R; being where he lives; made out.

1864. Jun. 14, 1746 David Smith enters 500 ac in Bladen Co on SW side of NW Cape Fear R and on N side of Lower Little R; made out.

1865. Jun. 14, 1746 John Easter enters 100 ac in Hyde Co on E side of Masons Bay; border: Thomas Mason's line, runs along the bay, & "back"; paid; made out.

1866. Jun. 14, 1746 Benja. Mason enters 125 ac in Hyde Co on E side of Oyster Cr and on Swan Quarter Bay; runs between Farster Jervis and Rogr. Mason jr; paid; made out.

1867. Jun. 14, 1746 Jas Hasell jr enters 200 ac in New Hanover Co on "the" main road up "the" NW [Cape Fear R] and about 4 miles from his father's land "of" Jas Hasell sr; made out.

page 219
1868. Jun. 14, 1746 Wm Gray enters 300 ac in Craven Co on Tuckahoe [Swamp]; known as "the" Springs; Mr. Griffith Dr; made out.

1869. Jun. 14, 1746 John Smith enters 500 ac in Beaufort Co; border: at head of Oyster Cr and runs through "the" swamp to Basset's head line at head of "mouse of arboun [or "fasbourn"] bay; paid; made out.

1870. Jun. 14, 1746 Joseph Kerr enters 100 ac in New Hanover Co on a branch of Maxwells Swamp on W side of Cape Fear R; paid; made out.

1871. Jun. 16, 1746 John Herrin enters 200 ac in Craven Co on N side of Neuse R; between Edward Williams' survey, Wm Wiggons, & on S side of Bear Harbour; rites returned "before"; paid; made out.

1872. Jun. 16, 1746 John Herrin enters 200 ac in Craven Co on S side of "Nuse" R; border: below George Roberts' survey on Saponey Cr, Wm Faris, & Christo. Harrison; rites returned "before"; paid; made out.

1873. Jun. 16, 1746 Jno Taylor enters 100 ac in Craven Co on "the" main road at head of Slocoms Cr; called Core Swamp and runs up the swamp; paid; made out.

1874. Jun. 16, 1746 "Conrid" Whitman enters 200 ac in New Hanover Co; border: Jacob Hanshy's corner and runs up "towards" Persimon Br; Mr. McCulloh Dr; made out.

page 220
1875. Jun. 16, 1746 Jacob Hanshy enters 200 ac in New Hanover Co; border: at

Stocking head Br on N side and runs "off & down" the branch; rites returned "before"; Mr. McCulloh Dr; made out.

1876. Jun. 16, 1746 John Dudley enters 300 ac in Onslow Co on both sides of NW fork of Grants Cr; made out.

1877. Jun. 16, 1746 Joseph Duks enters 100 ac in New Hanover Co on W side of NE River and on head of Horse Br; rites returned; paid; made out.

1878. Jun. 16, 1746 Jno Davis enters 400 ac in New Hanover Co on NE side of NW River; border: John Davis' upper corner and down to Neal's lower corner; Rogr. Moor Dr; made out.

1879. Jun. 16, 1746 Wm Grassett enters 100 ac in New Hanover Co on S side of Waggamaw R about a mile above mouth of Lon gBr; Rogr. Moor Dr; made out.

1880. Jun. 16, 1746 Robt. Park enters 200 ac in Bladen Co on S side of Great P D River, below mouth of Cyder Cr, & runs "out and up"; paid.

1881. Jun. 16, 1746 Robt. Park enters 500 ac in Bladen Co on Bare Cr, in "the" fork, & runs up both sides; paid.

1882. Jun. 16, 1746 Thos Jarmain enters 200 ac in Craven Co on Tuckahoe [Swamp] "on N side of S side" Trent R; made out.

page 221
1883. Jun. 16, 1746 Wm Dupee enters 300 ac in Craven Co on S side of Trent R and W side of Punch Bowl Br; Mr. Starky Dr; rites returned.

1884. Jun. 16, 1746 Saml Berry enters 200 ac in Craven Co on S side of Neuse R and on Williams Br; made out.

1885. Jun. 16, 1746 Wm Mills enters 100 ac in New Hanover Co on W side of northermost branch of Black R; Saml Johnston esq Dr; made out.

1886. Jun. 16, 1746 Jas Burns enters 150 ac in Bladen Co on N side of Great P D River and up Mountain Cr; [being] a place called White Oak Springs; paid; made out.

1887. Jun. 16, 1746 Jas Williams enters 100 ac in Craven Co on S side of Nuse R in the fork of Mill Cr; Jno [sic] Williams Dr; made out.

1888. Jun. 16, 1746 Nathan Smith enters 300 ac in Carteret Co on S side of Newport R; being the land formerly called Charles Glover's; rites proved; paid; made out.

North Carolina Land Entries 1735-1752

1889. Jun. 16, 1746 Jas Howell enters 100 ac in Craven Co on S side of Falling Cr, below "the" falls at a red oak, & runs "up"; made out.

1890. Jun. 16, 1746 Jas Wallace enters 600 ac in Craven Co on both sides of Enoe R [at] "the first fording place".

page 222
1891. Jun. 16, 1746 Saml Johnston esq enters 400 ac in Onslow Co; being the surplus land on Mark Ratcliffe's resurvey; border: joins said Johnston's lines; made out.

1892. Jun. 16, 1746 Joseph Williams enters 400 ac in Currituck Co on or near SW end of Cape Hatteras; border: Joseph Oliver and Thos Oliver; made out.

1893. Jun. 16, 1746 Frances Rowan enters 1,500 ac in New Hanover Co on SE side of Livingstons Cr; border: SE corner of her tract; being "the" surplus land and within the lines of the same; made out.

1894. Jun. 16, 1746 Jacob Farrow enters 640 ac in Currituck Co on Hatteras Banks; border: a live oak on Follies Cr, runs along the creek to the sound, along Pamplico Sound, along Wm Bryan's line, along the sea shore, & along Hezekiah Farrow's line; made out.

1895. [entire entry lined out] Joseph Williams enters 500 ac in Currituck Co on SW end of Harreras [Banks]; border: Joseph Oliver's back line and runs "back".

page 223
1896. Jun. 26, 1746 Wm Salter enters 300 ac in Carteret Co on "the" banks near Occacock Inlet and between the Three Hatts [Islands ?]; border: joins Thos Nelson's land; rites returned; made out.

1897. Jun. 26, 1746 John Clitheral enters 150 ac in Carteret Co at "Bottle a Rum" Hammock, "in the" sound, N and E of the upper Whale Camps on Shacklefords Banks "with" the contiguous marshes, runs W to "those" hamocks in "the" marshes on N and E of Jas Shackleford's houses on said banks with adjacent marshes, to "those" marshes N and W of "the" Ship Fare on Harkers Island, begins at SE end of "the same", runs N on E side of a creek, & W and S with the creek to the beginning; made out.

1898. Jun. 26, 1746 Benja Fuzzell enters 150 ac in New Hanover Co; border: on W side of his own land whereon he lives; made out.

1899. Jun. 26, 1746 Rd James enters 150 ac in New Hanover Co on S side of a large swamp of Black R; border: joins upper end of a marsh; made out.

page 224 [only 2 entries on this page]

162

1900. Jun. 26, 1746 Robt. Lee enters 200 ac in Craven Co on S side of Neuse R ["Middlesex Count"--lined out]; border: joins the land where he lives; Mr. Conner; paid; made out.

1901. Jun. 26, 1746 Bennet Blackman enters 150 ac in Craven Co on S side of Neuse R; border: a large marsh; known as Buck Island; Mr. Conner; paid; made out.

page 225 "Entry Book of Warrants" for Feb. Court 1746
page 226 [blank page]

page 227 "Entries of Feb. Court 1746" [out of order by date]
1902 (1). Feb. 25, 1746/7 Magnus Cowen [Jas Stoney--lined out] enters 200 ac in New Hanover Co; at a place called Pursley's place about 3 miles E of Black R; Pet. made out.
1903 (2). Feb. 25, 1746/7 Thos Stoakley enters 150 ac in Onslow Co in the fork of Goose Cr; border: Jno King; Pet. made out; paid.

1904 (3). Feb. 25, 1746/7 George Crandall enters 100 ac in Onslow Co; between Thos Beasly and Jos Sadbury on Beaslys Swamp; Pet. made out; paid.

1905 (4). Feb. 25, 1746/7 Joseph Mason enters 200 ac in Craven Co on N side of Neuse R and on the River Pecoson; between Mr. Griffith's line and the place where Moses Fog lives; Pet. made out; paid.

1906 (5). Feb. 25, 1746/7 Edward Frank enters 640 ac in Craven Co; border: Saml Johnston's upper line on both sides of Chinkapin Cr; Pet. made out.

1907 (6). Feb. 25, 1746/7 Elias Lagerdere enters 150 ac in Craven Co on Beaverdam branches and Bathelders Cr; P made out.

1908 (7). Feb. 25, 1746/7 James Marshall enters 200 ac in Craven Co on W side of White Oak "Peconson" at mouth of Iron mine Cr; Pet. made out.

page 228
1909 (8). Feb. 25, 1746/7 JohnRussell enters 200 ac in Craven Co on easternmost side of Back Cr; border: Thos Jones; paid; P made out.

1910 (9). Feb. 25, 1746/7 Levi Truhitt enters 800 ac in Craven Co on head of Moselys Cr, on S side of Neuse R, & above Nichs Culbert; Pet. made out.

1911 (10). Feb. 25, 1746/7 Josias Jones enters 100 ac in Beaufort Co on S side [of] head of Great Bay, "a small" distance from head of Lamberts Cr, & runs on both sides of said creek; paid; P made out.

1912 (11). Feb. 25, 1746/7 Nathaniel Everit enters 200 ac in Onslow Co on NE

New R, below mouth of Horse Swamp, & joins the lands "taken up"; P made out.

1913 (12). Feb. 25, 1746/7 Jonathan Taylor enters 200 ac in New Hanover Co; border: Jona Taylor "his father" and runs up N side of Goshan [Swamp]; paid; P made out.

1914 (13). Feb. 25, 1746/7 Elias Legardere enters 150 ac in Craven Co on S side of Neuse R, oposite Charltons ferry, & being "the" low grounds; P made out.

1915 (14). Feb. 26, 1746/7 Major Croom enters 200 ac in Johnston Co on N side of Neuse R; border: back of Jno Williams and William Williams line; paid; P made out.

page 229
1916 (15). Feb. 26, 1746/7 John Windows enters 200 ac in Johnston Co on head of Fork Br; border: Lester's line on N side of Neuse R; P made out; paid.

1917 (16). Feb. 27, 1746/7 George Kernegee enters 100 [written over 70] ac in Craven Co on Vine Swamp and on Rattlesnake Br; border: Fredrick Isler and his own land; P made out.

1918 (17). Feb. 27, 1746/7 George Kernegee 50 ac in New Hanover Co on "the" Beaverdam and W side of Spring Br; border: his lines; Pet. made out.

1919 (18). Feb. 27, 1746/7 Saml Silby enters 600 ac in Hyde Co on S side of Maramasket Lake; border: a place called the pines, runs down the lake, & "back"; paid; Pet. made out.

1920 (19). Feb. 27, 1746/7 David Dunn enters 200 ac in Craven Co; border: his head line, runs "up and down", & over a branch a prong of Swifts Cr; Griffith Dr; P made out.

1921 (20). Feb. 27, 1746/7 John Lingfield enters 200 ac in Craven Co; border: N side of land where he lives and runs up to John Arthur's; Griffith Dr; P made out.

1922 (21). Feb. 27, 1746/7 Edmund Wiggins enters 200 ac in Craven Co; border: Eves' line at Deep Cr, runs "out", & to "the" river; Griffith Dr; P made out.

page 230
1923 (22). Feb. 27, 1746/7 Moses Fogg enters 300 ac in Craven Co on N side of Neuse R; border: John Arthur's line and runs "out & up"; Mr. Griffith Dr; P made out.

1924 (23). Feb. 27, 1746/7 Thomas Dudley enters 100 ac "of marsh land" in Onslow Co; border: Thos Week's [or Wick] land on "the" island opposite "Boague" Inlet; Mr. Starkey Dr; paid; P made out.

North Carolina Land Entries 1735-1752

1925 (24). Feb. 27, 1746/7 Anthony Charlescraft enters 100 ac in Onslow Co on mouth of Pometa Br and runs on both sides; being the land where he lives; Mr. Starkey Dr; paid; P made out.

1926 (25). Feb. 27, 1746/7 William Stevens enters 200 ac in Johnston Co on S side of Neuse R and on Falling Cr; border: joins his own line; paid; P made out.

1927 (26). Feb. 27, 1746/7 Jacob Farrow enters 400 ac in Currituck Co; border: a live oak on head of Folleys Cr, runs N5E 780 poles along his own line to a water oak, E 160 poles to the sea side, & along the sea to the beginning; Mr. Craven Dr; P made out.

1928 (27). Feb. 27, 1746/7 Jas Perkins enters 200 ac in Beaufort Co on N side of Bear [or Baar] R, on N side of Vandemos Cr, & both sides of "the same"; W "Carrethirs" Dr; P made out.

page 231
1929 (28). Mar. 3, 1746/7 Jno Willison enters 200 ac in Carteret Co; being where he lives on Nelsons Bay; paid; P made out.

1930 (29). Mar. 3, 1746/7 William Sheppard Foster enters 300 ac in Craven Co on S side of Brices Cr; includes his improvements; R Moore esq Dr; P made out.

1931 (30). Mar. 3, 1746/7 John Simpson enters 200 ac in Carteret Co on the next island E of Great Island in Core Sound; Col. Lovick Dr; P made out.

1932 (31). Mar. 3, 1746/7 Gilbert Clark enters 150 ac in Bladen Co on NE side of Upper Little R, about a mile below "the" falls, & four miles from "the" main river; Armstrong Dr; P made out.

1933 (32). Mar. 3, 1746/7 Joseph Carruthers enters 100 ac in Johnston Co on W side of Loosing Swamp; border: Thomas Rollins; between Loosing Swamp and "the Survanna"; Jos Carruthers Dr; P made out.

1934 (33). Mar. 3, 1746/7 John Bell enters 200 ac in New Hanover Co on E side of Waggamaw R; border: about 0.75 miles above Thomas Bell's; R Moor Dr; P made out.
1935 (34). Mar. 3, 1746/7 Jas Alston enters 300 ac in Craven Co; between Spring's line and land of George Linnington deceased on Core Cr; paid; P made out.

page 232
1936 (35). Mar. 3, 1746/7 Stephen Wallis enters 200 ac in Craven Co on Bogue Banks, at the first swatch next to "the" great hamock, N of said hamock, & runs NE; paid; P made out.

1937 (36). Mar. 3, 1746/7 Jno Hicks enters 100 ac in Carteret Co on "the" fork of Newport R; Col. Lovick Dr; Pet. made out.

1938. Mar. 3, 1746/7 Edward Clark enters 200 ac in New Hanover Co on Bear Br, on NE side of Black R, & about a mile from the river; border: about 8 miles from James Portwint; S Swann Dr; P made out.

1939. Mar. 3, 1746/7 Anthony Laeir [or Lavir] sr enters 150 ac in Onslow Co; border: his own land on N side of NW New R; S Swann Dr; P made out.

1940. Mar. 6, 1746/7 Alexr. McCulloch enters 400 ac in Craven Co on S side of Neuse R; between Graves' land, Arapnall's land, & the river; being "partly" an island opposite Beaslys Island; P made out.

page 233 "Entry Book begun at Wilmington" Nov. 16, 1746
page 234 [blank page]

page 235 "Entrys of Land [entered] at Wilmington" Nov. 18, 1746 [out of order by date; belongs before No. 1902 above]
1941. Nov. 18, 1746 Jno Chapman enters 200 ac in Craven Co on N side of Neuse R; border: begins at Duck Cr and runs down the river; Mr. Griffith Dr.

1942. Nov. 18, 1746 Nathl. Waters enters 200 ac in Johnston Co on E side of Bear Cr; border: Jos Dawson and runs up the creek; Mr. Griffith Dr.

1943. Nov. 18, 1746 Jas "Mcelwean" enters 640 ac in Craven Co; between said Mcelwean's "plantation" and Neuse R on N side "thereof"; border: Stringer's line; Mcelwean Dr.

1944. Nov. 19, 1746 Saml Richardson enters 100 ac in Bladen Co; border: Russell's upper line on N side of Cross Creek and runs "up"; paid.

1945. Nov. 19, 1746 Wm Kellet enters 300 ac in Johnston Co on S side of Buck Br and on Falling Cr; being the "plantation" where he lives; paid; rites returned [Mat Whitfield Dr--lined out].

1946. Nov. 19, 1746 Edwd. Vann enters 300 ac in New Hanover Co on N side of Goshen Swamp; being the "plantation" where he lives; paid; rites returned [Mat Whitfield Dr--lined out].

1947. Nov. 19, 1746 Jonatha. Murray enters 100 [or 130] ac in New Hanover Co on E side of Cypress Cr; border: a red oak and runs up the creek; Mathew Whitfield Dr; paid "I R".

page 236
1948. Nov. 20, 1746 John Fonvielle enters 288 ac in Craven Co on N side of

North Carolina Land Entries 1735-1752

Neuse R and upper side of Batchelders Cr; border: his own corner; McWean Dr.

1949. Nov. 20, 1746 Robt Mills enters 200 ac in Bladen Co on S side of Little R; border: Jno McCoy's upper line and runs "up and out".

1950. Nov. 20, 1746 Jno Arrington enters 200 ac in Bladen Co on S side of Great P D River; border: Gallahorn's upper line and runs "up and out".

1951. Nov. 20, 1746 Jno Berry [Solomn. Hughes--lined out] enters 200 ac in Bladen Co; border: Sena's back line and runs up his line.

1952. Nov. 20, 1746 Jas Adams enters 300 ac in Bladen Co on lower side of Hitchcocks Cr; border: his line and runs "up & out".

1953. Nov. 20, 1746 Robt. Lee enters 200 ac in Bladen Co on S side of Rocky R; border: below McCulloh's line, at mouth of a little branch, & runs "out and up".

page 237
1954. Nov. 20, 1746 Wm Fryar enters 100 ac in New Hanover Co on S side of Little Coharee Cr, on the marsh on the creek, & runs "up"; Mr. Swann Dr.

1955. Nov. 20, 1746 Jno "Fitzjarrald" enters 200 ac in Bladen Co; border: Thos Red's lower line on S side of Great P D River; at a place called Pleasant Hill.

1956. Nov. 20, 1746 David Provender enters 100 ac in Bladen Co; border: Wm Phillips' lower line on S side of Great P D River and runs "out & up".

1957. Nov. 20, 1746 Jos Lahaune enters 200 ac in Craven Co on a branch of Falling Cr; border: Wm Stevens' land; at a place called Thunder Swamp on S side of Neuse R.

1958. Nov. 20, 1746 Wm Gourly enters 400 ac in Johnston Co on N side of Neuse R and N side of Mockison Swamp; border: said Gourley's [sic] line and runs up the swamp.

1959. Nov. 20, 1746 John Harper enters 320 ac in Craven Co on N side of Trent R; border: on W side of Wm Owens land, joins "the same", begins on the river side, & runs "up".

page 238
1960. Nov. 20, 1746 Wm Forskue enters 100 ac in Hyde Co; border: on S side of Mathias Tyson's line, on E side of Matchapungo R, & E side of Slades Cr.

1961. Nov. 20, 1746 Benjamin Fordham enters 100 ac in Craven Co on N fork of Batchelders Cr on S side; at a place called Limbo.

1962. Nov. 20, 1746 John Benson enters 150 ac in Craven Co on N and S sides of Batchelders Cr; border: above Saml Mackubin's land.

1963. [entire entry lined out] John Wilkins [or Willims] enters [blank] ac in Craven Co; [being] a warrant for running the surplus of his resurvey.

1964. Nov. 20, 1746 Johna. Calkins enters 200 ac in New Hanover Co; border: his own land on NW side of Waucomaw R and "chiefly" swamp.

1965. Nov. 20, 1746 Benja. Brocket enters 200 ac in Craven Co on Black Br; border: Mr. Fred Jones, Mr. Wm Willson, & near Brices Cr; Herritage Dr.

1966. Nov. 21, 1746 Geo Gould esq enters 640 ac in Bladen Co on the "third" northern branch of Jones Cr and E side of Pee Dee R; Mr. Gould Dr.

1967. Nov. 21, 1746 Geo Gould esq enters 1,000 ac in Bladen Co on S side of Browns Cr and "out".

1968. Nov. 21, 1746 Geo Gould esq enters 640 ac in Bladen Co in the fork of Mountain Cr and on E side of Pee Dee R.

page 239
1969. Nov. 21, 1746 Joseph Ford and Anne Smith enter 400 ac in Bladen Co on N side of Great P D River; border: James Denson's upper line and runs "out & up"; paid.

1970. Nov. 21, 1746 John Clark enters 500 ac in Bladen Co on N side of P D River; border: Phil Hinson and runs "out & down"; paid.

1971. Nov. 21, 1746 Jno Clark enters 400 ac in Bladen Co on S side of P D River; border: John Westfeild's [sic] upper line and runs "out & up"; paid.

1972. Nov. 21, 1746 Wm Herritage enters 350 ac in Craven Co; border: ["the corner tree of"--lined out] his own line on E side of Jimmys Cr; Herritage Dr.

1973. Nov. 21, 1746 Edwd. Outlair enters 100 ac in New Hanover Co in the fork of Indian old field Br; border: Wm Whitefield; Jas McWaine Dr.

1974. Nov. 21, 1746 Wm Cheek enters 200 ac in Bladen Co on N side of Little R; border: Jno Cheek's upper corner and runs "out & up"; Jas McWaine Dr.

1975. Nov. 21, 1746 Wm Sawser enters 300 ac in Johnston Co on N side of Neuse R, at Marshy Br, & runs on both sides; J Rice Dr.

page 240
1976. Nov. 21, 1746 Rice Price enters 150 ac in Johnston Co on a branch of

Stoney Cr; includes his improvement; J Rice Dr.

1977. Nov. 21, 1746 Wm Coleman enters 200 ac in Bladen Co on N side of P D River; border: Jolus Francis' land; J Rice Dr.

1978. Nov. 21, 1746 Abra. Boyd enters 300 ac in Bladen Co on N side of P D River, on N side of Little R, & on Cheeks Cr; J Rice Dr.

1979. Nov. 21, 1746 Abra. Colson enters 100 ac in Bladen Co on N side of P D River and Hinsons Cr; border: an oak and runs on "both sides"; J Rice.

1980. Nov. 21, 1746 Walter Gibson enters 200 ac in Bladen Co on S side of P D River; being where he lives; J Rice.

1981. Nov. 21, 1746 John Oates enters 400 ac in New Hanover Co on N side of Goshan Swamp and on White Oak Swamp ["begins at a white oak being the land he lives on"--lined out]; paid.

1982. Nov. 21, 1746 Pat. McVicers enters 300 ac in New Hanover Co; border: on N side of Red "Crea" [or brea], 0.5 miles "on" N side of Pursley's old place, & on W side of Widows Cr on Black R.

page 241
1983. Nov. 21, 1746 Pat. McVicers enters 300 ac in New Hanover Co; border: Alexr. Calven's upper line near Black R.

1984. Nov. 21, 1746 John "Dicson" enters 640 ac in New Hanover Co on NW side of NE Cape Fear R; border: a small branch that makes out of the main branch called Elder Br, "a little" below said Dixon's Path, & runs "down"; paid.

1985. Nov. 21, 1746 David Bumpos enters 50 ac in Onslow Co near mouth of NE New R; border: Mr. Mabson's corner, runs down the NE [River], & up the NW [River]; paid.

1986. Nov. 21, 1746 Jacob Powell enters 100 ac in Johnston Co on Bucks Br, below Marsh Br, & "up"; paid.

1987. Nov. 21, 1746 Heny. Jacob Wells enters 200 ac in New Hanover Co on Stocking head Br; border: Timo. Murphy's line and runs down both sides of the branch.

page 242
1988. Nov. 21, 1746 Fras. Irvin enters 300 ac in Bladen Co on S side of great Pedee R; border: Jno Giles' lower line, in Walker's Island, & runs "out and down".

1989. Nov. 21, 1746 Edwd. Stofford enters 100 ac in New Hanover Co on S side of Waggomau R; border: Thos Bell's land; R Moor Dr.

1990. Nov. 21, 1746 Jno Williams enters 400 ac in Craven Co; border: his own line in Mill Creek Marshes and runs up the same; includes Isaac Williams' "plantation"; J W Dr.

1991. Nov. 21, 1746 Jno Hollaway enters 150 ac in Craven Co on Half Moon Swamp; between the land he bought of Corns. Loften, "his" bounded tree, & Russell's; paid J R.

1992. Nov. 21, 1746 Jno Hilliard enters 100 ac in Craven Co; between Danl Simons' land and Pollock's line; paid J R.

1993. Nov. 21, 1746 Jno Hilliard enters 150 ac in Craven Co on S side of Trent R; border: Jno Simons and Martin Bender's land; paid J R.

1994. Nov. 22, 1746 Richd. Miller enters 200 ac in New Hanover Co on Maxwells Swamp; border: a red oak and runs on both sides; known as Chambers folley; paid.

page 243
1995. Nov. 22, 1746 John Miller enters 200 ac in New Hanover Co; border: on S side of Mr. McCullock's land and "his" line on the branches of Black R; Jno Samson Dr.

1996. Nov. 22, 1746 John [or Jehu] Davis enters 400 ac in Bladen Co on S side of Pe Dee R and on Thomas Cr; border: a hickory; R M Dr   "made out to this".

1997. Nov. 22, 1746 Daniel Shipman enters 300 ac in Bladen Co on NW side of Brown marsh Swamp about a mile above "the" western prong; paid.
1998. Nov. 22, 1746 Wm Hester enters 300 ac in Bladen Co on W side of White Marsh; border: on upper side of Roger Haynes' land; paid.

1999. Nov. 22, 1746 Wm Cheek enters 200 ac in Bladen Co on Cheeks Cr, above Buffelow licks, & runs "out and up"; paid.

2000. Nov. 22, 1746 Heny. Faltenberry enters 100 ac in Bladen Co on N side of P D River, at mouth of Naked Cr, & runs down "the same".

2001. Nov. 22, 1746 Jno Hornbeack enters 200 ac in Bladen Co on N side of P D River at mouth of Mountain Cr.

2002. Nov. 22, 1746 Brewer Simsson [or Simxson] enters 200 ac in Bladen Co on S side of P D River; border: a marked oak at the mouth of a branch and runs up the river.

North Carolina Land Entries 1735-1752

page 244
2003. Nov. 25, 1746 Fras. Stringer enters 100 ac in Johnston Co on N side of Loosing Swamp; border: Mr. McClendon's line and runs up both sides of the swamp.

2004. Nov. 25, 1746 Christ. Harrison enters 100 ac in Johnston Co on W side of Bear Cr; between said Harrison and Robt. Parks.

2005. Nov. 25, 1746 John Yeates enters 300 ac in Craven Co in the fork of Juniper Swamp and on SE side "thereof"; paid McWaine Dr.

2006. Nov. 25, 1746 John White enters 100 ac in Bladen Co on Jones Cr; includes his "Dary" house; called Poplaar Springs; M Rowan Dr.

2007. Nov. 25, 1746 John Clark enters 250 ac in Bladen Co on N side of great P D River; border: said Clark's lower line and runs "up"; paid; P made out.

2008. Nov. 26, 1746 Edward Greffeth enters 400 ac in Bladen Co at mouth of Solomon Cr on N side of Great P D River and runs "down"; known as Suchberry folley; P made out.

2009. Nov. 26, 1746 Wm Dry enters 300 ac in Bladen Co on S side of Rocky R about 3 miles above mouth of said river; border: below Mr. McCulloh's land and runs "up"; P made out.

page 245
2010. Nov. 26, 1746 Wm Dry enters 400 ac in Bladen Co on Thompsons Cr; border: Jehu Davis, "his" upper line, & runs on both sides of the creek "upwards"; P made out.

2011. Nov. 26, 1746 Wm Dry enters 300 ac in Bladen Co on Jones Cr, at mouth of a little branch, &runs on both sides of the branch; P made out.

2012. Nov. 26, 1746 Wm Dry enters 300 ac in Bladen Co on Thompsons Cr; at a place called Jack in the Ashes "his" Camp and runs on both sides of the creek; P made out.

2013. Nov. 26, 1746 Jno Wright and Wm Dry enter 200 ac in New Hanover Co; being "several" isalnds "on" Cape Fear R; border: opposite [Gov.--lined out] Burrington's and Wm Lithgow's lands; P made out.

2014. Nov. 26, 1746 Hector McNeal enters 200 ac in Bladen Co on SW side of NW Cape Fear R, in the fork of Gum Br, &on upper side of Lower Little R; Mr. McCullock; P made out; paid.

page 246

North Carolina Land Entries 1735-1752

2015. Nov. 27, 1746 Allen Sloan enters 200 ac in New Hanover Co on "a place" called White Oak Br and on E side of Black R; includes his improvement; paid; P made out.

2016. Nov. 27, 1746 Jno Sampson enters 400 ac in Bladen Co on S side of great Pedee R; border: John Westfield's upper line and runs "out & up"; P made out.

2017. Nov. 27, 1746 Jno Sampson enters 368 [written over 300] ac in New Hanover Co on Cohera R on E side and about 4 miles from said Sampson's "plantation"; P made out.

2018. Nov. 27, 1746 Edwd. Griffith enters 320 ac in New Hanover Co; border: Jno Simpson's line; includes Hoop Pole Br part of Turky Br; P made out.

2019. Nov. 27, 1746 Alexr. McCulloh enters 500 ac in Bladen Co about 1.5 miles above the mouth of Great Cr and runs "out & up"; P made out.

2020. Nov. 27, 1746 Job How [or Hore] enters 500 ac in New Hanover Co on Smiths Cr; border: Thos Axom's line; Patn. made out.

2021. Nov. 27, 1746 Moordock McCraney enters 200 ac in Bladen Co on SW side of Little R, at Barbecu Cr, & runs "up"; Pet. made out.

page 247
2022. Nov. 28, 1746 Mordock McCraney enters 100 ac in Bladen Co on SW side of NW Cape Fear R; border: his own upper line and runs "up"; P made out.

2023. Nov. 29, 1746 Samuel Baker enters 200 ac in Bladen Co; border: on upper part of Mr. Wyer's land on Baker's Mill Cr; paid; P made out.

2024. Nov. 29, 1746 Jno Wright enters 320 ac in New Hanover Co on Burnt Coat Br on NE Cape Fear R; border: Jas Green's land and runs "up"; P made out.

2025. Nov. 29, 1746 Henry Simons [Roger Moore--lined out] enters 1,000 ac in New Hanover Co on N side of Old Town Cr; border: Col. Maurice Moore deceased's land and on said creek; R Moor Dr; P made out.

2026. Dec. 1, 1746 Antho. Miller and Geo Miller enter 240 ac in New Hanover Co on S side of SE branch of Black R; border: 3 miles below Jas Williams, begins at a cypress, & runs up the branch; paid; P made out.

2027. Dec. 3, 1746 Rufus Marsden enters 640 ac in Bladen Co on S side of NW branch of Black R; border: about 5 miles "by land" above George Moore's "late" survey and begins at a hickory "levell" about a mile above Poplar Cr; P made out.

page 248

2028. Dec. 3, 1746 Thos Johns enters 150 ac in New Hanover Co on Island Cr; between Jno Cook's "plantation" where he lives and NE River; J Smallwood Dr; Pet. made out.

2029. Dec. 4, 1746 Thos Harrold enters 200 ac in Craven Co on S side of Trent R; border: Alexr. Steel and Christr. Stanbough; P made out.
2030. Dec. 4, 1746 Thomas Hobber enters 300 ac in Johnston Co on S side of Neuse R; border: a little marsh on S side of Buck Br; includes his improvements; P made out.

2031. Dec. 4, 1746 Thos Nelson enters 300 ac in Craven Co on W side of a branch of [or "at"] mouth of South R; R Lovet Dr; P made out.

2032. Dec. 4, 1746 Benja. Fuzzell enters 320 ac in New Hanover Co; border: Rd James' [or Jones] upper line on S side of NE River; being where he lives; N R; P made out.

2033. Dec. 5, 1746 John Rice enters 400 ac in Craven Co [being] a marsh; between Thos Graves and Jno Deep's "front" lines, above Graves ferry, & on S side of Neuse R; P made out.

2034. Dec. 5, 1746 James McWean enters 60 ac in Craven Co; being an island of marsh opposite Linkfield's ferry on Neuse R; P made out.

page 249
2035. Dec. 5, 1746 Richd. Lovett enters 10 ac in Craven Co; border: about 0.75 miles above his "plantation", "in the middle" of Trent R, & "opposite" the land where he formerly lived.

page 250 [blank page]
page 251 "Entry Book for Land" Mar. 1747
page 252 [blank page]

page 253
2036. Mar. 15, 1747/8 Jonathan Taylor enters 200 ac in New Hanover Co on head of Bare Marsh, on "the" branch, & runs "up"; Pet. made out and W made out.

2037. Mar. 15, 1747/8 Peter Hendrickson enters 150 ac in Craven Co; border: Arthur Johnston and Mr. Warranton on Wahoe Cr, joins Neuse R, & up "the" great savannah.

2038. Mar. 15, 1747/8 Philip Trapnal enters [blank] ac in Craven Co on Williams Br of "the" Southwest [Cr ?].

2039. Mar. 15, 1747/8 William Smith enters 150 ac in Johnston Co on S side of Neuse R in the fork of Falling Cr; border: Paces ferry and runs "up" to Edwd.

Dudley's bounds.

2040. Mar. 15, 1747/8 William Smith enters 200 ac in Johnston Co on N side of Neuse R; border: "from" Jno Fitzgerald's to Bass' upper line and then to Philip Pearce's.

2041. Mar. 15, 1747/8 Wm Baston Whitford enters 640 ac in Craven Co on N side of Neuse R and NW side of "the main" Swifts Cr; border: "a" Poplar Br, runs up the branch, & down.

2042. Mar. 15, 1747/8 James Calef enters 640 ac in Beaufort Co on S side of Pamplico R "on Blounts" [Cr ?]; border: joins land formerly Samuel Slade's.

page 254
2043. Mar. 15, 1747/8 Jacob Folkenburry enters 100 ac in Bladen Co on S side of Pedee R; being where he lives.

2044. Mar. 15, 1747/8 John Bush enters 200 ac in New Hanover Co on Beaverdam Br and on S side of Cohera R.

2045. Mar. 15, 1747/8 Joseph Jackson enters 300 ac in Craven Co on both sides of Hen Coop Br and runs up the branch.

2046. Mar. 15, 1747/8 Southey Rew enters 300 ac in Craven Co on S side of Neuse R; between land formerly beloning to Gould and William Hodgson; paid; P made out; W made out.

2047. Mar. 15, 1747/8 Florence Sex enters 100 ac in Craven Co "on" mouth of Crooked Run; border: Thos Frederick and Stephen Swilley; P made out.

2048. Mar. 15, 1747/8 John Stanly enters 100 ac in Craven Co; border: George Counce and runs up Chinkapin Cr; P made out; W made out.

2049. Mar. 15, 1747/8 Nathan Smith enters 150 ac in Craven Co on S side of Neuse R and W side of Slocums Cr; border: Jno Colling's.

2050. Mar. 15, 1747/8 James Paget enters 200 ac in Onslow Co on W side of New R; border: Thos Johnson's beginning tree "at" a gum on the river side and runs up the river to Cox's Cr.

page 255
2051. Mar. 15, 1747/8 Martin Futch enters 100 ac in Craven Co; border: Edwd. Frank's land on White Oak Pecoson.

2052. Mar. 15, 1747/8 Edward Outlaw enters 200 ac in New Hanover Co on Bear Marsh; border: Heny. Goodman's line and runs up the marsh; Pet. made out.

2053. Mar. 15, 1747/8 William Islar enters 100 ac in Craven Co at Poplar Spring and runs down Beaver Cr; paid; P made out; W made out.

2054. Mar. 15, 1747/8 Edmd. Barnecastle enters 350 [written over 300] ac in Craven Co on S side of Neuse R and on Adams Cr; border: Thos Nelson and Jno Freebody; Pet made out; W made out.

2055. Mar. 15, 1747/8 William Teague enters 100 ac in Johnston Co on S side of Neuse R; between George Roberts' land and land where Robt. Hinds lives; Petn. made out; W made out.

2056. Mar. 15, 1747/8 Robert Jones enters 250 ac in New Hanover Co on N side of Goshen [Swamp]; known as the Beaverdam where John Moor has built a log house.

2057. Mar. 15, 1747/8 William Dunbar enters 300 ac in Beaufort Co on S side of Pamplico R and E side of main branch of Blounts Cr; border: said Dunbar's upper corner tree and runs a miles; paid; made out.

2058. Mar. 15, 1747/8 Jno Williams enters 640 ac in Craven Co; border: Col. Moseley's back line and runs up Aligator Br.

page 256
2059. Mar. 15, 1747/8 Joseph Carruthers enters 125 [written over 175] ac in Johnston Co on N side of Neuse R; border: Lazarus Turner; "Dec. 20, 1747"; P made out; W made out.

2060. Mar. 15, 1747/8 Mark Harefoot enters 200 ac in Beaufort Co; border: his own land; includes the "Cod" of Bells Neck; paid; P made out; W made out.

2061. Mar. 15, 1747/8 John Hoard enters 300 ac in Beaufort Co on S side of Bear R and head of Trent Cr on both sides "thereof"; border: James Hume; includes Thos Smith's improvements; paid; P made out; W made out.
2062. Mar. 15, 1747/8 Cason Brinson enters 200 ac in Currituck Co on N side of old Maramuskeet Cr; border: Joseph Midget; paid; P made out; W made out.

2063. Mar. 15, 1747/8 Willm, Carruthers jr enters 300 ac in [blank] Co on W side of "Goone" Cr; includes Tager's [or Fager's] old field; paid; P made out; W made out.

2064. Mar. 15, 1747/8 John Hover enters 300 ac in Craven Co on E side of Little Cotentnea Cr; border: the upper fork and runs down "towards" the lower fork; known as the Hen Cook [? page torn]; Griff. Dr; W made out.

2065. Mar. 15, 1747/8 Charles Hopkin enters 150 ac in Craven Co; border: Edwd.

Bryan's "side" line,runs up the creek taking in an island, & "towards" Joseph Dawson's; Griff. Dr; W made out.

2066. Mar. 15, 1747/8 Charles Hopkin enters 100 ac in Craven Co; border: Edwd. Bryan's "other" side and runs up to Bear Br; Griff. Dr; W made out.

page 257
2066A. [the following lined out] Thomas Armstrong [blank] in Bladen Co on S side of NW Cape Fear R [this probably relates No. 2078 on page 259 below].

2067. Mar. 15, 1747/8 Philip Shute enters 450 ac in Beaufort Co on S side of Pamplico R, on W side of Blounts Cr, runs up Herring Run, & back; paid; W made out; P made out.

2068. Mar. 15, 1747/8 Nathan Archibald enters 250 ac in Beaufort Co on S side of Tar R; known as Indian Wells; paid; P made out; W made out.

2069. Mar. 15, 1747/8 WmAlligood enters 100 ac in Beaufort Co on N side of Pamplico R; border: John McReil's line on N side of White oak Pond and runs "back"; paid; P made out; W made out.

2070. Mar. 15, 1747/8 James Adams enters 600 ac in Beaufort Co on S side of Pamplico R, head of Blounts Cr, on "main" Herring Run, on main Beaverdam Neck, runs "both sides", & down the main run; paid; made out.

2071. Mar. 15, 1747/8 Robt. Ryley enters 250 ac in Johnston Co on NW of Mrs. Powell's Br and on S side of Neuse R; paid; P made out; W made out.

2072. Mar. 15, 1747/8 Robt. Ryley enters 300 ac in Johnston co on S side of Neuse R; between mouth of Sleepy Cr and Mrs. Powel's [sic] line along the river side; paid; P made out; W made out.

2073. Mar. 15, 1747/8 Saml Pikes enters 350 ac in New Hanover Co on Porter "or" Carvers Cr "NW"; border: Chas Benbow on N side; P made out; W made out.

page 258 [only 4 entries on this page]
2074. Mar. 15, 1747/8 Isaac Overman enters 200 ac in New Hanover Co on a branch of "said" creek; border: W side of Chas Benbow; P made out; W made out.

2075. Mar. 15, 1747/8 Mary [written over Geo] Musgrove enters 640 ac in New Hanover Co on "the" fork of Old Town Cr; between Benson and Musgrove; P made out; W made out.

2076. Mar. 15, 1747/8 James Willis enters 200 ac in Craven Co; between Randolph Fisher and Christian Ipock; border: begins at Hardy Bryan's tan kill; Jno Carruthers Dr; P made out; W made out.

2077. Mar. 15, 1747/8 Henry Bishop enters 100 ac in [Onslow Co ?] in the fork of "the" prong of Beasley's Swamp; N R Dr; P made out; W made out.

page 259
2078. Mar. 15, 1747/8 Thomas Armstrong enters 160 ac in Bladen Co on S side of NW Cape Fear R and on Boyle [or Coyl] Spring Br of Rockfish Cr; border: below Roberts' Path and runs "up"; paid; W made out.

2079. Mar. 15, 1747/8 Howel Brewer enters 200 ac in Bladen Co on NE side of Deep R above Tyces Cr; border: an oak marked "four paths"; paid; W made out.

2080. Mar. 15, 1747/8 John Page enters 300 ac in Johnston Co on N side of Little R; border: near Robert Rayford's line and runs down the river; paid; P made out.

2081. Mar. 19, 1747/8 [sic] Thomas Coor, of Little R, enters 300 ac in Johnston Co on N side of Neuse R and on Charles' Br; paid; P made out.

2082. Mar. 15, 1747/8 James Herburt enters 640 ac in Johnston Co; border: Wm Pate's upper line and runs "up with the" swamp; paid; Pet. made out; Warrt. made out.

2083. Mar. 15, 1747/8 James Herburt enters 200 ac in Craven Co; border: "Lawyer" Lovet's lower bounded tree and runs down great Cotentnea Cr with said creek; paid; made out.

2084. Mar. 15, 1747/8 Jacob McClendon enters 300 ac in Bladen Co on S side of Deep R, below the mouth of Buck Cr, runs "up", & "turns to" the river; paid; P made out.

page 260
2085. Mar. 15, 1747/8 Edwd. Rawlins enters 100 [written over 200] ac in New Hanover Co on NE Cape Fear R at a "place" called Rattlesnake Br; being where he lives; paid; P made out.

2086. Mar. 15, 1747/8 Joel McClendon enters 300 ac in Bladen Co on S side of Deep R, about 2 miles above Buck Cr, at Rocky ford, & runs "up"; paid; P made out.

2087. Mar. 15, 1747/8 Thos Holmes enters 200 ac in Bladen Co on E side of Little R of Pedee R [or Little Peedee R], below mouth of Thickety Cr, & runs "up"; paid; Pet. made out; W made out.

2088. Mar. 15, 1747/8 James Jewers [or Tewers] enters 400 ac in Bladen Co on Bufflow Br running into Little R of P D River on E side about 3 or 4 miles above mouth of Buffelow "Cr"; P made out.

2089. Mar. 15, 1747/8 Nicholas Porter enters 100 ac in Johnston Co; border: a pine on W side of Pole Cat Swamp and runs "up"; P made out.

2090. Mar. 15, 1747/8 Wm Palmer enters 100 ac in Johnston Co; border: Richd. Wiggins' corner near "the" Race Ground, runs down said Wiggins' line to "the" river, down the river to Jno Blackman's corner, up "said" line, & "off"; P made out.

page 261
2091. Mar. 15, 1747/8 Aaron Smith enters 200 ac in Johnston Co on S side of Neuse R, at mouth of "a" mirey branch on Stoney Run, & runs down the run; P made out.

2092. Mar. 15, 1747/8 Jno Coupland enters 150 ac in Bladen Co; between Henry Philips and Duncan Campbell on NW Cape Fear R on N side; P made out.

2093. Mar. 15, 1747/8 Moses Binton enters 100 ac in Johnston Co on S side of Black R; where he lives near Greens Path; P made out.

2094. Mar. 15, 1747/8 Abra. Taylor enters 100 ac in Johnston Co on N side of "SW" [Southwest] Creek and on a Gum Br; paid; Pet. made out.

2095. Mar. 15, 1747/8 James Cheyne enters 300 ac in Craven Co; at a place where Robt. Hays [or Nays] lives; includes Wm Anderson's Spring Br; paid; P made out.

2096. Mar. 15, 1747/8 Abra. Coulston enters 150 ac in Bladen Co on N side of Great P D River; border: Saml Bay's land and runs "down"; paid; Pet. made out.

2097. Mar. 15, 1747/8 Moses Tyler enters 400 ac in New Hanover Co on S side of Cohera Swamp and on White oak Br; bruns "up" from mouth of said branch; paid; Pet. made out.

page 262
2098. Mar. 15, 1747/8 Benjamin Blount enters 300 ac in Johnston Co in the fork of Bear Cr, on lower side of Peter's Br, & runs "up"; paid; Pet. made out.

2099. Mar. 15, 1747/8 Joseph Bryan enters 200 ac in Craven Co on N side of Swifts Cr; border: on Hart's line and runs down Pameta Swamp.

2100. Mar. 15, 1747/8 Hardy Bryan enters 200 ac in Craven Co on S side of Neuse R; border: a red oak on Mark Philips' line and runs up the lower side of "a" Cain Br.

2101. Mar. 15, 1747/8 Rd. Bass enters 200 ac in New Hanover Co; border: John Bush's line on N side of Black R and runs down Cohera Cr; paid.

2102. Mar. 15, 1747/8 Owen Jones and Thos Cummins enter 250 ac in Onslow Co; border: Col. Goodward's "front" and runs W to Snoad's "front" on the mouth of Queens Cr; paid; Pt. made out; W made out.

2103. Mar. 15, 1747/8 Henry Oberry enters 640 ac in Bladen Co on N side of Drowning Cr below "the" path; paid; P made out; W made out.

2104. Mar. 15, 1747/8 Henry Oberry enters 350 ac in Bladen Co in the fork of Little P D River and below "the" path; paid; P made out; W made out.

2105. Mar. 15, 1747/8 Robt. Lee enters 200 ac in Johnston Co in the fork of Mill Cr and on Watery Br; Smith Dr; P made out; W made out.

2106. Mar. 15, 1747/8 Jno Holley enters 300 ac in New Hanover Co on N side of Great Cohera R, on a marsh branch, & runs "down"; paid; P made out; W made out.

2107. Mar. 15, 1747/8 Jas Perdue enters 100 ac in Craven Co on N side of Nuce R and E of Swifts Cr; between his own line and Abraham Warren; paid; made out; P made out.

page 263
2108. Mar. 18, 1747/8 Moses Arnold enters 50 ac in Craven Co in John Hill's Neck; border: runs between his own line and Jno Holts' on N side of Great Swamp; Forbes paid; made out; P made out.

2109. Mar. 18, 1747/8 John Williams enters 200 ac in Craven Co on N side of Neuse R and on Bear Br; border: Christn. Ipock's line and runs "out"; Forbes Paid; made out; P made out.

2110. Mar. 18, 1747/8 Joseph Gadd enters 300 ac in Beaufort Co on S side of Tarr R and W side of "Chi-codd" Swamp; bat mouth of the Second Bottom from Pine log Br, runs up the swamp, & "back"; Forbes paid; made out; P made out.

2111. Mar. 18, 1747/8 Robert Thompson enters 250 ac in Beaufort Co on S side of Tarr R, on S side of Indian "Wai" Swamp, & in Clay Root Meadow; Forbes paid; made out; P made out.

2112. Mar. 18, 1747/8 Arthr. Blackman enters 150 ac in New Hanover Co on N side of Great Cohera Cr; being the "plantation" where Thos Odam lives; paid; P made out; W made out.

2113. Mar. 18, 1747/8 Joseph Taylor enters 300 ac in Johnston Co on S side of Neuse R; border: his own land; paid; Pet. made out.

page 264

2114. Mar. 18, 1747/8 Major Croom enters 100 ac in Johnston Co on N side of Nuce R and upper side of Lower faling Cr; Jas Carruthers Dr; P made out.

2115. Mar. 18, 1747/8 Andrew Bass enters 400 ac in Johnston Co; border: John Pait's and Martin Trantom's lines on N side of Nuce R; Jas Carruthers Dr; P made out.

2116. Mar. 18, 1747/8 John Taylor [or Taytor] enters 300 ac in Johnston Co on S side of Nuce R and near head of Faling Cr on S side; Jas Carruthers Dr; P made out.

2117. Mar. 18, 1747/8 Thomas McClendon enters 640 ac in Johnston Co; border: Daniel Streen's [or Stran] upper corner and runs up Rainbow [Cr] to his own line; Jas Carruthers Dr; P made out.

2118. Mar. 18, 1747/8 Saml Rollings enters 200 ac in Johnston Co on both sides of Joy's Marsh; border: Williams, Harper, & Joyl; Jas Carruthers Dr; P made out.

2119. Mar. 18, 1747/8 Saml Rollings enters 200 ac [in Johnston Co] on S side of Rainbo Cr; border: joins "a" Long Br and runs across Rainbo Cr; Jas Carruthers Dr; P made out.

2120. Mar. 18, 1747/8 George Bruton enters 200 ac [in Johnston Co ?] on Loosing Swamp; border: below John Powel's land and on upper side of "said" branch; Jas Carruthers Dr; P made out.

2121. Mar. 18, 1747/8 Thos Blake enters 200 ac in Johnston Co; border: Blunt's upper corner, on Peters Br, & runs up said branch; Jas Carruthers Dr.

page 265

2122. Mar. 18, 1747/8 Samuel Beasley enters 150 ac in Craven Co; border: his own land where he lives; paid; Pt. made out.

2123. Mar. 18, 1747/8 Robert Taylor enters 100 ac in Johnston Co on Indian Cabbin Br; border: near Gilbert Dever's line; paid; P made out; W made out.

2124. Mar. 18, 1747/8 Wm Taylor enters 200 ac in New Hanover Co on Goshen Swamp; border: near Jonathan Taylor's line; paid; P made out; W made out.

2125. Mar. 21, 1747/8 [sic] Joseph Oates enters 100 ac in New Hanover Co on N side of "Gosham" Swamp; between White oak Br and Dry Pond Br; known as Indian Old Field and runs "out and up"; being the land where he lives; paid by Jno [sic] Oates; mo; W made out; Pet. made out.

2126. Mar. 21, 1747/8 John Rouse enters 50 ac in Johnston Co on N side of Neuse

R; border: his own head line and runs "out"; paid; Pet. made out; Wart. made out.

2127. Nov. 16, 1747 [sic] Richard Caswell jr enters 200 ac in Johnston Co on N side of Neuse R; border: lands "taken up by" John Williams & Gilbert Dever and runs "out"; Pet. made out; Wart. made out.

page 266
2128. Mar. 21, 1747/8 William Rutledge enters 100 ac in Craven Co on S side of Nuse R and on a place called Stumpy Point; between Wm Handcock sr and Wm Handcock jr; being his "plantation"; paid to Hodges; P made out; paid Apr. 5, 1749 to I R.

2129. Jan. 1747 [sic] Richard Caswell jr enters 200 ac in Johnston Co on N side of Nuse R; border: Lazarus Turner; includes the improvement made by Thos Hussleton; paid; Pet. made out; Wart. made out.

2130. Mar. 21, 1747/8 Mathew Wilkes enters 200 ac in Craven Co on S side of Trent R; known as Deep Neck; paid; Pet. made out; W made out.

2131. Mar. 21, 1747/8 John Collins enters 200 ac in Craven Co on W side of Slocumbs Cr; border: Robt. Coleman's line and runs up said creek; E G Dr.

2132. Mar. 22, 1747/8 Sml Middleton enters 100 ac in Onslow Co on N side of Half Moon Swamp and at a place called Beaverdams; border: Joseph Sumner; Starkey Dr; paid; P made out.

2133. Mar. 22, 1747/8 Lewis Trott enters 200 ac in Onslow Co in Sherlows Swamp, on White Oak R, & on each side of the swamp; includes where he lives; Starkey Dr; paid; P made out.

page 267
2134. Mar. 22, 1747/8 John Lambert enters 300 ac in Craven Co on N side of Little [River--lined out] Contenty [Cr], about a mile from mouth of Sandy Run, & runs up said run; E G Dr.

2135. Mar. 22, 1747/8 Simon Jones enters 400 ac in Beaufort Co on S side of Tarr R, on lower end of Round Island, at head of Chicod Cr, & runs "back"; paid to Mr. Rice; P made out; W made out.

2136. Mar. 22, 1747/8 Coleman Roe enters 200 ac in Beaufort Co on S side of Pamplico R and E side of head of Durham's Cr; known as Perdue's; paid to Mr. Rice; P made out; W made out.

2137. Mar. 22, 1747/8 Henry Goodman enters 100 ac in New Hanover Co on N side of NE Cape Fear R, on both sides of Sam's Br, begins at mouth of said branch, & runs "up"; paid T C; P made out; W made out.

2138. Mar. 22, 1747/8 Reading Blount enters 640 ac in Beaufort Co on S side of Pamplico R; border: his own line at Chocawinity Bay and runs up "the" great swamp; paid; Pet. made out.

page 268
2139. Mar. 22, 1747/8 Jas McRee enters 200 ac in New Hanover Co; border: an oak on NW side of Dark Br and joins his brother William's line; paid; P made out; W made out.

2140. Mar. 22, 1747/8 John [written over Solo] Smith enters 100 ac in New Hanover Co on John McRee's Br; includes said branch about 0.25 miles from Wm McRee's line; paid; P made out; W made out.

2141. Mar. 22, 1747/8 Alexa. Blackshire enters 100 ac in Onslow Co on Rattlesnake Br above Tuckahoe Cr; E G Dr; P made out; W made out.

2142. Mar. 23, 1747/8 James Roads enters 200 ac in Johnston Co on S side of Falling Cr; border: Wm Bush's upper line and runs "up & back"; P made out; W made out.

2143. Mar. 23, 1747/8 John Holmes enters 100 ac in Onslow Co on E side of NW [written over NE] New R; border: Benjamin Essom; paid; P made out; W made out.

2144. Mar. 23, 1747/8 Wm Williams enters 360 ac in Onslow Co; border: a hickory on Smiths Cr and runs up the branches of the creek; paid; P made out.

2145. Mar. 23, 1747/8 Wm Williams enters 360 ac in Onslow Co; border: mouth of Persimon Br near John Mayner and joins David Jones; paid; P made out.

2146. Mar. 24, 1747/8 Abra. Boyd enters 350 ac in Johnston Co; border: the beginning tree of Ambros Ayres' upper survey on Falling Cr; includes the land between Thos McClendon, said Ayres, & said Boyd; paid; P made out; W made out.

page 269
2147. Mar. 24, 1747/8 John Tison enters 350 ac in Bladen Co on N side of Deep R, at a little creek below Merry Maid Camp, & about 5 miles from the "plantation" where "one" Richardson lives; paid; P made out; W made out.

2148. Mar. 24, 1747/8 John Rogers enters 200 ac in Craven Co [on E side of--lined out]; border: Caldom's line on Cotentnea Cr and runs along said line; paid; P made out; W made out.

2149. [entire entry lined out] John Franks enters 100 ac in Craven Co; between

North Carolina Land Entries 1735-1752

John Worsley and Martin Frank; [paid--erased].

2150. Mar. 24, 1747/8 Joseph Pitman enters 100 ac in Craven Co on E side of mouth of Adams Cr and on "the end" of Live oak Hamock Cr; border: runs ESE, then "across" to Thos Nelson's line, & to Pine Point; Col. Lovick Dr; paid; P made out; W made out.

2151. Mar. 24, 1747/8 Henry Smith enters 250 ac in Craven Co; border: a red oak on N side of Beseley's Swamp and runs along the swamp to "the" road; P made out; W made out.

2152. Mar. 24, 1747/8 George Eiland enters 150 ac in Johnston Co on S side of Neuse R, "a little" above mouth of Sleepy Cr, & on "the" high hills at mouth of "the" Beaverdams; paid; P made out; W made out.

page 270
2153. Apr. 1, 1748 John Mead enters 100 ac in Onslow Co in "the" fork of White Oak R [path--lined out]; border: a "piece" of land now in possession of John Starkey esq; George Johnson Dr; P made out; W made out.

2154. Apr. 2, 1748 James Conner enters 400 ac in Johnston Co on N side of Little R; being the place where Denns. Foley lives; paid to Mr. Rice; P made out; W made out.

2155. Apr. 2, 1748 James Conner enters 200 ac in Craven Co on N side of Falling Cr, on "the" great marsh, & runs down the marsh from upper end of the marsh; paid to Mr. Rice; P made out; W made out.

2156. Apr. 2, 1748 Hope Willets enters 100 ac in New Hanover Co on SW side of Lockwoods folley R; border: mouth of Doe Cr at Scenkin Moore's corner, runs W along his line, & S down the river; N R Dr; P made out; W made out.

2157. May 4, 1748 John Campbell enters 200 ac in Craven Co on N side of Neuse R, on Northwest Cr, "a little" above mouth of Upper Broad Cr, & runs up Northwest Cr; recd. per "7.6".

page 271 [only two entries on this page]
2158. May 11, 1748 George Cogdell enters 200 ac in Carteret Co on E side of White "Oake" R; border: James Noble's back line and "into the woods"; Col. Lovick, the collector, Dr.

2159. May 12, 1748 Joseph Bailey enters 200 ac in Carteret Co; border: David Bailey's land at Piney Point, in Core Sound, & runs up Nelsons Cr; recd. per "7.6".

page 272 [blank page]
page 273 "Entries of Land at Sept. Court of Claims 1747"

North Carolina Land Entries 1735-1752

2160 (1). Sept. 29, 1747 Moses Tyler enters 150 ac in New Hanover Co; border: Oates' line on E side of White Oak Br and runs up the branch; P made out.

2161 (2). Sept. 29, 1747 Joshua Sarsnutt enters 100 ac in Johnston Co; between Sarsnutt's line and Col. Roberts deceased; P made out.

2162 (3). Sept. 29, 1747 Peter Mathews enters 200 ac in Craven Co on Vine Swamp; between John Isler and Mr. Lane; at a place called old cabbin; P made out.

2163 (4). Sept. 29, 1747 Philip Trapnall enters 200 ac in Craven Co on S side of Neuse R; between Thomas Graves and Cullen Pollock; P made out.

2164 (5). Sept. 29, 1747 Henry Goodman enters 200 ac in New Hanover Co N of Bear Marsh and along "the" side of the same; border: Jonathan Taylor's line and runs up the marsh from his line; P made out.

2165 (6). Sept. 29, 1747 Thos Hardy enters 100 ac in Beaufort Co being an island known as Beacon Island; P made out.

2166 (7). Sept. 29, 1747 Edward Outlaw enters 100 ac in New Hanover Co on N side of Goshen Swamp and on Indian Br; P made out.

2167 (8). Sept. 29, 1747 George Outlaw enters 100 ac in New Hanover Co on N side of Goshen Swamp and on Miln Br; P made out.

2168 (9). Sept. 29, 1747 Richard Malpas enters 550 ac in New Hanover Co on N side of Goshen Swamp, on Great Br, & begins "below and runs up"; P made out.

2169 (10). Sept. 29, 1747 Jno Baker enters 100 ac in Johnston Co; border: the land he bought of Thomas Rawlins on N side of Loosing Swamp, runs up N side, "across", & down to his land bought of Wm Johnston; P made out.
page 274
2170 (11). Sept. 29, 1747 William Coleman enters 200 ac in Bladen Co on N side of Pedee R, on Mountain Cr, & above "the" great fork; P made out.

2171 (12). Sept. 29, 1747 John Grigg enters 100 ac in Bladen Co on S side of Pedee R; border: joins the waggon ford at "the" Grassy Island and runs "up"; P made out.

2172 (13). Sept. 29, 1747 Thos Smith enters 200 ac in Craven Co on S side of Neuse R and on E side of Slocums Cr; border: runs "up" from Turkey Neck; known as Indian Landing; P made out.

2173 (14). Sept. 29, 1747 William Islar enters 100 ac in Craven Co; border: Jacob Ipack's line on S side of Bever Cr and runs "up"; P made out.

North Carolina Land Entries 1735-1752

2174 (15). Sept. 29, 1747 Hardy Bryan enters 100 ac in New Hanover Co on W side of Great Cohera Cr; border: Gardner's head line on Great Marsh and runs "up"; P made out.

2175 (16). Sept. 29, 1747 Edward Griffith enters 640 ac in Craven Co in the main fork of Swifts Cr and on S side of the main branch; border: Willis' line and runs up to the great Crane Ponds; P made out.

2176 (17). Sept. 29, 1747 William Smith enters 300 ac in Craven Co on S side of Neuse R; border: the "side" line of his own land, runs down Ferry neck on S side of Slocoms Cr, & down said creek; P made out.

2177 (18). Sept. 29, 1747 Thomas Mason enters 200 ac in Hyde Co; border: his own land on N side and runs to Row [or Rose] Bay; P made out.

2178 (19). Sept. 29, 1747 Hardy Bush enters 200 ac in New Hanover Co on Little Cohera Cr of Black R on "the" West side; border: a prong of said creek about 1.5 miles below where Wm Frayar formerly lived and runs "up"; P made out.

2179 (20). Sept. 29, 1747 Jacob Reasonover [Jno Grenade--lined out] enters 150 [100--lined out] ac in Craven Co on E and W sides of Mill Cr "without side" of Pollock's line; P made out.

2180 (21). Sept. 29, 1747 Thomas Campean enters 640 ac in Beaufort Co on S side of Pamplico R and on E side of Goose Cr; between Jno Tindall & Robt Campean and runs to Jno May's line; P made out.

2181 (22). Sept. 29, 1747 Richd. Mason enters 250 ac in Craven Co; border: Wm Storey's line "called" Cabbin Br "whereon" said Mason lives and runs on both sides of said branch; P made out.

page 275
2182 (23). Sept. 29, 1747 Jno mann enters 300 ac in Johnston Co on S side of Bear Cr; border: Christo. Harrison's line and runs "up"; P made out.

2183 (24). Sept. 29, 1747 Robt. Rayford enters 100 ac in Johnston Co on both sides of Little R; being the land where he has a mill; P made out.

2184 (25). Sept. 29, 1747 Jno Rouse enters 350 [640--lined out] in Johnston Co on Bare Creek Marsh; border: near a place called Horse Point on both sides of the creek and runs down in the marsh; P made out.

2185 (26). Sept. 29, 1747 Wm Powell enters 200 ac in Johnston Co on S side of Neuse R; border: on upper side of and joins upper part of land of John Powell deceased known as Sapona land; P made out.

2186 (27). Sept. 29, 1747 Jno Echolls enters 50 ac in Beaufort Co on head of Goose Cr on S side; known as Putnell's Ridge; P made out.

2187 (28). Sept. 29, 1747 Wm Simpson enters 200 ac in New Hanover Co; between James Moor & the late Archibald Hamilton on Old Town Cr and runs along the creek; P made out.

2188 (29). Sept. 29, 1747 Jno Stewart enters 100 ac in Craven Co on N side of Herritages Br and on N side of Trent R; P made out.

2189 (30). Sept. 29, 1747 Jno McCurray enters 100 ac in New Hanover Co on Cypress Cr; border: runs up said creek from a pine; P made out.

2190 (31). Sept. 29, 1747 Wm Foscue enters 250 ac in Beaufort Co on S side of Pamplico R, in the fork of Oyster Cr, [on] a ridge know as Ray's Ridge, & runs "over" the head of each branch; P made out.

2191 (32). Sept. 29, 1747 Joseph Sanderson enters 50 ac in Craven Co; border: Frederick Jones' back line and on upper end of Round Pecoson at a place called the Sand Hills; P made out.

page 276
2192 (33). Sept. 29, 1747 Richd. Foscue enters 100 ac in Craven Co being a savannah; border: a line in dispute between Wm Brice and Benja. Sanderson; at a place called the Race Paths; P made out.

2193 (34). Sept. 29, 1747 James Clayton enters 640 ac in Hyde Co on N side of Maramuskeet Lake; border: "the" Willows and runs West; P made out.

2194 (35). Sept. 29, 1747 John "New berry" enters 500 [written over 300] ac in Bladen Co on Jno Harmor's mill Cr; border: "the" river, Stones Island, & begins at Camp's upper corner; P made out.

2195 (36). Sept. 29, 1747 Wm Ellet enters 100 ac in Craven Co on N side of Neuse R; between Swifts Cr and the prong of said creek called Fork Swamp in "the" point; P made out.

2196 (37). Sept. 30, 1747 Wm Pate enters 150 ac in Johnston Co on both sides of Little R; border: at "the" Stoney hill and runs down the river; P made out.

2197. Sept. 30, 1747 Stephen Howard enters 300 ac in Onslow Co on N side of New R and at head of Kings Cr; border: a pine; P made out.

2198. Sept. 30, 1747 Habakuk Rusell enters 200 ac in Carteret Co; border: his own land, Bartrim, & runs "out"; P made out.

North Carolina Land Entries 1735-1752

2199. Sept. 30, 1747 Jno Piggot enters 200 ac in Carteret Co inthe fork of old Ned's Cr and on White Oak R; being where said Piggot lives; P made out.

2200. Sept. 30, 1747 Rd. Leath enters 350 ac in Hyde Co in New Currituck [Twsp]; border: Francis Banks; P made out; paid.

2201. Sept. 30, 1747 Thomas Williams enters 200 ac in Beaufort Co on S side of Pamplico R and in the fork of Cuckolds Cr; border: his own line; P made out; paid.

page 277
2202. Sept. 30, 1747 Jno Tuley enters 100 ac in Hyde Co on SE side of Rose [or Row] Bay; border: mouth of Thos Mason's pasture Cr, runs up the bay, & "back"; paid; P made out.

2203. Sept. 30, 1747 Moses Arnold enters 200 ac in Craven Co on N side of Great Swamp of Swifts Cr and in Jno Hill's Neck; paid; P made out.

2204. Sept. 30, 1747 Lancaster Lovit enters 200 ac in Carteret Co on N side of Bogue Sound; between Wm Russel and Wm Reed deceased; paid; P made out.

2205. Oct. 1, 1747 Mathias Camp enters 300 ac in Craven Co on S side of Swifts Cr, at a pecoson, & runs up a branch; known as the "fast" land; E G paid; P made out.

2206. Oct. 1, 1747 Thos Stephens enters 200 ac in Craven Co on Hoods Cr near the mouth and runs to Frederick Jones' line; E G paid; P made out.

2207. Oct. 1, 1747 Thos Mason enters 1,000 ac in Hyde Co on E side of Masons Bay, runs to Swan Quarter Bay, & "back"; E G paid; P made out.

2208. Oct. 1, 1747 Wm Fryar enters 100 ac in New Hanover Co at Beaverdam Swamp and on S side of great Cohera Cr; paid; P made out.

2209. Oct. 1, 1747 Moses Tyler enters 150 ac in New Hanover Co on E side of Goshen [Swamp], at head of a little branch, & runs up the swamp; paid; P made out.

page 278
2210. Oct. 1, 1747 Edward Weaver enters 200 ac in New Hanover Co on NE Cape Fear R; border: Edwd. Carter's upper line, runs up "the" swamp, & back of Carter's line; McCulloh Dr; paid; P made out.

2211. Oct. 1, 1747 Jno Phillips enters 150 ac in Bladen Co on Upper Little R about 3.5 miles from "the" main river; paid; P made out.

2212. Oct. 1, 1747 Josiah Chadwick enters 100 ac in Bladen Co on Upper Little R about 2 miles from Jno Philips' "settlement"; paid; P made out.

2213. Oct. 1, 1747 Benja. Foreman enters 300 ac in Bladen Co on N side of Deep R, above mouth of Buck Cr, & runs "up"; paid; P made out.

2214. Oct. 1, 1747 Henry Kingsberry enters 300 ac in Bladen Co on great Pedee R, at the fork of Hedgecocks Cr at a forked pine, runs westerly "over" the main creek, & "down"; paid; P made out.

2215. Oct. 1, 1747 Benja. Adams enters 150 [written over 100] ac in New Hanover Co on Angola Cr, in the swamp of said creek, & runs along said swamp; paid; P made out.

2216. Oct. 1, 1747 Jeremiah Swann enters 200 ac in Bladen Co; border: S of McCulloh's land on S side of Rocky R, a white oak, & runs "down"; paid; P made out.

2217. Oct. 1, 1747 Jeremiah Swann enters 200 ac in Bladen Co on Lanes Cr and S side of Rocky R; border: S of McCulloh's land; paid; P made out.

page 279
2218. Oct. 1, 1747 Jno Newberry enters 545 ac in Bladen Co on N side of Great Pedee R, at the fords of Grassy Islands, & runs "up"; paid; P made out.

2219. Oct. 1, 1747 Thomas George [Jno Hamore--lined out] enters 320 ac in Bladen Co on SW side of Great Pedee R, at Tuckeho Br at a path, & runs "down" [Wm Kemp's upper corner and runs up--lined out]; paid; P made out.

2220. Oct. 1, 1747 Nichs. Smith enters 450 ac in Bladen Co on Buck Cr running out of S side of Deep R; border: runs "down" from a white oak; paid; P made out.

2221. Oct. 1, 1747 Joseph Waters enters 200 ac in Bladen Co on S side of Rocky R; border: S of McCulloh's land above Poplar Springs; paid; P made out.

2222. Oct. 2, 1747 Edward Cox enters 100 ac in Craven Co; border: upper corner tree of Jabez Mott's land on S side of Neuse R; paid; P made out.

2223. Oct. 2, 1747 James Salter enters 100 ac in Carteret Co on S side of Three hatt Swash and on Core banks "in Carteret Co"; P made out; W H.

2224. Oct. 2, 1747 Henry Bush enters 200 ac in New Hanover Co on a long marsh at a branch on S side of great Cohera Cr and runs up said marsh; E G; P made out.

2225. Oct. 2, 1747 Mark Philips enters 100 ac in New Hanover Co at a marsh on W side of Little Cohera Cr and runs up said marsh & a swamp; E G; P made out.

North Carolina Land Entries 1735-1752

page 280

2226. Oct. 3, 1747 Benja. Peyton enters 640 ac in Currituck Co between Cape Hateras and Kings Point; border: West line of James Wahab's land; Dr; paid; P made out.

2227. Oct. 3, 1747 Mark Philips enters 640 ac in New Hanover Co; border: Jno Blackman's head line at a branch and runs up said branch; E G paid; P made out.

2228. Oct. 3, 1747 Needham Bryan enters 250 ac in Johnston Co on S side of Black Cr and on a reedy branch about a mile above Green's Path; paid; S Smith Dr; P made out; paid [sic].

2229. Oct. 3, 1747 Thos Castellaw enters 200 ac in New Hanover Co; border: Moses Tyler's lower line, runs from there to head of Maple Br, & down; paid; P made out.

2230. Oct. 3, 1747 Thos Pugh enters 300 ac in New Hanover Co on S side of Six Runs Cr and "in" mouth of Rowans br; P made out.

2231. Oct. 3, 1747 Joseph Carruthers enters 300 ac in Craven Co; border: Jno Carruthers sr "his" line and runs up "the" River Ridges; Dr; P made out.

2232. Oct. 3, 1747 Joseph Carruthers enters 300 ac in Johnston Co; border: Spears' line on S side of Nuce R, runs "across" to Southwest Cr, & down said creek; Dr; P made out.

page 281

2233. Oct. 4, 1747 John [write over] Grenade enters 100 ac in Craven Co on westmost branch of Mill Cr "without side" Pollock's lines; [this entry same as No. 2179 except for enterer's name] I R; P made out.

2234. Oct. 4, 1747 James Innis [or Innes] enters 400 ac in New Hanover Co on Mulberry Br, Long Cr, & W side of NW Cape Fear R; border: Capt. Innis' own line; McCulloh; paid; P made out.

2235. Oct. 4, 1747 William Farris enters 100 ac in New Hanover Co; border: said Farris' "plantation" called Fairfield on upper branches of Rockfish Cr, runs "off" his own line, & "back"; McCulloh; paid; P made out.

2236. Oct. 4, 1747 Jacob Thompson enters 50 ac in Johnston Co; being the "plantation" where he lives near head of Gum Br; J Carruthers Dr; P made out.

2237. Oct. 4, 1747 Saml Willis [John Abetee ?--lined out] enters 300 ac in Craven Co in the fork of Swifts Cr, on Little Swifts Cr, runs across to the main creek swamp, & down the same; E G Dr; paid; P made out; Warrant made out.

2238. Oct. 4, 1747 William Routledge enters 100 ac in Craven Co on eastermost prong of Slocumbs Cr; border: William Wickliff; paid; P made out.

page 282
2239. Oct. 5, 1747 George Clemment enters 200 ac in Bladen Co on Little R of Pedee R [or Little Peedee R]; border: Charles Robinson's upper line and runs up both sides of Little R; paid; P made out.

2240. Oct. 5, 1747 James Mackilwean enters 300 ac in Bladen Co on N side of Great Pede R; border: Mr. Edwd. Griffith's line and runs "up"; Dr; P made out.

2241. Oct. 5, 1747 Philip Millar enters 200 ac in Bladen Co on S side of NW Cape Fear R and on a branch on the head of Upper Little R beyond the head of "Leek" Cr; paid; P made out.

2242. Oct. 5, 1747 Francis Britten enters 100 ac in Bladen Co on S side of Ash pole Swamp; part of which is "an" Indian old field and is known as Howard's old field; Swann Dr; P made out.

2243. Oct. 5, 1747 Fras. Faulks enters 150 ac in Bladen Co on Willow Br; between Bear Swamp and Ash pole [Swamp] on S side of Ash pole Swamp; Swann Dr; P made out.

2244. Oct. 5, 1747 Othniel Strahawn enters 200 ac in New Hanover Co on S side of the main branch of Rockfish Cr and near the fork of the branch Mr. Farris' land is on; Swann Dr; P made out.

2245. Oct. 5, 1747 James Portevint enters 200 ac in New Hanover Co on Bear Br and on Black R; border: about 3 miles from the "plantation" where said Portevint lives on NE side of Black R; Swann Dr.

page 283
2246. Oct. 5, 1747 Stephen Lee enters 100 ac in Onslow Co; border: Wallis' upper line on head of Chappel Br; W Hedges Dr; P made out.

2247. Oct. 5, 1747 George Brinn enters 640 ac in Craven Co between Goose Cr and Broad Cr; known as Pitts' Neck; Hedges Dr; P made out.

2248. Oct. 5, 1747 Thomas Smith enters 640 ac in Craven Co on S side of Neuse R; border: Nathan Smith's upper corner tree at head of Otter Cr and joins Jacob Taylor's land; T Smith Dr; P made out.

2249. Oct. 5, 1747 George Ward enters 100 ac in New Hanover Co in the fork of Poplar Swamp; border: on NE side of James Barnes' "plantation"; N R Dr; I R paid; P made out.

North Carolina Land Entries 1735-1752

2250. Oct. 5, 1747 George Kernegee enters 100 ac in Craven Co on E side of Musle Shell Cr and N side of Chinkapin Road; Kernegee Dr; P made out.

2251. Oct. 5, 1747 Joshua [written over Cashua] Grainger enters 200 ac in New Hanover Co on Wolf Swamp and near Barran Inlet Cr; Grainger Dr; P made out.

2252. Oct. 5, 1747 Isaac Overton enters 200 ac in Bladen Co on Carver's Mill Cr "near or joins" Charles Benbow's "plantation"; N R Dr; [P made out--lined out].

2253. Oct. 5, 1747 Saml Pike enters 300 ac in Bladen Co on Carver's Mill Cr; N R Dr; [P made out--lined out].

2254. Oct. 5, 1747 Saml Tindall enters 200 ac in Beaufort Co on S side of Pamplico R and on Campbells Cr; between John Echolls and John Tindall; border: "the" swamp and marsh; Dr; P made out.

2255. Oct. 6, 1747 Wm Whithurst enters 600 ac in Carteret Co on head of Capt. John Nelson's Bay at Hunting Quarter; border: Jno Nelson jr; Col. Lovick Dr.

page 284
2256. Oct. 6, 1747 Thomas Nelson enters 200 ac in Carteret Co on Core Banks; border: John Nelson's live oak Hamock, runs N to Thos Nelson's whale bone survey, & joins "thereto"; paid; P made out; [David _?_ --lined out].

2257. Oct. 6, 1747 Jno Nelson enters 300 ac in Carteret Co on Core Banks; between Three hatts [Swamp ?] and runs South to "the" white hill; paid; P made out.

2258. Oct. 6, 1747 Saml Johnston esq enters 1,000 ac in Bladen Co about 8 miles below "the" Governor's land on Deep R; Pet. made out.

2259. Oct. 6, 1747 Alexander Chambers enters 200 ac in New Hanover Co on NE branch of Maxwells Cr; border: runs "up" from a white oak; includes his improvements; paid; P made out.

2260. Oct. 6, 1747 James Heaton enters 150 ac in Johnston Co on S side of Nuce R and below Irons' land; Dr; P made out.

2261. Oct. 6, 1747 Charles Ryal enters 480 ac in New Hanover Co on Beverdam Br of Falling Cr; border: William Kellet's upper corner, runs up the branch, & "back"; paid; P made out.

page 285
2262. Oct. 7, 1747 Andrew "Morgin" enters 300 ac in Craven Co on NW "run" of Upper Broad Cr; border: the "plantation" where said Andrew Morgin lives; P made out; fees paid W H; to be paid to I R; paid; paid [sic].

191

North Carolina Land Entries 1735-1752

2263. Oct. 7, 1747 John Prescot enters 100 ac in Craven Co on S side of Swifts Cr; border: a creek "pacoson" and runs down the creek; P made out; [Mr. Graves--lined out]; since paid to Hedges; to be paid to I R.

2264. Oct. 7, 1747 Henry Everit enters 300 ac in Beaufort Co on S side of Pamplico R and on W side of Goose Cr; border: Aaron Spring's line and runs "up" James Campean; Peyton Dr; P made out; paid.

2265. Oct. 7, 1747 Henry Heaton enters 150 ac in Johnston Co on N side of Neuse R; being Chietly [or chiefly] Pecoson; Dr; P made out.

2266. Oct. 7, 1747 Chas Cogdale enters 200 ac in Carteret Co on W side of Newport R and near or joins Glovers Hamock; paid by "H"; P made out.

2267. Oct. 8, 1747 John Holland enters 200 ac in New Hanover Co on a branch of Cohera Cr on E side and runs up the branch; paid; P made out.

page 286 [only 5 entries on this page]
2268. Oct. 8, 1747 Michl. Higgins enters 200 ac in Johnston Co; border: on E side of a "piece" of land "taken up" by Robt. Parks and joins said Parks' Walnut Creek land; paid; P made out.

2269. Oct. 9, 1747 Anthony Lewis enters 200 ac in Onslow Co; border: at Half Moon Swamp, runs S20E 120 poles, N75E 180 poles, N20W 200 poles, S5W 80 poles to Sumner's line, & a "straight" line to the beginning; Swann Dr; Pet. made out.

2270. Oct. 9, 1747 Wm McDead enters 200 ac in New Hanover Co on S side of Six Runs Cr about 4 miles below Jno Sampson and near a marsh; Sampson Dr; P made out.

2271. Oct. 9, 1747 Andw. Moorman enters 400 ac in Bladen Co about 3 miles above mouth of Rockey R on E side; F McWaine Dr; paid; P made out.

2272. Oct. 9, 1747 Philip Mew enters 100 ac in Craven Co on Joshua's Cr whereon he has made improvements; Fonvielle Dr; P made out.

page 287 [blank page]

page 288 Septr. Entry book shows warrants chd. by I R whole fees he accounts with Secretary
page 289 Entry Book of Sept. Court 1748
d
page 290 [blank page]
page 291

North Carolina Land Entries 1735-1752

2273. Sept. 27, 1748 Thomas Jones enters 600 ac in Johnston Co on W side of Bear Creek "run"; border: on said run near the horse ford and runs "down".

2274. Sept. 27, 1748 Florence "Sex" enters 200 ac in Craven Co on N side of Trent R and runs E; at a place called Haw Neck.

2275. Sept. 27, 1748 Jno Williams enters 300 ac in Craven Co on N side of Trent R; at a place called Joshua's Resolution; P made out; I R Dr.

2276. Sept. 27, 1748 Jno Row enters 560 [written over 640] ac in Johnston Co on Ground Nut Swamp on N side of Neuse R, on both sides of Beaverdam Cr, & runs "up"; Pet. made out; T R Dr.

2277. Sept. 27, 1748 George Bell enters 200 ac in Carteret Co on Core Sound; border: a line formerly called Nicholas Daws line, runs with said line, & "round" to the beginning "by water"; Pet. made out; [paid--lined out]; T R Dr.

2278. Sept. 27, 1748 Jno Beck enters 400 ac in Johnston Co on S side of Neuse R; border: Wm Teague's back line and runs "out" to "the" great marsh.

2279. Sept. 27, 1748 Richard Byrd enters 200 ac in Johnston Co on S side of Falling Cr and on N side of Neuse R above Gum Swamp; border: George Wiggin's land and runs up the creek.
page 292
2280. Sept. 27, 1748 James Clerk enters 100 [written over 150] ac in New Hanover Co on W side of Black R, where "one" Larkins formerly built a cabbin, & about 2 miles below Fewoxes; paid; P made out.

2281. Sept. 27, 1748 Jno Turner enters 400 ac in Beaufort Co on W side of Darhams Cr; border: Wm Davis' line on the creek swamp and runs up the swamp of said creek to Juniper Swamp; paid.

2282. Sept. 27, 1748 Lamuel Hatch enters 100 ac in Craven Co near head of Brices Cr.

2283. Sept. 27, 1748 Jno Rouce enters 150 ac in Johnston Co on N side of Neuse R; border: at Wolf trap Br and runs up said Rouce's line.

2284. Sept. 27, 1748 Wm Baker enters 100 ac in Johnston Co on N side of Neuse R; called Jas Muckilroy's clearing.

2285. Sept. 27, 1748 Jno Crowson enters 200 ac in Johnston Co on N side of Neuse R; border: Belk's old house and runs up the river.

2286. Sept. 27, 1748 Saml Ratcliff enters 200 ac in Johnston Co on N side of Neuse R, on N side of Falling Cr, & on both sides of Cabbin Br.

2287. Sept. 27, 1748 Thomas Farmer enters 640 ac in Johnston Co on both sides of Wheat Swamp and on a branch on S side of Great Cotentnea Cr; J R Dr; [paid--lined out]; Pet. made out.

page 293
2288. Sept. 27, 1748 John Abett enters 100 ac in Craven Co on N side of Trent R and on Beverdam Br; border: Edwd. Cummins; paid; Pet. made out; [faint] to J Carruthers.

2289. Sept. 27, 1748 Jno Fonvielle enters 100 ac in New Hanover Co on a small branch on "the" eastermost side of Six Runs Cr above Gardner's Path; includes both sides of the main run; J R Dr; P made out.

2290. Sept. 27, 1748 James Clayton enters 200 ac in Hyde Co on SW side of Marmuskeet Lake at head of Hyrne Bay; J R Dr; P made out.

2291. Sept. 27, 1748 Richard caswell jr enters 200 ac in Johnston Co on N side of Neuse R and on each side of the forks of Briery Br; border: above Mr. Rice's land and about a mile below Cotentnea Path; paid; P made out.

2292. Sept. 27, 1748 Andrew Killet enters 100 ac in Johnston Co on Buck Swamp of S Falling Cr and S side of Neuse R; where a little house stands; P made out.

2293. Sept. 27, 1748 Jno Rice enters 200 ac in Craven Co on S side of Trent R; border: Jno Frederick and the land that was formerly Jno Hilliard's which "the latter" sold to Stephen Swilley.

2294. Sept. 27, 1748 Wm Cole enters 200 ac in Johnston Co on S side of Neuse R and on Squirrel Br; border: Jno Grady; J R Dr; P made out.

page 294
2295. Sept. 27, 1748 Patrick White enters 1,000 ac in Hyde Co on S side of Maramuskeet Lake; between Waterman Emery and George Turner; includes the land he bought of Saml Stow; made out; warrant granted.

2296. Sept. 27, 1748 Jno Irons enters 300 ac in Johnston Co on N side of Neuse R; border: Plowman's line "where Belk's lives" and runs "up" to the river; includes "some" part of "the" pecoson; paid by Mr. Boyd; P made out.

2297. Sept. 27, 1748 Wm Belks enters 100 ac in Johnston Co on S side of Neuse R and "high up" Southwest Cr; known as Rd. Roberts folley; paid; P made out.

2298. Sept. 27, 1748 Hams Clark enters 200 ac in Craven Co on Core [or Cow] Cr and at a place called Turkey Delight on E side of said creek; includes both sides "thereof"; J Fonvielle Dr; J R Dr; P made out.

2299. Sept. 27, 1748 Thos Nughs enters 100 ac in Johnston Co on N side of Neuse R and upper side of Falling Cr; paid; Pet. made out.

2300. Sept. 27, 1748 Abraham Boyd enters 100 ac in Johnston Co on N side of Neuse R; border: Alexr. Rouce's survey on S side of Briery Br.

2301. Sept. 27, 1748 Joseph Mercer enters 100 ac in Johnston Co on Cotentnea Cr; border: joins the land where he lives.

page 295
2302. Sept. 27, 1748 Wm Middleton enters 100 ac in New Hanover Co on N side of Cohera Cr and on "a" Beaverdam Br; border: near and above Jno Herring's land.

2303. Sept. 27, 1748 Fras. Benton enters 300 ac in Johnston Co on S side of Neuse R and on Panther Cr; being where he lives; paid; P made out.

2304. Sept. 27, 1748 Jno "Matchitt" enters 200 ac in New Hanover Co on Reedy Br, on W side of Maxwells Cr, & runs "up"; paid; P made out.

2305. Sept. 27, 1748 Edwd. Frank enters 200 ac in Craven Co on Acron Br on N side of Trent R.

2306. Sept. 27, 1748 Elizabeth Hill enters 150 ac in Onslow Co; border: Corns. Bumpos on E side of New R, on both sides of NE New R, & runs up both sides; paid; P made out.

2307. Sept. 27, 1748 Robert Jones enters 300 ac in New Hanover [Johnston--lined out] Co on N side of Goshen Swamp and on a branch that runs out of Goshen Swamp where Jery Railey built a cabbin; J RIce Dr; P made out.

page 296 [only 2 entries on this page]
2308. Sept. 27, 1748 Richd. Becton enters 400 ac in New Hanover Co on NW side of Nichs. Gunnels Folley, where Joseph Esom lives, & near Beverdam Marsh.

2309. Sept. 27, 1748 Mark Driggers enters 100 ac in Craven Co on the branches of Swifts Cr and on S side of Great Swamp; Walter Lane Dr; P made out.

page 297
2310. Sept. 27, 1748 Danl. Connely enters 300 ac in New Hanover Co on NE Cape Fear R and near mouth of Rattlesnake Swamp.

2311. Sept. 27, 1748 Benjamin Clements enters 640 ac in Johnston Co on W side of Bear Cr; between Jumping Run and Christopher Hamson's.

North Carolina Land Entries 1735-1752

2312. Sept. 27, 1748 Benjamin Meridith enters 100 ac in New Hanover Co on E side of Moors Cr; border: below Samll. Averidge; paid; P made out.

2313. Sept. 27, 1748 Simon Player enters 200 ac in New Hanover Co in the fork of Porters [Moors--lined out] Cr; border: Thomas Merick, runs along his back line, & "back"; paid; P made out.

2314. Sept. 27, 1748 John Peterson enters 200 ac in New Hanover Co on a branch of Goshen Swamp where he lives; includes his improvements; paid; P made out.

2315. Sept. 27, 1748 David Smith enters 100 ac in Bladen Co on N side of Lower Little R and NW side of NW Cape Fear R; paid; P made out.

2316. Sept. 27, 1748 William Henderson enters 640 ac in Johnston Co on N side of Ducking Run and runs "across" to Wheats Swamp; Jos Carruthers Dr; P made out.

2317. Sept. 27, 1748 Anthony Arnol enters 200 ac in Johnston Co; between John Wilson and Howel Jones on N side of Nuce R; Jos Carruthers Dr; P made out.

page 298
2318. Sept. 27, 1748 David Smith enters 100 ac in Bladen Co on SW side of NW Cape Fear R, on lower side of Upper Little R, & above the fork of Barbacue Cr; Pet. made out.

2319. Sept. 27, 1748 James Ard enters 60 ac in Johnston Co on great Cotentnea Cr and on Great Marsh; border: near "a tract" said Ard bought of Jno Beverly; paid.

2320. Sept. 27, 1748 Gilbert Kerr enters 200 ac in Johnston Co on S side of great Cotentnea Cr, on S side of Sellers Marsh, & on Walnut old field; paid.

2321. Sept. 27, 1748 Wm Han [or Harr] enters 200 ac in Johnston Co on Button Br; between head of Bear Cr and Cow Br; paid.

2322. Sept. 27, 1748 Wm Mackintosh [Joseph Rd. Nickson--lined out] enters 200 ac in Johnston Co near Powell's Br and on S side of Neuse R; paid; P made out.

2323. Sept. 27, 1748 Wm Williamson enters 150 ac in Johnston Co; border: Blount's line at mouth of Peters Br on E side of Bear Cr; paid.

page 299
2324. Sept. 27, 1748 Richd. Stevens enters 500 ac in Onslow Co on W side of White oak R; border: at a place called Starkey's on head of Ismael Taylor's piney land; paid; P made out.

North Carolina Land Entries 1735-1752

2325. Sept. 27, 1748 Severus Gereld enters 500 ac in Onslow Co on E side of NW New R; between Arther Mopson and Richard Farr [or Fares]; paid; Skibbo Dr; P made out.

2326. Sept. 27, 1748 Samll. Thomas enters 200 ac in Johnston Co on "Horce" Br a prong of Southwest Cr; includes his improvement; Jos Carruthers Dr; P made out.

2327. Sept. 27, 1748 William Collins enters 350 ac in [omitted] Co; border: on Bryri Br below Lov. Homs' land and runs to Bruton's land; Jos Cartuthers Dr; P made out.

2328. Sept. 27, 1748 Jno Witherinton enters 50 ac in Johnston Co; border: his own land he bought of Stringar; Jos Carruthers Dr.

2329. Sept. 27, 1748 Major Croom enters 200 ac in Johnston Co on S side of Neuse R; border: near William Belt's land; J Carruthers Dr; P made out.

2330. Sept. 27, 1748 Henry Canedy enters 200 ac in Johnston Co on N side of Rainbo Cr; [being] a place called Long Marsh; Jos Carruthers Dr; P made out.

page 300
2331. Sept. 27, 1748 Joseph King enters 400 ac in Craven Co on N side of Neuse R, near head of Cypress Br, runs down said branch to Morgans Run, & up said run; Mr. Griffith Dr.

2332. Sept. 27, 1748 Thomas Turnbull enters 800 ac in Bladen Co on Edward Jones' Cr and N side of NW Cape Fear R; paid; P made out.

2333. Sept. 27, 1748 Robt. Nicolson enters 150 ac in Johnston Co on Beils Cr; being the place where he lives; paid; P made out.

2334. Sept. 27, 1748 Thos Farmer enters 200 ac in Johnston Co on N side of Neuse R; border: Benja. Williams' line and runs up the river; paid; P made out.

2335. Sept. 27, 1748 Isaac Willaims enters 200 ac in New Hanover Co on W side of great Cohera Cr and at a place called Bane [or Bare] Marsh; border: a red oak on "said" swamp below where Roger Hodge lives and runs "up"; paid; P made out.

page 301
2336. Sept. 27, 1748 James McManus enters 640 ac in Bladen Co on S [? faint] side of Pedee R, aout 6 miles "or upwards" below Camps ferry, & at a "place" called Mill Cr where there is a small "plantation"; paid; Pet. made out.

2337. Sept. 27, 1748 James McManus enters 300 ac in Bladen Co on S side of Pedee R; border: Camp "the ferryman's" land, below said Camp's land, & runs down the river; paid; P made out.

2338. Sept. 27, 1748 Jno Dees enters 100 ac in Johnston Co on S side of Neuse R, on Black Cr, & on both sides "thereof"; paid; P made out.

2339. Sept. 30, 1748 George Clements enters 100 [written over 200] ac in Bladen Co on upper side of Little R of Pedee R; border: above Chas Robertson's upper line and runs "up" [both sides of Little R--lined out]; Robertson Dr; paid; P made out.

page 302
2340. Sept. 30, 1748 Henry Walker enters 200 ac in Bladen Co on Rockey R; border: mouth of a small branch on upper side of said river about 2 miles from mouth "thereof"; "Roberson" Dr; paid; P made out.

2341. Sept. 30, 1748 Wm Brown enters 100 [written over 200] ac in Bladen Co on Little R; border: a pine near John Stone's line on upper side of said river and runs "down" [both sides of Little R--lined out]; Roberson Dr; paid; P made out.

2342. Sept. 30, 1748 Michl. Mixson enters 100 ac in New Hanover Co on S side of Rowans Swamp below "the" path; SampsonDr; paid; P made out.

2343. Sept. 30, 1748 Thomas Suggs enters 500 ac in New Hanover Co on Peacock Swamp; border: on great Cohera Cr on E side above George Smith; Sampson Dr; paid; P made out.

2344. Sept. 30, 1748 Philip Mew enters 100 ac in Craven Co in the fork of Southwest Cr on S side; Fonvielle Dr; P made out.

page 303
2345. Sept. 30, 1748 Peter Dobuske enters 200 ac in New Hanover Co on Cypress Br at a place called "the" Lake; border: said Lake and runs down S side of the branch; Skibbo Dr; paid; P made out.

2346. Sept. 30, 1748 Henry Philips enters 150 ac in Bladen Co on S side of NW Cape Fear R; border: Duncan Campbell; paid; Pet. made out.

2347. Sept. 30, 1748 Henry Philips enters 80 ac in Bladen Co on S side of NW Cape Fear R; border: upper side of Duncan Campbell; paid; P made out.

2348. Sept. 30, 1748 John Lee enters 400 ac in Johnston Co; between Jno Lee and Jno Ward esq on Neuse R; Petn. made out; paid.

2349. Sept. 30, 1748 Moses Titman enters 500 ac in Johnston Co; border: Col.

Roberts' corner tree, runs 0.5 miles up "the" marsh, to Peter Prevat's land, & up his line; paid; P made out.

2350. Sept. 30, 1748 John Lee enters 400 ac in Johnston Co; between Jno Lee and Jno Ward; border: a hickory and runs up Neuse R; paid; P made out.

page 304
2351. Sept. 30, 1748 Nesbie Mills enters 200 ac in Beaufort Co; border: Moses Tyson's line, runs up Swift Creek Swamp, & "back"; paid; made out; P made out.

2352. Sept. 30, 1748 James Baker enters 300 ac in Beaufort Co on S side of Pamplico R; border: Thos Wessly [or Worsely], Mr. Saltor on Bear Cr, runs "towards the" dividing line, & over "the" main road; made out; paid; Pet. made out.

2353. Sept. 30, 1748 Patrick White enters 1,000 ac in Hyde Co on S side of Maramaskeet Lake; between Wateman Emerey and Geo Turner; includes the land he bought of Saml How; made out; paid; Pet. made out.

2354. Sept. 30, 1748 Isaac Buck enters 200 ac in Beaufort Co at mouth of Cross Swamp and runs up "the" branch of Chicod Swamp; made out; paid; Pet. made out.

2355. Sept. 30, 1748 Simon Barney enters 100 ac in Beaufort Co on S side of Tar R, on SW side of Chicod Swamp, runs down the swamp, & "out"; made out; paid; Pet. made out.

page 305
2356. Sept. 30, 1748 John Clark enters 150 ac in Johnston Co; border: near Roe's line at mouth of Harleys Marsh and runs "down"; [paid--lined out].

2357. Sept. 30, 1748 John Clark enters 100 ac in Johnston Co; border: "a little" above Thomas Banke's line and runs "uptowards" head of Tyson's Marsh; [paid--lined out].

2358. Sept. 30, 1748 Frs. McWean [and ?] Edward Frisbie enters 300 ac in Bladen Co; border: an oak marked "E F" near Thickete Br on S side of Great P D River and runs "down"; paid; P made out.

2359. Sept. 30, 1748 Jno Eleby enters 100 ac in Bladen Co on N side of Great P D River; border: his own land where he lives; paid; P made out.

2360. Sept. 30, 1748 Entheny Cox enters 200 ac in New Hanover Co on E side of Little Cohare Cr above Mark "Fillips" land; paid; P made out.

2361. Sept. 30, 1748 Walter Murrey enters 640 ac in Johnston Co on N side of

Nuce R; between Wilm. Qunney and Wilm. Tegue; border: on the river and runs "out" to Great Marsh; paid; P made out.

2362. Sept. 30, 1748 Jno Temple enters 200 ac in Johnston Co; border: Jno Bracher, on both sides of "Rede" Br, begins "below", & runs "up"; paid; P made out.

2363. Sept. 30, 1748 Thos Temple enters 200 ac in Johnston Co; being where he lives; paid; P made out.

2364. Sept. 30, 1748 Thos Holms enters 150 ac in Bladen Co on N side of Great P D River; border: William Colman's corner in "Beare" Island; being where he lives; paid; P made out.

page 306
2365. Sept. 30, 1748 Jno Gillet sr enters 50 ac in Craven Co on S side of Tuckahoe Cr; border: Alexander Blackskin and runs South.

2366. Sept. 30, 1748 Thos. Williams enters 100 ac in Craven Co on N side of Trent R and runs up Horse Br; paid; P made out.

2367. Sept. 30, 1748 Jno Gillet enters 50 ac in Craven Co on S side of Cypress Cr on upper side thereof at the mouth; Starkey Dr; P made out.

2368. Sept. 30, 1748 Robert Park enters 640 ac in Bladen Co on S side of great Pedee R and above mouth of Brown Cr; border: near his own line and runs "down"; chd.

2369. Sept. 30, 1748 Martin Trentham enters 200 ac in Bladen Co on SW side of NW Cape Fear R; border: a white oak on N side of McFerson's Cr about 3 miles from the river and runs "up"; paid; P made out.

page 307
2370. Oct. 1, 1748 George Cogdale enters 200 ac in Carteret Co on E side of White oak R, on Black Swamp, & runs through said swamp from "high" land to "high" land; Lovick Dr; P made out.

2371. Oct. 3, 1748 Thos Saucer enters 150 ac in Johnston Co on Stoney Cr on N side of Neuse R; border: David Williams; paid; P made out.

2372. Oct. 3, 1748 Abra. Boyd enters 1,000 ac in Johnston Co on N side of Neuse R and on N side of Bucklesberry Pecoson; border: at Horse Point and runs "out"; paid; Pet. made out.

2373. Oct. 3, 1748 Wm Atkins enters 150 ac in Bladen co on S side of Great Pedee R; being the place where he lives; paid; Pet. made out.

2374. Oct. 3, 1748 Burling Hamrudd [Ham Rudd] enters 300 ac in Bladen Co on S side of Great Pedee R and S side of Jones Cr; border: runs "up" from a red oak paid; Pet. made out.
page 308
2375. Oct. 3, 1748 Jno Parsley enters 200 ac in Bladen Co on N side of Rockey R; border: runs "up" from a red oak; paid; P made out.

2376. Oct. 3, 1748 Thos Brooks enters 100 ac in Bladen Co on W side of NW Cape fear R; border: a red oak on upper side of S fork of Cross Cr about a mile from the river; paid; P made out.

2377. Oct. 3, 1748 Martin Trentham enters 100 ac in Bladen Co on S side of NW Cape Fear R and on a branch of Upper Little R known as Martin's vinyard Br; paid; P made out.

2378. Oct. 3, 1748 Jno Williams enters 200 ac in Bladen Co on S side of W prong of Waggamaw R; border: a red oak about 3 miles from Adam's survey; paid; P made out.

2379. Oct. 3, 1748 Thos Armstrong enters 200 ac in Bladen Co on S side of NW Cape Fear R and on Caines Cr, a North branch of Lower Little R; paid; P made out.

page 309
2380. Oct. 3, 1748 Jno Cannon [or Camon] enters 130 ac in Craven Co; border: the upper part of his land and runs up "the" creek.

2381. Oct. 3, 1748 Jno Cannon enters 150 ac in Craven Co on Swifts Cr; between two Horse Branches and runs along "the" branch; Jos Carruthers Dr.

2382. Oct. 3, 1748 Wm Powell enters 200 ac in Craven Co on Swifts Cr; border: Price's land and runs to Vine's land; Jos Carruthers Dr.

2383. Oct. 3, 1748 Ebenezar Ram enters 200 ac in Craven Co; border: Moses Tyce's land and runs to Mills' land; Jos Carruthers Dr.

2384. Oct. 3, 1748 Wm Runn enters 300 ac in Craven Co; border: his own land and runs to Linnington's [or Sinnington] on both sides of Grindal Cr; Jos Carruthers Dr.

2385. Oct. 3, 1748 John Windes enters 100 ac in Johnston Co near head of Walnott Rigg Br; border: Walter Jones; Jos Carruthers Dr; P made out.

page 310
2386. Oct. 3, 1748 Georg. Miller enters 100 ac in Craven Co on N side of Trent

R and on or near head of Joshua's Neck; paid; P made out.

2387. Oct. 3, 1748 Jacob Taylor enters 200 ac in Craven Co on S side of Southwest Cr; known as Great Neck at Ironmine Hill and about 4 miles above Jno Taylor's; paid; P made out; W made out.

2388. Oct. 3, 1748 Joseph Everitt enters 200 ac in Johnston Co on S side of Nuse R and on each side of Horse Marsh; border: Killingsworth; paid; P made out.

2389. Oct. 3, 1748 William Teague enters 200 ac in New Hanover Co at head of NE Cape Fear R and joins Juniper Pond; paid; P made out.

2390. Oct. 3, 1748 William Teague enters 100 [written over 200] ac in Johnston [sic] Co on S side of Nuse R near Slocumbs Marsh; paid; P made out.
2391. Oct. 3, 1748 James Barber enters 150 ac in Johnston Co on N side of Neuse R; border: near Wm Lasser [or Tasser], near Marshy Br, & on E side "thereof".

page 311
2392. Oct. 3, 1748 Mark Mevis enters 100 ac in Craven Co; border: "widdow" Killet's corner on S side of Trent R; Jno Carruthers Dr; P made out.

2393. Oct. 3, 1748 Jno Williams enters 300 ac in Beaufort Co; border: Moses Tyson's line on S side of Swift Cr and runs down the creek.

2394. Oct. 3, 1748 Edwd. Salter enters 400 ac in Beaufort Co on upper side of Chicod Swamp, runs down a branch to "the " dividing line, down the line to a swamp, & up "the same"; paid; Pet. made out.

2395. Oct. 3, 1748 Edwd. Salter enters 1,000 ac in Beaufort Co on lower side of Chicod Swamp, below Round Island, runs up the swamp, & "round"; paid; P made out.

page 312
2396. Oct. 3, 1748 John Clark enters 200 ac in Bladen Co on N side of Great P D River, "on" mouth of Clarks Cr, & runs "up"; R Moor Dr; P made out.

2397. Oct. 3, 1748 John Clark enters 400 ac in Bladen Co on S side of Great P D River and on Rocky R about 3 or 4 miles from the mouth; R Moor Dr; P made out.

2398. Oct. 3, 1748 Jehu Davis enters 640 ac in Bladen Co on Drowning Cr, about a mile or two below "the" old ford, & joins the swamp of the creek on N side; paid; Rowan; P made out.

2399. Oct. 3, 1748 Jno Grooms enters 200 ac in Bladen Co on Drowning Cr; known as Errington's Cowpen; paid; Rowan; P made out.

2400. Oct. 3, 1748 Joshua Herrin enters 300 ac in Johnston Co on the branch where he lives, runs down "the" marsh to "the" creek, & down the creek; paid; P made out.

2401. Oct. 4, 1748 John Adkinson enters 100 ac in Johnston Co on S side of Nuse R; border: John Gradies corner red oak at Herwags Windals "on" Robinsons; paid; P made out.

page 313
2402. Oct. 4, 1748 Nathan Smith enters 250 ac in Craven Co on S side of Neus R and E side of Southwest Cr; border: Mr. Herritage's land which was taken up by Col. George Roberts and being the "plantation" where James Clapt formerly lived; N Smith Dr; P made out.

2403. Oct. 4, 1748 William Ric [or Rie] enters 300 ac in New Hanover Co on S side of Great Cohera Cr and on Mirtle Swamp; border: near mouth of said swamp; E Griffith Dr; John Williams Dr; P made out.

2404. Oct. 4, 1748 Benja Moore enters 250 ac in Bladen Co where Great Swamp joins Little Pedee R and on "the" East side; includes the place called the Bluff; paid; P made out.

2405. Oct. 4, 1748 John Green sr enters 300 ac in Bladen Co; border: a red oak on Water's lower line and joins Warring & James Balding's back line; paid; P made out.

2406. Oct. 4, 1748 Gershon Benbow enters 200 ac in Bladen Co; between his own line and his brother Charles Benbow on S branch of Porters Cr; paid; P made out.

2407. Oct. 4, 1748 George Brown enters 150 ac in Bladen Co on Horse Pond Swamp about a mile from Little Pedee R; includes an old Indian Field; paid; P made out.

page 314
2408. Oct. 4, 1748 William Bartram enters 150 [written over 160] ac in Bladen Co on NE side of NW Cape Fear R; border: on "back" part of Thos Hall's land and "taking up" both sides of "the" creek or branch; paid; P made out.

2409. Oct. 4, 1748 John Dunn enters 100 ac in Bladen Co on W side of White Marsh; border: Mr. Clayton's lower corner tree; paid; Rowan Dr; P made out.

2410. Oct. 4, 1748 Horatio Woodhouse enters 330 ac in Onlsow Co; border: runs N35E 280 poles from a sweet gum on the river to a sweet gum; paid; P made out.

2411. Oct. 4, 1748 John Paina enters 200 ac in Craven Co on SE side of "Indian landen" on Goose Cr, runs down the creek, & "out"; P made out; Griffith [or Snffith].

2412. Oct. 4, 1748 Col. Fras. Stringer enters 300 ac in Craven Co on N side and "upper" side of Stoneton Cr; border: his own corner white oak on said creek, runs up his line, & to "the" river; paid; P made out.

2413. Oct. 4, 1748 Thos "Armsrong" enters 400 ac in Bladen Co on SW side of NW Cape Fear R; border: the upper corner red oak of a piece of land laid off for John McGombery and runs "up"; paid; P made out.

page 315
2414. Oct. 4, 1748 Silvanus Soul enters 300 ac in Bladen Co; border: a gum on S side of Hester's Swamp and runs up said swamp; paid; P made out.

2415. Oct. 4, 1748 Thos Austin enters 500 ac in Carteret Co; border: Smiths Hamock on Bogue Sound, on "said" Smith's back line, & runs up the creek; paid; Col. Lovick Dr; Pet. made out.

2416. Oct. 4, 1748 Jno Prescot enters 150 ac in Johnston Co on upper side of Trotters Cr and at mouth of Spring Br; border: runs "across" to Ben Thompson's line and up to Goose Pond; [paid--lined out].

2417. Oct. 4, 1748 Jno Prescot enters 100 ac in Johnston Co in the fork of Buck Marsh Swamp; [paid--lined out].

2418. Oct. 4, 1748 Wm Beasley enters 200 ac in Craven Co on N side of Neuse R and on Gum Swamp; border: a little branch and runs "down"; paid; P made out.

2419. Oct. 6, 1748 Edward Ward jr enters 200 ac in Onslow Co on W side of Kings Cr; border: Arthur Powel's land and Stephen Howard's survey; Starkey Dr; P made out.

page 316
2420. Oct. 10, 1748 Joseph Bores [or Bows] enters 100 ac in Craven Co; called Bluff Savanna on S side of Trent R; between the branches of Island Cr and Racoon Cr; paid by "H"; P made out.

2421. Oct. 11, 1748 Abra. Boyd enters 300 ac in Bladen Co on N side of P D River; border: Jno McCoy on Cheeks Cr; paid; P made out.

2422. Oct. 11, 1748 Jno Pender enters 100 ac in Onslow Co on Bare Cr; border: the land that was formerly Jno Huggin's "plantation"; Balch Dr.

2423. Oct. 11, 1748 Saml Wright enters 500 ac in Bladen Co; border: on "head" of Richd. Dunn's land, Jno Dunn, & Robt. Dunn on NW River.

2424. Oct. 13, 1748 Jno Atkenson enters 100 ac in Johnston Co on S side of Neuse R, on N side of Southwest Cr, & on Mushes Br; paid; P made out.

2425. Oct. 13, 1748 Gibson Martin enters 200 ac in Johnston Co on N side of Neuse R; being in the fork of Falling Cr; paid; P made out.

page 317
2426. Oct. 13, 1748 Wm Arrendall enters 100 ac in Johnston Co on N side of Neuse R; being the land where he lives; paid; P made out.

pages 318 and 319 [blank pages]
page 320 [some random addition on this page]

page 321
2427. Sept. 26, 1749 John Rice enters 280 ac in Craven Co on S side of Trent R; border: on E side of Notgomery's [or Montgomery] land and joins Jno Gillet & the river; P made out; entered Apr. 1749.

2428. Sept. 26, 1749 Thomas Hardy enters 640 ac in Beaufort Co; border: Joseph Lockey's line and runs along Bares' line; entered Apr. 1749; P made out; Dr no rights filed.

2429. Sept. 26, 1749 Samuel Uxford enters 200 ac in Craven Co on N side of Neuse R and on Beasley's Swamp; border: John Beasley; entered May 15, 1749; P made out; not "grd" Oct. 1749.

2430. Sept. 26, 1749 James Johnston enters 320 ac in Carteret Co on Oyster Cr; border: William Davis' "first bounded" line and runs on the sound to David Bailey's line; entered May 31, 1749; P made out; W made out and issued.

2431. Sept. 26, 1749 John Hilliard enters 100 ac in Craven Co on S side of Trent R and in the fork of Little Limestone Cr; entered Jun. 2, 1749; P made out; Dr.

2432. Sept. 26, 1749 Benjamin Clements enters 400 ac in Johnston Co on N side of Neuse R and S side of Bear Cr; border: Martin Fryar's line and runs "up" to Robert Park's; entered Jun. 3, 1749; P made out; W made out and issued.

2433. Sept. 26, 1749 Joseph Willington enters 500 ac in Johnston Co on N side of Nuce R and S side of Bear Cr; entered Jun. 3, 1749; P made out; not grd Oct. 1749.

page 322
2434. Sept. 26, 1749 John Oates enters 400 ac in Johnston Co on N side of Neuse R; between Col. Wilson and mouth of Simons Br, runs up the river, & "out" to James Oates' line; entered Jun. 5, 1749; P made out; W made out and issued.

2435. Sept. 26, 1749 William Curlee enters 50 ac in Johnston Co on W side of Rainbow Cr and runs "up"; entered Jul. 10, 1749 per Vernom; P made out; not grd Oct. 1749.

2436. Sept. 26, 1749 Samuel Uxford enters 200 ac in Craven Co on N side of Neuse R; border: joins Beaver Cr and runs to Lionel Leighs; entered Jul. 10, 1749; P made out; rejected.

2437. Sept. 26, 1749 Jacob Jernagan enters 640 ac in New Hanover Co on N side of Cohera Cr, at "the" side of Forked Marsh, & runs up "the" creek; entered Jun. 23, 1749; P made out; R C; vid [asked] if rights proved; not grd Oct. 1749.

2438. Sept. 26, 1749 Robert Fellow enters 200 [written over 150] ac in Johnston Co on E side of Falling Cr and in the fork of Brooks Swamp; entered Jun. 23, 1749; P made out; R C; vid if rights proved; issued.

2439. Sept. 26, 1749 John New [or Nen] enters 100 ac in Johnston Co on N side of Rainbow Cr, at Cattail Marsh, & runs down Rainbow Cr; entered Jun. 15, 1749; P made out; J Carruthers Dr 50/; issued.

2440. Sept. 26, 1749 James Carter enters 300 ac in New Hanover Co on NE Cape Fear R and on "the" great branch; border: Edward Carter's land; entered Jun. 15, 1749; P made out; J Carruthers Dr 50/; vid if rights proved.

page 323
2441. Sept. 26, 1749 John Tutle enters 50 ac in Craven Co; border: Mrs. Nixon and John Becton on the branches of Southwest Cr; entered Jun. 15, 1749; P made out; J Carruthers Dr 50/.

2442. Sept. 26, 1749 William Mills enters 100 ac in Craven Co on a branch of Trent R; between mouth of Patrick's Br and Beaverdam Cr; entered Jul. 25, 1749; P made out.

2443. Sept. 26, 1749 John Dunn enters 100 ac in New Hanover Co on the mouth of Buck Hall [Br] a branch of Limestone Cr; known as Indigo Hill; entered Jul. 25, 1749; P made out.

2444. Sept. 26, 1749 William Brice enters 50 ac in New Hanover Co on White oak Swamp a branch of Limestone Cr at the fork of Soracte Road; entered Jul. 25, 1749; P made out.

2445. Sept. 26, 1749 John Rice enters 150 [written over 100] ac in Craven Co on Wilsons Cr, on Trent R, & in the fork of the creek; entered Jul. 28, 1749; P made out.

2446. Sept. 26, 1749 John Rice enters 100 ac in Craven Co; border: Saml Johnston esq's corner and runs down "the" river to Gillyard's line; entered Jul. 28, 1749; P made out.

2447. Sept. 26, 1749 Jacob Thomson enters 100 ac in Johnston Co on S side of Neuse R and N side of Pates Br; border: James Barber; entered Aug. 1, 1749; P made out; J Carruthers Dr 50/.

2448. Sept. 26, 1749 Samuel Jasper enters 150 ac in Hyde Co on E side of Swan Quarter Bay and runs back to Foster Jervis' line; entered Sept. 16, 1749; P made out; W made out; Forbes Dr 10/; vid if rights proved.

page 324
2449. Sept. 26, 1749 William Pringle enters 100 ac in Hyde Co on E side of Matchapungo R; runs between Jno Leith and Willoby Richards; entered Sept. 16, 1749 per Forbes; Forbes Dr 10/; P made out; W made out.

2450. Sept. 26, 1749 Richard Adams enters 100 ac in Beaufort Co on N side of Pamplico R and on Whitehouse's Cr; border: runs "back" of William Foreman and Henry Lucas; entered Sept. 16, 1749 per Forbes; Forbes Dr 10/; P made out; W made out.

2451. Sept. 26, 1749 John Leigh jr enters 150 ac in Hyde Co on E side of Matchapungo R in new Currituck [Twsp]; border: Richard Jasper's line and runs on E side of Long Cr; entered Sept. 16, 1749.
2452. Sept. 26, 1749 Samuel Sinclair enters 300 ac in Beaufort Co on Pamplico R below Runney Marsh; border: "a tract" belonging to Mr. Wyriot Ormand and William Price; entered Sept. 16, 1749 per Vail; Dr 50/; P made out.

2453. Sept. 26, 1749 Arthur Mabson enters 400 [written over 640] ac in Craven Co in the fork of Clubfoots Cr; border: John Bishop and Robt Blake; entered Sept. 16, 1749; vid if rights proved; P made out.

2454. Sept. 26, 1749 Jeremiah Vail enters 200 ac in New Hanover Co on Holley Shelter Cr; border: his own land; entered Sept. 20, 1749; chd; vid if rights proved; P made out.

page 325
2455. Sept. 26, 1749 Henry Snoad [? faint] enters 640 ac in Beaufort Co on [page torn] Derhams Cr; border: above Sarah Payton's, runs up a creek, & "back"; entered Sept. 19, 1749; Dr 50/; vid if rights proved; P made out.

2456. Sept. 26, 1749 John Smith enters 250 ac in Bladen Co on E side of NW River; border: near Volen [page torn] Hollingsworth's upper line; entered Sept. 20, 1749; Hamson Dr 50/; rights to be filed; P made out.

2457. Sept. 26, 1749 Roger Moor esq enters 500 ac in Craven Co; being white oak timbered land about 3 miles above his "milns"; Dr; P made out.

2458. Sept. 26, 1749 Roger Moore esq enters 500 ac in Craven Co; being white oak timbered land; border: joins Ainsworth's land on E; entered Sept. 20, 1749; Dr; P made out.

2459. Sept. 26, 1749 William Whitty enters 100 ac in Craven Co on N side of Neuse R and on head of Dawsons Cr; border: his own land; entered Sept. 20, 1749; P made out.

2460. Sept. 26, 1749 Thomas Norwood enters 100 ac in Craven Co on Trent R and on S side of Sawpit Br; border: runs WNW from Trent Road to Wm Norwood's land; P made out.

2461. Sept. 26, 1749 William Gibson enters 66 ac in Onslow Co on Wild "Cate" Br, on S side of White Oak R, & on "back" side of Andrew's land; P made out.

page 326
2462. Sept. [page torn], 1749 John Philips enters 150 ac in Craven Co; between John Derham and Lionel Leigh; includes the "plantation" and mill "thereon"; paid; P made out.

2463. Sept. [page torn], 1749 Henry Sumerlin enters 100 ac in Anson Co in "the" fork of Little P D River, about 10 or 12 miles above "the" ford, & runs "down"; P made out.

2464. Sept. [page torn], 1749 Peter Gustaves and Josts. Nobles enter 300 ac in Anson Co on S side of Great P D River; border: Gustaves' Mill and runs "across" to N fork of Jones Cr; P made out.

2465. Sept. [page torn], 1749 Andrew Carthy enters 400 ac in Anson Co at mouth of Joseph McDowels Cr and runs up & down both sides of the creek on N side of "Ketanbo" R; P made out.

2466. Sept. [page torn], 1749 Jean Adams enters 300 ac in Anson Co; border: a white oak marked "J A", below "the waggen" road to the "Adkee" [Yadkin R ?] on N side of Ketaubo R; P made out.

2467. Sept. [page torn], 1749 Robert Brevard enters 640 ac in Anson Co on "a" Reedy Cr; includes the Great Bever Dam on W side of Rocky R; P made out.

2468. Sept. [page torn], 1749 Alexr. Dobbin enters 550 ac in Anson Co on N side of Ketaubo R about a mile above "the" fork; P made out.

page 327

North Carolina Land Entries 1735-1752

2469. Sept. 27, 1749 Joseph McDowel enters 400 ac in Anson Co on N [page torn] River and on both [sides of; page torn] Great Meadow; border: joins his own land; P made out.

2470. Sept. 27, 1749 Rachel Price enters 400 ac in Anson Co on N side of Kavtabo R; border: joins her own land where she lives; P made out.

2471. Sept. 27, 1749 John Chithalm enters 400 ac in Anson Co on S side of Kavtabo R, on Stoney Br, & runs up the branch; P made out.

2472. Sept. 27, 1749 Abbiton Sherrel enters 400 ac in Anson Co on S side of Kavtabo R below the Goose Ponds; P made out.

2473. Sept. 27, 1749 William Sherrel enters 600 ac in Anson Co on S side of Kavtabo R, on Jumping Run, & runs up both sides [of run ?]; P made out.

2474. Sept. 27, 1749 Preston Goforth enters 400 ac in Anson Co on N side of S fork of Kavtabo R; between Tyre Harris and the Goose Pond; P made out.

2475. Sept. 27, 1749 Tyre Harris enters 600 ac in Anson Co on N side of S fork of Cautabo R; border: a red oak marked "T H" and runs "down"; P made out.

2476. Sept. 27, 1749 Thomas Potts enters 400 ac in Anson Co on S side of S fork of Cautabo R; border: below Clark's on Fishers Cr; P made out.

2477. Sept. 27, 1749 Fracs. McWean enters 600 ac in Anson Co on S side of S fork of Cautaubo R and on Fishers Cr; includes the Great Medow; P made out.

page 328
2478. Sept. 27, 1749 Benjn. Jackson enters 400 ac in Anson Co on N side of Tomsons Cr, on N side of Great P D River, & on "both" sides of the creek; P made out.

2479. Sept. 27, 1749 Jordan Gibson enters 100 ac in Anson Co on S side of Drowning Cr and on lower side of "Showeheel" Cr; P made out.

2480. Sept. 27, 1749 Thomas Holems enters 200 ac in Anson Co on N side of Great P D River and on S fork of Mountain Cr; P made out.

2481. Sept. 27, 1749 John Ikaller [written over Isler] enters 640 [written over 600] ac in Anson Co on Rocky Cr; babove Joseph McDowel; includes a large "beever" dam; P made out.

2482. Sept. 27, 1749 Habakuk Russell enters 50 ac in Carteret Co on E side of head of Goose Cr; border: on Reed's "head" line; P made out.

2483. Sept. 27, 1749 David Shepard enters 100 ac in Carteret Co on S side of Newport R; at a place called Snow's Neck; P made out.

2484. Sept. 27, 1749 Thomas Lovick [Joseph Butt--lined out] enters 200 ac in Craven Co on S side of Neuse R and in the fork of Handcocks Cr; border: Francis Alway's corner, runs up the creek to Master's line, & "back"; P made out.

2485. Sept. 27, 1749 Robert Manker enters 100 ac in Beaufort Co on N side of Bear Cr; between Reding Blunt's line and Thomas Worsley's; includes David OBrian's clearing; P made out; W made out.

page 329
2486. Sept. 27, 1749 Reding Blunt enters 650 ac in Beaufort Co S [page torn] River and on S side of [page torn] pecoson; border: runs between "Joshsua" Port[page torn; Porter ?] and Thomas Worsley; P made out; W made out.

2487. Sept. 27, 1749 John Smith enters 300 ac in New Hanover Co on a "branch" called Crane Cr and runs West; P made out.

2488. Sept. 27, 1749 James Adams enters 100 ac in Beaufort Co on head of "ould" Town Cr; border: SE corner of Richd. Adams' corner, runs up his line, & "back"; P made out; W made out.

2489. Sept. 27, 1749 Charles Gavin enters 500 ac in New Hanover Co on W side of Six Runs Cr; being the place where he lives; Dr; P made out.

2490. Sept. 27, 1749 Griffith Jones enters 100 ac in Bladen Co on W side of S branch of Black R about 2 miles from "Governour's" ford; border: a cypress tree near a beaver dam; includes his cowpen; entered Sept. 26, 1749; P made out.

2491. Sept. 27, 1749 William Askins enters 100 ac in Onslow Co on NE of New R and on upper side of Mirey Br; where he lives; Starkey Dr; P made out.

2492. Sept. 27, 1749 Jno Vandrick enters 200 ac in Craven Co in the main fork of Beards Cr; border: on the South prong where the creek forks, runs up said prong, across to the other prong, & "down"; Griff Dr; P made out.

page 330
2493. Sept. [page torn], 1749 [George ? faint] Starkey enters 250 ac in Onslow Co; between Mr. Starkey's line on White Oak R and Grant's line; includes the swamp; entered Sept. 23, 1749; Starkey Dr; P made out.

2494. Sept. [page torn], 1749 Joseph Roads enters 100 ac in Carteret Co on White Oak R and N side of Hadnots Cr; called Flat Neck; entered "rits uprd."; Starkey Dr; P made out.

North Carolina Land Entries 1735-1752

2495. Sept. [page torn], 1749 Edward Ward enters 640 ac in Onslow Co on Bear Cr; border: Philip Dexter; Starkey Dr; P made out.

2496. Sept. [page torn], 1749 Roger Moore enters 500 ac in Craven Co on N side of Trent R and runs up each side of "Muscel" shell Cr; P made out.

2497. Sept. [page torn], 1749 Roger Moore enters 1,000 ac in Craven Co; border: runs "round" his mill and joins Brices Cr; P made out.

2498. Sept. [page torn], 1749 Roger Moore enters 100 ac in Craven Co; border: line of late Col. Wilson's land, Francis Brice, & Handcock; known as Green Spring; P made out.

2499. Sept. [page torn], 1749 Saml. Uxford enters 600 ac in Craven Co; border: near "the" little fort on N side of Cotentnea Cr and runs up the creek; P made out; not grd Oct. 1749.

2500. Sept. [page torn], 1749 Wendel Blyler enters 200 ac in Johnston Co on S side of Neuse R; border: joins his own line; P made out.

2501. Sept. [page torn], 1749 Jacob Taylor enters 100 ac in Craven Co on head of Slocombs Cr, at mouth of Black Swamp, & runs "down"; P made out.

page 331
2502. Sept. 28, 1749 Jno Smith enters 250 ac in Craven Co on [page torn] Stewarts Swamp [page torn] from the lower line; Gavin Dr; P made out.

2503. Sept. 28, 1749 William Belk enters 100 ac in Johnston Co on S side of Neuse R; border: back of Peter O[page torn]; P made out.

2504. Sept. 28, 1749 Jno Hollingsworth enters 200 ac in Craven Co on N side of Neuse R and on Cat tail Br; includes Cedar Island; "Nil".

2505. Sept. 28, 1749 Henry Snoad and Elinor Peyton, executors of Benja Peyton [see Beaufort Co "Old" Will Book p. 35], enter 640 ac in Beaufort Co; border: Joseph Lockey's line and runs along Barress' line; P made out; W made out.

2506. Sept. 28, 1749 Andrew Moreman jr enters 300 ac in Anson Co; border: James Adams' land and runs up Hedgcock Cr; P made out.

2507. Sept. 28, 1749 Andrew Moreman jr enters 600 ac in Anson Co; border: Hedgcock's line and runs "down & out"; P made out.

2508. Sept. 28, 1749 William Rainey enters 300 ac in Johnston Co on S side of Neuse R and on Brooks Swamp; includes Brooks' and Barlow's improvements; R C Dr; P made out.

2509. Sept. 28, 1749 Stephen Cade enters 150 ac in Johnston Co on N side of Neuse R and W side of Walnut Cr; border: Anthony Herring sr; R C Dr; P made out.

page 332
2510. Sept. [page torn], 1749 [page torn and water stain] enters 600 ac in Anson Co on N side of Great Peedee R, E side of Little R, & each side of the fork of Cheeks Cr [page torn].

2511. Sept. [page torn], 1749 Hugh Blaning enters 200 ac in New Hanover Co on Seven miles Cr; border: "back" from his mill standing on Beaverdam Cr [page torn].

2512. Sept. [page torn], 1749 Hugh Blaning enters 200 ac in New Hanover Co about 5 or 6 miles "back" of his mill on Beaverdam Cr.

2513. Sept. [page torn], 1749 Thos "Keunan" enters 50 ac in New Hanover Co on Cabbin Br of Maxwell Cr and on S side of Maxwell Cr; border: runs up the creek from a pine; Pet. made out; W made out.

2514. Sept. [page torn], 1749 Edward Grantham enters 200 ac in New Hanover Co on N side of Goshen Swamp; border: Monk and Edwd. Vann; R C Dr; P made out.

2515. Sept. [page torn], 1749 Wm McKinney enters 300 ac in Johnston Co on S side of Neuse R and on lower side of mouth of Simmons Run; R C Dr; P made out.

2516. Sept. [page torn], 1749 John Wilson enters 200 ac in Craven Co on E side of Swifts Cr at mouth of Horsepen Br; R C Dr; P made out.

2517. Sept. [page torn], 1749 Henry Best enters 640 ac in Johnston Co on S side of Norhunty Cr; border: on the beaverdam at his own line and runs up "the same"; R C Dr; P made out.

page 333
2518. Sept. 29, 1749 Gilbert Werr [or Kerr] enters 200 ac in Johnston Co on S side of great Cotentnea [? water stain] Cr; border: on S side of Sellar's [smudge] walnut old field; R C Dr; P made out.

2519. Sept. 29, 1749 Saml [written over John] Guilliard enters 100 ac in Craven Co on Poplar Savanna [smudge] on Roman Br and on Trent R.

2520. Sept. 29, 1749 Jno Cook enters 100 ac in New Hanover Co on W side of NE Cape fear R and Bergaw Cr; border: on "Welech" Path near the [page torn]

North Carolina Land Entries 1735-1752

and runs on "both sides"; Skibbow; P made out.

2521. Sept. 29, 1749 William Armstrong enters 100 ac in New Hanover Co on W side of "Mores" Cr, a "branch" of Holley Shelter Cr; includes his improvements; P made out.

2522. Sept. 29, 1749 Richard James enters 200 ac in New Hanover Co on SE side of Six Runs Cr, a "branch" of Black R; border: about 0.5 miles above his other "tract" and in the River Swamp; P made out.

2523. Sept. 29, 1749 John Clarke enters 100 ac in New Hanover Co on SE side of Six Runs Cr, a branch of Black R, on upper sides of "Strabery" Br, runs down Six Runs Cr, & back; P made out.

2524. Sept. 29, 1749 Michl. Lowber [or Lowbor] enters 320 ac in New Hanover Co on S side of Cotskin Br of Porters Cr; border: a red oak, runs up said branch, & "back"; includes his improvement; P made out.

page 334
2525. Sept. 29, 1749 Jno [smudge] enters 200 ac in New Hanover Co on upper side of Six Runs "prong" [Cr], on Cain Cr, & on S side of said prong; P made out.

2526. Sept. 29, 1749 John Williams enters 40 ac in Bladen Co on SW side of NW Cape Fear R and on each side of Lick Cr; border: near Capt. Armstrong's survey [smudge].

2527. Sept. 29, 1749 Moses Tilman enters 150 ac in Craven Co on each side of Mosleys Cr; border: Richard Carlton's upper corner tree; P made out.

2528. Sept. 30, 1749 Daniel Short enters 200 ac in Anson Co on S side of P D River and on both sides of Jones' Cr; includes his improvements; P made out.

2529. Sept. 30, 1749 John Hill enters 100 ac in Anson Co in the fork of Little P D River; border: "at & in" the fork and runs up & "out" both forks; P made out.

2530. Sept. 30, 1749 Abrahm. Boyd enters 350 ac in Anson Co on N side of P D River, lower side of Little R, & on Cheeks Cr; border: his own land, begins at a white oak on his own line, runs "up, & round some part" of said land; P made out.
2531. Sept. 30, 1749 Ephraim Lyles enters 200 ac in Anson Co on N side of P D River; border: "a little" below mouth of Lake Cr, runs "out, & up"; includes his improvement; P made out.

page 335
2532. Sept. 30, 1749 Jno Smith enters 300 ac in Anson Co on N side of P D River, [smudge] side of Little R, & on Thickette Cr; border: a red oak and runs up "both sides"; P made out.

North Carolina Land Entries 1735-1752

2533. Sept. 30, 1749 Edmund Cartlidge enters 400 ac in Anson Co on N side of P D River and on [smudge] Fork of Cartlidges Cr; border: below the new road and runs up on both sides; P made out.

2534. Sept. 30, 1749 Benja. Wheatley enters 200 ac in Craven Co [Roger Moore enters 200 ac in Craven Co--lined out]; border: his own land and land that was Martin F[faint]; P made out.

2535. Sept. 30, 1749 John Cletheral enters 640 ac in Carteret Co on SW side of Newport R; border: in Snows Neck, runs up the river above Cedar Swamp [faint] SW branch of the river, & "back"; Dr; P made out.

2536. Sept. 30, 1749 Peter "Eellet" enters 300 ac in Anson Co on N side of Catauba R about 23 miles up Ellets Cr; P made out.

2537. Sept. 30, 1749 Abraham Boyd enters 400 [written over 300] ac in Anson Co on N side of Great P D River; border: James Denson's upper line, runs "out, & up"; P made out.

2538. Sept. 30, 1749 Abra. Paul enters 200 ac in Anson Co on S side of great Pedee R and on both sides of Thompsons Cr; border: Dry's line; P made out.

page 336
2539. Oct. 2, 1749 John Kolls [or Stolls] enters 150 ac in Beaufort Co in a fork of a cypress swamp at the head of Campbells Cr; P made out; W made out.

2540. Oct. 2, 1749 James Cook enters 300 ac in New Hanover Co on W side of NE Cape Fear R and on the main branch of Rockfish Cr; border: [Josp ?] Merriddith's lower line and runs down both sides; includes his improvement.

2541. Oct. 2, 1749 Joseph Lamb enters 200 ac in New Hanover Co on E side of Long Cr; between Capt. Rowan and James Thomas; border: Capt. Rowan's corner on E side of said creek, runs along the creek, & "back"; Skibbow; P made out.

2542. Oct. 2, 1749 Wm Peebles enters 60 ac in Johnston Co on N side of Norhunte [Swamp]; between Beverdam Br and Button Br; chd. to Fontaine.

2543. Oct. 2, 1749 Robert Beaverly enters 200 ac in New Hanover Co on NE of Cape Fear R and on a place called Burn Coat Swamp on S side of said river; chd. to Fontaine.

2544. Oct. 3, 1749 Edwd. Williams enters 150 ac in Craven Co on S side of Tuckahoe Cr in "the" great fork; border: on lower side of "the" runing branch, runs up the same, & Trent R; F Fonvielle Dr; P made out.

North Carolina Land Entries 1735-1752

2545. Oct. 3, 1749 William Wilkison enters 100 ac in Craven Co on S side of Neuse R and E side of Southwest Cr; [being] the place where he lives; P made out.

page 337
2546. Oct. 3, 1749 Gilbert Buy enters 100 ac in Bladen Co on S side of NW Cape Fear R; border: upper line of "Maraeen" McCraine; Smith Dr; P made out.

2547. Oct. 3, 1749 James Anderson enters 100 ac in Craven Co on N side of [smudge] in the fork of Great Br and runs "back"; P made out.

2548. Oct. 3, 1749 Joseph Jackson enters 400 ac in Craven Co on Little Cotentnea Cr; border: James Blunt; includes his improvements; P made out.

2549. Oct. 3, 1749 Joseph Letchworth enters 200 ac in Craven Co on upper side of Clay root [Swamp] and runs "along"; P made out.

2550. Oct. 3, 1749 William Barber enters 100 ac in Craven Co; border: Jno Barber's land on N side of Neuse R; includes his improvements; P made out.

2551. Oct. 3, 1749 Samuel "Keight" enters 200 ac in Craven Co on a prong of Swifts Cr; border: Williams' land and runs along the swamp; P made out.

2552. Oct. 3, 1749 Jno Stanly enters 100 ac in Craven Co on N side of Trent R; border: near George Kornegee's line and runs up into the fork of Musell Shell Cr; P made out.

page 338
2553. Oct. 3, 1749 William Hales enters [page torn]65 ac in Johnston Co on S side of Neuse R, on Sleepy Cr, & below Spring Br; R C; P made out; War. made out.

2554. Oct. 3, 1749 William Teague enters 300 ac in Johnston Co on S side of Neuse R and in the lower S Roundabout; border: "late" Col. Wilson's land; R C; P made out; War. made out.

2555. Oct. 3, 1749 Martin Foyer enters 100 ac in New Hanover Co in the fork of Great Cohera Cr and Little Cohera Cr; border: above Jno Fryer; R C; P made out; War. made out.

2556. Oct. 3, 1749 John Smith enters 140 ac in Bladen Co on S side of Deep R and both sides of Bear Cr; border: a white oak on E side of said creek and runs down; R C; P made out; W made out.

2557. Oct. 3, 1749 Farnifold Green jr enters 200 ac in Bladen Co on S side of Deep R and near the Great Cain Patch; includes Reid's improvements; R C; P made out; W made out.

2558. Oct. 3, 1749 Martin Caswell enters 100 ac in Bladen Co on S side of Deep R and on & in the fork of Bear Cr; known as Hassle Neck; R C; P made out; W made out.

2559. Oct. 3, 1749 Richd. Caswell jr enters 400 ac in Johnston Co on S side of Neuse R; border: "back" of Henry Owens, Joshua Sarsnett, & Wm Teague; R C; P made out; W made out.

2560. Oct. 3, 1749 Stephen Herring enters 640 ac in Johnston Co on N side of Neuse R and in & on each side of the forks of Black Walnut Cr.

2561. Oct. 3, 1749 James Thomas enters 150 ac in New Hanover Co on Long Cr; border: Thomas Rowan and Martin Jinkengs [or Jinhengs]; Murray chd; P made out.

page 339
2562. Oct. 3, 1749 DuncanBuy enters 100 ac in Bladen Co on N side of Deep R below "the" great fork; Smith Dr; P made out.

2563. Oct. 3, 1749 David Smith enters 200 ac in Bladen Co on Lower Little R on N side [smudge] on Tranthams Cr; Smith Dr; P made out.

2564. Oct. 4, 1749 Stephen cade enters 200 ac in Johnston Co on Bever Creek Marsh; border: Christopher Harrison's land where he lives and runs down the creek; P made out; W made out.

2565. Oct. 4, 1749 William Hancock enters 100 ac in Anson Co on E side of "Pdee" River; border: Mr. Blewart's upper line on the river side; James McWain Dr "3 entries"; P made out.

2566. Oct. 4, 1749 John Bone enters 300 ac in Anson Co on W fork of Drowning Cr; called "the" rich lands; P made out.

2567. Oct. 4, 1749 John Craford enters 300 ac in Bladen Co on a branch of Hetchcocks Cr and on a small branch "thereof" called Craford Br; P made out.

2568. Oct. 4, 1749 Thomas Brooks enters 400 ac in Bladen Co on SW side of Cape Fear R; border: a pine at John McFashion's line, upper line of John Russell on [Kurts ? smudge] Cr; Dr 5 entries; P made out; arm. chd.

page 340
2569. Oct. 4, 1749 Thomas Brooks enters 100 ac in Bladen Co on John Locks Cr; border: a red oak about a mile from NW Cape fear R; P made out; arm. chd.

2570. Oct. 4, 1749 Alexander [write over] McAllester enters 640 ac in Bladen Co; border: Wm Stephens' lower corner and runs "down"; P made out; arm. chd.

2571. Oct. 4, 1749 Alexander McAllester enters 100 ac in Bladen Co; border: a red oak at the "back" of Isaac Waine's line; P made out; arm. chd.

2572. Oct. 4, 1749 Jacob Blocker enters 200 ac in Bladen Co on Upper Little R; border: about 2 miles above Josiah Shadock's land; Pet. made out; arm. chd.

2573. Oct. 4, 1749 Thomas Castelow enters 500 ac in Johnston Co; border: Andrew Bass' upper line [corner--lined out] on S side of Beaverdam Swamp of Falling Cr, runs "out, & up"; P made out; chd to Oates.

2574. Oct. 4, 1749 Georg Lane enters 100 ac in Craven Co on E side of Core Cr; border: mouth of Mirery Br; P made out.

2575. Oct. 4, 1749 Stephen Cade enters 200 ac in Johnston Co on N side of Neuse R and E side of Walnut Cr; border: Wm Starley's line; chd; P made out.

2576. Oct. 4, 1749 Thomas Armstrong enters 200 ac in Bladen Co on head of main branch of Rockfish Cr, about 2 miles above Roberts' Path, & on S side of Cape "Fair" R; P made out; chd.

page 341
2577. Oct. 4, 1749 Charles Hurd enters 100 ac in Bladen Co on a branch of Lower Little R, about 3 miles from Crane's "Settlement", & about 1.5 miles below Shadocks' Path; P made out; arm. chd.

2578. Oct. 4, 1749 Abram. Boyd enters 200 ac in Anson Co on S side of Great P D River and both sides of Lains Cr; border: about 12 or 15 miles above Robert Lain's; charged; P made out.

2579. Oct. 4, 1749 Amns [or Anens] Cutterel enters 300 ac in Craven Co on N side of Neuse R, on head of Goose Cr, & on both sides "thereof"; P made out.

2580. Oct. 4, 1749 John Edmundson enters 300 ac in Craven Co on West [written over North] side of Cushaw Cr, a prong of Smiths Cr, and on N side of Nuse R; P made out.

2581. Oct. 4, 1749 James Green enters 100 ac in New Hanover Co on E side of NE Swamp and about a mile below Jumping Run; charg; P made out.

2582. Oct. 4, 1749 John Smith enters 600 ac in Craven Co on W side of Hancocks Cr; border: Marshal's line and runs up the creek; P made out.

2583. Oct. 4, 1749 Jno Hollingsworth [Saml Uxford--lined out] enters 600 ac in

Craven Co; border: Oxford Beasley's corner tree in "the" island and runs "down" the island; P made out.

2584. Oct. 4, 1749 James Clayton enters 400 ac in Hyde Co on S side of "Maremuskeet" Lake; called Fort Point.

2585. Oct. 4, 1749 Timothy Allen enters 200 ac in Hyde co on W side of Matchapungo R and on a branch of Jones Cr; border: joins land of said Allen and Jones.

page 342
2586. Oct. 5, 1749 Jno Porter jr enters 100 ac in Bladen Co on E side of Cubbages Swamp where "the" path crosses the swamp; P made out.

2587. Oct. 5, 1749 William Porter enters 100 ac in Bladen Co on E side of Cubbages Swamp near and below "the" fork; includes a small marsh; P made out.

2588. Oct. 5, 1749 Thomas Mims enters 200 ac in Bladen Co on S side of Waggamaw R; includes a place called Gray's Bluff or Long Bluff; about 2 miles below "Pyriva"; P made out.

2589. Oct. 5, 1749 Cyprian Shepard enters 300 ac in Bladen Co; border: Jas Grange's land and runs up Plomers Br; P made out.

2590. Oct. 5, 1749 Thomas Moor enters 100 ac in New Hanover Co on ath; [grant abstract #67].

2591. Oct. 5, 1749 Thomas Moor enters 200 ac in New Hanover Co on Black R at a place called Wallis' Bluff; P made out.

2592. Oct. 5, 1749 Coleman Roe enters 400 ac in Beaufort Co on head of Core Cr on both sides; includes the places called Sigley's and Bettey More's.

page 343
2593. Oct. 5, 1749 Mark Forgirson [or Forgisson] enters 200 ac in Craven Co on S side of Nuse R and E side of Bectons Cr; P made out.

2594. Oct. 5, 1749 David Lewis enters 200 ac in Craven Co on N side of [Nuse ? smudge] River in the fork of Upper Broad R; border: Isaac Barrinton's land; P made out.

2595. Oct. 5, 1749 Jno Peters enters 300 ac in Craven Co; border: John Hollingsworth's line on N side of Neuse R, runs up the River Pecoson, & "out"; P made out; "to next Court, not being grd Oct. 1749".

2596. Oct. 6, 1749 John Williams enters 150 ac in Craven Co on S side of Nuse

North Carolina Land Entries 1735-1752

R, opposite Beasly Island, & runs up the river; charged; P made out.

2597. Oct. 6, 1749 Richard Ogden enters 300 ac in Bladen Co on W side of White Marsh Swamp, at Turkey Br, & runs up said swamp; P made out; W made out.

2598. Oct. 6, 1749 George Gresset enters 100 ac in New Hanover Co on W side of White Marsh Swamp; border: Thomas Bell's lower corner and runs down said swamp; P made out; W made out.

page 344
2599. Oct. 6, 1749 Richard Curtes enters 150 ac in Onslow Co on NE side of NW New R and on the fork of Half Moon Swamp; P made out; chd Mr. Swann.

2600. Oct. 6, 1749 Robt. Peyton enters 640 ac in Beaufort Co; border: Barrus' East corner on Barrus' Cr; P made out.

2601. Oct. 6, 1749 Robert Fellow enters 300 ac in Johnston Co on S side of Norhunty [Swamp] in the fork; border: Solomon Johnston's line; P made out.

2602. Oct. 7, 1749 John Becton enters 150 ac in Craven Co on N side of Little "Conttenee" Cr "right against" Henry Bradley's land; P made out; chd Dr.

2603. Oct. 9, 1749 Alexr. McKikin enters 100 ac in Bladen Co on NE side of NW Cape Fear R and below Leonard Lockes Cr; known as Lewis L Favour's place; P made out.

2604. Oct. 9, 1749 James Pugh enters 100 ac in Bladen Co on S side of NW River; border: a red oak on upper side of S fork of Cross Cr; P made out; T James.

2605. Oct. 9, 1749 Jno Williams enters 100 ac in Bladen Co on W side of White Marsh; border: Roger Haine and Edmund Rourk; P made out; Armstrong.

page 345
2606. Oct. 10, 1749 Robt. Caldwell enters 200 ac in Bladen Co on S side of Bea[page torn] Cr; between Col. Forbes and Capt. Blaning; P made out; Mr. Clark to bring cert. of rights.

2607. Oct. 11, 1749 James Davis enters 200 ac in Craven Co in the fork of Hancock Cr; border: the "back" line of Col. Thomas Lovick; P made out.

2608. Oct. 11, 1749 Samuel Baker enters 200 ac in Bladen Co near Blackburn Br on Rockfish Cr; P made out.

2609. Oct. 13, 1749 William Peters jr enters 200 ac in Craven Co on N side of Nuce R on an island; border: William Peters sr and John Beasley; P made out.

2610. Oct. 14, 1749 Thos. Armstrong enters 100 ac in Bladen Co; border: Edwd. Conner's lower line, Col. Forbes' upper line, & Thos Davis' "back" line; P made out.

2611. Oct. 14, 1749 Margt. Green enters 50 ac in Bladen Co on E side of White Marsh and "fronting" the "plantation" of "late" Jno Green; P made out.
2612. Oct. 16, 1749 Peter Griffith enters 100 ac in Anson Co on N side of Great Peedee R and lower side of Little R; border: beginning tree of John McCoy's lower survey, runs "out" with said survey, & "down"; P made out.

page 346
2613. Oct. [page torn], 1749 Peter Griffith, Samuel Gent, Abraham Boyd, & James Green enter 1,000 ac in Anson Co on S side of Great Pedee R, S side of Browns Cr, on Camp Cr, & runs up "both sides".

2614. Oct. [page torn], 1749 Thomas Stevens enters 200 ac in Carteret Co at Mill Cr on E side of White Oak R; border: on the front of the land formerly beloning to Robert Atkins.

2615. Oct. [page torn], 1749 Wm Crain enters 200 ac in Bladen Co on S side of Deep R and W prong of Buck Cr; P made out.

2616. Oct. [page torn], 1749 Robert Taylor enters 100 ac in Craven Co; border: his own corner on W side of Core Cr; P made out.

2617. Oct. 18, 1749 Henry Hylands enters 50 ac [in Craven Co] on Beacon Island; being the part fronting Core Island; P made out.

2618. Oct. 18, 1749 John Anderson jr enters 120 [written over 200] ac in Bladen Co on E side of S branch of Black R; at a place called Spring Hill.

2619. Oct. 18, 1749 "Jho." Oats enters 300 ac in Johnston Co on S side of Nuse R; border: his own land and runs "up"; entered.

page 347 [writing on this page very faint]
2620. Mar. 29, 1749 [page torn and faint for whole entry; P made out.

2621. Mar. 29, 1749 James M[page torn and faint for rest of entry]; P made out.

2622. Mar. 29, 1749 Georg Nichols [page torn and faint for rest of entry]; P made out.

2623. Mar. 29, 1749 John Rice enters 300 ac in Craven Co on N side [page torn and faint] S side [page torn and faint].

2624. Mar. 29, 1749 John Rice enters [100 ?] ac in Craven Co on N side of [page torn and faint] S side [page torn and faint] Indian cabbin [faint].

2625. Mar. 29, 1749 John Rice enters 150 ac in Craven Co [faint].

2626. Mar. 29, 1749 John Rice enters 640 ac in Craven Co on S side of Rainbow Cr below [faint] road; border: Saml [faint].

2627. Mar. 29, 1749 John Rice enters 320 ac in Craven Co on "the" prong of Rainbow "Swamp"; border: a red oak [faint].

page 348 [writing on this page is faint]
2628. [page torn] on S side of NW [page torn] land formerly taken [page torn] and both sides of [page torn].

2629. [page torn] New Hanover Co on S side [page torn]ms Swamp on the marsh [page torn] William McDead's land.

2630. [page torn] enters 100 ac in New Hanover Co on N side of Goshen Swamp "a little" below the fish trap of [faint].

2631. [page torn] Richard Caswell [jr ? faint] enters 100 ac in Johnston Co on both sides of Black Walnut Cr; being the land Robert Parks obtained a warrant for; border: [faint] survey.

2632. [page torn] Stephen Batt [? faint] enters 50 ac in Bladen Co on N side of Vine Swamp; border: George McCarty's upper line and runs up the swamp.

2633. Mar. 29, 1749 John Waine enters 300 ac in Beaufort Co on S side of Swifts Cr; border: Vine's line and runs to Nesby Mills' line; being where William Powell formerly lived.

2634. Mar. 29, 1749 Francis Clark enters 200 ac in New Hanover Co on Stewards Cr on lower side thereof and on a branch of Black R; being where he lives; P made out.

page 349 [writing on this page is faint]
2635. Mar. 29, 1749 John W[page torn] enters 300 ac in Bladen Co on W side of NW River [faint] Lick Cr [faint]; paid; P made out.

2636. Mar. 29, 1749 James C[faint] enters 200 ac in Bladen Co on [faint] River [faint] Great Cain Patch; paid; P made out.

2637. Mar. 29, 1749 Dennis Cannon enters 100 ac in Craven Co [faint] Swamp [faint] Ellet's lines; paid; P made out.

2638. Mar. 29, 1749 John Maddocks enters 500 ac in Craven Co; border: John

North Carolina Land Entries 1735-1752

Philips' land and runs along [said ? faint] line; paid; P made out.

2639. Mar. 29, 1749 John Powell enters 100 ac in Craven Co; border: Price [faint], Samuel Vine's line, & runs along said lines; paid; P made out; Wart. made out by mistake returned into "the" office.

2640. Mar. 29, 1749 John Fishpoole enters 150 ac in Johnston Co; border: Archd. Whitehouse, on N [faint] of Gumb Swamp [faint], & runs on both sides; P made out; "whole fees paid".

page 350
2641. Mar. 29, 1749 [faint] enters 150 ac [faint]; border: near Roe's [faint] branch of Stanleys Marsh and runs down [faint].

2642. Mar. 29, 1749 [faint; same person as in 2641] enters 150 ac [written over 100] ac in Johnston Co; border: "a little" above James Banks' line and runs up "towards" [faint] Tysson's [faint].

2643. Mar. 29, 1749 Alexander McKeithan enters 200 ac in Bladen Co on NE side of main branch of Waccamaw R; border: Edmund [Rourk's ? smudge] lower corner and John McCauslin's land; at a place called [faint] Marsh Swamp; paid; P made out.

2644. Mar. 29, 1749 Hugh Blaning jr enters 200 ac in Bladen Co on Beaverdam Cr about 1.5 miles above Capt. Blaning's saw mill; P made out.

2645. Mar. 29, 1749 Mathew Rowan esq enters 50 ac in New Hanover Co on Horse Cr; between [Conner ? faint] Halton and the creek; P made out.

2646. Mar. 29, 1749 William Waite enters 100 ac in Bladen Co on [smudge] side of Little Pedee R; includes his improvement; paid; P made out.

2647. Mar. 29, 1749 James Welch jr enters 300 ac in Bladen Co on E side of White Marsh; border: on lower side of his father's land; paid; P made out.

page 351
2648. Mar. 30, 1749 John [faint] enters 50 ac in Bladen Co [page torn] on Little Pedee R [rest of entry page torn and faint]; paid; P made out.

2649. Mar. 30, 1749 Thomas Bryan jr enters 100 ac in Bladen Co [page torn] on Little Pedee R; border: [page torn] above a branch called [page torn] and runs "up"; paid; P made out.

2650. Mar. 30, 1749 Isaac Odam enters 640 ac in Bladen Co on S side of Little Pedee R; border: [faint] branch above his house and runs down the river; paid; P made out.

North Carolina Land Entries 1735-1752

2651. Mar. 30, 1749 James Odam jr enters 250 ac in Bladen Co on S side of Little Pedee R, at Spring Br, & runs down the river; paid; P made out.

2652. Mar. 30, 1749 Saml Carver enters 500 ac in Bladen Co on E side of White Marsh; border: on upper side of Joseph Soul's land; paid; P made out.

2653. Mar. 30, 1749 William Maltsby [or Mattsby] enters 250 ac in Bladen Co on Carvers Cr and on Little Beaver Pond; paid; P made out.

page 352
2654. [page torn] enters 200 ac in Craven Co on Clayroot Swamp; between Swift Cr and Tar R.

2655. [page torn] David [Noyus ? smudge] enters 100 ac in Carteret Co on E side of Newport R; between Deep Cr and David Sheppard's cowpens; border: the River Swamp; [page torn] chd.

2656. [faint] Lazarus Pearce jr enters 200 ac in Beaufort Co on S side of Pamplico R and W side of Chocaminica Cr; border: on said creek, runs "up, & back"; paid; P made out; Warrant made out.

2657. Mar. 31, 1749 [no name] enters 200 ac in Craven Co; border: on or near Arthur Johnston's line on Nuse R and Thomas [faint]ortsnine's creek [faint].

2658. Mar. 31, 1749 Ralph Miller enters 300 ac in Anson Co on S side of Great Pedee R on Browns Cr; border: Mr. Goold's upper corner and runs "up"; paid; P made out.

2659. Mar. 31, 1749 Ralph Miller enters 300 ac in Anson Co on S side of Great Pedee R and on Browns Cr; border: John McCoy's upper corner and runs "upwards"; paid; P made out.

page 353 [writing on top part of this page is faint]
2660. Mar. 31, 1749 Aaron [rest of entry faint and page torn]; paid; P made out.

2661. Mar. 31, 1749 Gideon Gibson enters 100 ac [rest of entry faint and page torn]; paid; P made out.

2662. Mar. 31, 1749 John Roberts enters 100 ac in Bladen Co [faint] side of Rowan's Marsh and on S [faint] near [Sampson ? faint] path; paid; P made out.

2663. Mar. 31, 1749 John Cannon enters 150 ac in Craven Co [faint] Swift Cr; border: [faint] part of his own land and runs up the creek; paid; P made out.

2664. Mar. 31, 1749 Peter Guilstrap enters 350 ac in Craven Co on [faint] side of

North Carolina Land Entries 1735-1752

Neuse R; border: Thomas Branton's land; paid; P made out.

2665. Mar. 31, 1749 Edmund Cullen enters 200 ac in Craven Co on S side of Neuse R, W side of Adams Cr, & runs up "the" fork; paid "5.12/6"; P made out.

2666. Mar. 31, 1749 Edmund Cullen enters 640 ac in Craven Co in the fork of [page torn] creek, runs down to [page torn] creek, & W side of Coate's Cr; paid; P made out.

page 354 [this page smudged and writing is very faint]
2667. [smudge] James Barber enters 100 ac in New Hanover Co on N side of Goshen Swamp at the [faint] below William Case; border: a white oak on the side of [faint] and runs "down".

2668. [faint] in Craven Co on N side of S Falling Cr; known as McFenkin's place on S side.

2669. [faint] enters 150 ac in Craven Co on N side of Nuce R [faint] fork of Thickete Marsh and includes "the same".

2670. [faint; maybe John Rice] enters 200 ac in Craven Co on N side of Nuce R and on Wheat Swamp; being an Indian old field and a place where Johnston "went to set down"; border: Cattail Pond.

2671. [faint; maybe John Rice] enters 640 ac in Craven Co on N side of Nuce R, N and S sides of [Briery ? smudge] Br, & "at and about" the Horse Pond; border: said Rice's land.

2672. [faint] Daniel McNeal enters 150 ac in Bladen Co on NE side of NW Cape Fear R; border: Saml Swann's upper line about 2 miles below the long pond; paid; P made out.

2673. [faint] Thomas Anderson enters 200 ac in Bladen Co on a branch of Lower Little R known as Craine Cr; paid; P made out.

page 355 [writing on top half of page is faint]
2674. [page torn] George [faint and rest of entry page torn].

2675. [page torn] John Rice enters 100 ac in Craven Co [rest of entry page torn and faint].

2676. [page torn] John Rice enters 400 ac in Craven Co [faint] Bright's [faint].

2677. [page torn] John Rice enters 100 ac in Craven Co on N side [smudge]; between Atkins [smudge] "the" Kills and the school house.

North Carolina Land Entries 1735-1752

2678. [page torn] John Rice enters 200 ac in Craven Co on N side [smudge] on Atkins Br on [smudge] East side; between Nichs. Green and Robt. Hays but now Her[smudge].

2679. [page torn] John Rice enters 50 ac in Craven Co on N side of Nuce R; border: on the river back of old John Rouce's line and Michl. Raisher.

2680. [page torn] John Rice enters 100 ac in Craven Co on N side of Nuce R, E side of Loosing Swamp, & "against" the mouth of Briery Br.

page 356 [page torn at top left]
2681. [page torn] in Craven Co on N side of [page torn] Falling Cr; where "one" Benjn. Creech lives [page torn].

2682. [page torn] enters 200 ac in Craven Co on head of Fork Br; between Briery Br and Jerico "or" Mirey Br [page torn].

2683. [page torn] John Wotherington [? faint] enters 100 ac in Craven Co on head of [Gap or Gum--faint] Br; where he lives [page torn].

2684. [page torn] John Bryan enters 200 ac in Craven Co on N side of Trent R; border: Capt. Rowan's line, runs along the same to Cullen Pollock's line, along said line to Adam Moor's land, & down his line; P made out.

2685. [page torn] William Bush enters 425 ac in New Hanover Co on W side of Cohera "Run"; border: a white oak on the run, runs "out, & down"; paid; P made out.

2686. [page torn] Robert Hines enters 50 ac in Johnston Co on S side of Neuse R, on both sides of Sleepy Cr, & near the mouth thereof; paid; P made out.

2687. [page torn] Alexr. Rouse enters 87 ac in New Hanover Co on N side of Goshen Swamp; border: above Absolom Wesson's land; includes Taylors Folley; paid; P made out.

page 357 [top right of page torn]
2688. [page torn] Wm [rest of entry page torn]; paid; P made out.

2689. [page torn] Robert Cook [rest of entry pate torn]; paid; P made out.

2690. [page torn] Saml Ratcliffe enters 200 ac in Johnston Co [page torn] Neuse R [page torn] Cabbin Br above [page torn] Pool's land; paid; P made out.

2691. [page torn] Abraham Boyd enters 600 ac in Bladen Co on S side of P D River and both sides of Mill Cr; border: a red oak about 0.25 miles below his improvements, runs up both sides, & includes "the same"; paid; P made out.

2692. [page torn] Abraham Boyd enters 200 ac in Bladen Co on S side of [smudge] River, "a little" above mouth of Persimon Cr at a white oak, & runs "down"; paid; P made out.

2693. [page torn] Abraham Boyd enters 100 ac in Bladen Co on S side of [P] D River; border: William Kemp's land on lower side "thereof"; paid; P made out.

2694. [page torn] Hopkin Howell enters 600 ac in Bladen Co on S side of P D River, on Jones Cr, & on Watery Br; paid; P made out.

2695. [page torn] William Forbes enters 100 ac in Bladen Co on S side of P D River; border: on lower side of Thomas Thomkins land; paid; P made out.

2696. [page torn] Edmund Cartledge enters 200 ac in Bladen Co on N side of [P] D River and both sides of "Cartlidges" [Creek ? smudge]; border: near Jones' land; paid; P made out.

page 358 [top left of page torn]
2697. [page torn] on the North [page torn] Cartledges [page torn] marked pine above [page torn] fork.

2698. [page torn] enters 150 ac in Bladen Co on N side of Pedee R and on upper side of Little R; border: "his" lower survey.

2699. [page torn] Horn enters 150 ac in Bladen Co on S side of Pedee R and N side of Jones' Cr; includes his improvements [page torn].

2700. [page torn] John Hilliard enters 1,280 ac in Craven Co on S side of Trent R and NE side of Steels Run [page torn].

2701. [page torn] John Blackman enters 200 ac in Johnston Co on S side of Nuse R, in Nuse Marshes, & near Fort Island; paid; Pet. made out.

2702. [page torn] Benje. Williams enters 200 ac in Johnston Co on S side of Nuse R; border: joins his own "plantation"; paid; Pet. made out.

2703. [page torn] Gideon Allen enters 200 ac in Johnston Co on S side of Nuse R and near a beaverdam on Reid Cr; paid; Pet. made out.

2704. [page torn] John Whitley enters 200 ac in Johnston Co on E side of Body Swamp; known as Spoil Conie Swamp and in the fork "thereof"; paid; P made out.

page 359 [top right of page is torn]
2705. [page torn] William Deel [page torn]; paid; Pet. made out.

North Carolina Land Entries 1735-1752

2706. [page torn] Jno Tindel [or Tinazl] enters 150 ac in Beaufort Co [page torn] of Campbells Cr [page torn] his own line, runs [faint], & "out"; paid; Petition made out.

2707. [page torn] Abraham Duncan enters 300 ac in Beaufort Co on S side of N prong of Swifts Cr; border: below the cowpen [smudge] and runs up the swamp; paid; Petition made out.

2708. [page torn] Jonathan Cullen enters 200 ac in Craven Co on W side of [smudge] Creek, on the head "thereof", & runs up the creek; paid; P made out.

2709. [page torn] Joseph Mott enters 200 ac in New Hanover Co on W side of NE Cape Fear R; border: Edward Pearcol and David Evans; paid; P made out.

page 360 [top left of page is torn]
2710. [page torn] on Beverdam Br.

2711. [page torn] Prescot enters 100 ac in Craven Co on N side of Nuse R and S side of Swifts Cr; border: at a small branch below his house and runs up the "creek fork" [page torn].

2712. Apr. 4, [page torn] Saml. Coburn enters 800 ac in Anson Co on S side of N fork "or" branch of Catabo R; border: George Carthey's lower line and runs down the river; includes Mill Cr and his improvements; paid; P made out.

2713. Apr. 4, [page torn] George Carthey jr enters 400 ac in Anson Co on S side of Catabo R; border: Robert Leeper's land on NW side; paid; P made out.

2714. Apr. 4, [page torn] George Carthey sr enters 400 ac in Anson Co on NE side of N branch of Catabo R; border: opposite Coburn's and Leapper's land; includes Dutchman's Camping Place; paid; P made out.

2715. Apr. 4, [page torn] Geo Carthey jr enters 400 ac in Anson Co on S side of Catabo R; border: opposite Robert Rinnes' land; paid; P made out.

2716. Apr. 4, [page torn] John Carthey enters 400 ac in Anson Co; border: a large bottom above his house on N side of Catabo R; includes part of the island opposite said land and runs down said river; paid; P made out.

page 361 [top right of page is torn]
2717. [page torn for entire entry]

2718. [page torn] Thos [page torn]; paid; P made out.

2719. [page torn] Tyree Harris enters 600 ac [page torn] on N side of [page torn]

River and runs "up"; paid; P made out.

2720. [page torn] Wm Shirrell enters 400 ac [in Anson Co] on S fork of Clarks Cr and N side of Catabo R; paid; P made out.

2721. [page torn] Saml. Beason enters 400 ac [in Anson Co] on E side of Clarks Cr about a [mile ? smudge] below a beaverdam; paid; P made out.

2722. [page torn] Jacob Faulkonbury enters 150 ac [in Anson Co] on N side of Great P D River; being where he lives; paid; P made out.

2723. [page torn] William Kemp enters 400 ac [in Anson Co] on S side of Great P D River and on Mill Cr; being where "Androw" [Coat ? page torn] lives; paid; P made out.

2724. [page torn] Geo Dobbs enters 150 ac [in Anson Co] on S side of Great P D River and on both sides of Thompsons Cr; paid; P made out.

2725. [page torn] Benja. Jackson enters 200 ac [in Anson Co] on S side of Great P D River and on both side of Thompsons Cr; paid; P made out.

page 362 [top left of page is torn]
2726. [page torn for entire entry]

2727. [page torn] [in Anson Co] on N side of P D River; border: his own line and Yearby [page torn].

2728. [page torn] Joseph White jr enters 250 [written over 200] ac [in Anson Co] on S side of P D River and on [faint] side of Browns Cr; includes a spring; paid [page torn].

2729. [page torn] Joseph White and Fras. Mackelwean enter 500 ac [in Anson Co] on S side of P D River and both sides of Smiths Cr; paid; P made out.
2730. [page torn] John Becton enters 100 ac in Craven Co on S side of Neuse R; border: "SW" John Williams' "plantation" and runs to Benoni Loftin's land where he lives; P made out.

2731. [page torn] James Adair enters 400 ac in Bladen Co on S side of Deep R and on head of Buffaloe Cr; called Golden Grove and Silver Spring; paid.

2732. [page torn] James Adair enters 100 ac in Johnston Co; border: Job Ive's land on N side of Neuse R; paid.

page 363 [top right and bottom right of page are torn]
2733. [page torn for entire entry].

North Carolina Land Entries 1735-1752

2734. [page torn] Edmund Mitchell enters [page torn]; paid; P made out.

2735. [page torn] Benjamin Fuzel [written over Fuzzel] enters 100 ac in New Hanover Co on W side of NE Cape Fear R at a place called the wells where Francis Park "lately" lived; paid; P made out.

2736. [page torn] John "Herris" enters 150 ac in Craven Co between Mott Swamp and Berr Swamp on S side of [Trent ? smudge] River; paid; P made out [Jos Carruthers Dr--lined ot].

2737. [page torn] Frs. Mackilwean and Jos Carruthers enter 200 ac in Johnston Co on S side of Nuce R; border: on the river [smudge] Stringar's Ferry and [faint]; P made out.

2738. Apr. 5, 1749 John Price enters 300 ac in Anson Co on [smudge] Cataba R "on" Price's [smudge] where his house stands; paid; P made out.

2739. Apr. 5, 1749 Peter Ellot enters 200 ac in Anson Co [page torn] of Cataba R [page torn] "miles" be [page torn]; paid; P made out.

2740. Apr. 5, 1749 Reese Price enters 600 ac in Anson Co on [page torn] river [page torn]; paid; P made out.

page 364 [top left and botton left of page are torn]
2741. [page torn for entire entry]

2742. [page torn] on Browns Cr a branch of Clarks "R".

2743. [page torn] 100 ac in Anson Co on Clarks R [faint] S part of Cataba R.

2744. [page torn] Thomas Cooks [or Hooks] enters 640 ac in Anson Co on S side of Clarks R; border: a hickory marked "T C"; paid; P made out.

2745. [page torn] Matthew Dill enters 400 ac in Anson Co on S fork of the creek where Alexr. Osburn lives and about 5 miles from said Osburn's "plantation"; paid; P made out.

2746. [page torn] James Dill enters 400 ac in Anson Co; border: S of Matthew Dill's land and joins said Matthew's land; paid; P made out.

2747. [page torn] Thomas Dill enters 400 ac in Anson Co on "the" [McCulloh's] manor line on Davisons Cr; paid; [page torn].

2748. [page torn] [following is lined out] McCullock enters 640 ac in Anson Co on N side of Third Cr opposite an old beaver dam marked "A M C" on a white oak; [page torn].

page 365 [top right half of page is torn]
2749. [page torn for entire entry]

2750. [page torn for entire entry]

2751. [page torn for entire entry]

2752. [page torn] James McGee enters 640 ac [page torn]; paid; P made out.

2753. [page torn] Andrew McGee enters 640 ac [page torn]; paid; P made out.

2754. [page torn] John McGee enters 300 ac in Anson Co on N side of [page torn] River on McGees Br [page torn] and runs "thro" said land; paid; P made out.

2755. [page torn] Andrew McGee enters 500 ac in Anson Co on both sides of [page torn] Creek, on N side of Cataba R, & about 5 miles from the river; paid; Pet. made out.

page 366 [top left half of is page torn]
2756. [page torn for entire entry]

2757. [page torn for entire entry]

2758. [page torn] on S side of [page torn] River and below Browns Cr.

2759. [page torn] enters 300 ac in Bladen Co on N side of Great Pedee R; border: [faint]mer's line; [page torn].

2760. [page torn] enters 300 ac in Bladen Co; between Henry Walker and "the" fork; [page torn].

2761. [page torn] McCulloh enters 100 ac in New Hanover Co on E side of "hod" [or hoe] branch of NE branch of Black R; border: near his 1,000 ac tract "lately" taken up by him on said branch.

2762. [page torn] James Thomas enters 120 ac in New Hanover Co on Long Cr; P made out.

2763. [page torn] Jno Fryer enters 200 ac in New Hanover Co in the fork of Little Cohery Cr and on N side of the creek; Lampson [or Sampson]; P made out.

[end of first folder in this box]

[The following entries are in the second folder in the box.]
"Crown Land Office Land Entry book 1741-1752" [actually second part of the

North Carolina Land Entries 1735-1752

book and includes some entries in Granville's District]
page 1 [blank page]

page 2
2764. Jul. 9, 1750 Thomas Williams enters 200 ac in Granville Co on S Hico Cr; [being] the "plantation" where said Williams lives; border: about 0.5 miles below the fork of said creek and runs up the creek; Churton.

2765. Jul. 9, 1750 William Wilson enters 200 ac in Granville Co on S "Hyco" Cr; [being] the "plantation" where said Wilson lives; border: at a place called the ford below said Wilson's "plantation" and runs up the creek; Churton.

2766. Jul. 9, 1750 George Bryant enters 150 ac in Edgecombe Co in the fork of Fishing Cr and Tar R; border: mouth of said creek, runs up the creek to mouth of Cove Br, up said branch to Thos Bryan's line, & down his line; Conner.

2767. Jul. 9, 1750 John Herring enters 200 ac in Johnston Co; border: John Giles line and runs "almost" East on "the" creek from N side of Neus R; Caswell.

2768. Jul. 9, 1750 James Mackleroy enters 300 ac in Johnston Co on N side of Walnut Cr; border: "a little" below his mill and runs up the creek; Caswell.

2769. Jul. 9, 1750 John Bockom enters 300 ac in Johnston Co on S side of Neus R; border: about a mile above John Bennifield and runs up the river; Caswell.

2770. Jul. 9, 1750 John Smith enters 400 ac in Johnston Co on S side of Middle Cr, [at] mouth of Beaverdam Br, & runs up the branch; Caswell.

page 3
2771. Jul. 9, 1750 Silus Monk enters 150 ac in Johnston Co on N side of Walnut Cr and joins both sides of Great Br; Caswell.

2772. Jul. 9, 1750 John Rouse enters 150 ac in Johnston Co on S side of Neus R, on Crabtree Cr, & on a place called Sycamore fork; Caswell.

2773. Jul. 9, 1750 Zechariah Martin enters 640 ac in Bladen Co on Cane Cr; includes Jos Griffith's improvement on S side of Haw R.

2774. Jul. 9, 1750 Zechariah Martin enters 300 ac in Bladen Co on S side of Haw R.

2775. Jul. 9, 1750 John Hammond enters 200 ac in Bladen Co on Cane Cr and on N side of Haw R; Caswell.

2776. Jul. 9, 1750 Joseph Wells enters 640 ac in Bladen Co on waters of Cane Cr and on S side of Haw R.

2777. Jul. 9, 1750 Zechariah Martin enters 640 ac in Bladen Co on John Williams' Mill Cr and on S side of Haw R.

2778. Jul. 9, 1750 Joseph Hardy enters 640 ac in Bladen Co on N side of Haw R; includes his own and Thomas Shiles' improvements; Caswell.

2779. Jul. 9, 1750 Anthony Chamness enters 640 ac in Bladen Co on waters of Cane Cr and S side of Haw R.

2780. Jul. 9, 1750 Henry Bellinger enters 640 ac in Bladen Co on Horsepen fork of Haw R.

2781. Jul. 9, 1750 David Myres enters 640 ac in Bladen Co on N side of Cane Cr and S side of Haw R.

page 4
2782. Jul. 9, 1750 Richard Burk enters 200 ac in Bladen Co on waters of Rocky R; border: on S side of John Landom's line.

2783. Jul. 9, 1750 Timothy Tyrrel enters 640 ac in Bladen Co on head of Stinking Quarter Cr, opposite the head of Sandy Cr, "against" head of middle prong of Rocky R; includes Gregory's cabin, "if suit".
2784. Jul. 9, 1750 Timothy Tyrrel enters 640 ac in Bladen Co on N side of Poll Catt Cr.

2785. Jul. 9, 1750 Timothy Tyrrel enters 640 ac in Bladen Co on N prong of Poll Catt Cr.

2786. Jul. 9, 1750 William Eaton enters "a resurvey" of land [number of acres omitted] where he lives in Granville Co; border: begins at his upper corner on "the" river bank, runs "out" along the "line or lines" to the corner at his mill, then to the road at Reedy Swamp, "down" along the edge of the marsh or swamp to Mr. Wm Parson's line, down Stonehouse Cr, & to the beginning; Weldan and Churton.

2787. Jul. 9, 1750 William Eaton enters 300 ac in Granville Co on Grassy Cr; between Bolleans Mountain and "the" Meadows.

2788. Aug. 31, 1750 Henry Harvey enters 640 ac in "said" County below "the" lick, S of Fourth Cr, & on upper side "thereof".

2789. Aug. 31, 1750 Henry Harvey enters 400 ac in "said" County on W side of a small mountain, on waters of Kers Cr, & about a mile from John Withraw's place.

North Carolina Land Entries 1735-1752

page 5
2790. Sept. 1750 James McKlewain enters 640 ac in Anson Co on both sides of Fourth Cr; border: John McCulloch's lower corner; includes "the good land" on both sides of Buffalo Br.

2791. Sept. 1750 Thomas McOwen enters 640 ac in Anson Co on a branch of Rocky R; border: about 3 miles below Mr. Carruthers' "plantation".

2792. Sept. 1750 Archibald Hamilton enters 340 ac in Anson Co on "a" back creek, about 1.5 miles above White Oak Lick, & "by" an old bridge.

2793. Sept. 1750 James Beel enters 640 ac in Anson Co on Fourth Cr; border: near George Davison's survey.

2794. Sept. 1750 Alexdr. Cathey enters 640 ac in Anson Co on W side of main fork of Grants Cr; between said Cathey's "plantation" and James Graham.

2795. Sept. 1750 John Nesbett enters 300 ac in Anson Co on head of Chas. Hart's Cr; border: about 2 miles above John Brandon's place.

2796. Sept. 1750 James Oliphant enters 640 ac in Anson Co on both sides of Fourth Cr; border: below James Mackilwain's place.

2797. Sept. 1750 John McConnel enters 300 ac in Anson Co on both sides of "Daviesons" Cr; border: Jno McDowall, Benja. Winslow, & his own line.

2798. Sept. 1750 Robt. Johnston enters 640 ac in Anson Co; border: John McConnel's "plantation".

2799. Sept. 1750 James Huggins enters 640 ac in Anson Co on E side of Buffaloe Cr; border: about 2 miles below Thoms. McOwen's place and where there are "considerable" falls in the creek.

page 6
2800. Sept. 1750 George Davieson jr enters 500 ac in Anson Co in the fork of Buffaloe Cr; border: about 3 miles below Andrew Mitchell's "plantation".
2801. Sept. 1750 John Thompson enters 640 ac in Anson Co on both sides of Fourth Cr; border: John Oliphant's "plantation" on lower side.

2802. Sept. 1750 John Thompson enters 640 ac in Anson Co on N side of Fifth Cr and near "which" there's a good spring by a tall hollow poplar; includes both sides of "the" fork.

2803. Sept. 1750 John Thompson enters 640 ac [in Anson Co] "said place and according to the above description".

2804. Sept. 1750 John Thompson enters 640 ac in Anson Co in the fork of Fifth Cr; includes both sides of the "forks" and main creek.

2805. Sept. 1750 John Thompson enters 640 ac in Anson Co "in the said last mentioned place".

2806. Sept. 1750 John Thompson enters 640 ac in Anson Co on S fork of Fifth Cr about a mile above the fork.

2807. Sept. 1750 John Thompson enters 640 ac in Anson Co on head "Drats" of Alexr. Cathey's Cr; border: Brandon's place; between "the above place" and George Cathey's place.

2808. Sept. 1750 James Mackilwain enters 640 ac in Anson Co on Second Cr where "the" road crosses said creek.

2809. Sept. 1750 Hanis Baum enters 300 ac in Anson Co on N side of S fork of Catawba R and on both sides of Hannis' Cr running into main Catawba R.

2810. Sept. 1750 Adam "Shirill" enters 640 ac in Anson Co on N side of Catawba R; border: the upper line of "the" manor.

2811. Sept. 1750 Christopr. Goodhart enters 640 ac in Anson Co on N side of S fork of Catawba R, in the fork of Clarks Cr, & runs "down".

page 7
2812. Sept. 1750 Jams McKilwain enters 640 ac in Anson Co on both sides of the mouth of Muddy Cr and on S side of "Catawby" R; includes the low ground of the creek and river.

2813. Sept. 1750 Thomas Tyson enters 300 ac in Bladen Co on both sides of Deep R, about 4 miles below "the" line, & near mouth of Great Cr.

2814. Sept. 1750 John Sallis "two entries directed according to his request to be surveyed and returned" [no number of acres or county mentioned].

2815. Sept. 1750 John Miatt enters 500 ac in Johnston Co on Swifts Cr; includes the improvements "thereon".

2816. Sept. 1750 Robert Jones jr enters 300 ac in Granville Co; border: Thos Pasher and William Eves; includes "th tenement" of Thomas Harding.

2817. Sept. 1750 Peter Elliot enters 400 ac in Anson Co on Catawba R; border: about 2.5 miles above John Cathey on said river, at the "bent" of the river, "against" a small island in the river, begins at a small branch, & runs up the river.

North Carolina Land Entries 1735-1752

2818. Sept. 1750 Henry Johnston enters 640 ac in Anson Co; border: Henry Lawson's line, "containing" Beaverdam Cr, runs down the creek, joins Mr. Winsley's line, & runs "up" "2 " Winslow "page 15" [may refer to 2923 below on p. 18 (sic)].

2819. Sept. 1750 "Squiar" Boon esq "seven entries" in Anson Co on Bear Cr and in the fork of Yadkin R [number of acres not mentioned].

2820. Sept. 1750 John Harry enters 640 ac in Anson Co on S side of N fork of Yadkin R, begins at mouth of Luken Cr, & runs "up".

page 8
2821. Sept. 17, 1750 Henry Slander enters 640 ac in Anson Co in the fork of Yadkin R and on S side of N fork [of Yadkin R].

2822. Sept. 17, 1750 James Deacon enters 640 ac in Anson Co; where George Henry's entry was.

2823. Sept. 17, 1750 Henry Dowland enters 640 ac in Anson Co on N fork of Yadkin R, below Reedy Cr, & at head of Beaverdam Meadow.

2824. Sept. 17, 1750 Isaac [write over] Hollyman enters 640 ac in Anson Co; border: at lower end of said Dowland's line.

2825. Sept. 17, 1750 Hugh McCrackden enters 640 ac in Anson Co; border: at lower end of Hollyman's line.

2826. Sept. 17, 1750 William Harrison enters 640 ac in Anson Co on N side of N fork of "the" river.

2827. Sept. 17, 1750 John Allen enters 640 ac in Anson Co on S side of Catawba R; border: about 3 miles above John Beats.

2828. Sept. 17, 1750 "Squiar" Boon enters 640 ac in Anson Co on Grants Cr and at Licking Cr; includes a great timber bottom and Paul Garrison's.

2829. Sept. 17, 1750 John Moy enters 640 ac in Beaufort Co on S side of Grindal Cr and N side of Pamplico R; border: Jacob Moor's line and runs up the creek; Bonner.

2830. Sept. 17, 1750 Seth Pilkington enters 640 ac in Beaufort Co on N side of Pamplico R; border: John Floyd's upper corner tree and runs E up South side of "the" Beaver Dam; Bonner.

2831. Sept. 17, 1750 John Willerd enters 60 ac in Tyrrell Co in the fork of Smithwicks Cr.

2832. Sept. 17, 1750 William Brown enters 640 ac in Tyrrell Co; border: John Smith's line and runs along Crane Pond.

page 9 [only five entries on this page]
2833. Sept. 17, 1750 James Bonner enters 450 ac in Beaufort Co on N side of Pamplico R and on both sides of Moy's Beaver Dam; border: John Snowd's corner tree, runs near Roanoak Road, & "round"; Bonner.

2834. Sept. 17, 1750 Thomas Bonner sr and Jas Bonner enter 400 ac in Beaufort Co; border: at Henry Snowd's line and runs up "the" river; includes the vacant land between Thos Bonner and William Adams; Bonner.

2835. Sept. 17, 1750 William Congleton enters 200 ac in Beaufort Co; border: at John Smith's line, near Crane Pond, on N side of Pamplico R, & runs "out and back"; Bonner.
2836. Sept. 17, 1750 James Tate enters 300 ac in Johnston Co; border: on the line James Jones "ran out" and runs up "the" creek.

2837. Sept. 17, 1750 Roger Turner enters 640 ac in Anson Co in the forks of Yadkin R and on N side of S fork of said river.

pages 10 and 11 [blank pages]
page 12
2838. Dec. 5, 1750 William Niel enters 400 ac in Anson Co; border: above his brother's place.

2839. Dec. 5, 1750 William Niel enters 400 ac in Anson Co on Meadow Br; between Rocky Hills and the place where Thos Boss lived; includes the Brushey Hill that Morsbey's Path runs "through".

2840. Nov. 23, 1750 Robert Mackferson enters 400 ac in Anson Co on S branch of Thos Potts mill Cr; border: William Shirill's line on S side of S fork of Cataba R.

2841. Dec. 1, 1750 William Marson enters 640 ac in Anson Co on Eight mile shole Cr and on N side of Catawba R.

2842. Dec. 1, 1750 William Marson enters 640 ac in Anson Co on Elk Shoal Cr and on N side of Cataba R.

2843. Dec. 1, 1750 John Oliphant enters "two tracts" of 640 ac each in Anson Co on Third Cr; border: at the uppermost large meadow and runs up both sides of the creek.

2844. Dec. 1, 1750 James Alexander enters 320 ac in Anson Co; border: Blyth's line and on both sides of "the" creek.

2845. Dec. 1, 1750 Richard "Morbee" enters 640 ac in Anson Co opposite mouth of a small run, on E side of Second Cr, & runs up both sides of said creek; being where he lives.

2846. Dec. 1, 1750 Francis McKilwain enters 640 ac in Anson Co on Quaker Meadow, on S side of "the Atkin" [Yadkin R], & on waters of Catawba R; includes the "good" upland on both sides of the meadow.

2847. Dec. 10, 1750 James Blyth enters 400 ac in Anson Co on Blyth's Cr; border: "up" said creek from his line; includes the Rocky Spring on both sides of said creek.

page 13
2848. Dec. 10, 1750 John Brandon enters 320 ac in Anson Co; between George Carthey on E side, James Carthey on W side, & Robt. Reed and John Little on S side; includes "the" Meeting House and Grave Yard; "said place" first improved by George Carthey and Thos Gillaspie.

2849. Nov. 24, 1750 James Ellison enters 320 ac in Anson Co; border: E of John Brandon's "plantation"; between Matthew Lock and John Nesbet on both sides of Crane Cr.

2850. Nov. 24, 1750 James Ellison enters 400 ac in Anson Co on both sides of Crane Cr; includes the Indian Camps and runs up to "the" path to Irish Settlement.

2851. Nov. 22, 1750 Andrew Ellison enters 640 ac in Anson Co on N side of "N" Creek; border: "round" John Thompson's entry; includes "the" stream of the creek.

2852. Nov. 23, 1750 Thomas Ellison enters 640 ac in Anson Co on N side of Fourth Cr; border "or near": Andrew Ellison's entry; includes "the" stream of the creek and Reedy Br.

2853. Nov. 23, 1750 Robert Ellison enters 640 ac in Anson Co on N side of Fourth Cr; border: John Oliphant's "plantation".

2854. Nov. 23, 1750 James Mackilwean enters 640 ac in Anson Co on and in the fork of Crane Cr, above the Indian Camps, & on both sides "thereof".

2855. Nov. 23, 1750 George Davieson enters 640 ac in Anson Co on Fourth Cr; border: John McCulloch's land on the upper side.

2856. Nov. 23, 1750 George Davieson enters 640 ac in Anson Co; border: John McCulloch's land and "the" upper entry; includes Jones' improvement.

2857. Nov. 23, 1750 Geoge Davieson enters 640 ac in Anson Co on the main Fourth Cr, above the upper entries, & where "the" path crosses the creek.

2858. Jan. 17, 1750/51 [sic] Fras Mackilwean enters 400 ac in Anson Co on S side of Catawba R, above Talk Shoals and Whitners Shoals, & on the main river; includes "the" Cherry Old Fields.

page 14
2859. Nov. 19, 1750 James Morrison enters 640 ac in Anson Co on Third Cr; border: Alexandr. McCulloch.

2860. Nov. 19, 1750 Willm. Morrison enters 640 ac in Anson Co; border: James Morrison on Third Cr.

2861. Nov. 19, 1750 Andrew Kart enters 640 ac in Anson Co on Second Cr; border: above James Carthey's place; being where he lives.

2862. Dec. 5, 1750 John Neale enters 400 ac in Anson Co on W side of Second Cr; border: opposite James Bast's [sic] place.

2863. Nov. 21, 1750 Samuel Davis enters 400 ac in Anson Co on Second Cr.

2864. Nov. 21, 1750 Samuel Davis enters 400 ac "on the same creek".

2865. Nov. 21, 1750 Samuel Davis enters 400 ac "on the same creek".

2866. Nov. 21, 1750 George Hise enters 500 ac in Anson Co "on the same creek".

2867. Nov. 21, 1750 Andrew "Craver" enters 600 ac in Anson Co "on the same creek".

2868. Nov. 21, 1750 Philip Haron "Hart" enters 300 ac in Anson Co "on the same creek".

2869. Nov. 21, 1750 Edward Davis enters 640 ac in Anson Co on N fork of Second Cr.

2870. Oct. 24, 1750 Robert Cade enters 400 ac in Bladen Co on S side of New Hope Cr and runs down the creek.

2871. Oct. 24, 1750 Robert Cade, for Jno Patterson, enters 640 ac in Johnston Co; border: Joseph John Alston's corner on E side of Pattersons Cr and runs down both sides of said creek.

2872. Oct. 24, 1750 Benjamin Bowling enters 300 ac in Johnston Co; border: a white oak on N side of Lick Cr and runs on both sides of the creek; includes his improvement where he dwells.

2873. Oct. 24, 1750 John Collins enters 300 ac in Bladen Co "alias" Duplin Co [sic] on N side of Haw R; border: a marked red oak on Pokeberry Cr.

page 15
2874. Oct. 24, 1750 William Speight enters 640 ac in Johnston Co on Great Swift Cr, runs on both sides of the creek, & includes where Stringer dwells; where John Stringer dwells.

2875. Oct. 24, 1750 James Paine enters 320 ac in Bladen Co on N side of Haw R; border: a red oak at the falls of Phills Cr and runs up the creek; includes the fork.

2876. Oct. 24, 1750 James Paine enters 300 ac in Bladen Co on N side of Haw R and at "Dooers" Folly; includes the rich land.

2877. Oct. 26, 1750 Phillip Johnston enters 600 ac in Johnston Co; being the improvements of Cornelius "Tyrrill"; Johnston purchased his [Tyrrill's] rights.

2878. Oct. 26, 1750 James Cane enters 640 ac in Johnston Co on S side of Neus R and on both sides of Middle Cr; includes said Cane's improvement.

2879. Nov. 11, 1750 [sic] John Dickson enters 640 ac in Anson Co on Muddy Cr between N and S forks of Yadkin R; border: about 2 miles above Willm. Grant's "plantation"; includes Paul Garrison's cabbin.

2880. Apr. 3, 1751 Andrew Berry enters 640 ac in Anson Co on both sides of Fourth Cr; border: upper line of George Davieson's upper tract on the "above" creek.

2881. Apr. 3, 1751 Andrew Berry enters 640 ac in Anson Co on both sides of Liles Cr; border: above James Mackilwean's place on S side of Cataba R.

2882. Apr. 3, 1751 John McGee enters 640 ac in Anson Co; border: in "the" corner of "the" manor and near Edward Givens' "plantation".

page 16
2883. Apr. 3, 1751 Alexander Read enters 640 ac in Anson Co on N side of Fourth Cr and near "the" Wild Dutchman's camp.

2884. Apr. 3, 1751 John Oliphant enters 640 ac in Anson Co on N fork of Swift Cr; border: Mrs. Thompson's land on said creek.

2885. Apr. 3, 1751 John Brandon enters 640 ac in Anson Co on middle fork of Crane Cr; includes both sides of the main creek; includes an old field where there are some walnuts.

2886. Apr. 3, 1751 John Brandon enters 400 ac in Anson Co on the "above said" fork; includes a bottom where there is a white oak marked "I B".

2887. Apr. 3, 1751 James Aston enters 640 ac in Anson Co; border: SE of Andrew Carthey on a branch of Catawba "Cr".

2888. Apr. 3, 1751 James Morrison enters 640 ac in Anson Co on Third Cr; border: Alexander McCulloch.

2889. Apr. 3, 1751 Willm. Morrison enters 640 ac in Anson Co on Third Cr; border: James Morrison's place.

2890. Apr. 3, 1751 John Slowan enters 640 ac in Anson Co on waters of Coddle Cr; between Alexdr. Osborn and George Davieson's place.

2891. Apr. 3, 1751 Andrew Mitchell enters 640 ac in Anson Co; border: on N and S sides of the ridge where he lives.

2892. Apr. 3, 1751 John Ireland enters 640 ac in Anson Co on N side of Cataba R and on both sides of Folk shole Cr; border: Wm Morrison.

2893. Apr. 3, 1751 Wm Shirill enters 200 ac in Anson Co on S side of Cataba R and about 1.5 miles below Elk Shoals.

2894. Apr. 3, 1751 Saml Head enters 640 ac in Anson Co on N side of Fourth Cr where there is a tree marked "S K".

2895. Apr. 3, 1751 John Oliphant enters 640 ac in Anson Co on Buffalo Br; border: James MacKilwean.

2896. Apr. 3, 1751 John Oliphant enters 320 ac in Anson Co on both sides of Fourth Cr; border: Jas MacKilwean and Ellison.

2897. Apr. 3, 1751 Mark Alexander enters 640 ac in Anson Co; border: "with" [within] 100 poles of Mr. Thompson's land and runs down S fork of Swifts Cr.

page 17
2898. Apr. 3, 1751 Robert Joyan enters 640 ac in Anson Co on S fork of Swifts Cr; border: Mark Alexander's place.

2899. Apr. 3, 1751 John McWrath enters 640 ac in Anson Co; border: Jno Caor's West line at "the lower entry" on Third Cr and runs "some part" of Carr's South line; includes two or three springs of Fourth Cr; includes his improvement and a white oak marked "I S".

North Carolina Land Entries 1735-1752

2900. Apr. 3, 1751 Robert Miller enters 640 ac in Anson Co on the branches of Fourth Cr; border: "back" of Geo Davieson's and McCulloch's [land].

2901. Apr. 3, 1751 Wm Archibald enters 640 ac in Anson Co on a large branch of S fork of Swift Cr; includes [the land] "about" a red oak marked "X".

2902. Apr. 3, 1751 Wm Brandon enters 640 ac in Anson Co; border: James Carthey on W side.

2903. Apr. 3, 1751 Henry Potts enters 640 ac in Anson Co on a branch of Forked Meadow Cr; border: "about" James Crawford.

2904. Apr. 3, 1751 Wm Morrison enters 640 ac in Anson Co on waters of Catawba R and on Eight mile Shoals; border: his other entry.

2905. Apr. 3, 1751 Jno Ireland enters 640 ac in Anson Co on waters of Catawba R near Elk Shoals; border: his "other" entry.

2906. Apr. 3, 1751 Adam Shirrill enters 400 ac in Anson Co on S side of Catawba R "over against" Quaker Meadow.

2907. Apr. 3, 1751 Geo Lamley enters 640 ac in Anson Co on N side of Catawba R on Lamleys Cr.

2908. Apr. 3, 1751 "Conread" Moll enters 640 ac in Anson Co on N side of Catawba R and on both sides of Molls Cr.

2909. Apr. 3, 1751 "Bastuan Chian" enters 300 ac in Anson Co on Clarks Cr and in the upper forks of said creek.

2910. Apr. 3, 1751 Barnet "Cheaan" enters 300 ac in Anson Co on Clarks Cr and near the above entry.

2911. Apr. 3, 1751 Jacob Beaver enters 300 ac in Anson Co on Clarks Cr and joining or near the above entry.

2912. Apr. 3, 1751 Geo Beaver enters 300 ac in Anson Co on Clarks Cr and joins the above entry.

page 18
2913. Apr. 3, 1751 David Viser enters 600 ac in Anson Co on N side of Catawba R and on the river.

2914. Apr. 3, 1751 David Viser enters 600 ac in Anson Co on N side of Catawba R and on the river.

North Carolina Land Entries 1735-1752

2915. Apr. 3, 1751 Bartlet Brown enters 600 ac in Anson Co on N side of Catawba R and on a large creek that runs "therein".

2916. Apr. 3, 1751 Philip Karr enters 640 ac in Anson Co on N side of Catawba R, on Table Mountain Cr, at the Great old field below Table Mountain, & at the forks of said creek.

2917. Apr. 3, 1751 Thos Karr enters 640 ac in Anson Co on N side of Catawba R on "some" of the three creeks "so called".

2918. Apr. 3, 1751 Jacob Karr enters 640 ac in Anson Co on N side of Catawba R and on "his" creek.

2919. Apr. 3, 1751 Josh. Gillespie enters 400 ac in Anson Co on N side of Catawba R and on head branches of Rocky R; border: John Brevard, Alexr. Osborn, & John McConnel.

2920. Apr. 3, 1751 Jas Hogans enters 640 ac in Anson Co on head branches of Rocky R and on "the" Waggon Road.

2921. Apr. 3, 1751 Alexr. Osborn enters 200 ac in Anson Co on that part of "said" creek where said Osborn lives and includes "both sides".

2922. Apr. 3, 1751 Alexdr. Carthey enters 200 ac in Anson Co on Grants Cr; border: his own line, John Brandon, & Richard Graham.

2923. Dec. 25, 1750 Benja. Winsley jr enters 640 ac in Anson Co; border: Edward Gibbons' N line and runs up "the" branches "towards" Catawba R.

2924. Dec. 25, 1750 Benja. Winsley jr enters 640 ac in Anson Co on W side of Catawba R, at Mountain Cr, & runs on both sides.

2925. Dec. 25, 1750 Benja. Winsley enters 640 ac in Anson Co; border: Hugh Lawson's line and runs down "said" creek; includes "the" beaver dam.

page 19
2926. Dec. 25, 1750 Thos. Andrew enters 640 ac in Anson Co; border: at George Davis' East [or "ast"] line and runs up both sides.

2927. Dec. 25, 1750 Thos. Andrew enters 640 ac in Anson Co on Catawba R, at Buck Cr a branch on E side of said river, & runs "down".

2928. Dec. 25, 1750 John Burnett enters 640 ac in Anson Co on middle branch of Crane Cr; includes James Bast's old place and on P D Road.

2929. Dec. 25, 1750 Henry Kirkhan enters 640 ac in Anson Co on S fork of Liles

North Carolina Land Entries 1735-1752

Cr and runs on both sides.

2930. Dec. 25, 1750 Jas Hoggan enters 640 ac in Anson Co; border: below Kirkhan's in the same fork of said creek and runs down both sides of said creek.

2931. Dec. 25, 1750 Henry Kirkhan enters 640 ac in Anson Co on both sides of "the same" creek; border: about a mile above his first entry.

2932. Dec. 25, 1750 Jas Hoggan enters 640 ac in Anson Co on both sides of "the same" creek.

2933. Dec. 25, 1750 Wm Morrison enters 640 ac in Anson Co on Liles Cr; includes a great meadow on both sides of said creek.

2934. Dec. 25, 1750 John McConnel enters 640 ac in Anson Co on a long branch of Catawba R and on E side of said river; includes a small Indian field and runs up said river & creek.

2935. Dec. 25, 1750 Moses Andrews enters 640 ac in Anson Co on E side of Catawba R, at a great bend of said river, at mouth of three small branches, & runs up the river.

2936. Dec. 25, 1750 Moses Andrews enters 640 ac in Anson Co on Fourth Cr; border: below James McCalwight's line, & "at or near" said line, & runs down said creek.

2937. Dec. 25, 1750 Wm Morrison enters 640 ac in Anson Co; border: Geo Davis' land on N side of his own line "a place" called Poplar Springs.

page 20
2938. Dec. 25, 1750 Wm Morrison enters 326 ac in Anson Co; border: Jno McDowell's line on waters of Daviesons Cr.

2939. Dec. 25, 1750 Geo "Davison" enters 640 ac in Anson Co on the third fork of Liles Cr and on both sides of an old Indian field on said creek; includes a great meadow.

2940. Jan. 15, 1750/1 Thos. Rich enters 640 ac in Anson Co on S side of Deep R, N side of Richland Cr, & about "the" Trading Path; border: Benja. Well and runs up the creek.

2941. Jan. 15, 1750/1 Thos. Rich enters 640 ac in Anson Co "to be laid out contagious" to the above entry.

2942. Jan. 15, 1750/1 Philip Miller enters two entries [no number of acres mentioned] in Anson Co on S side of Deep R and S side of Richland Cr; border:

Benja. Well and runs "up".

2943. Jan. 15, 1750/1 Thos. Davis enters 640 ac in Anson Co on Richland Cr, S side of Deep R, at "the" Poplar Springs, & runs up the creek.

2944. Oct. 23, 1750 Alexdr. Parker enters 200 ac in Johnston Co on S side of Neus R, on head of Poplar Cr, & about 3 miles from Buncoms Ferry.

2945. Oct. 23, 1750 Geo Whitley enters 400 ac in Johnston Co on N side of Neuse R and S side of Buffalo Swamp.

2946. Oct. 23, 1750 Jno Patterson enters 150 ac in Johnston Co on both sides of Pattersons Cr; border: Joseph Jno Alston's line.

2947. Oct. 23, 1750 Jno Williams enters 200 ac in Bladen Co on N side of Deep R; border: upper corner of Richard Johnston's survey.

2948. Oct. 23, 1750 Richd. Caswell jr enters 640 ac in Bladen Co on N side of Haw R and on Cane Cr; border: John Hammonds.

2949. Oct. 23, 1750 John Cornelious enters 400 ac in Johnston Co on Little R; includes his own improvement.

page 21
2950. Mar. 5, 1750/1 Benja. Boon enters 640 ac in Anson Co on Third Cr on [page torn; probably South] side of Yadkin R and below the path from Grants to the Irish "tract".

2951. Mar. 5, 1750/1 Benja. Boon enters 640 ac in Anson Co in the fork of Yadkin R; border: below Wm Grant's; includes Grindston Quarry.

2952. Mar. 5, 1750/1 Benja. Boon enters 640 ac in Anson Co on S side of Dutchmans Cr; border: 4 miles below Grant's old place; includes a small white oak marked "B" on No Creek.

2953. Mar. 5, 1750/1 Benja. Boon enters 640 ac in Anson Co in the fork of Yadkin R, at a great cane brake, & a great pine marked "B".

2954. Mar. 5, 1750/1 Wm Winters enters 640 ac in Anson Co; border: "Squar" Boon's entry; includes both sides of Dutchmans Cr.

2955. Mar. 5, 1750/1 Wm Winters enters 640 ac in Anson Co on both sides of the path from Swan Creek ford to "Squiar" Boon's.

2956. Mar. 5, 1750/1 Wm Winters enters 640 ac in Anson Co on "the" fork of Grants Cr; includes "the" three forks and a white oak marked "W" at the head of a spring.

2957. Mar. 5, 1750/1 Moses Ellsworth jr enters 640 ac in Anson Co on a small branch that emptys into Grants Cr "alias" Lickin Cr; border: on E side of Wm Grant's.

2958. Mar. 5, 1750/1 Moses Ellsworth sr enters 640 ac in Anson Co on the small branch as the above entry.

2959. Mar. 5, 1750/1 Matthew Gallaspy enters 640 ac in Anson Co on a branch of Grants Cr; includes James Pattent's improvements.

2960. Mar. 5, 1750/1 Thos Donald enters "(12)" 640 ac "tracts" [in Anson Co] on waaters of S fork of Saxapahaw [Haw] R and waters of Buffalo Cr.

2961. Mar. 5, 1750/1 John Conningham enters "two (2)" 640 ac "tracts described as above" [in Anson Co].

2962. Mar. 5, 1750/1 Robt. Rankin enters "six (6)" 640 ac "tracts described as above" [in Anson Co].

2963. Mar. 5, 1750/1 Wm McClintock enters "five (5)" 640 ac "tracts described as above" [in Anson Co].

2964. Mar. 5, 1750/1 Thos. McCuiston enters "two (2)" 640 ac "tracts described as above" [in Anson Co].

2965. Mar. 5, 1750/1 Harmon Cox enters 640 ac in Anson Co on middle prong of Pole catt Cr.

page 21
2966. Mar. 5, 1750/1 Peter Hilton enters 640 ac in Anson Co on Stinking Quarter Cr; includes Jane Boy's place.

2967. Mar. 5, 1750/1 Zachh. Martin enters 640 ac in Anson Co on waters of Sandy Cr; includes the cabins built by Gregory Aldrick.

2968. Mar. 5, 1750/1 Wm Holmes enters 200 ac in Anson Co on Cane Cr; includes the place where he lives.

2969. Mar. 5, 1750/1 Wm Leakey enters 640 ac in Anson Co on middle branch of Rocky R and on both sides of "the" old hunting path.

2970. Mar. 5, 1750/1 John Wright enters 300 ac in Anson Co on the place where he lives; includes his improvements.

2971. Mar. 5, 1750/1 Jos Griffith enters 640 ac in Anson Co on waters of Cane

Cr; includes his improvements.

2972. Mar. 5, 1750/1 Zachh. Martin enters 640 ac in Anson Co on S fork of Cane Cr.

2973. Mar. 5, 1750/1 Wm "Vistiol" enters 640 ac in Anson Co on S side of N fork of Rocky R.

2974. Mar. 5, 1750/1 Jas Crawford enters 640 ac in Anson Co on waters of Stinking Quarter Cr; includes his own improvements.

2975. Mar. 5, 1750/1 Geo Cathey enters 640 ac in Anson Co on S side of Yadkin R; border: below Robt Reed's, "the" waggon road, & Mark Chambers cabbin.

2976. Mar. 5, 1750/1 Jno Brandon enters 640 ac in Anson Co on S side of Yadkin R and on each sides of the waggon road from Yadkin R to the Irish Settlment; called the Poplar "land".

2977. Mar. 5, 1750/1 Jno King enters 400 ac in Anson Co on N side of Yadkin R; border: "next" above Danl. Grant's land.

2978. Mar. 5, 1750/1 Edwd. Dycus enters 400 ac in Anson Co on mouth of Reedy Br, on N side of Yadkin R, begins above mouth of said creek, & runs down the river.

2979. Mar. 5, 1750/1 Jas McGowan enters 640 ac in Anson Co on middle South fork of Eno R.

2980. Mar. 5, 1750/1 Thos. Hunter enters 640 ac in Anson Co between Saxapahaw R & Deep R on Horsepen Br and on N side of Buffaloe Cr.

2981. Mar. 5, 1750/1 Thos. Mathaes [or Mathaos] enters 640 ac in Anson Co between Haw R and Deep R.

2982. Mar. 5, 1750/1 Jane Corrooth "widow" enters 640 ac in Anson Co; between Robt. Bravard & Walter Carooth and joins both tracts; includes her own improvements.

page 23
2983. Mar. 5, 1750/1 Wm Ellis enters 640 ac in Anson Co on waters of Deep R.

2984. Mar. 5, 1750/1 Wm Ellis enters 640 ac in Anson Co on waters of Deep R.

2985. Mar. 5, 1750/1 Wm Ellis enters 640 ac in Anson Co on Polecat Cr; border: above Duke Kimbrough and joins "the same".

North Carolina Land Entries 1735-1752

2986. Mar. 5, 1750/1 Wm Ellis enters 640 ac [in Anson Co] on "the" Trading Path; between Pollcat Cr and Stinking Quarter Cr.

2987. Mar. 5, 1750/1 Wm Ellis enters 640 ac [in Anson Co] "as last described".

2988. Mar. 5, 1750/1 Wm Ellis enters 640 ac [in Anson Co] on waters of Deep R.

2989. Mar. 5, 1750/1 Thomas Turner enters 640 ac in Anson Co; border: on S side of Abraham Caroon.

2990. Mar. 5, 1750/1 Morgan Bryan enters 640 ac in Anson Co; border: two miles below Linville's on "the same" side of "the" river.

2991. Mar. 5, 1750/1 Wm Linville enters 640 ac in Anson Co on S side of N fork of Yadkin R [on] Linville's Cr.

2992. Mar. 5, 1750/1 Jos Bryan enters 640 ac in Anson Co on William Linville's Cr on [page torn; probably South] side of Yadkin R.

2993. Mar. 5, 1750/1 John Fisher enters 640 ac in Anson Co on Second Cr, at mouth of Beaverdam Br, & runs up Third Cr on both sides.

2994. Mar. 5, 1750/1 Jno Patterson enters 640 ac in Anson Co; border: Felix Kenneday on S side.

2995. Mar. 5, 1750/1 Jno Carr enters 640 ac in Anson Co on the ridge between Third Cr and Fourth Cr; border: his lower survey.

2996. Mar. 5, 1750/1 Jno Cunningham enters 640 ac in Anson Co on S side of Ciles Cr; border: on SW side of James Hill.

2997. Mar. 5, 1750/1 Thos McKetheney enters 640 ac in Anson Co on "the" fork of Reedy Br "of a Beaver Dam" that runs into Grants Cr on N side and below the road to Yadkin R.

2998. Mar. 5, 1750/1 Wm Carr enters 640 ac in Anson Co on Witherow's Cr; border: "next" [to] James Huey's on both sides of said creek.

2999. Mar. 5, 1750/1 Wm Carr enters 640 ac in Anson Co; border: "next below" John Hoan's entry on both sides of his creek.

3000. Mar. 5, 1750/1 John McKilwrath enters 640 ac in Anson Co on both sides of Fifth Cr and about a mile above "the" Great fall; includes his improvements.

page 24
3001. Mar. 5, 1750/1 Thos McKithenney enters 640 ac in Anson Co on both sides

of Back Cr; border: above Archibald Hamilton's entry.

3002. Mar. 5, 1750/1 Thos McKithenney enters 640 ac in Anson Co on Third Cr; between Madill's entry and Rev. John Thomson.

3003. Mar. 5, 1750/1 Jos White enters 640 ac in Anson Co on Back Cr; border: the land of Henry White "upwards".

3004. Mar. 5, 1750/1 Thos. Gallaspy enters 640 ac in Anson Co on Back Cr; border: opposite his own place.

3005. Mar. 5, 1750/1 Thos. Gallaspy enters 640 ac in Anson Co on both sides of Third Cr; border: above Madill's survey; includes a mill place at "the" Indian Camp.

3006. Mar. 5, 1750/1 Thos. Gallaspy enters 640 ac in Anson Co on Back Cr; between his own entry and Henry White's entry.

3007. Mar. 5, 1750/1 Thos McKilhenney enters 640 ac in Anson Co on Third Cr; between Madill's East line and John Parr's West line "where" there's a meadow running through this entry.

3008. Mar. 5, 1750/1 John McDowall enters 320 ac in Anson Co; border: his own entry on both sides of Lambarth's mill Cr.

3009. Mar. 5, 1750/1 James Graham enters 640 ac in Anson Co on head waters of Coldwater Cr and joins a branch of Crane Cr; border: about 2 miles SE of his own house; between him and "the" Trading Path.

3010. Mar. 5, 1750/1 Archibald Hamilton enters 640 ac in Anson Co on Coldwater Cr, at Buffalo Cr, & below "the" Beaver Pond; includes a "spring black oak" marked "A H" on S side of said creek and includes "both sides".

3011. Mar. 5, 1750/1 Edmund Hynds enters 640 ac in Anson Co on both sides of "the" creek; between Ferguson Grimes and Saml Burnet.

3012. Mar. 5, 1750/1 John Sill enters 400 ac in Anson Co on both sides of Third Cr; border: David Fullerton.

3013. Mar. 5, 1750/1 Thos "Rogerman" enters 640 ac in Anson Co on Liles Cr and on S side of Catawba R.

3014. Mar. 5, 1750/1 Wm Grant enters "two (2)" 640 ac adjoining "tracts" in Anson Co on N fork of Bear Cr; "encompassing" both sides of said creek.

page 25

North Carolina Land Entries 1735-1752

3015. Mar. 5, 1750/1 Hugh Dickson enters 640 ac in Anson Co on Third Cr.

3016. Mar. 5, 1750/1 Abrahm. Potter enters 640 ac in Anson Co on N side of Yadkin R; border: on lower side of Willm. Bryan's land.
3017. Mar. 5, 1750/1 Roger Turner enters 640 ac in Anson Co on S side of Yadkin R; includes mouth of Turners Cr.

3018. Mar. 5, 1750/1 Jacob Rees enters 640 ac in Anson Co on Deep R; border: a beech tree marked "R I" and runs "up".

3019. Mar. 5, 1750/1 Jno Reedy enters 640 ac in Anson Co on E branch of N fork of Muddy Cr, begins 10 chains below the fork at a white oak, & runs "up".

3020. Mar. 5, 1750/1 Fras. Pincher enters 640 ac in Anson Co on S side of Yadkin R; includes his "plantation".

3021. Mar. 5, 1750/1 Saml Steward enters 320 ac in Anson Co on S side of Yadkin R; border: "the" corner of Bean's land and runs "up".

3022. Mar. 5, 1750/1 Robt. Forbes enters 640 ac in Anson Co begins at upper side of Roaring R that comes into Yadkin R on N side and runs down Yadkin R below Roaring R.

3023. Mar. 5, 1750/1 Isaac Free enters 640 ac in Anson Co on S side of Dutchmans Cr; includes a spanish oak marked "I F".

3024. Mar. 5, 1750/1 Isaac Free enters 640 ac in Anson Co on S side of Yadkin R; between Dogwood Bottom and "the" Mulberry Fields.

3025. Mar. 5, 1750/1 Edwd. Hughs enters 640 ac in Anson Co on S side of Yadkin R; border: about 2 miles below Linville's and Bryan's.

3026. Mar. 5, 1750/1 Saml Bryan enters 640 ac in Anson Co; includes "the" Great Meadow on S side of Yadkin R and about 4 miles above the Mulberry Fields.

3027. Mar. 5, 1750/1 Roger Turner jr enters 640 ac in Anson Co on Sweet Cr, a branch of Dutchmans Cr; border: below Morgan Bryan jr.

3028. Mar. 5, 1750/1 Jno Witherow enters 640 ac in Anson Co on the lower side of the path that goes to Grant's; includes "a" Beaver Pond Br.

3029. Mar. 5, 1750/1 Jno Davieson enters 640 ac in Anson Co on W side of Daviesons Cr; border: Mr. McDowell's land on N side; includes part of a Beaver Pond.

page 26

North Carolina Land Entries 1735-1752

3030. Mar. 5, 1750/1 Wm McCulloch enters 640 ac in Anson Co on Mill Cr, a branch of Fourth Cr; border: W side of Geo Reed; includes Mill Cr and the walnut land.

3031. Mar. 5, 1750/1 Jno McCulloch enters 640 ac in Anson Co on Third Cr and above Oliphant's Path; includes "a" Great Meadow and runs "upward".

3032. Mar. 5, 1750/1 John McWherton enters 640 ac in Anson Co; border: Alexander Osborn's East line, "part" of John Bravard's West line, & "part" of Robert Bravard's line.

3033. Mar. 5, 1750/1 Mark Alexander enters 640 ac in Anson Co; border: Saml Blythe on S side.

3034. Mar. 5, 1750/1 Jno Thomas enters 640 ac in Anson Co; border: on S side of lower end of John Dill's and runs down "the" river; includes an island "along side" the place.

3035. Mar. 5, 1750/1 John Nesbitt enters 500 ac in Anson Co on both sides of the path from John Brandon's to "the" waggon road; between Grants Cr and "the" trading path.

3036. Mar. 5, 1750/1 John Whitesides enters 400 ac in Anson Co on head branches of Grants Cr; includes the branches of Bear Cr and in the forks of Yadkin R.

3037. Mar. 5, 1750/1 Benja. Boon enters 640 ac in Anson Co on Hunting Cr; includes a large forked poplar lying across said creek about 2 or 3 miles above "the canoe" tree.

3038. Mar. 5, 1750/1 Geo. Forbes enters 640 ac in Anson Co on N side of Yadkin R and on the Shallow ford of N fork [of Yadkin R]; border: on upper side of Capt. Davis' survey.

3039. Mar. 5, 1750/1 Edwd. Parnold enters 640 ac in Anson Co on Belues Cr; includes Robert Rutlidge's cabbin.

3040. Mar. 5, 1750/1 Edwd. Parnold enters 640 ac in Anson Co "up" Belues Cr from Rutlidge's cabbin on a branch of said creek.

3041. Mar. 5, 1750/1 Edwd. Parnold enters 640 ac in Anson Co on Reedy Cr that emptys into N side of N fork of Yadkin R.

3042. Mar. 5, 1750/1 Edwd. Parnold enters 640 ac in Anson Co on Swearing Cr; border: above Weaton's and Smith's surveys.

North Carolina Land Entries 1735-1752

3043. Mar. 5, 1750/1 Charles Davis enters 300 ac in Anson Co on Cane Cr; border: above "Euing's" improvement.

3044. Mar. 5, 1750/1 Wm Ludford enters 640 ac in Anson Co on the branches of Uwharey R "if not entered before, but if entered" then on "the" branch of Muddy Cr.

page 27
3045. Mar. 5, 1750/1 James Carter enters 640 ac in Anson Co on Muddy Cr or the branches thereof.

3046. Mar. 5, 1750/1 Martin Wallick enters 640 ac in Anson Co on N side of Yadkin R; called Locust Bottom; between Horseshoe Neck and Swan Cr.

3047. Mar. 5, 1750/1 Lewis Fisher enters 640 ac in Anson Co "on" the mouth of Abbots Cr "on each side or on either side as suits".

3048. Mar. 5, 1750/1 Jno McKilhenney enters 640 ac in Anson Co on N side of "a" Reedy Br, on the path from William Grant's to S fork of Yadkin R "Great Shoals", & runs S; includes said branch and another branch that lies S from "thence".

3049. Mar. 5, 1750/1 Sylvanus Smith enters 640 ac in Anson Co on Swearing Cr; border: Robert Heaton and "round his" upper corner.

3050. Mar. 5, 1750/1 Jno Holmes enters 640 ac in Anson Co; border: on N side of his own place and joins Thomas Fillaspy's line.

3051. Mar. 5, 1750/1 Jno Sidwell enters 640 ac in Anson Co on waters of Rocky Cr [River--lined out]; includes "the" Molatto's improvements.

3052. Mar. 5, 1750/1 Wm Bues enters 640 ac in Anson Co on the branches of Muddy Cr.

3053. Mar. 5, 1750/1 Jas Carter enters 400 ac in Anson Co in "the" Bushey fork; between Swearing Cr and the fork "on either side as suits".

3054. Oct. 26, 1750 Michl. Synnot enters 300 ac in Granville Co on Little R; between "the" Governor's land and John Donnagan and near a fall of said river.

3055. Oct. 26, 1750 Abrahm. Nelson enters 320 ac in Granville Co near Great Cr; below Occoneecheys Cr and a branch called Three Springs Br.

3056. Oct. 26, 1750 Thos. Hawkins enters 640 ac in Granville Co on Grassy Cr, at Little Bearskin Cr at a maple marked "T H", & runs down both sides.

3057. Oct. 26, 1750 Thos. Hawkins enters 640 ac in Granville Co on W fork of Grassy Cr, at a "Lodge of Thicks", & runs "down".

3058. Oct. 27, 1750 Michl. Synnot enters 640 ac in Granville Co on head of Buck Quarter Cr; border: a red oak and runs E; includes his "plantation".

3059. Oct. 27, 1750 Thos. Parker enters 640 ac in Granville Co "on or near" Tar R and on Mill Cr "otherwise called" Wolf Pit Cr; border: Mr. James' line and runs up "both sides".

page 28
3060. Jul. 16, 1750 Jno Terrell enters 640 ac in Granville Co on S side of Lyons Cr; border: Benjn. Rush's corner and runs "the same line he did before".

3061. Jul. 16, 1750 Jno Terrell enters 640 ac in Granville Co between Tar R and Lyons Cr; border: a red oak near the fork of Capt. Lancer's Road where that road comes into Simms' [or Simons'] Road that goes to Fishing Cr.

3062. Jul. 16, 1750 Jno Terrell enters 640 ac in Granville Co; border: a marked pine between Sandy Cr and Shocco [or Shouo] Cr.

3063. Jul. 16, 1750 Jno Terrell enters 640 ac in Granville Co; border: near a branch of Tar R that Robt. Southerland lives on, at a white oak marked "I", & runs up both sides of the branch.

3064. Jul. 16, 1750 Jno Terrell enters 640 ac in Granville Co; border: near Roger Thornton's upper line and runs on both sides of Sandy Cr.

3065. Jul. 16, 1750 Jacob Bledso enters 640 ac in Granville Co on Crabtree Br and on S side of Sandy Cr; border: a white oak and runs up on "both sides".

3066. Jul. 16, 1750 Jacob Bledso enters 640 ac in Granville Co on S side of Sandy Cr; border: Roger Thornton's line and runs up a branch.

3067. Jul. 16, 1750 Jno Egerton 640 ac in Granville Co on both sides of Tar R, above Rocky Ford, & at Oulder Springs; includes "the" Indian Old Fields.

3068. Jul. 20, 1750 Jno Robertson enters 640 ac in Granville Co on "the" County [or State] line and runs up both sides of Nutbush Cr.

3069. Jul. 20, 1750 Jno "Terrel" enters 640 ac in Granville Co at a marked tree in the fork of Red Bird Cr and runs up in the fork.

3070. Jul. 20, 1750 Jno Terrel enters 640 ac in Granville Co on Cypruss Swamp at a red oak marked "T" and runs "up".

North Carolina Land Entries 1735-1752

3071. Jul. 20, 1750 Chas. Dodson enters 640 ac in Granville Co at "the" Bogg on Great Nutbush Cr and runs down N side of said creek.

3072. Jul. 23, 1750 Richd. Hargrove enters 500 ac in Granville Co; border: his "plantation" where he lives and crosses Little Nutbush Cr.

3073. Jul. 23, 1750 Robt. Callier enters 640 ac in Granville Co; border: his own line and runs on both sides of "the" Trading Path.

3074. Jul. 23, 1750 Wm Eaton enters 300 ac in Granville Co; includes the three forks of Tabbs Cr; border: near Jonathan White's Path and below Thomas Morris.

3075. Jul. 23, 1750 Wm Eaton enters 200 ac in Granville Co on both sides of Tabbs Cr; border: Chavis' upper line; [being] where Thomas Smith lives.

3076. Jul. 24, 1750 Thos. Cook enters 300 ac in Granville Co; border: John Liles upper line and runs up Flat Br.

3077. Jul. 23, 1750 Jno Bird enters 640 ac in Granville Co on Bow House Cr; border: a poplar marked "I B" on S side of said creek and runs up both sides; "vacant land".

3078. Jul. 25, 1750 Jas Trivelion enters 400 ac in Granville Co on both sides of Little Nutbush Cr; border: Luke Waldrop's upper "or North" line; includes his "plantation" where he lives.

3079. Jul. 25, 1750 Jno Bishop enters 640 ac in Cumberland Co; border: a pine marked "I " near mouth of Tims Br and runs down Summes' "ats" line.

page 29
3080. Jul. 25, 1750 Jno Sullivant enters 640 ac in Granville Co on Little Bear Swamp and runs up both sides; includes the "plantation" where John Richardson "went from".

3081. Jul. 28, 1750 Robt. Callier enters 300 ac in Granville Co on Smith Cr; border: Willm. Paschal's upper line and runs on both sides of said creek to the fork of Bowhouse Cr; includes Gibbe Bunch's clearing.

3082. Jul. 31, 1750 Robt. Taylor enters 640 ac in Granville Co on Wolf Pit Br of Reedy Cr; border: near the forks of said branch and runs from the mouth of said branch on Reedy Cr.

3083. Jul. 31, 1750 Thos. Petty enters 640 ac in Granville Co on both sides of Sandy Cr; border: Hopkin Wilder's lower line and runs "down".

3084. Jul. 31, 1750 Jno Adcock enters 400 ac in Granville Co on S side of Tar R,

253

on S side of Indian field Cr, & at New litte [or litle] Path.

3085. Aug. 1, 1750 Robt. Callier enters 200 ac in Granville Co on Hawtree Cr; border: Thos Havet's North line and runs up the branch; includes Jno Shaves' improvement.

3086. Aug. 3, 1750 Jno Searcy sr enters 640 ac in Granville Co on S side of Nutbush Cr, at mouth of a branch, & below the fork of Andersons Swamp; includes his improvements.

3087. Aug. 4, 1750 Wm Smith enters 640 ac in Granville Co on S side of Tar R; border: his own corner in Wolf Pit Swamp and runs up both sides.

3088. Aug. 4, 1750 Leonard Hartline enters 640 ac in Granville Co on Second fork of Tar R; border: Richd. Giggs' line and runs up both sides of Sheldons Cr.

3089. Aug. 4, 1750 Geo. Jordan jr enters 640 ac in Granville Co on S side of N fork of Haw R, at Hogens Beaver Pond, & runs "down".

3090. Aug. 6, 1750 Ellis Marens enters 200 ac in Granville Co on Rocky Cr; border: John Knight's upper line and runs on both sides of the creek.

3091. Aug. 6, 1750 Benja. Ward enters 400 ac in Granville Co on Great Shocco Cr; border: his own corner pine, runs "near" Edwd. Jones' corner pine, & down said Jones' line.

3092. Aug. 11, 1750 Jno Duke enters 300 ac in Granville Co on Possom Quarter Cr; border: Jos Duke's upper line and runs up "both sides".

3093. Aug. 11, 1750 Jno Duke enters 600 ac in Granville Co on Reedy Cr; border: a white oak above Peter Green's and runs up both sides of Little fork.

3094. Aug. 13, 1750 Nathl. Dohurty enters 250 ac in Granville Co on Island Cr; border: Josiah Mitchell's East line near "the" Main Road.

3095. Aug. 16, 1750 Jacob Braswell enters 300 ac in Granville Co on both sides of Tar R; border: Richd. Williams' line; includes the "waste" land between said Williams, Robt. Butler, Jacob Powel, Jas Ben, & Wm Wilder.

3096. Aug. 16, 1750 Micajh. Gustavus enters 640 ac in Granville Co on S side of Little Cr; border: Jno Dogger's line, runs down the creek to Henry King's line, & over said creek.

3097. Aug. 22, 1750 Geo Glover enters 300 ac in Granville Co at "a" Great Br; border: above Jos Linsey's Lick and runs up both sides of Andersons Swamp & said branch.

North Carolina Land Entries 1735-1752

3098. Aug. 22, 1750 Henry Jones enters 400 ac in Granville Co on Eno R; border: a white oak in "the" fork and runs "across" to Little R.

3099. Aug. 27, 1750 Jno Adcock enters 400 ac in Granville Co on S side of Tar R, on S fork of Old Mill Cr, & at small branch of said creek; includes "the land" called Winder's cabbin and runs down the creek.

3100. Aug. 28, 1750 Jas Knot enters 640 ac in Granville Co on head of a marsh; border: above Jonath. Parker's, at a small red oak marked "I K", on Tar River Path, & on "the" SE side.

3101. Aug. 31, 1750 Jos Person enters 640 ac in Granville Co; border: Wm Clark's line, runs to Wm Mangum's line on head of Rocky Br, down said branch to Saintling's line, & joins "his" line to Fishing Cr; being the vacant land between Rocky Br and Wm Clark.

3102. Sept. 4, 1750 Wm Chavers enters 640 ac in Granville Co; border: his upper line on Tabbs Cr, runs up said creek, across said creek, & down to Tar R.

3103. Sept. 4, 1750 Wm Clayton enters 200 ac in Granville Co on S side of Pine Mountain; border: a white oak at the mouth of a branch and runs to Jonathans Cr on S side of said mountain.

3104. Sept. 4, 1750 Giles Bowers enters 300 ac in Granville Co on Linches Cr; border: his own line and runs "down".

3105. Sept. 5, 1750 Jonathn. Parker enters 640 ac in Granville Co; border: his own line on Grassy Cr and runs down said creek to Capt. James Mitchell's line.

3106. Sept. 4, 1750 Jos Green enters 640 ac in Granville Co on N side of Fishing Cr; border: Philemon Bradford's corner tree and runs North.

3107. Sept. 5, 1750 Geo Jordan, son of Anthony Jordan, enters 300 ac in Granville Co on Hall "Widvers" Cr, on a branch below Hickory Br, & runs up the creek.

3108. Sept. 6, 1750 Jno Dickson enters 400 ac in Granville Co on Sandy Cr; border: a "Ledge of Rocks" at the fork of said creek and runs up both sides.

3109. Sept. 11, 1750 Edwd. Killingsworth enters 640 ac in Granville Co; border: Jno Roberson's upper line, runs "out", & then up both sides of "said" creek.

3110. Sept. 18, 1750 Jno Byrd enters 400 ac in Granville Co on a branch [on] N side of Deep Cr; includes Thomas Ward's improvements.

3111. Sept. 29, 1750 Wm Nichols enters 640 ac in Granville Co; border: near John

Robertson's upper corner and runs down John Dozer's & his own lines.

3112. Oct. 5, 1750 Thos. Hughs enters 640 ac in Granville Co; border: John Smith's line and runs up Nutbush Cr.

3113. Oct. 6, 1750 Jas Mitchell enters 640 ac in Granville Co "about" the head of a small branch of Island Cr and runs over the branch to "the" beaver pond; [being] the place caalled Robert Mitchell's Hay Meadows.

3114. Oct. 6, 1750 Jno West sr enters 640 ac in Granville Co on Stony Cr, one of head branches of Haw R, runs down N side of said river, at mouth of Toms Cr, & runs on both sides of Stony Cr.

page 31
3115. Oct. 6, 1750 Jno West sr enters 640 ac in Granville Co; border: joins the aforesaid [previous] entry.

3116. Oct. 6, 1750 Jas Pace enters 600 ac in Granville Co on Cypress Swamp.

3117. Oct. 10, 1750 Leonard Hartlin [or Hastlin] enters 640 ac in Granville Co on S fork of Tar R; border: about a mile above Roce's, "near" said fork, & runs "up".

3118. Oct. 6, 1750 Capt. James Mitchell enters 640 ac in Granville Co on S side of Grassy Cr; border: at a white oak corner tree on his own line, runs up a small branch, "along" crossing the branches of Grassy Cr, over the creek, & down it.

3119. Oct. 19, 1750 Nathl. Doherty enters 300 ac in Granville Co near head of Tar R; includes the "plantation" where Isaac Devenport deceased lived and "made".

3120. Oct. 22, 1750 Jos Devenport enters 400 ac in Granville Co on N side of Little Island Cr; border: his West corner tree, runs on Lick Br, & down the branch.

3121. Oct. 22, 1750 James Pace enters 640 ac in Granville Co on Moony Cr; includes the school house and runs down both sides of the creek.

3122. Oct. 22, 1750 John Gillum enters 600 ac in Granville Co on Little Island Cr; border: a white oak marked "I G" in the fork of Cornfield Br and runs up both the branches.

3123. Oct. 25, 1750 John Wade enters 400 ac in Granville Co; border: a white oak near the falls of Little R, above "Brdley's" cabbin, & runs "down".

3124. Oct. 26, 1750 Joseph Collins enters 60 ac in Granville Co on Flat R, above mouth of Cattail Br, & runs from Flat R by "said" Horse Lick to Mountain Cr.

North Carolina Land Entries 1735-1752

3125. May 20, 1751 Wm Dawson and Wm Hodges enter 640 ac in Bladen Co on S side of Deep R, about 1.25 miles above mouth of said river, & runs up said river.

page 32
3126. May 20, 1751 Jeremiah Vail and [blank] Smith enters "2 tracts" in [blank] Co; "2P".

3127. May 20, 1751 Daniel Garret [or Gaviet] enters 640 ac in Anson Co; "1P".

3128. May 20, 1751 John Garret enters 640 ac in Anson Co; "1P".

3129. May 20, 1751 Robert Jones jr enters "2 tracts" in [blank] Co; "2P".

page 33 The following eight entries were made by Mr. Child at Col. Haywood's Apr. 25, 1751 and not accounted for with Mr. Corbin.
3130. Apr. 25, 1751 Daniel Hill enters 320 ac in Johnston Co on N side of Neuse R, on S side of Richland Cr, & at the mouth of "a" Reedy Br.

3131. Apr. 25, 1751 John Blacklock enters 640 ac in Johnston Co on both sides of Neuse R; includes his own improvement; to be laid out according to a "former" entry.

3132. Apr. 25, 1751 John Johnston enters 100 ac in Johnston Co on N side of Little R; includes his own improvements.

3133. Apr. 25, 1751 William Coupland enters 300 ac in Bladen Co on S side of Haw R opposite mouth of New Hope Cr; includes the improvements he purchased of Nicholas Coupland.

3134. Apr. 25, 1751 Thomas Durham enters 640 ac in Bladen Co; border: on [page torn] side of Morgan's, near the fork of a branch, & runs "down".

3135. Apr. 25, 1751 Mark Morgan enters 640 ac in Bladen Co on E side of New Hope Cr and at a pine on the third fork of said creek.

3136. Apr. 25, 1751 Mark Morgan enters 640 ac in Bladen Co on "the" heads of the branches of Lick Cr and New Hope Cr; border: a red oak [pine--lined out].

3137. Apr. 25, 1751 Mark Morgan enters 640 ac in Bladen Co; border: a red oak "against" the mouth of NE branch of New Hope Cr and runs up the creek; includes the fork.

3138. Apr. 29, 1751 John Hatcher enters 140 ac in [omitted] county; border: Willm McLemore's lower corner tree and runs down "the" creek.

page 34 [blank page]

page 35 [Nos. 3139 through 3241 are grants most of which are found in N. C. Colonial Grants volume 1; noted at end of each number is abstract number from the published book of grants; Nos. 3140, 3141, & 3142 contain complete abstracts; after that, complete abstracts are done only when the grant isn't in the colonial grant book; town mentioned at end probably indicates where grant issued, not necessarily where the rights were proved.]

3139. [only part of this grant survives] Apr. 10, 1752 [grant to George Cowan] "then" S20E 400 poles [page torn], S60W 165 poles to a stake, [page torn] line to the beginning; Bath; rites; [grant abstract #69].

3140. Oct. 11, 1752 Hopkin Howell granted 600 ac in Anson Co on S side of great Pedee R, on Jones Cr, & on Watery Br of said creek; border: begins at 3 scrubby white oaks on the point of a hill, runs N15W 52 poles to a poplar, S75W 240 poles to a black jack, S15E 400 poles to a black oak, N75E 240 poles to a hickory, & with [page torn] line to the beginning; N Bern; [grant abstract #70].

3141. Apr. 7, 1752 James Adams granted 100 ac in Beaufort Co on head of Old Town Cr; border: begins at SE corner poplar of Richard Adams' "tract", runs S62E 100 poles to a pine, N2[page torn] 160 poles to a pine, N62W 100 poles to Richard Adams' second line, S28W 160 poles along said line to the beginning; Bath; rights; [grant abstract #71].

3142. Apr. 14, 1749 Thomas William granted 225 ac in Beaufort Co on S side of Pamplico R and in the fork of Cuckals Cr; border: begins "in" a point near the mouth of said creek, runs S55W 24 poles, S35W 82 poles, S65W 120 poles to a pine, S15E 120 poles to a pine, S7[page torn]E 84 poles to a pine, N65E 144 poles to a white oak on NE of Core Creek Swamp, N 20 poles to a pine, & to the beginning; [grant abstract #72].

page 36
3143. Apr. 13, 1752 [John Bryan granted 350 ac] in Craven Co on N side of Nuce R, NW side of Goose Cr, & runs along "the" swamp; [grant abstract #73].

3144. Apr. 13, 1752 William Shirrell granted 200 ac in Anson Co on N side of Broad R and on a creek thereof; [grant abstract #74].

3145. Apr. 7, 1752 [John] Davis granted 240 ac in Craven Co; border: a sweet gum on S side of his former line and joins his "plantation"; [grant abstract #75].

3146. Apr. 8, 1752 John Williams granted 295 ac in Craven Co; border: a white oak at the "mouth" of Joshuas "resolution"; [grant abstract #76].

page 37
3147. Apr. 8, 1752 John Rice granted 640 ac in Craven Co; border: a white oak at mouth of Miery Br and near mouth of Horse Br; [grant abstract #77].

North Carolina Land Entries 1735-1752

3148. Apr. 13, 1752 Isley Kilpatrick granted 400 ac in Johnston Co on S side of great Contentnee Cr; border: a hickory on Mill Run formerly James Jones' line and runs along the Mill Pond; Bath; [grant abstract #78].

3149. Apr. 20, 1745 [sic] Rigdon Smith granted 200 ac in Craven Co between mouth of Northwest Cr and Duck Cr on N side of Neuse R; border: Capt. John Bryan's land, a small creek in a marsh, & head of Northwest Cr; [grant abstract #3441].

page 38 "To Be Recorded" [written at top of page]
3150. Mar. 28, 1751 Thomas Lovick granted 1,000 ac in Anson Co on both side of the path from the Cherokee Nation to the Catawba River Settlement and about 6 miles from the Nation; [grant abstract #91].

3151. Apr. 11, 1745 Ephraim Vernon granted 300 ac in Bladen Co on W side of Black R; border: begins at a pine, runs S10E 310 poles to a pine, S10W 110 poles to a pine, N10W 440 poles to a dogwood by "the" side of a swamp, & with the swamp to the beginning; [not in grant book].

3152. Apr. 20, 1745 Catherine Dimick granted 200 ac in Craven Co on N side of Neuse R; between Thomas McClendon and Little Cr; [grant abstract #3133].

3153. Oct. 12, 1748 Joseph Bryan granted 200 ac in Craven Co on N side of Neuse R; border: begins a poplar near John Hart's line, runs N32W 120 poles to a red oak, S38W 240 poles to a white oak on a branch, S32E 120 poles down the branch to a dogwood, & up Pometo Swamp [Br--lined out] to the beginning; fees paid G J; [not in grant book].

page 39
3154. Apr. 20, 1745 John Gatlin granted 86 ac in Craven Co on N side of Neuse R called Thoroughfare land; border: begins a pine near Pamplico Road, runs S76E 48 poles, N80E 46 poles to a gumb, S45E 140 poles to a black oak, S25W 70 poles to a pine, S30E 44 poles to a pine, W 100 poles to a pine, & along a branch and pocosan to the beginning; [not in grant book].

3155. Nov. 17, 1743 Richard Lovett granted 320 poles in Craven Co; border: begins at Acorn Br between Neuce and Trent Rivers, runs S80E 60 poles to a pine, N10E 220 poles to a pine, N80W 220 poles to a pine, S10W 220 poles to a pine, & to the beginning; rights; G J; [not in grant book].

3156. Nov. 17, 1743 Richard Lovett granted 66 ac in Craven Co; between John Murphy's land on N side of Trent R and said river; border: begins at said Murphy's corner red oak, runs S16E 60 poles to the river, S38W 153 poles up the river, N37W 85 poles to Murphy's corner beech, & N48E 176 poles along Murphy's line to the beginning; rights; G J; [not in grant book].

page 40

3157. Sept. 29, 1741 Richard Lovett granted 130 ac in Craven Co on N side of Trent R; border: begins at a white oak corner of the land where he lives, runs N65E 60 poles to a hickory stump "another" border of his land, the same course 36 poles, S72E 64 poles, N65E 26 poles, N3W 26 poles, N24W 78 poles to a black oak, S86W 134 poles, S35W 40 poles to a white oak by a branch, S89W 20 poles, S30W 72 poles to a scrubby oak on a hill side near Samuel Cr, & down the creek to the beginning; "one white person"; [not in grant book].

3158. Oct. 6, 1752 James Ellison jr granted 640 ac in Beaufort Co on S side of Checod Swamp; border: begins at Joseph Godley's corner tree, runs S20W 366 poles, W 280 poles to a pine, N 366 poles to "the" swamp, & E 280 to the beginning; N R; [not in grant book].

3159. Oct. 6, 1752 John Tindall granted 200 ac in Beaufort Co on S side of Pamplico R; between Goose Cr & Oyster Cr and joins "the" Great Marsh; border: begins at a pine on the river side, runs S13E 140 poles to a bay tree in Bald Eagle Pocosan [Swamp--lined out], S85E 208 [written over 228] poles to a pine by the Great Marsh, N13W 148 poles to the river, & up the same to the beginning; N R; [not in grant book].

page 41

3160. Oct. 6,1752 James Rigney granted 200 ac in Beaufort Co on S side of Pamplico R, W side of Blounts Cr, & in a place called Mauls Neck; border: begins at a pine, runs S54E 100 poles, S10E 320 poles to a pine in the edge of "the" pecosan, N52W 100 poles to a gumb, & N10W 320 poles to the beginning; N R; [not in grant book].

3161. May 5, 1742 John Starkey and John Bryan granted 300 ac in Craven Co on N side of Neuce R and on or near Linkfield's "plantation" at Neuce Ferry; border: begins at a pine, runs S80E 219 poles to a pine, N10E 219 poles to a pine, N80W 219 poles to a pine, & S10W 219 poles to the beginning; G Johnston; [not ingrant book].

3162. Apr. 7, 1749 Thomas King granted 450 ac in Craven Co on N side of Neuce R and called "high hills"; border: begins at Thos. Bass' corner white oak, runs N80W 360 poles to a red oak, N20W 100 poles to a pine, N5E 70 poles to a red oak, N75E 250 poles to a red oak at a branch, & to the beginning; [not in grant book].

page 42

3163. Sept. 28, 1745 Catherine Dimick granted 200 ac in Craven Co on N side of Neuse R and S side of Rainbow Cr; border: begins at a pine by the creek, runs S45W 160 poles up "a" Marsh Br to a pine, N45W 200 poles to a pine by "a" Great Br, N45E 160 poles along the branch to a gumb by the creek, & to the beginning; G J; [not in grant book].

3164. Apr. 20, 1745 David George granted 60 ac in Craven Co on S side of Trent R; border: begins at a pine on "the" marsh side, runs S20E 90 poles to a pine, S70W 110 poles to a pine, N20W 90 poles to a pine, & N70E 110 poles to the beginning; G J; [not in grant book].

3165. Apr. 20, 1745 David George granted 40 ac in Craven Co on N side of Trent R; border: begins at a pine on a marsh, runs N 80 poles to a pine, E 80 poles to a pine, S 80 poles to a lightwood stake in the marsh, & W 80 poles to the beginning; G J; [not in grant book].

"this book consists of 16 leaves delivered to me Q if these are copied in the Record book" [signed] Ja Murray, Sec. [8 pages survive]
"The foregoing Patents Recorded [sic] in the Secretary's Office by Mr. Murray's Directions, not having been before recorded per Jams. Green".

page 43
3166. Jul. 26, 1743 John Lee granted 100 ac in Craven Co on S side of Neuse R; border: on Prickly Pear Marsh at Williams' corner live oak and on a pecoson; in "proportion" to rights; Edenton; [grant abstract #3825].

3167. Sept. 30, 1749 Andrew Killin granted 1,000 ac in Anson Co on S side of Cataba R and on "Kilins's" Cr; according to rights; New Bern; [grant abstract #3826].

3168. Sept. 30, 1749 John Killin granted 1,000 ac in Anson Co on S side of Cataba R and on Leapers Cr; border: Leonard Killin's corner red oak and white oak; according to rights at New Bern; [grant abstract #3827].

page 44
3169. Sept. 30, 1749 Leonard Killin granted 950 ac in Anson Co on S side of Cataba R and on Killins Cr; according to rights; Newbern; [grant abstract #3828].

3170. Jul. 25, 1743 John Wallis granted 300 ac in Onslow Co above the mouth of War Tom Swamp; border: an oak in War Tom Swamp and runs down War Tom Swamp to "the" main swamp; "1 white person"; [grant abstract #3829].

3171. Apr. 20, 1745 Jno Hardy granted 400 ac in Beaufort Co on S side of Tar R; border: his own line at his lower corner in "the" low ground, Ellison, & Hardy's "back" corner; rights; "lest of at"; [grant abstract #3830].

3172. Sept. 30, 1745 Andrew "Killens" jr granted 850 ac in Anson Co on Killens Cr and on S side of Cataba R; rites; [grant abstract #3831].

page 45 "Don't Record this til you ask me. P S"

3173. Apr. 20, 1745 James Blount granted 500 ac in Beaufort Co on S side of Tar R; border: joins land that was formerly John Hardy's, begins at a pine on S side of Mill's Run, runs S35E 120 poles to a pine "one" of Forbes' line trees, with his line to a pine, S 164 poles to a pine, S55W 284 poles to a pine, N 164 poles to a pine, N35W 120 poles to the run, & with the run to the beginning; rights; "Note this is one of the patents from Maj. Edwards [page torn] vide Forster's marble covered abstracts, if not recorded already"; "recorded already" [sic]; fees £1.17.6 Vir.; [not in grant book].

3174. Apr. 20, 1745 Cornelius Tyson granted 100 ac in Craven Co in the forks of Little Contentne Cr; border: a white oak by the marsh of the creek; rights; [grant abstract #3832].

3175. Oct. 7, 1749 John Price granted 250 ac in Anson Co on N side of Cataba R and on Prices Br where his house stands; rights; [grant abstract #3833].

page 46
3176. Apr. 4, 1750 [page torn--George] Clements granted 100 ac in Anson Co on W side of Little R of Peedee R [Little Pee Dee R]; border: Charles Robinson and the river; rights; [grant abstract #1].

3177. Apr. 4, 1751 Charles McDowell granted 200 ac in Anson Co on S side of Broad R, on second big creek that runs into said river above mouth of Pacolet R, & runs along Broad R; rights; [grant abstract #2].

3178. Oct. 4, 1751 John Hall granted 200 ac in Anson Co; border: a poplar on S bank of Peedee R below "the" Alegator Pond and runs along Peedee R; rights; [grant abstract #3].

3179. Apr. 1, 1751 Thomas Brooks granted 400 ac in Bladen Co on SW side of NW Cape Fear R on Crass [sic--Cross] Cr; border: John Russell; rights; [grant abstract #4].

page 47
3180. Nov. 18, 1748 John Holton granted 100 ac in Bladen Co on W side of NW River; border: on the river at upper corner of land "laid out" for Thomas Jones "BlackSmith", runs up Jones' upper line, & along said river; [grant abstract #5].

3181. May 2, 1742 Hugh McLaughlan granted 140 ac in Bladen Co on NE side of NW Cape Fear R; border: Doncan Campbell's upper corner, lower line of Mr. Neil McNeil's land, runs with McNeil's line to the river, & down the river; [seat the same in P--lined out]; [grant abstract #6].

3182. Jun. 4, 1743 William Stevans granted 300 ac in Bladen Co on SW side of NW Cape Fear R; border: a white oak opposite the lower point of Fox's Island and runs along the river; Wilmington; [grant abstract #7].

North Carolina Land Entries 1735-1752

page 48
3183. Apr. 6, 1750 James Davis granted 100 ac in Johnston Co on S side of Neuce R and on N side of Southwest Cr; being the land where he lives; rights; [grant abstract #8].

3184. Feb. 22 [26--lined out], 1743/4 Robert Halton esq granted 640 ac in New Hanover Co on Eastermost Br of Smiths Cr; border: a topless pine by a marsh or pond on SW side of Mr. Gray's corner and runs along Gray's line; rights; "North Car."; [grant abstract #9].

3185. Nov. 21, 1744 David Morely granted 80 ac in Bladen Co on S side of NW Cape Fear R; border: Henry Sims' lower corner stake at the river and runs along the river; according to rights; [grant abstract #10].

3186. Apr. 3, 1752 Samuel Donlap granted 240 ac in Anson Co on N side of Cataba R; between Ramsey and the river; border: Cane Cr and runs along the river; Bath; [grant abstract #12].

page 49
3187. Apr. 3, 1752 Robert Ramsey granted 300 ac in Anson Co on N side of Cataba R and on both sides of Cane Cr; includes a tree marked "R R"; rights Bath; [grant abstract #13].

3188. Apr. 3, 1752 Wm Robinson granted 400 ac in Anson Co on N side of Cataba R and on "the" South branch of Cane Cr called Rum Cr; rights Bath; [grant abstract #14].

3189. Apr. 3, 1752 Rob. Ramsey granted 400 ac in Anson Co on N side of Cataba R and on both sides of Cane [written over Cata] Cr; includes a tree marked "R R"; border: "the" line of his first survey; rights Bath; [grant abstract #15].

3190. Apr. 20, 1745 James Hamilton granted 150 ac in Beaufort Co on S side of Gum Br and on Pamplico R; border: Cedar Swamp, the main dismal, & runs along Gum Br; according to rights; [grant abstract #16].

3191. Mar. 10, [1740--page torn] James Hamilton granted 100 ac in Beaufort Co on Pamplico Road, on W side of "a" Cypress Br, & runs along Cedar Swamp; Edenton; [grant abstract #17].

page 50
3192. Jun. 21, 1746 Edward Stephens granted 200 ac in New Hanover Co; border: an oak at Cohera Swamp; according to rights; "not issued"; [grant abstract #18].

3193. Oct. 7, 1749 Joseph Oates granted 100 ac in New Hanover Co on N side of Goshan Swamp; between White oak Br & Pond Br and runs along the swamp;

according to rights; "not issued"; [grant abstract #19].

3194. Oct. 6, 1748 Abraham Taylor granted 100 ac in Johnston Co on N side of Southwest Cr and Gumb Br; according to rights; "not issued"; [grant abstract #20].

3195. Apr. 20, [1745--page torn] Edward Stephens granted 100 ac in Craven to on S side of Neuse R and in the fork between Mill Cr & Neuse R; border: Robert Mills; according to rights; "not issued"; [grant abstract #21].

page 51
3196. Apr. 3, 1752 Geyan Moore granted 600 ac in Anson Co on N side of Broad R and [on Beaverdam--page torn] Cr; includes a meadow above "the" mouth; Bath; [grant abstract #28].

3197. Sept. 29, 1750 John Harmer granted 170 ac in Anson Co on N side of Great Peedee R; border: a maple on the river below the mouth of Mountain Cr and runs along the river; N Bern; [grant abstract #29].

3198. Apr. 3, 1752 Joseph White granted 200 ac in Anson Co on N side of PeeDee R; border: Denson's [written over Henson] line on the river and runs along the river; Bath; [grant abstract #30].

3199. Apr. 3, 1752 Andrew Allison granted 640 ac in Anson Co on S side of Cataba R and on Indian Camp Cr; includes the Indian Old Fields on S side of said creek "running into" Cataba R; Bath; [grant abstract #31].

page 52
3200. Apr. 3, 1752 [John Clark--page torn] granted 600 ac in Anson Co on S side of Broad R "where Clark was settled" and runs along the river; Bath; [grant abstract #32].

3201. Sept. 27, 1751 John "Large" sr granted 250 ac in Anson Co on S side of Cataba R; being the place where he lives; border: John McConnel and runs along the river; N Bern; [grant abstract #33].

3202. Apr. 3, 1752 Geyan Moore granted 600 ac in Anson Co on N side of Broad R and on Beaverdam Cr; known as Beauty "Spott" and runs along the river; Bath; [grant abstract #34].

pages 52 and 53
3203. Apr. 3, 1752 Thomas "McHenney" granted 600 ac in Anson Co on N side of Cataba R; includes an improvement bought of Thom[page torn] Gills on Reedy Cr; border: begins at a red oak on the creek, runs S70W 192 poles to a hickory, S50E [or West--ink blob] 100 poles to a red oak, S32E 122 poles to a white oak, S17E 166 poles to a red oak, S65E 112 poles to a pine, N80E 292 poles to a spanish oak, & to the beginning; Bath; [not in grant book].

page 53
3204. Apr. 3, 1752 Matthias Dick granted 380 ac in Anson Co on S side of Cataba R, on "Cheagles" Cr, & joins his line; border: begins at a red oak, runs S40W 96 poles to a stake in Cheagles line, S79W 69 poles to a hickory, N24W 350 poles to a pine, N58E 190 poles to a pine, & to the beginning; Bath; "not recorded"; [not in grant book].

3205. Apr. 3, 1752 Geyan Moore granted 800 ac in Anson Co on both sides of Broad R; known as Mount Pleasant; border: begins at a white oak on S side of said river, runs N83E 200 poles to an ash, S18W 730 poles to a stake, S60W 160 poles to a stake on the river, & "up" to the beginning; Bath; "not recorded"; [not in grant book].

3206. Sept. 29, 1750 John Battey granted 400 ac in Anson Co on S side of Cataba R; border: a live oak below Lord Granville's "manner" and runs along the river; [Bath town Apr. 7, 1752--lined out]; according to rights; New Bern; [grant abstract #35].

3207. Apr. 7, 1752 John Battey granted 500 ac in Anson Co on S side of Cataba R and "back" of his own line; Bath; [grant abstract #36].

page 54
3208. Sept. 30, 1752 George Fagan granted 200 ac in Bladen Co on Deep R, about 4 miles above Great Falls, & runs along the river; N Bern; [grant abstract #37].

3209. Apr. 7, 1752 Samuel McGaw granted 100 ac in Bladen Co; border: lower corner of "a tract" of land "supposed" to be Hugh Ward's on N side of NW Cape Fear R; Bath; [grant abstract #38].

3210. Apr. 7, 1752 Daniel McFee granted 100 ac in Bladen Co on S side of Cape fear R and on Cross Cr; being the place where he lives; Bath; [grant abstract #39].

3211. Oct. 11, 1749 Habakuk Russell granted 144 ac in Carteret Co; border: Reed's corner oak on the head of a bay on Bogue Sound, "Habakkuk" Russell's corner, & a branch; New "Bn"; rights; [grant abstract #40].

page 55
3212. Jan. 26, 1746 John Roberts granted 100 ac in Craven Co on both sides of a branch of Whitleys Cr; rights; New Bern; [grant abstract #41].

3213. Jun. 26, 1746 John Roberts granted 200 ac in Anson Co on S side of Neuse R; between the land that was widow Stevenson's, Henry Roberts, & the river; rights; N Bern; [grant abstract #42].

3214. Apr. 7, 1752 James Ellison granted 100 ac in Beaufort Co on N side of

Pamplico R and W side of Deep Run; border: James Dudley's corner tree in Deep Run "Br" and runs down Deep Run; rights; Bath; [grant abstract #43].

page 56
3215. Apr. 11, 1752 Leonard Keaton [written above "Kealon"] granted 315 ac in Anson Co on N side of Leopards Cr and on a stoney hill; Bath; [grant abstract #44].

3216. Apr. 11, 1752 John Brevard granted 400 ac in Anson Co; border: Hugh Lawson and Winslow; rights; Bath; [grant abstract #45].

3217. Apr. 11, 1752 John Brevard granted 636 ac in Anson Co; border: Robert Brevard; rights; Bath; [grant abstract #46].

pages 56 and 57
3218. Apr. 13, 1752 Richard Newman granted 25 ac in Beaufort Co on N side of Pamplico R and NE side of Bath Town Cr; border: John Sullivant's patent, John Barris, mouth of Bath Town Cr, & Mr. Newman's house; being surplus land found in a resurvey; [grant abstract #47].

page 57
3219. Apr. 7, 1752 William Blackburn granted 400 ac in Duplin Co on S side of Black R, above Reedy Br, & runs along the river; rights; Bath; [grant abstract #48].

3220. Apr. 13, 1752 John Price granted 400 ac in Anson Co on N side of Cataba R; rights; Bath; [grant abstract #49].

3221. Apr. 13, 1752 Henry White granted 800 ac in Anson Co on N side of Cataba R, above mouth of Waxhaw Cr, & runs along the river; Bath; [grant abstract #50].

page 58
3222. Apr. 13, 1752 Andrew Pickins granted 551 ac in Anson Co on N side of [Cataba R--lined out] Waxhaw Cr; rights; Bath; [grant abstract #51; grant book indicates 500 ac].

3223. Apr. 11, 1752 Alice Marsden, widow in trust "to and for the uses" mentioned in will of Rufus Marsden deceased, granted 300 ac in Bladen Co on W side of South R; border: John Andrews jr's home place and runs along the river; rights; Bath; [grant abstract #52].

3224. Apr. 20, 1745 Alexander Steel granted 100 ac in Onslow Co on W side of Flat Swamp; border: a pine "a little above the" bridge and runs across the swamp; Bath; rights; [grant abstract #53].
3225. Apr. 11, 1752 Alexander Steel granted 200 ac in Craven Co on N side of Eves Br; rights; Bath; [grant abstract #54].

North Carolina Land Entries 1735-1752

page 59
3226. Apr. 13, 1752 John Peterson granted 200 ac in Johnston Co on a branch of Falling Cr; border: a red oak on N side of said branch opposite Charles Ryal's land; Bath; rights; "left off all this"; [grant abstract #55].

3227. Apr. 11, 1752 John Andrews jr granted 120 ac in Bladen Co on South R a branch of Black R and runs along South R; rights; Bath; [grant abstract #56].

3228. Apr. 10, 1752 George "Doncan" and Abraham Doncan, legatees of Abraham Doncan deceased, granted 320 ac in Beaufort Co on S side of N prong of Swifts Cr; border: "the" swamp; rights; Bath; [grant abstract #57].

3229. Apr. 10, 1752 George Doncan and Abraham Doncan, legatees of Abraham Doncan deceased, granted 271 ac in Beaufort Co on N side of Southermost Br of Swifts Cr; border: on E side of "the" swamp and a pine near a pond "back" of Wheelers Br; rights; Bath; [grant abstract #58].

page 60
3230. Apr. 10, 1752 Col. Robert Halton granted 300 ac in New Hanover Co; border: on the head of Col. Halton's land on Mill Cr and Col. Halton's SE corner; rights; Bath; [grant abstract #59].

3231. Apr. 10, 1752 John Smith granted 180 ac in Johnston Co on S side of Neuse R, N side of Mill Cr, & runs along the creek; rights; Bath; [grant abstract #60].

3232. Apr. 10, 1752 James Purvis [or Pervis] granted 200 ac in Johnston Co on S side of Neuse R; border: on S side of Mill Cr at Joseph Langston's last corner; rights; [grant abstract #61].

pages 60 and 61
3233. Nov. 22, 1746 Thomas Red granted 300 ac in Bladen Co on S side of P D River; border: a hickory at Mount Pleasant; "recorded before; vide if not recorded in great Book already"; [grant abstract #3634].

page 61
3234. Apr. 7, 1752 John Lee granted 270 [written over 200] ac in Johnston Co on S side of Neuse R; border: John Wood and runs along the river; rights; Bath; [grant abstract #62].

3235. Apr. 7, 1752 Needham Brant granted 320 in Johnston Co on S side of Black R; border: a white oak near "a" reedy branch about a mile above Greens Path; rights; Bath; [grant abstract #63].

3236. Apr. 4, 1752 Edward Lee [or Leae] granted 400 ac in Johnston Co on S side of Neuse R and N side of Mill Cr; rights; Bath; [grant abstract #64].

page 62
3237. Apr. 7, 1752 Robert Knowles granted 200 ac in New Hanover Co; border:

267

about 4 miles below John Andrews and a hickory near "his" house; rights; Bath; [grant abstract #65].

3238. Oct. 4, 1752 Daniel Short granted 200 ac in Anson Co on S side of Great P D River and on both sides of Jones Cr; New Bern; [grant abstract #66].

3239. Apr. 7, 1752 Evan Lewis granted 600 ac in Anson Co; border: a hickory on N side of first branch "next" to S fork of Cataba R and on S side of said South fork; rights; Bath; [grant abstract #67].

3240. Apr. 7, 1752 Evan Lewis granted 600 ac in Anson Co; border: a black oak on S side of Indian Cr and S side of Cataba R; rights; Bath; [grant abstract #68].

3241. [Apr. 10, 1752] George Cowan granted 400 ac in Anson Co; border: a black oak marked "G C" on N side of Broad R near the bank of the river [only first part of this grant on the page]; [grant abstract #69].
End of the folders in this box

Index to North Carolina Land Entries 1735-1752

Index to North Carolina Land Entries 1735-1752

Arnold, Moses   437, 2108, 2203
Arrendall, Wm   2426
Arrington, Jno   1950
Arthur, John   198, 1921, 1923
Ashburne, thos   1262
Ashe,   476
Ashe, John   1015, 1585
Askins, William   2491
Assop,   1013
Assop, Thomas   118
Aston, James   2887
Atkenson, Jno 2424
Atkins,   2677
Atkins, Jas   701
Atkins, Robert   2614
Atkins, Wm   2373
Austin, Thomas   555, 2415
Averidge, Samll   2312
Axom, Thos   2020
Ayres, Ambros   2146
Ayress, Ambrose   977

Baggot, Nicks   1569
Bailey, David   1844, 2159, 2430
Bailey, Joseph   2159
Baily, Thos   1392
Baker,   197, 1598
Baker (Bakar), Henry   564, 566
Baker, James   2352
Baker, Jno   2169
Baker, Richard   222
Baker, Robert   990
Baker, Samuel   2023, 2608
Baker, Thomas   642
Baker, Wm   2284
Balch,   2422
Balch, Joseph   1371
Baldwin (Balding), James   132, 1360, 2405
Baleaa (Balead), Wm   1035
Ballance, John   886, 1248, 1587
Ballard,   1310, 1464, 1474

Ballard, Elisha   613
Ballard, Jno   656
Balling, Benja   1494
Banfield, Richd   1287
Banke, Thomas   2357
Banks, Francis   2200
Banks, James   2642
Banks, John   1029
Banks, Thos   1006
Barber, James   2391, 2447, 2667
Barber, Jno   2550
Barber, William   1065, 2550
Barefield,   1310, 1766
Barefield (Barfiel), Richard   576, 1089
Bares,   2428
Barfield, Thos   1212
Bargeroon, Elias   727
Barlow,   2508
Barlow, Henry   1769
Barnecastle, Edmd   2054
Barnes, Jacob   751
Barnes, James   2249
Barnes, Joseph   1065
Barnes (Barns), Nathan   751, 752
Barnes, Wm   984
Barney, Simon   2355
Baron,   1113
Baron, Wm   1324
Barradell, Josh   1695
Barress,   2505
Barret, Wm   930
Barrinton, Isaac   2594
Barris, John   3218
Barrow, James   1478, 1828
Barrow, John   322, 325, 1099, 1519, 1673
Barrow, Joseph   311
Barrow (Barron), Nathan   623
Barrow, Richard   311
Barrus,   2600
Barton, James   1503
Bartram, William   2408
Bartrim,   700, 1841, 2198

Index to North Carolina Land Entries 1735-1752

Index to North Carolina Land Entries 1735-1752

Index to North Carolina Land Entries 1735-1752

Index to North Carolina Land Entries 1735-1752

Index to North Carolina Land Entries 1735-1752

Index to North Carolina Land Entries 1735-1752

Index to North Carolina Land Entries 1735-1752

Index to North Carolina Land Entries 1735-1752

Index to North Carolina Land Entries 1735-1752

Index to North Carolina Land Entries 1735-1752

Index to North Carolina Land Entries 1735-1752

Index to North Carolina Land Entries 1735-1752

Index to North Carolina Land Entries 1735-1752

Index to North Carolina Land Entries 1735-1752

Index to North Carolina Land Entries 1735-1752

Index to North Carolina Land Entries 1735-1752

650, 1365, 1615, 1651, 1807,
2117, 2146, 3152

McClintock, Wm 2963

McClure, Richd (R) 1248,
1585, 1587, 1606

McColvin, Alexr 885

McConkee, Mary 664

McConnel, John 2797, 2798,
2919, 2934, 3201

McCoulsky, Duncan 804

McCoy, John 1794, 1949,
2421, 2612, 2659

McCrackden, Hugh 2825

McCraine, Maraeen 2546

McCraney, Mordock
(Moordock) 2021, 2022

McCubbins (McKubbins,
Mackubin), Saml 1358

McCuiston, Thos 2964

McCull, 1808, 1809

McCullen (McCullin), Bryan
550, 1250

McCulloh (McCulloch,
McCullock, McCullo),
614, 895, 896, 946, 996,
997, 1109-1112, 1247, 1249,
1809, 1831, 1832, 1857,
1874, 1875, 1953, 1995,
2009, 2014, 2210, 2216,
2217, 2221, 2234, 2235,
2747, 2748, 2761, 2900

McCulloh (McCullo,
McCulloch), Alexander
1602, 1614, 1823, 1824,
1940, 2019, 2859, 2888

McCulloh (McCulloch), John
2790, 2856, 3031

McCulloh (McCulloch), Wm
3030

McCurray, Jno 2189

McDaniel, John 1209

McDead, William 2270, 2629

McDonohow, Chas 1703

McDoule, Peter 309

McDowel, Jas 1262

McDowel, Joseph 2465, 2469,
2481

McDowell, 3029

McDowell, Charles 3177

McDowell (McDowall), John
2797, 2938, 3008

McFashion, John 2568

McFee, Daniel 3210

McFenkin, 2668

McFerson, 2369

McGaw, Samuel 3209

McGee, Andrew 2753, 2755

McGee, James 2752

McGee, John 2754, 2882

McGee, Wm 1476

McGombery, John 2413

McGowan, Jas 2979

McGuffee, Daniel 1564

McHenney, Thomas 3203

McIlroy (Mcilroy, Muckilroy),
Jno 807, 2284

McIlroy, Wm 1167

McKay, Alexr 614

McKeithan, Alexander 2643

McKetheney (McKithenney),
Thos 2997, 3001, 3002,
3007

McKikin, Alexr 2603

McKikin, Donald 1733

McKilhenney, Jno 3048

McKilwain (Mackelwean),
Francis 2846, 2858

McKilwain (Mackelwean,
McKlewain), James 2790,
2812

McKilwrath, John 3000

McKinne, Barny. 17, 26

McKinney, Wm 2515

McKinny, Joyn. 9

McKinsey, John 1847

McKlewean, 905

McLaughlan, Hugh 3181

McLemore, Willm 3138

McLendon, Thos 758

Mcleary, Robt 849

McLewaine, Jos 799

McManus, James 2336, 2337

Index to North Carolina Land Entries 1735-1752

McMek, Jno 909, 910
McNaire, 647-661, 831
McNeal, Daniel 2672
McNeal, Hector 2014
McNeil, Malcolm 1773
McNeil, Neil (Neal) 1109,
 3181
McOwen, Thomas 2791, 2799
McRee, Jas 2139
McRee, John 2140
McRee, William 2139, 2140
McReil, John 2069
McVicers, Pat 1982, 1983
McWaine (McWean),
 1286, 1289, 1613, 1819,
 1821, 1846, 1858-1860,
 1948, 2005
McWaine (McWean), Francis
 (F) 1727, 2271, 2358, 2477
McWaine (McWain,
 McWaiane, McWean), James
875, 1138, 1731, 1973, 1974,
 2034, 2565
McWherton, John 3032
McWrath, John 2899
Mead, 1258
Mead, John 2153
Mealson (Meolson), Thos 863
Mears (Mear), Wm 1037,
 1205
Meazall, Jno 1020
Mecham, Joseph 101
Medcalf, 408
Melton, Jonathan 1459
Menture, Patrick 1098
Mercer, Joseph 2301
Mercor, Thos 671
Meredith (Merridith), Joseph
 130, 131, 2540
Merick, Thomas 2313
Meridith, Benjamin 2312
Merrick, Richard 73
Merriday, Thos 105
Metcalf, Caleb 333
Metcalf, Col. 249
Mevis, Mark 2392

Mew, Philip 1117, 1118,
 2272, 2344
Mew, Wm 1501
Miatt, John 2815
Middleton, Jno 489
Middleton, Sml 2132
Middleton (Midleton), Wm
 97, 1502, 2302
Midget, Joseph 103, 2062
Miles, David 1295-1297
Miller, 1243
Miller, Antho 2026
Miller (Millar), Evan 886,
 1587
Miller, Georg. 2026, 2386
Miller, John 183, 201, 213,
 223, 224, 227-229, 236, 237,
 1995
Miller, Jonathan 203, 204,
 206
Miller (Millar), Philip (Phillip)
 1246, 2241, 2942
Miller, Ralph 2658, 2659
Miller, Richd 1994
Miller, Robert 2900
Mills (Mill), 2383, 3173
Mills, George 396
Mills, John 264, 321, 597,
 1404
Mills, Nesby (Nisby, Newbie)
 1399, 2351, 2633
Mills, Robert 847, 1949, 3195
Mills, Thos 286
Mills, William 661, 1885,
 2442
Mims, Thomas 62, 2588
Miner, James 236
Ming, Nathl 1028
Ming, Thos 1028, 1305
Mitchell, Andrew 2800, 2891
Mitchell, Edmund 2734
Mitchell, James 3105, 3113,
 3118
Mitchell, Josiah 3094
Mitchell (Mitchel), Robert
 1107, 3113

Index to North Carolina Land Entries 1735-1752

Index to North Carolina Land Entries 1735-1752

Index to North Carolina Land Entries 1735-1752

Index to North Carolina Land Entries 1735-1752

Index to North Carolina Land Entries 1735-1752

Index to North Carolina Land Entries 1735-1752

Index to North Carolina Land Entries 1735-1752

Index to North Carolina Land Entries 1735-1752

Index to North Carolina Land Entries 1735-1752

Wilder, Wm 1149, 3095
Wiley, James 669
Wilkes (Wilks), Chas 803
Wilkes, Mathew 2130
Wilkins, 1531
Wilkins, John 780, 781, 1963
Wilkins, Joseph 1675
Wilkinson, 1022, 1197, 1531
Wilkison, William 1676, 1738, 2545
Will, Thomas 133
Willard (Willerd), John 1481, 2831
Willets, Hope 1251, 2156
Williams (William), 498, 1249, 2118, 2551
Williams, Anthy 1188
Williams, Benjamin 419, 673, 945, 2334, 2702
Williams, David 2371
Williams, Deborah 29
Williams, Edward 797, 1871, 2544
Williams, Isaac 670, 1990, 2335
Williams, Jas 768, 1887, 2026
Williams (Willims), John 64, 375, 376, 420, 457, 518-524, 526-532, 485, 503, 731, 799, 858, 902, 903, 924, 959, 1103, 1104, 1345, 1887, 1915, 1963, 1990, 2058, 2109, 2127, 2275, 2378, 2393, 2403, 2526, 2596, 2605, 2730, 2777, 2947, 3146
Williams, Joseph 1892, 1895
Williams, Richd 1335, 3095
Williams, Robt 899
Williams, Rowland 101
Williams, Sampson 953, 954
Williams, Samuel 38, 104, 1041, 1146, 1576
Williams, Stephen 947, 1349
Williams, Theophs 680, 1209

Williams (William), Thomas 422, 1007, 1637, 2201, 2366, 2764, 3142
Williams, Tullee (Talle, Jullee) 822
Williams, William 697, 764, 1831, 1832, 1838, 1915, 2144, 2145
Williamson, Chas 1525
Williamson, Wm 606, 1151, 1537, 2323
Williford (Wilifore), Richd 1334, 1484
Willington, Joseph 2433
Willis, 2175
Willis, James 2076
Willis, Jno 1487
Willis, Saml 2237
Wills, 582
Wilson (Willson), Col. 372, 1201, 1324, 1531, 2434, 2498, 2554
Wilson (Willson, Willison), John 312, 425, 1004, 1929, 2317, 2516
Wilson, Mrs. 1755
Wilson (Willson), William 329-332, 362, 363, 385, 620, 621, 1965, 2765
Wimberly, Thos 767, 768
Wimbey (Wimbee), 575
Windals, Herwags 2401
Winder, 3099
Windows (Windes), John 1916, 2385
Winfield, John 890, 1686
Wingate, Edward 171
Wingate, John 481, 504, 506
Winnright (Winright), James 536-541, 547-556, 558-565, 568
Winns (Winn), John 84, 101
Winns, Joseph 1332
Winsley, 2818
Winsley, Benja 2925
Winsley, Benja jr 2923, 2924

312

Index to North Carolina Land Entries 1735-1752

Index to North Carolina Land Entries 1735-1752

Index to North Carolina Land Entries 1735-1752

Index to North Carolina Land Entries 1735-1752

Index to North Carolina Land Entries 1735-1752

Index to North Carolina Land Entries 1735-1752

Index to North Carolina Land Entries 1735-1752

Index to North Carolina Land Entries 1735-1752

Index to North Carolina Land Entries 1735-1752

Index to North Carolina Land Entries 1735-1752

Index to North Carolina Land Entries 1735-1752

Index to North Carolina Land Entries 1735-1752

Index to North Carolina Land Entries 1735-1752

Marsh, White   664, 915, 1351,
  1360, 1530, 1998, 2409,
  2597, 2598, 2605, 2611,
  2647, 2652
Marshes, Cheraws   666
Marshes, Mill Creek   1990
Marshes, Neuse   2701
Meadow, Beaverdam   2823
Meadow, Clay Root   2111
Meadow, Great (great)   1478,
  2469, 2477, 2933, 2939,
  3026, 3031
Meadow, large   2843
Meadow, little   1371
Meadow, long   854
Meadow, pine   1140
Meadow, Quaker   2846, 2906
Meadow (Meddow, Meadows),
  the   62, 69, 223, 317, 909,
  1046, 2787, 3007, 3196
Meadow, Tuckahoe
  (Tuckahow)   457
Meadow, Turkey   451
Meadows, R. Mitchell's hay
  3113
Meadows, upper   1409
Meeting house, the   2848
Mill, Baker's   2023
Mill, Blaning's   1278
Mill, Capt. Alston's   1500
Mill, Capt. Blaning's saw
  2644
Mill, Carvers   2252, 2253
Mill, G. Moore's   1348
Mill, Gustaves'   2464
Mill, H. Blaning's   2511, 2512
Mill, Hellow's   883
Mill, J. Ferrill's   1128
Mill, J. Harmor's   2194
Mill, J. Mackleroy's   2768
Mill, J. Smith's   860
Mill, J. Williams'   2777
Mill, Keatley's (Keithly's)
  608, 672
Mill, Lambarth's   3008
Mill, M. Rowan's   1339, 1347,

  1361
Mill, M. Rowan's saw   234
Mill, Mrs. Rowan's   1341
Mill, Pratt's   1030
Mill, R. Moore's   2457, 2497
Mill, R. Rayford's   2183
Mill, saw   139
Mill, T. Harris'   316
Mill, T. Potts'   2840
Mill, the   127, 2462, 3005
Mill, W. Eaton's   2786
Mill (miln), W. Faris'   1810
Mill, Wilder's   1701
Mill, Willson's   372
Mill, Willson's saw   362
Miller, the   1358
Mount, Pleasant   1189, 1713,
  1725, 1795, 3205, 3233
Mountain, Bolleans   2787
Mountain, D. Jackson's   83
Mountain, Pine   3103
Mountain, small   2789
Mountain, Table   2916
NC, Albemarle Co   1-100,
  102-104, 562-575
NC, Anson Co   2463-2481,
  2506, 2507, 2510,
  2528-2533, 2536-2538, 2565,
  2566, 2578, 2612, 2613,
  2658, 2659, 2712-2716,
  2720-2725, 2727-2729,
  2738-2740, 2743-2748, 2754,
  2755, 2790-2812, 2817-2828,
  2837-2864, 2866-2869,
  2879-2943, 2950-3053, 3127,
  3128, 3140, 3144, 3150,
  3167-3169, 3172, 3175-3178,
  3186-3189, 3196-3207,
  3213, 3215-3217, 3220-3222,
  3240, 3241
NC, Bath   251, 292, 1134,
  1784, 3139, 3141, 3148,
  3186-3189, 3196, 3198-3200,
  3202-3207, 3209, 3210,
  3215-3217, 3219-3229,
  3234-3237, 3239, 3240

Index to North Carolina Land Entries 1735-1752

Index to North Carolina Land Entries 1735-1752

2632, 2635, 2636, 2643,
2644, 2646-2653, 2662,
2672, 2673, 2691-2696,
2698, 2699, 2731, 2759,
2760, 2773-2785, 2813,
2870, 2873, 2875, 2876,
2947, 2948, 3125,
3133-3137, 3151, 3179-3182,
3185, 3208-3210, 3223,
3227, 3233
NC, Bladen Prect. 246
NC, Brunswick   125, 183
NC, Carteret Co   622, 624,
    625, 700, 1003, 1004, 1121,
    1122, 1250, 1300, 1419,
    1420, 1431, 1487, 1644,
    1675, 1677, 1678, 1841,
    1843, 1844, 1888, 1896,
    1897, 1929, 1931, 1937,
    2158, 2159, 2198, 2199,
    2204, 2223, 2255-2257,
    2266, 2277, 2370, 2415,
    2430, 2482, 2483, 2494,
    2535, 2614, 2655, 3211
NC, Carteret Prect.   533-559,
    561
NC, Chowan Co   609, 615,
    645, 706, 748, 780, 835,
    839, 858, 927, 967, 1028,
    1305, 1308, 1310, 1332,
    1598, 1622
NC, Chowan Prect.   562-568
NC, Craven Co   589, 598,
    605, 606, 608, 617, 620,
    621, 623, 629, 649-660,
    668, 671-673, 675, 694, 695,
    716-721, 723, 724-727, 729,
    730, 736, 737, 739, 741,
    743, 745, 746, 758, 759,
    764, 771, 778, 779, 786,
    791, 793-799, 803, 807-809,
    814, 816, 821, 831, 842,
    845-848, 850, 851, 853-856,
    860, 861, 864, 875-877,
    882-884, 895, 896, 903-905,
    910-915, 923, 942-945, 952,

955, 963, 964, 968, 970,
971, 973, 984, 992, 993,
1000-1002, 1005, 1006,
1022, 1043, 1044, 1046,
1048, 1049, 1054, 1056,
1069, 1071, 1074-1083,
1085-1095, 1097, 1098,
1105, 1106, 1108, 1113,
1115, 1117-1120, 1125,
1128, 1129, 1133,
1136-1138, 1154, 1160,
1163, 1165-1169, 1171,
1173-1176, 1182, 1183,
1186, 1187, 1189, 1193,
1195-1197, 1199, 1201-1208,
1213, 1216, 1217, 1220,
1221, 1224, 1237,
1244-1246, 1249, 1263-1267,
1279, 1280, 1286-1290,
1292, 1293, 1299, 1311,
1317, 1323, 1324, 1326,
1327, 1335, 1350, 1351,
1358, 1364-1366, 1368,
1371, 1375-1384, 1386,
1388-1391, 1400, 1403-1408,
1410, 1411, 1415, 1416,
1418, 1421, 1437-1439,
1450-1452, 1457, 1462-1465,
1467, 1469, 1470, 1485,
1486, 1488-1493, 1496-1499,
1501-1507, 1517, 1522,
1523, 1527, 1531, 1532,
1537, 1547, 1560, 1561,
1573-1575, 1580, 1594-1596,
1599, 1604, 1605, 1608,
1610, 1615, 1617,
1618-1621, 1623-1635,
1637-1643, 1645-1651,
1653-1668, 1670-1672, 1687,
1691, 1703-1706, 1709,
1711, 1712, 1715, 1723,
1724, 1729-1731, 1737-1741,
1746-1748, 1750-1760,
1762-1765, 1767-1770,
1774, 1775, 1781,
1783-1785, 1798-1800, 1801,

249, 333-335, 338, 339, 342,
345, 347-349, 355-358, 361,
363, 368, 371, 373, 376-380,
383, 384, 386-388, 390, 393,
394, 397, 407, 408, 412,
413, 415, 418-423, 424, 428,
429, 433, 434, 442, 444-447,
449, 451-454, 458-460,
465-469, 471, 508, 623, 629,
649, 651, 653-655, 670, 673,
675, 695, 719, 743, 746,
758, 778, 779, 784, 786,
791, 794, 796, 799, 807-809,
831, 844, 847, 853, 856,
860, 882-884, 895, 896, 903,
912-915, 928, 945, 952, 955,
963, 981, 1002, 1069,
1077-1079, 1081, 1082,
1105, 1119, 1120, 1133,
1160, 1163, 1165-1167,
1169, 1169, 1187, 1203,
1204, 1206-1208, 1224,
1249, 1263, 1264, 1288,
1293, 1323, 1326, 1350,
1364-1366, 1371, 1377,
1381, 1386, 1388, 1390,
1400, 1403, 1404, 1411,
1416, 1418, 1437, 1448,
1452, 1457, 1463, 1488,
1489, 1493, 1502-1507,
1523, 1532, 1547, 1573,
1599, 1604, 1605, 1608,
1615, 1615, 1617, 1623,
1625-1627, 1629, 1632,
1633, 1638, 1640-1642,
1645-1647, 1649-1651,
1653, 1660-1662, 1664,
1667, 1668, 1670-1672,
1715, 1729, 1730, 1739,
1741, 1747, 1748, 1758,
1762, 1763, 1765, 1769,
1770, 1784, 1785, 1798,
1801, 1819, 1850-1855,
1859, 1860, 1871, 1872,
1884, 1887, 1900, 1901,
1905, 1910, 1915, 1916,

1923, 1926, 1940, 1941,
1943, 1948, 1957, 1958,
1975, 2030, 2033, 2034,
2037, 2039-2041, 2046,
2049, 2054, 2055, 2059,
2071, 2072, 2081, 2091,
2100, 2107, 2109,
2113-2116, 2126-2129, 2152,
2157, 2163, 2172, 2176,
2185, 2195, 2222, 2232,
2248, 2260, 2265, 2276,
2278, 2279, 2283-2286,
2291, 2292, 2294, 2296,
2297, 2299, 2300, 2303,
2317, 2322, 2329, 2331,
2334, 2338, 2348, 2350,
2361, 2371, 2372, 2388,
2390, 2391, 2401, 2402,
2418, 2424-2426, 2429,
2432-2434, 2436, 2447,
2459, 2484, 2500, 2503,
2504, 2508, 2509, 2515,
2545, 2550, 2553, 2554,
2559, 2560, 2575, 2579,
2580, 2593-2596, 2609,
2619, 2657, 2664, 2665,
2668, 2669, 2671, 2679,
2680, 2686, 2690,
2701-2703, 2730, 2732,
2737, 2767, 2769, 2772,
2878, 2944, 2945, 3131,
3143, 3149, 3152-3155,
3161-3163, 3166, 3183,
3195, 3213, 3231, 3232,
3234, 3236
River, New   478, 480, 482,
484, 492, 495, 496, 498,
499, 501, 503, 515, 516,
530, 532, 610, 922,
1190-1192, 1782, 2050,
2197, 2306, 2491, 2599
River, Newport   544, 548,
1419, 1888, 1937, 2266,
2483, 2535, 2655
River, North   546, 551, 559,
584, 1576, 1675

Index to North Carolina Land Entries 1735-1752

Index to North Carolina Land Entries 1735-1752

Index to North Carolina Land Entries 1735-1752